ETHICS IN A BRAVE NEW WORLD

PROFESSIONAL RESPONSIBILITY, PERSONAL ACCOUNTABILITY,
AND RISK MANAGEMENT FOR IMMIGRATION PRACTITIONERS

AILA Publications

AILA's Occupational Guidebook Series
Immigration Options for Physicians
Immigration Options for Nurses & Allied Health Care Professionals
Immigration Options for Religious Workers (Fall 2004)
Immigration Options for Professors & Researchers (Fall 2004)

Statutes, Regulations & Agency Materials
Immigration & Nationality Act (INA)
CFR, Title 8
CFR Titles 6, 20, 22, 28, 42 (Immigration-Related Provisions)
Agency Interpretations of Immigration Policy (Cables, Memos, and Liaison Minutes)

Core Curriculum
Selected Fundamentals: General Immigration Concepts
Selected Fundamentals: Employment-Based Immigration
Selected Fundamentals: Admission, Removal, and Relief

Government Reprints
BIA Practice Manual
Immigration Judge Benchbook (Print or CD)
Citizenship Laws of the World
Affirmative Asylum Procedures Manual

CD Products & Toolbox Series
AILALink CD-ROM
The AILA Immigration Practice Toolbox
The AILA Litigation Toolbox

Treatises & Primers
AILA's Asylum Primer by Regina Germain
Immigration Consequences of Criminal Activity by Mary E. Kramer
Kurzban's Immigration Law Sourcebook by Ira J. Kurzban
Professionals: A Matter of Degree by Martin J. Lawler

Other Titles
Immigration & Nationality Law Handbook (two-volume set)
Ethics in a Brave New World
AILA's Guide to Technology and Legal Research for the Immigration Lawyer
Global Immigration Guide
Client Brochures (10 Titles)
Countering the Culture of "No": Strategies for Business Immigration in 2004
Immigration Litigation: Winning in Federal and Immigration Courts
DOL Directory for Immigration Lawyers
Homeland Security, Business Insecurity: Immigration Practice in Uncertain Times
Immigration Practice & Procedure Under NAFTA
The Visa Processing Guide

AILA Periodicals
Immigration Law Today *(bimonthly magazine)*

Advocacy Publications*
(Washington Update; Restrictionist Watch; Immigrants Action Alert; Connect!)

Tables of Contents and other information about these publications can be found at *www.ailapubs.com*. Orders may be placed at that site or by calling 1-800-982-2839.

*These electronic publications, prepared by AILA's Advocacy Department, are freely available at *www.aila.org*.

ETHICS
In a Brave New World

Professional Responsibility, Personal Accountability, and Risk Management for Immigration Practitioners

Editor-in-Chief
John L. Pinnix

Associate Editor
C. Lynn Calder

Contributing Editors
Robert E. Juceam
Michael Maggio
Edwin R. Rubin

Managing Editor
Tatia L. Gordon-Troy

Executive Editor
Randy P. Auerbach

AMERICAN IMMIGRATION LAWYERS ASSOCIATION
918 F Street, NW, Washington, DC 20004 • (202) 216-2400 • *www.aila.org*

> **Web Site for Corrections and Updates**
>
> Corrections and other updates to AILA publications
> can be found online at: *www.aila.org/BookUpdates.*
>
> If you have any corrections or updates to the information in this book,
> please let us know by sending a note to the address below,
> or e-mail us at *books@aila.org.*

This publication is designed to provide accurate and authoritative information in regard to the subject matter covered. It is distributed with the understanding that the publisher is not engaged in rendering legal, accounting, or other professional service. If legal advice or other expert assistance is required, the services of a competent professional should be sought.

—from a Declaration of Principles jointly adopted by a Committee of the American Bar Association and a Committee of Publishers

Copyright © 2004 by the American Immigration Lawyers Association

All rights reserved. No part of this publication may be reproduced or transmitted in any form or by any means, electronic or mechanical, including photocopy, recording, or any information storage retrieval system, without written permission from the publisher. No copyright claimed on U.S. government material.

Requests for permission to make electronic or print copies of any part of this work should be mailed to Director of Publications, American Immigration Lawyers Association, 918 F Street NW, Washington, DC 20004, or e-mailed to *books@aila.org*.

Printed in the United States of America

ISBN 1-57370-145-9
Stock No. 81-45

"Law is a compromise between moral ideas and practical possibilities."

—Reinhold Niebuhr

"... to do right is noble: to advise others to do right is also noble and much less trouble for yourself."

—Mark Twain

"A good lawyer can always get mad if somebody pays him for it, but after you've been paid a few times for getting good and mad, you hate like the deuce to get mad on your own when nobody's paying for it."

—Perry Mason
(Erle Stanley Gardner's *The Case of the Amorous Aunt*)

ETHICS IN A BRAVE NEW WORLD

PROFESSIONAL RESPONSIBILITY, PERSONAL ACCOUNTABILITY, AND RISK MANAGEMENT FOR IMMIGRATION PRACTITIONERS

FOREWORD: AILA'S COMMITMENT TO INTEGRITY AND ETHICAL PRACTICE
    by Paul L. Zulkie ix

PREFACE: WHY AN ETHICS BOOK, WHY NOW?
    by John L. Pinnix xi

Have You Considered ...?

MATTER OF ETHICS ...
    by Michael Maggio 1

ETHICAL ISSUES FOR IMMIGRATION LAWYERS
    updated by Hamel Vyas 4

UTILIZING IMMIGRATION PARAPROFESSIONALS
    by Mark J. Newman and Russell C. Ford 15

DUAL REPRESENTATION IN IMMIGRATION PRACTICE
    by Bruce A. Hake 28

Safeguarding Your Practice

RISK MANAGEMENT FOR THE IMMIGRATION PRACTITIONER
    by John L. Pinnix 36

UTILIZING A RECORDS RETENTION PROGRAM TO PROTECT THE CLIENTS' INTERESTS, TOO!
    by Donald S. Skupsky 45

THE MALPRACTICE INSURANCE "GODS" ARE MORE LIKELY TO HELP THOSE WHO HAVE HELPED THEMSELVES: RISK MANAGEMENT SUGGESTIONS FOR THE IMMIGRATION LAWYER
    by David E. Walker 54

SAFEGUARDING AGAINST CRIMINAL PROSECUTION AND MALPRACTICE IN IMMIGRATION LAW—AN OUTLINE OF KEY TOPICS
    by Robert E. Juceam 57

FILING IMMIGRATION APPLICATIONS AND PETITIONS: ETHICAL RESPONSIBILITIES AND CRIMINAL PENALTIES
    by Edwin R. Rubin 76

Following the Rules

MULTI-JURISDICTIONAL DISCIPLINARY ENFORCEMENT
    by James G. Gavin 82

AN IMMIGRATION PRACTITIONER'S GUIDE TO THE RULES AND PROCEDURES OF PROFESSIONAL CONDUCT WHEN REPRESENTING CLIENTS BEFORE THE EOIR, BIA, AND DHS
    by Roy F. Berg and Moises Hernandez 89

A Brave New World

INTERNATIONAL SECURITY, CIVIL LIBERTIES, AND HUMAN RIGHTS AFTER 9/11—AN OUTLINE
    by Robert E. Juceam 98

Professional and Personal Fulfillment

TWELVE STEPS TOWARD FULFILLMENT IN THE PRACTICE OF LAW
    by Carl Horn III 122

TESTIMONIALS:
    The Path of an Immigration Attorney, *by Elizabeth Gervais-Gruen* 147
    My Name Is Lynn, and I am a Volunteer, *by C. Lynn Calder* 149
    Immigration Advocacy Is a Matter of Professional Responsibility, *by John L. Pinnix* . 152

FOREWORD

AILA's Commitment to Integrity and Ethical Practice

by Paul L. Zulkie[*]

"No brilliance is needed in the law. Nothing but common sense, and relatively clean fingernails."

These are the words of John Mortimer, the British author best known for the "Rumpole" series of short stories. While lawyers often laugh at such observations about our profession, the issues of competence and ethics in the practice of immigration law have never been more important and vital to our success in representing our clients.

I sincerely believe that most AILA members hold themselves to the highest standards of practice skills and ethical behavior because they think it's the right thing to do. While the fear of malpractice suits or disciplinary actions are realities that must be taken seriously, the fact that we have our clients' lives in our hands remains all the motivation most of us need to take these obligations to heart.

Regrettably, in the last few years we have witnessed an unprecedented shift in the practice environment for immigration lawyers. The post-9/11 emphasis on enforcement has significantly increased the pressure on attorneys seeking relief for their clients. When does creative lawyering and zealous representation cross the line and subject attorneys to accusations of obstruction of justice? The "Culture of No" that continues to hold federal agency personnel in a trance-like state has converted what once were routine business-immigration matters into nightmare scenarios none of us could ever have foreseen. Nevertheless, our clients have become increasingly demanding about what they expect from their attorneys and less forgiving of what they perceive to be errors or excuses when attorneys fail to meet their expectations.

There is another reason AILA members must continually strive to maintain the highest ethical standards. Along with our competence and training, a focus on ethical behavior sets us apart from the ever-growing cabal of individuals engaged in the unauthorized practice of law. Stories about the broken lives of immigrants and exploitation of the innocent are all too familiar. Combating those that exploit immigrant communities in court, before legislative bodies, and in the media is far easier when the standard against which UPL providers are measured is an immigration bar that takes self-regulation and integrity seriously.

At AILA, we have made raising the ethical standards of our membership a priority. This publication is being distributed to all members free of charge. All of our panels at CLEs and teleconferences are instructed to integrate ethical considerations into the presentations. Articles addressing professional responsibility have become commonplace in AILA publications. Our Ethics and Professionalism Committee serves as a clearing house for information on ethics-related cases around the country and brings emerging trends to the attention of our members. AILA's chapters are encouraged to have standing ethics committees that serve as a resource and sounding-board for individual AILA members with concerns about ethical issues arising in their practices.

If Horace Rumpole were an AILA member, he would read *Ethics in a Brave New World* cover-to-cover, and never forget the importance of common sense and clean fingernails.

---

[*] **Paul L. Zulkie** is managing principal in the Chicago law firm of Zulkie Partners LLC and presently serves as President of AILA. Listed in *Best Lawyers in America* and *International Who's Who of Corporate Immigration Lawyers*, his practice is concentrated in business immigration law and employer sanctions enforcement.

Preface

WHY AN ETHICS BOOK? WHY NOW?

*by John L. Pinnix**

Just months before the 9/11 attacks, *The Washington Post* quoted an INS spokesperson as saying immigration "is a mystery and a mastery of obfuscation, and the lawyers who can figure it out are worth their weight in gold."

I couldn't agree more; yet as we begin practicing in the new millennium, evidence of some tarnishing mounts.

Reflecting on today's "Culture of No," the remarkable Elizabeth Gervais-Gruen, who is among the deans of actively-practicing immigration attorneys, expresses bewilderment as to why "they [the government] want to make it so hard." Not that, Elizabeth attests, it was ever easy during her nearly 50 years of immigration practice.

On the first anniversary of the Department of Homeland Security (DHS), my local newspaper, the *News and Observer*, asked me to evaluate the success of the DHS immigration provisions, and my (fair and balanced) conclusion was, "It's too early to tell." No one can fairly lay the blame for a broken immigration system on the legitimate national security concerns that were highlighted in the aftermath of 9/11. Dry rot and neglect of the institutional infrastructure and the corrosive bureaucratic culture is decades old and never has proven amenable to cosmetic fixes on the cheap.

But if the *News and Observer* asked me to revisit the question today, I would now have fewer reservations and little reluctance in concluding that the promised life supports were lost in transit and that the patient is comatose and terminal.

Technology has made us better able to serve our clients; yet despite our being available 24/7, we often can't get the simplest response from U.S. Citizenship and Immigration Services (USCIS). USCIS's promise of reducing processing backlogs is illusory, even as quota backlogs loom on the horizon. Fundamental liberties are suspended in the name of national security. Frustrated clients are increasingly—and fortunately thus far figuratively—tempted to kill the messenger. To sustain lifestyles unimaginable to any previous generation, we are tempted, or sometimes feel forced, to chase incredible billable hours.

Immigration attorneys, once almost immune to the pervasive jokes told at the expense of other lawyers on talk shows, at social functions, and within their own families, now face a reality that is no joke. Recently, AILA immediate past-President Palma Yanni, noted in an *Immigration Law Today* (ILT) article that a former Florida AILA member was "sentenced to more than eight years in prison after being convicted of fraud and conspiracy in the filing of thousands of religious worker and multinational executive petitions." Afterwards, another AILA member was convicted in Virginia, in connection with filing phony labor certifications.

Palma also noted, "Three other members in Washington, D.C., Maryland, and Virginia have been arrested on similar charges, and an assistant U.S. attorney in northern Virginia has announced his intention to prosecute AILA members."

This year, the North Carolina State Bar's Grievance Committee transferred a veteran Carolinas Chapter member "to disability inactive status pursuant to a consent order," stipulating that the attorney suffers from "mental disorders that significantly impair her ability to practice law." Shortly thereafter, the attorney was indicted for allegedly arranging a sham marriage, and "filing legal papers with authorities falsely claiming

---

* **John L. Pinnix** is a past president of the American Immigration Lawyers Association (2002–2003) and a founding member of AILA's Carolinas Chapter. He attained B.A. and M.A. degrees in History at the University of North Carolina at Greensboro and his J.D. at the Wake Forest University School of Law. He has served as an adjunct professor at North Carolina Central University School of Law and as a senior lecturing fellow at Duke University School of Law. Pinnix is a principal in the Raleigh law firm, Allen and Pinnix, P.A., and is a North Carolina Board-Certified Immigration Specialist.

that another immigrant was gay and would be persecuted if sent back to Egypt." The clients in the 19-count indictment were working as government informants. Also indicted was the attorney's 27-year-old daughter, who worked as her paralegal.

Times are changing. Palma Yanni noted that in the District of Columbia, immigration matters now "receive the lion's share of complaints against attorneys." She went on to say: "In a distressing corollary, AILA members increasingly find themselves filing complaints against other members for ineffective assistance of counsel under the *Matter of Lozada* rubric. The BIA has left us little choice."

Yet, should this prove to be, in King Richard III's words, "the winter of our discontent,"[1] it would be irresponsible to simply damn the system and not make every effort to wrest control of our own destinies. We must acknowledge that at least some of the fault is, after all, in ourselves and not in our stars.

In a changing world, AILA's leadership has sought to respond to its members' needs for mentoring and to provide tools addressing a wide range of professional development issues. Even with powerful tools, such as the AILA InfoNet, the challenge can be daunting. In 1994, AILA had 3,700 members; in 10 years, our rolls have grown by nearly 5,000 and will soon reach 9,000. A comprehensive member survey conducted in late 2002 indicated that a quarter of our membership are under the age of 35; more than half of the survey participants have belonged to AILA less than six years; and 25 percent have been members for less than three years. In 1998, AILA's Board of Governors passed a resolution urging each chapter to establish an ethics committee and to hold an annual continuing legal education event devoted to ethics. In her ILT article, Palma Yanni wrote that "ethics must be more than an annual event; it must be ingrained in every action we take each day we represent a client."

The all-member distribution of this ethics and professional responsibility anthology is to further awareness of the landmines we traverse daily, and to hopefully serve as a trip-wire for our individual and collective consciences. And it is distributed with the hope that it will be a tool to help its readers start to wrest control of their personal destinies. Despite the turbulent times we practice in—no, more accurately because of the turbulent times we practice in—the author fervently believes that the practice of law, particularly of immigration law, is both a high calling and a privilege.

Elsewhere in this book is quoted the late Carrol W. Weathers who said an attorney "occupies a preferred station of leadership, possesses exceptional influence, and it not only is his privilege but his duty to use his influence and position on behalf of a better social order, and live as a worthy example to others." The quote bears repeating.

Before Garry Trudeau, there was Walt Kelly. Kelly's daily Pogo comic strip, at its zenith, was arguably more influential than Doonesbury, and indisputably better drawn. Kelly was a fearless opponent of Joseph McCarthy and all that he stood for. The message of one of my favorite strips is conveyed on a sweet note. One of the animal children is talking with Porky, the porcupine, a featured bit player who is the swamp's resident curmudgeon. The child has evidently heard a sermon by the Deacon, a card carrying member of the Okefenokee Swamp Chapter of the Jack Acid (read, John Birch) Society. The Deacon would still be readily recognizable in the political world of the 21st century:

> "The Deacon," relates the child, "says how can GOD be DEAD when He's always in the BOOK?" Porky responds: "Does he mean pressed in the PAGES? Like a DRIED FLOWER? A nostalgic MEMENTO? The Everlovin' real flowers are OUT, living in the fields, in the forests, in the world ... fair, and fragrant, and WITH us."

While "Stop to Smell the Roses" is but a part of the message shared by Judge Carl Horn, III, in his article, "Twelve Steps Toward Fulfillment in the Practice of Law," it is a message often neglected by busy attorneys. Neglected at our own peril!

In addition to Judge Horn, the following people deserve their share of the blame for this publication: at the AILA National Office—Tatia L. Gordon-Troy, AILA's Associate Director of Publications and this vol-

---

[1] William Shakespeare (1564–1616), "King Richard III," Act 1 scene 1.

ume's Managing Editor; Randy P. Auerbach, Director of Publications; Executive Director Jeanne Butterfield; Amy Novick, AILA's former Programs Director; and Susan D. Quarles, Deputy Director of Finance & Administration. Also my sincere thanks to Palma R. Yanni and Paul L. Zulkie, under whose watches this project was conceived and executed, as well as the other members of AILA's Executive Committee for their vision and support; my wife, Sally Pinnix; Margaret Murray; Sidney Gill; my law partner and associate editor, Lynn Calder; my assistant, Sue Grasso-Bocchino; Alice Glover and the other members of my firm of Allen and Pinnix, P.A., who took up some of the slack to free me for this project; former Congressman Nick Galifianakis; contributing editors Edwin R. Rubin and Michael Maggio; David E. Walker; Bruce A. Hake; Peter Williamson; Kay Adams; Mark J. Newman; Russell C. Ford; Royal F. Berg; Moises Hernandez; Alfonso Caprara; Hamel Vyas; Donald S. Skupsky; James G. Gavin; Elizabeth Gervais-Gruen; Denise C. Hammond; Judge Horn's clerk, David Grigg; and contributing editor Robert E. Juceam and his colleagues at Fried, Frank, Harris, Shriver & Jacobson LLP—Dian R. Gray and Nia Fripp, as well as summer associates Jeremy Goldman, Marc Romanoff, and Victor Suthammanont, and intern Raquel Aragon.

In Ben Schott's words, "To them my thanks are due for suggestions, advice, encouragement, expert opinions, and other such things. If glaring errors exist within this book, it's probably their fault."[2]

Seriously, thank you.

JOHN L. PINNIX
RALEIGH, NORTH CAROLINA
SEPTEMBER 2004

---

[2] Ben Schott, *Schott's Original Miscellany* (Bloomsbury, 2002).

ABOUT AILA

The American Immigration Lawyers Association (AILA) is a national bar association of more than 8,500 attorneys and law professors who practice and teach immigration law. AILA member attorneys represent tens of thousands of U.S. families who have applied for permanent residence for their spouses, children, and other close relatives. AILA members also represent thousands of U.S. businesses and industries that sponsor highly skilled foreign workers seeking to enter the United States on a temporary or permanent basis. In addition, AILA members represent foreign students, entertainers, athletes, and asylum seekers, often on a pro bono basis. AILA is also the premier publisher of immigration law titles and periodicals. Founded in 1946, AILA is a nonpartisan, not-for-profit organization that provides its members with continuing legal education, information, professional services, and a multitude of publications on immigration topics, while providing expertise through its 35 chapters and over 50 national committees. AILA is an affiliated organization of the American Bar Association and is represented in the ABA House of Delegates.

American Immigration Lawyers Association
918 F Street, NW
Washington, DC 20004
Tel: (202) 216-2400
Fax: (202) 783-7853
www.aila.org
AILA Publications: 1-800-982-2839

MATTER OF ETHICS...

by Michael Maggio[*]

A few months back, *The Washington Post* ran numerous stories about the shameful escapades of a former AILA member, Samuel Kooritzky. In case you have not heard of him, Kooritzky was convicted of filing more than 2,700 bogus §245(i) labor certification applications in an 18-month period. According to the *Post*, Kooritzky charged his unwitting clients between $7,000 and $20,000 for bogus job offers with nationally known companies. He was assisted by Kinkos-generated company letterheads, the real names of human resources directors, and G-28s, orienting decisions from DOL back to his enormous and seemingly successful office until DOL mistakenly notified an employer that dozens of labor certification applications had been approved.

In March 2003, Kooritzky was sentenced to 10 years in prison, ordered to pay restitution to his victims, and ordered to forfeit $2.3 million in unlawful proceeds. No amount of money or prison time can make his victims whole. Their most important dream is now a nightmare, and, for most, with §245(i) gone, there is no waking up.

Other criminal investigations against immigration lawyers are underway in the Washington, D.C., area, and almost certainly elsewhere. Last summer, an AILA member in downtown D.C. had virtually everything in his office carted away by dozens of FBI, DOL, and INS agents. Apparently, attorneys who have filed an enormous number of §245(i) labor certification applications are in the government's cross-hairs. DOL agents think that some attorneys allegedly paid sponsoring employers to file §245(i) labor certification applications. These attorneys are said to have charged foreign nationals a substantial additional fee for the service of "finding" a sponsoring employer.

---

[*] This article first appeared at 23 *Immigration Law Today* 34 (Jan./Feb. 2004), as the first installment of the Matter of Ethics column. Readers are encouraged to submit ethical questions to *ILT@aila.org* to appear in a future Q&A as part of the Matter of Ethics column.

Michael Maggio is a partner with the Washington, D.C., firm of Maggio & Kattar, PC. He serves on AILA's Ethics Committee and writes the Matter of Ethics column for ILT.

ETHICS, LIKE SEX, IS...

Immigration ethics is not thought of as a particularly sexy topic. But ethics in the immigration field and good sex have much in common, believe it or not. This observation is not merely made to get an article read on a subject most prefer to avoid.

More and better immigration ethics, like more and better you know what, is enriching, satisfying, and, yes, fun. More and better immigration ethics also results in more clients, and, therefore, more revenue. AILA has a well established history of improving the lot of its members, and immigrants, too. Making ethics the centerpiece of AILA's educational programs and daily practice will help us as attorneys, and it will help our clients. A greater focus on ethics will also enhance AILA's standing and effectiveness as advocates for immigrants' rights at a time when those rights are under constant attack.

Ethics cannot merely mean mastering the dual-representation problem that characterizes immigration practices. Ethics cannot mean meeting boring mandatory CLE requirements that seem to have little relevance to our work. If this perspective prevails, the collective ethical reputation of the immigration bar will suffer as never before because of these and other highly publicized incidents.

RAISING THE BAR

The nation's capital, of course, is where all immigration law, other than judge-made law, is made. AILA's stature and role in shaping immigration law will be helped if there is a well-justified public perception that nothing is more important to AILA than enhancing ethical standards in our profession and protecting our clients from unethical lawyers.

AILA also must address the fact that foreign nationals are damaged by lawyers, some of whom are members of our association, who either do not know the law or elect to ignore it. The vulnerability of our clients to attorney abuse is well known. AILA, at its peril, will be perceived in the same light as those medical associations that refuse to adequately police their profession. Indeed, AILA's ability to help those clients hurt by our colleagues—as well as its ability to defend immigration lawyers wrongly accused—will be enhanced if AILA's commitment to the highest ethical standards also is well known.

Most AILA members are unaware, for example, that in the late 1980s—which is not really the too distant past—AILA's national president was wrongly indicted for immigration fraud. A U.S. attorney decided that it constituted submitting false statements to the government upon filing an immigrant visa petition for a corporate officer shortly after filing for an extension of a nonimmigrant visa that required nonimmigrant intent. In other words, our then-president allegedly lied about his client's intentions. Although the charges were ultimately dismissed, the financial, emotional, and political costs were huge. The defenders of immigrants are much more easily cast as "evil doers" now, and AILA cannot properly defend wrongly accused lawyers today until its commitment to the highest ethical standards is clearly established.

FOLLOWING A CODE

Although every state bar association has a Code on Professional Responsibility that governs attorney conduct, an additional code must guide the conduct of immigration attorneys. Moreover, improving the ethical standards of immigration lawyers, as AILA's immediate past President, Palma Yanni, has stated, must be one of AILA's highest and most public priorities. The four-part code that this author believes should govern the conduct of immigration lawyers will help achieve Palma's goal. This code also takes us back to the theme of this article.

Always be openhearted and unfailingly honest with clients.

Yes, be emotionally and intellectually intimate with your clients, for your own good, if for no other reason. There will be reciprocity as you both learn more, and you will be better equipped to meet your client's needs. It is infuriatingly true that some immigration lawyers routinely lead their clients into believing that their case is likely to succeed when failure is preordained. Unfortunately, an open and honest assessment of many immigration problems today requires the lawyer to tell the client there is little chance of success. Some immigration attorneys view such candor as an invitation to financial ruin. They believe that they cannot afford to be honest with their clients. In fact, the opposite is true. Our clients, for better or for worse, are walking billboards. They either extol our virtues or heap derision upon us to a very wide audience. "Honest" is how every successful immigration lawyer wishes to be characterized by his or her clients. Sure, "smart" is important, but "honest" more so because dishonest lawyers are correctly seen as definitionally dumb. Honesty in the attorney-client relationship requires that attorneys put the needs of their clients before their own. Hiding behind "I never guarantee success" is a porous mask, and wrong.

Always be honest with the government.

Every state's Code on Professional Responsibility mandates this, and violating this rule can send both the client and the attorney on an unwelcome trip to "Club Fed." Lying about employment experience, the time, manner and circumstances of entry, and previous misrepresentations on visa is, of course, a crime but in more than the usual sense. An attorney helping or turning a blind eye to a client's efforts to submit false statements to the government is like a physician who writes false pain killer prescriptions. Neither the lawyer nor the physician can hide behind "I was only trying to help" because in the end, the lawyer and the physician are doing harm to those they are obligated to assist. Also, always being truthful to the government enhances what is most important, your reputation.

Immigration lawyers must know their craft.

Making a mistake, of course, is not an ethical violation, but not putting in the time required to master what is without question one of the most complicated areas of law easily does lead to ethical violations. Immigration attorneys cannot satisfy their clients unless they know what they are doing. This requires mindfulness, constant study, and attorneys helping each other master the vast and ever changing landscape of American immigration law and procedure.

Do pro bono work.

It is good for your soul, and for your wallet. Start by helping someone pro bono who was taken advantage of by another immigration attorney. Or accept a pro bono case from the immigration court, your religious institution, or a local immigrant's rights organization. The community of immigrants that ultimately feeds, houses, and clothes us desperately needs pro bono assistance. This mitzvah always is repaid by good will, good karma, and many referrals. Yes, pro bono work also makes you feel good to be alive. No immigration lawyer can afford not to do pro bono work.

INTEGRATING ETHICS

It would go a long way toward improving the ethical standards of the immigration bar if ethics is integrated into every aspect of all AILA educational programs. In other words, rather than a separate ethics panel, every panel at every conference should discuss ethical issues that arise within the context of each individual topic, be it asylum, labor certification applications, or waivers of inadmissibility. Concern for ethics also must be reflected in all written materials. This would not be an artificial exercise because there is no area of immigration law and procedure that does not involve ethical issues. Hopefully the need and benefits of such an approach now are evident.

AILA and our membership would also benefit tremendously if every AILA chapter has an ethics officer who can respond to ethical questions and concerns of chapter members. Ethics officers should also serve as a liaison between AILA and each chapter's local Board on Professional Responsibility. AILA should encourage its members to bring to the attention of their chapter's ethics officer unethical conduct of other immigration lawyers, including the all-too-common practice of charging clients, who are frequently among the working poor, for unattainable immigration benefits.

Like sex, immigration ethics is discussed frequently but rarely in a meaningful fashion. More and better ethics clearly is in the interest of AILA and its members. AILA has an obligation to do more to enhance the ethical standards of our profession and to better help our clients avoid the consequences of unethical lawyering.

ETHICAL ISSUES FOR IMMIGRATION LAWYERS

updated by Hamel Vyas[*]

INTRODUCTION

Historically, the practice of immigration law has involved unique issues of ethical conduct. The increasingly complex practice of immigration law in the 21st-Century promises to continue to challenge the immigration lawyer's ability to understand and abide by different codes of professional discipline that may apply in a given situation. In addition to complying with the formal rules, the immigration lawyer must also conform to appropriate mores of conduct for responsible professionals. In the immigration field, more than most areas of the legal profession, ethical behavior may not be moral behavior.[1]

Much is at stake in immigration matters. Lawyers must react to a body of law that is constantly changing. They deal with clients whose entire future may depend on the outcome of the lawyer's work. The law and regulations impose increasingly harsh penalties for noncompliance with even the most minor provisions.

Issues that arise frequently in the context of immigration practice include the question of whether an application submitted was frivolous and whether a lawyer's conduct was dishonest, neglectful, or involved an unusual delay. Additionally, certain areas of immigration law inherently involve dual representation, and its attendant ethical issues. These include cases involving labor certifications, marriage-based relative cases, cases requiring the use of Form I-864 Affidavit of Support, and H-1B/LCA cases.

Furthermore, each addition to the immigration laws has added new requirements, both from substantive and ethical perspectives. Thus, the lawyer has been regularly faced with the prospect of grappling with how to adapt his or her practice to each change in the law, while at the same time endeavoring to remain in compliance with the ethical rules that govern our practices.

The obligations unique to immigration practice are not the end of the immigration lawyer's responsibilities. Every lawyer, regardless of field of practice, plays multiple roles in the execution of his or her duties. The lawyer is a representative of clients, a public citizen having special responsibility for the quality of justice, and a member of a learned profession.[2]

As a representative of clients, the lawyer may be called upon to act as advisor, advocate, counselor, negotiator, intermediary, and evaluator. In carrying out these roles, the lawyer must be competent, prompt, and diligent. The lawyer must maintain communication with the client concerning representation and must keep confidences.

As a public citizen having special responsibility for the quality of justice, the lawyer must seek improvement of the law, the administration of justice, and the quality of service rendered by the legal professional.

As a member of a learned profession, the lawyer must cultivate knowledge of the law beyond its use for clients, and help the bar regulate itself in the public interest.

These multiple roles can be a source of conflict. According to the ABA Model Rules of Professional Conduct, "Virtually all difficult ethical problems arise from conflict between a lawyer's responsibilities to clients, to the legal system and to the lawyer's own interest in remaining an upright person while earning a satisfactory living."[3]

---

[*] Reprinted from 1 *Immigration & Nationality Law Handbook* 34 (2004–05 ed.).

Hamel Vyas received a B.A. in Political Science (with honors) from York University, Toronto, and her J.D. from the Widener University School of Law, Wilmington, Delaware. Vyas began her immigration law career in Buffalo in 1997 after her admission to the New York State Bar. She currently practices immigration law in Philadelphia. She served a one-year term as chair (2002–03) and co-chair (2001–02) of AILA's Young Lawyers Division.

[1] *See* B. Hake, "Attorney Misconduct—A Rebuttal," 4 *Geo. Immigr. L.J.* 727 (Fall 1990). *See also* B. Hake, "We Represent *People*, Not Files!—Reflections on the *Valinoti* Case," 8 *Bender's Immigration Bulletin* 859 (May 15, 2003).

[2] American Bar Association Model Rules of Prof'l Conduct, at 5 (2001 ed.) (hereinafter Model Rules).

[3] *Id.* at 6.

As licensed professionals who regularly counsel corporate and individual clients on how to remain in compliance with the governing schema, it is ironic that we are often ill-prepared to address our own internal issues of compliance with the ethical rules that govern our practice as lawyers.

Therefore, as was suggested in an AILA roundtable on this topic that took place more than a decade ago,[4] the best advice for a lawyer who is uncertain whether an ethical dilemma exists is to stop, assess, and consider the issues before proceeding further. The purpose of this article is to provide resources that will help immigration lawyers with that process. Hopefully, this article will aid immigration lawyers in evaluating their own ethical dilemmas, and resolving them in a legal, ethical, and moral manner.

SOURCES OF ETHICS RULES

The practice of immigration law is governed by a diverse assortment of rules, requirements, suggestions, options, and prohibitions. Those which are most likely to apply to the immigration lawyer are listed in this section.

State Rules on Professional Responsibility

Your state rules of professional responsibility are the first resource you should consult when confronted by ethical issues. To locate and review the rules of the state in which you are licensed to practice, you may refer to one of the following: *www.legalethics.com*, or *www.law.cornell.edu/ethics/index.html*.

However, immigration practice is complicated by the fact that it is a federal administrative practice. Thus, immigration lawyers—admitted to the Bar of a certain state—frequently practice in another state (even multiple states). This can create what one commentator calls a "jurisdictional gap" if an attorney licensed in one state commits an act of alleged malpractice against a client in a second state while filing an application with a government office located in a third state. Which state's rules apply?[5] This is why looking to immigration laws and regulations, as well as multi-jurisdictional rules, is also important.

Immigration Statutes

INA §240(b)(6)(C)—This section defines the conduct of removal proceedings. In addressing the treatment of frivolous behavior, the law states:

> The Attorney General shall, by regulation—
>
> (A) define in proceeding before an immigration judge or before an appellate administrative body under this subchapter, frivolous behavior for which attorneys may be sanctioned,
>
> (B) specify the circumstances under which an administrative appeal of a decision or ruling will be considered frivolous and will be summarily dismissed, and
>
> (C) impose appropriate sanctions (which may include suspension and disbarment) in the case of frivolous behavior.
>
> Nothing in this paragraph shall be construed as limiting the authority of the Attorney General to take actions with respect to inappropriate behavior.

INA §274C(a)(5)—This statute among other things, prohibits any person or entity to knowingly:

> Prepare, file, or assist another in preparing or filing any application for benefits under this chapter, or any document required under this chapter, or any document submitted in connection with such application or document, with knowledge or in reckless disregard of the fact that such application or document was falsely made or, in whole or in part, does not relate to the person on whose behalf it was or is being submitted.

The term "falsely make" is defined in §1324c(f) as:

> to prepare or provide an application or document, with knowledge or in reckless disregard of the fact that the application or document contains a false, fictitious, or fraudulent statement or material representation, or has no basis in law or fact, *or otherwise fails to state a fact which is material to the purpose for which it was submitted* (emphasis added).

---

[4] *See* M.S. Frisch, H. Gee, Jr., W.E. Grauer, B.A. Hake, M.D. Patrick, L.G. Ripley, R.E. Rosen & W.V. Whelan, "Ethical Issues in Immigration Practice: A Roundtable Discussion," 90-08 *Immigration Briefings* (Aug. 1990) (hereinafter Roundtable); *see also* B. Hake "Some Professional Responsibility Issues in Law Firm Management," *Ethics and Your Immigration Practice: Have you Considered...*, p. 1 (AILA 1998).

[5] Sheard, "Ethical Issues in Immigration Proceedings," 9 *Geo. Immigr. L.J.* 719, 721 (Fall 1995).

The subject of false statements will be discussed in further detail in the "Document and Presentation Fraud" section.

Immigration Regulations

8 CFR §103.2(a)(3)—This regulation provides that when filing applications, petitions, and other documents with the Department of Homeland Security:

> An applicant or petitioner may be represented by an attorney in the United States, as defined in §1.1(f) of this chapter, by an attorney outside the United States as defined in §292.1(a)(6) of this chapter, or by an accredited representative as defined in §202.1(a)(4) of this chapter.

8 CFR §292.3, duplicated at 8 CFR §1292.3— 8 CFR §292.3 now describes practice before the Department of Homeland Security (DHS). 8 CFR §1292.3 describes practice before the Executive Office for Immigration Review (EOIR). This duplication was made "because representation of aliens before INS and EOIR has historically been considered as a single process and will continue to be so considered for the foreseeable future."[6]

These sections provide the authority for adjudicatory officials and the Board of Immigration Appeals to impose sanctions against immigration lawyers. Their provisions provide:

> It will be in the public interest to impose disciplinary sanctions against a practitioner who is authorized to practice before the Service when such person has engaged in criminal, unethical, or unprofessional conduct, or in frivolous behavior, as set forth in §3.102[7] of this chapter.

The sections go on to list sanctions and to provide the procedure for imposing them.

8 CFR §1003.102—EOIR has promulgated its own rules governing the practice of lawyers and representatives appearing before it.[8] As part of those rules, the EOIR has provided a list of thirteen examples of conduct that will provide grounds for imposing sanctions. Since this list is now referenced by both DHS and EOIR regulations, all immigration lawyers, not just those who practice before EOIR, should be familiar with this list.

However, the list is not exclusive. The preamble to 8 CFR §1003.102 notes:

> It is deemed to be in the public interest for an adjudicating official or the Board to impose disciplinary sanctions against any practitioner who falls within one or more of the categories enumerated in this section, *but these categories do not constitute the exclusive grounds for which disciplinary sanctions may be imposed in the public interest*. Nothing in this regulation should be read to denigrate the practitioner's duty to represent zealously his or her client within the bounds of the law (emphasis added).[9]

ABA Model Rules of Professional Conduct

Initially, in 1908, the ABA adopted the original Canons of Ethics. In 1969, the ABA established the Model Code of Professional Responsibility (Code) and then in 1983, the Model Rules of Professional Conduct (Model Rules). In August 2001 and February 2002, the ABA adopted revised Model Rules that differed significantly from previous versions. Although the new revisions have not yet been adopted by any state, they are beginning to appear for reference purposes in some state's rules. Given the history of state adoption of all or part of the ABA rules, the revisions will probably be incorporated into states' rules. For this reason, they are incorporated into this article.[10]

PENALTIES FOR NONCOMPLIANCE

The penalties for noncompliance range in severity depending upon the gravity of the infraction. Attorneys may be faced with possible suspension, disbarment, sanctions (including judicial), malpractice and other tort liability, as well as criminal prosecution. Judicial sanctions from a federal district court do not affect a lawyer's activities in administrative proceedings. However from a practical perspective, they will most certainly affect the lawyer's ability to practice. For example, a prerequisite to entering an appearance on behalf of a client is that the attorney must be a member of the Bar in good standing and not under a court order suspending, disbarring, or otherwise restricting him or her from practicing law. This is a specific feature of the G-28 Notice of Ap-

---

[6] 68 Fed. Reg. 9824 (Feb. 28, 2003).

[7] Now 8 CFR §1003.102. *See* 68 Fed. Reg. 9824, 9830, 9846 (Feb. 28, 2003); 68 Fed. Reg. 10349, 10350 (Mar 5, 2003).

[8] *See* 8 CFR §1003.101 *et seq.*

[9] For a more complete discussion, see 77 *Interpreter Releases* No. 25 (June 30, 2000).

[10] The revisions, including an explanation of the changes, can be found at *www.abanet.org/leadership/2002/401.html*.

pearance.[11] Therefore, judicial sanctions may therefore impinge upon a lawyer's ability to practice in the administrative immigration setting.

Although disciplinary action remains infrequent in the immigration context, the threat of losing one's livelihood is still an effective motivator for immigration lawyers to carefully evaluate their professional conduct on a regular basis. Furthermore, it is unclear whether the heightened national attention upon immigration law, coupled with new rules of enforcement and an EOIR Web site,[12] which publishes a list of sanctioned and expelled lawyers, will focus more attention on lawyers' conduct. Since the terrorist attacks of September 11, 2001, and the transfer of functions of the INS into DHS, other areas of substantive immigration law have experienced a more rigorous enforcement climate. It stands to reason that this climate will spill over into the arena of attorney professional responsibility as well.

COMMUNICATION

Keeping Clients Informed

Few aspects of practice are more important than keeping clients informed. The Model Rules recognize this with clarity and force. Model Rule 1.4 provides:

(a) A lawyer shall:

(1) promptly inform the client of any decision or circumstance with respect to which the client's informed consent, as defined in Rule 1.0(e), is required by these rules;

(2) reasonably consult with the client about the means by which the client's objectives are to be accomplished;

(3) keep the client reasonably informed about the status of the matter;

(4) promptly comply with reasonable requests for information; and

(5) consult with the client about any relevant limitation on the lawyer's conduct when the lawyer knows that the client expects assistance not permitted by the Rules of Professional Conduct or other law.

(b) A lawyer shall explain a matter to the client to the extent reasonably necessary to permit the client to make informed decisions regarding the representation.[13]

Note 1 to Model Rule 1.4 provides an effective summary: "Reasonable communication between the lawyer and the client is necessary for the client effectively to participate in the representation."

The need to keep the client informed is especially important in immigration practice. Government processing is anything but smooth and timely. Deadlines and expiration dates mark the calendar on every case. Clients are nervous before they hire you. After you tell them all the things that can and might go wrong, their nervousness doubles. Ethnic communities, regardless of the level of sophistication, are excellent sources of horror stories and misinformation. Each change, and proposed change, in immigration laws is reported by the ethnic media, and by word of mouth.

Effective Communication

In addition to keeping clients informed, the immigration lawyer must exercise special care in communicating with foreign nationals. In this regard the lawyer's conduct should be governed by the rules akin to the rules governing clients who have a disability; *i.e.*, the lawyer has a special responsibility to communicate with the client so the client can make decisions as to the scope and objectives of the representation.[14] In at least one case, an attorney was reprimanded for allowing another individual to handle this duty.[15]

In some cases, the client's inability to effectively participate in his or her case may be obvious. The client will not speak English. The client will be unfamiliar with the culture of the United States. The client will demonstrate a lack of understanding of the lawyer's role in the United States legal system.

In other cases, the client may appear to be able to completely understand and participate in his or her case. However, that understanding may be incomplete, or flawed. The prudent immigration attorney cannot assume that the client understands legal terminology in English, despite an apparent English flu-

---

[11] Matthew Bender, *Imm. Law and Procedure* Pt. 2, Ch. 4, at 2.

[12] See www.usdoj.gov/eoir/profcond/chart.htm.

[13] Model Rules, *supra* note 2, R. 1.4—"Communication."

[14] *ABA/BNA Lawyer's Manual on Prof'l Conduct*, "Lawyer-Client Relationship, Client Under a Disability" at §31:601 (Jan. 31, 2001) (hereinafter *ABA Manual*).

[15] *Mays v. Neal*, 938 S.W.2d 830 (Ark. Sup. Ct. 1997) (attorney reprimanded for allowing assistant to handle all communications with non–English speaking client).

ency. Cross-cultural issues (both the attorney's and the client's) may impede effective communication.

The prudent immigration attorney will take each client's unique cultural situation into account, and use a variety of tools to insure that his or her clients are kept fully and properly informed. If there is any doubt whether the attorney is effectively communicating with the client, the attorney must make sure such doubt is eliminated.

WHEN IS THE ATTORNEY-CLIENT RELATIONSHIP ESTABLISHED?

What Constitutes Representation

The point at which a lawyer-client relationship is established is determined primarily by principles of agency and contract law. The relationship begins when the client acknowledges the lawyer's capacity to act in his or her behalf and the lawyer agrees to act for the benefit and under the control of the client. Usually the agreement is explicit: the client consults the lawyer, relates his or her problem, and the lawyer agrees to take the case.

However, in other cases, the lawyer's acceptance may be implied by actions the lawyer takes on the client's behalf or by the client's reasonable reliance.[16] Whether a form of attorney representation exists depends not on what the lawyer thinks, but what the reasonable client would think. No express contract is required if there are good reasons to find that the client believed that the lawyer was acting as the person's lawyer.[17]

Consultations—A lawyer's duty to the client is created when an attorney-client relationship is formed. Therefore, it is critical for the immigration attorney to communicate clearly to potential clients both when an attorney-client relationship exists, and the parameters of the relationship. "The duty of confidentiality attaches to all prospective clients even before a client-lawyer relationship is created and even if a client-lawyer relationship is never created."[18] In other words, a lawyer may not divulge information gained in the context of an initial consultation even when the prospective client ultimately decides against engaging the lawyer's services for future work. It is also not necessary for a lawyer to receive payment from a client for the duty of confidentiality to attach and for the attorney-client relationship to exist.[19]

A good lawyer makes sure to explain to a prospective client the nature of the relationship and the responsibilities that flow thereafter. Many prominent lawyers recommend using nonengagement letters when clients do not hire them so as to make clear that the lawyer does not represent the client merely by the fact that the client had once consulted with the lawyer. Other lawyers make it a practice not to answer legal questions over the telephone and require an in-person consultation.[20] The manner in which a lawyer chooses to manage his or her practice and professional conduct is indeed largely stylistic, depending upon the type of practice. However, each immigration attorney must apply sound judgment and good law office management in resolving this issue.

Declining Representation—When the lawyer does not wish to represent a person, the lawyer must make this clear to the person seeking counsel. Again, the issue will be whether a reasonable person would have properly perceived that the attorney communicated his or her clear intention to decline representation in the specific situation at hand. Even lawyers who do not send nonengagement letters to clients who do not hire them may send nonengagement letters to decline representation.

DUAL REPRESENTATION

Dual representation in immigration law arises in any situation where an attorney provides services to two or more parties seeking an immigration benefit in one case. For example, an immigration attorney will represent a corporation as well as a foreign national employee.

---

[16] *ABA Manual, supra* note 14, "Lawyer-Client Relationship" at §31:101. *See also Bays v. Theran,* 418 Mass. 685; 639 N.E.2d 720 (Mass. 1994) (attorney-client relationship involving confidential communications can be established simply through telephone conversations and letters, even if the attorney never meets the client, never bills the client, and is never retained formally by the client).

[17] B. Hake "G-28 Notice of Appearance and the Client-Lawyer Relationship", 72 *Interpreter Releases* 757, 767 (June 5, 1995).

[18] *Id.*

[19] *Nichols v. Village Voice Inc.,* 417 NY.S.2d. 415, 418 (N.Y. Sup. Ct. 1979); *Kurtenback v. Tekippe,* 260 N.W.2d 53 (Iowa 1977).

[20] Allott, Montiel Davis, Kaye, Lawler & Webber, "Law Office Management Roundtable," 93-08 *Immigration Briefings* (Aug. 1993).

The basic concern with dual representation is that the lawyer may subordinate one party's interests to those of the other. Usually the interests of both parties will remain the same throughout the process and the concern is only theoretical. However, when one party's interests diverge in a material way from the other party's interests, or where one party shares with the lawyer information that he or she does not wish to share with the other party, the lawyer must address the concern, and resolve it.

In order for the lawyer to continue to represent both parties if a conflict arises, the lawyer must obtain consent (written consent is required by the revised Model Rules) notwithstanding the conflict; *i.e.*, both parties must knowingly waive the lawyer's duty of full confidentiality and loyalty.

Rule 1.7 of the Model Rules provides the following general rule regarding conflicts of interest:[21]

> (a) Except as provided in paragraph (b), a lawyer shall not represent a client if the representation involves a concurrent conflict of interest. A concurrent conflict of interest exists if:
>
> (1) the representation of one client will be directly adverse to another client; or
>
> (2) there is a significant risk that the representation of one or more clients will be materially limited by the lawyer's responsibilities to another client, a former client or a third person or by a personal interest of the lawyer.
>
> (b) Notwithstanding the existence of a concurrent conflict of interest under paragraph (a), a lawyer may represent a client if:
>
> (1) the lawyer reasonably believes that the lawyer will be able to provide competent and diligent representation to each affected client;
>
> (2) the representation is not prohibited by law;
>
> (3) the representation does not involve the assertion of a claim by one client against another client represented by the lawyer in the same litigation or other proceeding before a tribunal; and
>
> (4) each affected client gives informed consent, confirmed in writing.[22]

As one lawyer points out, "the key here in dual representation is to prevent impairment of one's ability to effectively represent clients."[23] This does not mean that the lawyer automatically has to withdraw, but that he or she needs to consult with both clients to determine whether representation may continue, considering the fact that an actual conflict, rather than a potential conflict has arisen.

However, even with informed consent, situations may arise where under the Model Rules, dual representation should not continue. In those instances, lawyers may need to withdraw from representation of both parties with respect to the specific case in question. In some immigration cases, however, continued representation of one client after the other client terminates a dual representation may be appropriate under the general rule that conflicts are construed less strictly in nonlitigation contexts.[24]

There are a number of possible solutions to handling a dual representation case before a conflict arises. One involves what has been criticized by one lawyer as the "Simple Solution"[25]; *i.e.*, regarding the foreign national as not being a client, when in fact the lawyer is involved in representing both the foreign national and the person or employer seeking an immigration benefit on the foreign national's behalf.

Another option involves using a retainer agreement, even in jurisdictions where it is not required. The agreement makes clear how potential conflicts will be handled. By having the agreement signed by all the parties, the attorney obtains the clients' informed consent at the outset.

In any dual representation situation, the lawyer needs to make it clear to both parties that there will either be no secrets between parties without their mutual consent. Therefore, what one party shares with the lawyer may also be assumed to be shared with the other party as well.

Finally, hiring separate counsel for the foreign national and the petitioner can avoid conflicts, although

---

[21] Model Rules, *supra* note 2, R. 1.7—"Conflict of Interest: General Rule."

[22] Note that in certain jurisdictions like California, a written waiver of conflict of interest is required at the outset of the relationship even before an actual conflict arises. *See* State
continued

Bar of California Rules of Prof'l Conduct (Jan. 1, 2000) at 3-310(C)(1), relating to potential conflicts, and (2), relating to actual conflict.

[23] Coven, *Ethical Issues in Immigration Practice*, 1209 PLI/Corp. 137 (33rd Annual Immigration and Naturalization Institute 2000 Practicing Law Institute) at 4.

[24] B. Hake, "Dual Representation in Immigration Practice: The Simple Solution is the Wrong Solution," 5 *Geo. Immigr. L.J.* 58 (Fall, 1991) (hereinafter Hake, Simple Solution).

[25] *Id.* at 4.

this option is often impractical for several reasons in the immigration context due to expense, difficulties in communication, and overlap in services.

DOCUMENT AND PRESENTATION FRAUD

A lawyer's obligation to present the truth and to refuse to participate in fraud is clear. Model Rule 3.3 states

(a) A lawyer shall not knowingly:

(1) make a false statement of fact or law to a tribunal or fail to correct a false statement of material fact or law previously made to the tribunal by the lawyer;

(2) fail to disclose to the tribunal legal authority in the controlling jurisdiction known to the lawyer to be directly adverse to the position of the client and not disclosed by opposing counsel; or

(3) offer evidence that the lawyer knows to be false. If a lawyer, the lawyer's client, or a witness called by the lawyer, has offered material evidence and the lawyer comes to know of its falsity, the lawyer shall take reasonable remedial measures, including, if necessary, disclosure to the tribunal. A lawyer may refuse to offer evidence, other than the testimony of a defendant in a criminal matter, that the lawyer reasonably believes is false.

(b) A lawyer who represents a client in an adjudicative proceeding and who knows that a person intends to engage, is engaging or has engaged in criminal or fraudulent conduct related to the proceeding shall take reasonable remedial measures, including, if necessary, disclosure to the tribunal.

(c) The duties stated in paragraphs (a) and (b) continue to the conclusion of the proceeding, and apply even if compliance requires disclosure of information otherwise protected by Rule 1.6.

(d) In an ex parte proceeding, a lawyer shall inform the tribunal of all material facts known to the lawyer that will enable the tribunal to make an informed decision, whether or not the facts are adverse:[26]

Model Rule 1.0(m) defines a "tribunal" as: a court, an arbitrator in a binding arbitration proceeding or a legislative body, administrative agency or other body acting in an adjudicative capacity. A legislative body, administrative agency or other body acts in an adjudicative capacity when a neutral official, after the presentation of evidence or legal argument by a party or parties, will render a binding legal judgment directly affecting a party's interests in a particular matter.

Immigration judges, USCIS examiners, and USCIS service centers all appear to meet this definition of tribunal. This is important because, with the new revisions, the Model Rules make the lawyer responsible not only for the lawyer's representations, but representations made by clients and third parties to the tribunal.

Furthermore, under the new revisions, the attorney-client privilege does not shield the client from attorney disclosure in certain situations. Neither does Model Rule 1.6, governing confidentiality. If the client has offered material evidence that is false, or if the client intends to engage in criminal or fraudulent conduct related to the proceeding, the lawyer may be required to disclose the situation to the tribunal. Note 11 to Model Rule 3.3 explains:

The disclosure of a client's false testimony can result in grave consequences to the client, including not only a sense of betrayal, but also loss of the case and perhaps a prosecution for perjury. But the alternative is that the lawyer cooperate in deceiving the court, thereby subverting the truth-finding process which the adversary system is designed to implement. See Rule 1.2(d). Furthermore, unless it is clearly understood that the lawyer will act upon the duty to disclose the existence of false evidence, the client can simply reject the lawyer's advice to reveal the false evidence and insist that the lawyer keep silent. Thus the client could in effect coerce the lawyer into being a party to fraud on the court.

Despite the ethical duties imposed on attorneys to be truthful to tribunals, the DHS and Congress recognize that ethical attorneys do not prepare all immigration applications. Deliberate misstatements and fraud on immigration-related applications prepared by applicants, by unlicensed practitioners, and even by unethical attorneys, are perceived as a serious problem. This has resulted in laws intended to penalize those who engage in fraudulent behavior. For example, IIRAIRA created civil liability:

---

[26] Model Rules, *supra* note 2, R. 3.3—"Candor Toward the Tribunal."

- for those who prepare, file, or assist another person in preparing or filing an application;
- the person filing must be doing so for benefits;
- with knowledge or in reckless disregard;
- of the fact that such an application or document was falsely made.[27]

The penalties for violations of this statute include $250–$2,000 per document for first offense and $2,000–$5,000 per document for subsequent offenses.[28]

The law significantly expanded the concept of "falsely making" to include false statements or misrepresentations on genuine immigration documents. IIRAIRA defined "falsely make" to mean:

- to prepare or provide an application or document;
- with knowledge or in reckless disregard;
- of the fact that the application or document contains
  - a false, fictitious, or fraudulent statement; or
  - a material representation or
  - has no basis in law or fact; or
  - otherwise fails to state a fact which is material to the purpose for which it was submitted;
- Changes apply retroactively to applications prepared before September 30, 1996, IIRAIRA's date of enactment.

The term "reckless disregard" has yet to be defined by the government[29] and as of March 2001, there has been no one charged in this regard.[30]

In addition to civil liability, IIRAIRA created criminal penalties for failure to disclose one's role as a document preparer. Specifically, INA §274C makes it a crime:

- For a person (attorney and nonattorney) to "knowingly and willfully" conceal; or
- Fail to disclose his or her role in preparing;
- For a fee or other remuneration;
- A false application for benefits under the INA.

Penalties under this section of the law include a fine and up to five years' imprisonment, plus permanent prohibition on any further preparing or assisting; for a second offense, penalties include a fine, and up to 15 years' imprisonment.[31]

In reviewing the scope of INA §274C, it is obvious that its effects are potentially far-reaching to members of immigrant communities who file applications for benefits, as well as those lawyers and nonlawyers who assist them in doing so.

Since the DHS possesses broad prosecutorial discretion in this arena, the preparer of documents to be filed should exercise caution. As indicated in a 1997 memorandum drafted by Paul Virtue, then-Acting Executive Associate Commissioner of the INS:

> [T]he term preparation should be construed broadly to include actually filling-out the form itself; completing other documents in support of the form (with knowledge at the time of completion that the information in the document is false and that the document will be attached to the form); instructing another about filling-out a form (with knowledge that the information entered on the form will be falsely made). The act of preparation may be related to a document other than a specific immigration benefit application form at the time that the document was prepared ... "[P]reparation" does not include giving general advice about immigration.[32]

In summary, an immigration lawyer must always remain vigilant in guarding against involvement with false or misleading information supplied by a client. Consequences can be severe, both in disciplinary and INA §274C proceedings.

FEES

Consultation Fees

Consultation fees are common in the practice of immigration law. Prospective clients sometimes do not end up engaging the attorney's services to handle a case. Furthermore, the level of knowledge required to accurately assess the options available to a

---

[27] INA §274C(a)(5).

[28] INA §274C(e).

[29] *But see US v. Sarantos*, 455 F.2d 877 (2d Cir. 1972) (an attorney who filed false documents with the INS engaged in reckless disregard for the truth in illegally planning to obtain permanent residence for his clients).

[30] 78 *Interpreter Releases* 473, 476 (Mar. 12, 2001).

[31] INA §274C(e)(2).

[32] INS Office of Program (HQPGM) memo (Sept. 3, 1997), "Criminal Penalties for Preparation of Falsely Made Applications for Immigration Benefits Added by Sections 213 & 214 of the Illegal Immigration Reform and Immigrant Responsibility Act of 1996 (IIRAIRA)," *reprinted in* 74 *Interpreter Releases* 1445 (Sept. 22, 1997).

prospective client, coupled with the amount of time generally required to obtain this information, together warrant some fee for this effort.

Factors that Influence Setting Fees

What attorneys charge for their services is primarily a matter of agreement between the lawyer and the client, not to mention "market forces." The one ethical guideline that governs attorney's fees is that a lawyer's fee must be "reasonable."[33] In determining whether a fee is reasonable the following factors are considered:

- The time and labor required, the novelty and difficulty of the questions involved, and the skill requisite to perform the legal service properly;
- The likelihood, if apparent to the client, that the acceptance of the particular employment will preclude other employment by the lawyer;
- The fee customarily charged in the locality for similar legal services;
- The amount involved and the results obtained;
- The time limitations imposed by the client or by the circumstances;
- The nature and length of the professional relationship with the client;
- The experience, reputation, and ability of the lawyer or lawyers performing the services; and
- Whether the fee is fixed or contingent.

The reasonableness test also applies to any interest charged on an unpaid client bill.[34] Many lawyers do not charge interest. Nevertheless, nearly every jurisdiction permits lawyers to charge interest on legal fees that remain unpaid, if the client has agreed to such an arrangement.[35] However, the interest rate must be within the legal limits. Furthermore, the total amount of fees plus interest sought from the client must be reasonable.

Under the Model Rules a lawyer is prohibited from sharing his or her legal fees with a nonlawyer, except in very limited situations.[36] The policy behind this general prohibition is to avoid the possibility of a nonlawyer's interference with the exercise of a lawyer's independent professional judgment and to ensure that the total fee paid by a client is not unreasonably high.[37]

One principle should always guide: Make sure the client understands the fee arrangement and agrees to it in advance, preferably in writing.

COMMON DISCIPLINARY COMPLAINTS MADE AGAINST IMMIGRATION LAWYERS

In the field of immigration law, there are a number of complaints that frequently arise.[38] Below, are the most frequent of those complaints. It is important to be mindful of these topics from the outset, and to take appropriate steps to prevent them from occurring in your practice.

Failure to Timely File Applications/Petitions with DHS

When a lawyer takes on a case, he or she must understand that all deadlines and expirations become his or her professional problem. Lawyers should not take cases where they cannot assure themselves and their clients that they can and will meet all necessary deadlines. In immigration, the possible consequences of failure are fairly obvious: risk of an overstay, unlawful presence, removal, or loss of important immigration benefits.

Failure to Provide Accurate and Timely Case Status Information

As discussed previously in the section on "Communication—Keeping Clients Informed," there is simply no substitute for a lawyer's adequate performance of this responsibility. The most common complaints in this area allege that the attorneys did not keep clients apprised of the progress of their cases, did not provide sufficient notice (or any notice) of deadlines, and simply failed to respond to repeated inquiries.

---

[33] Model Rules, *supra* note 2, R. 1.5—"Fees."

[34] Michigan Informal Ethics Opinion RI-40 (1989).

[35] *See* ABA Manual, *supra* note 14, "Conduct, Fees" at §41:2017.

[36] *See* Model Rules, *supra* note 2, R. 5.4—"Professional Independence of a Lawyer" (addressing issues regarding the professional independence of a lawyer, and the limited situations in which fee sharing and affiliation is permissible).

[37] ABA Formal Ethics Opinion 87–355 (Dec. 14, 1987).

[38] Heiserman, Clark, "Professional Responsibility in Immigration Practice and Government Service," 22 *San Diego L. Rev.* 971, 980 (1985). The specific professional responsibility problems in immigration practice listed in this law review article of 1985 still hold true today. The primary problems listed are frivolous actions, fraud, dishonesty, neglect, and delay.

Incompetence

Even attorneys who are neither negligent nor dishonest are sometimes just "over their head" in the substantive law they attempt to practice. It is a trap to proceed believing that some aspects of immigration law are no more complicated that completing forms. Mistakes in strategy can result in creating bars to adjustment of status or inadmissibility. As the Model Rules simply state: "Competent representation requires the legal knowledge, skill, thoroughness and preparation reasonably necessary for the representation."[39]

Generally, members of the immigration bar are willing to share information and discuss cases. Making inquiries through the local AILA chapter, or contacting an AILA Mentor[40] (after making a reasonable effort to inform yourself of the applicable law, regulations, and procedures) are excellent methods for avoiding problems of competency.

PRACTICE POINTERS

Retainer Agreements—Retainer agreements are useful tools for good law office practice. The immigration field is no exception. Regular use of retainers is generally recommended even when not mandated by state law. The retainer agreement can serve a number of important functions. First, it establishes the lawyer's relationship with the client. Second, it serves as a memorialization of the written consent to joint representation. Third, an effective retainer agreement will explain the limits of representation, address the waiver of confidentiality in joint representation situations, and explain how the firm would handle potential conflicts should they arise. Finally—and in some respects most importantly—the retainer agreement sets forth the fee arrangement: how much, when due, and covering what. While retainer agreements are a useful tool to the lawyer, it is important to recognize from a public policy standpoint, that the lawyer cannot opt out of future malpractice liability through language in the retainer agreement.

Technological Advances—The growth of technology and near-universal availability of the Internet makes it easier to stay in touch with clients and keep them apprised of milestone events in their case. Technological developments have created greater opportunities to effectively track deadlines. E-mail, cellular telephones with roaming capabilities, and fax-machines have made it possible to communicate nearly instantly with clients, regardless of their geographical location.

Lawyers should consider the pros, as well as the possible cons, of automating some aspects of communication with clients. For example, an e-mail or tickler may be automatically generated to remind the lawyer to communicate with the client with respect to a particular milestone. In this way, the client will be regularly updated and informed, thus minimizing the possibility for misunderstanding. Many routine communications can be drafted in advance and generated automatically, adding individual case information from a client database. In "automating", the lawyer should not only have back-ups, but should take steps to avoid a client perception that that he or she is being offered a "one size fits all", "canned" service.

The lawyer should not expect technology to replace service. Any examination of ethical behavior will hinge upon the manner of service provided by the lawyer to the client. Even in this day of Palm Pilot "beaming," intranets, voicemail, e-mail, and voice-recognition telephone systems, there is still no substitute for face-to-face or telephone conversations with clients to answer questions, explain a specific area of law, or to alleviate the concerns and anxieties surrounding the immigration process.

Best Practice Methods—Best practices may differ depending upon your clientele and the governing state rules. However, it is critical to thoughtfully consider best practices in a preventive posture, rather than as a result of specific ethical complaints lodged against you or a lawyer you know.

There are a variety of methods employed by lawyers to ensure the utmost ethical compliance. Some will not provide legal advice to clients over the phone. Some will follow up with the advice in writing. Some will use a written agreement signed by both parties in a dual representation context, even when not required to do so by state law. Some will send a nonengagement letter to clients after a consultation to ensure that the client does not mistakenly believe that the lawyer is representing them.[41]

---

[39] Model Rules, *supra* note 2, R. 1.1—"Competence."

[40] *See* www.aila.org/infonet under "Member Network."

[41] Two lawyers offer sound practical advice in an easy to read checklist format. *See* B. Hake, "Some Professional Responsibility Issues in Law Firm Management" and H. R. Klasko, "Ethical Issues Affecting Immigration Law Practice
continued

One strong recommendation is to have both parties, petitioner and beneficiary, sign a Form G-28 upon the commencement of representation. In addition to the client engagement letter (also strongly recommended), the execution of the G-28 will serve to further solidify the notion of representation to all parties involved, as well as to any agency or organization before whom the attorney may enter an appearance.[42] Also, it is generally advisable to indicate on the Form G-28 the specific nature of the representation, (e.g., I-140 Immigrant Visa Petition as a Multinational Manager or Executive)[43] since this helps to clarify the scope of the lawyer-client relationship.

Additionally, when attorneys enter their appearance with immigration court and file an EOIR-28, the scope of representation is not limited to the master calendar hearing. The lawyer is expected to represent the client for the duration of the removal proceedings. If the lawyer wishes to withdraw from the matter, a motion to withdraw must be filed outlining the reasons requesting the motion. The immigration judge will exercise discretion when granting the motion and may chose to deny the motion and the attorney will be expected to appear for every scheduled court appearance. Lawyers should check local operating procedures of the immigration court for Motions to Withdraw Representation.

CONCLUSION

For many lawyers, the myriad of ethical issues that arise in the practice of immigration law will remain a theoretical consideration, with few of us likely to face actual disciplinary proceedings. A larger percentage of us will be the subject of complaints lodged by clients. As in many other areas of life, you can avoid many potential problems by setting in place effective safeguards to address them before they occur.

One lawyer who represents other lawyers facing disciplinary proceedings advises that a lawyer's best protection is to practice defensively.[44] Again, the manner in which this advice translates into one's daily practice will vary. However, in structuring your conduct it is helpful to visualize what your colleagues would think if you were accused of committing an ethical violation. In this era of strict scrutiny from the media, your reputation can easily be marred by even the appearance of impropriety. Thus, as officers of the court, we must strive to avoid even the appearance of impropriety and always err on the side of caution in representing our clients.

KEY RESOURCES IN THE ETHICAL ARENA

There are many effective resources available regarding ethics issues. Resources include: Web sites, hotlines, bar associations, mentors, and colleagues. Additionally, the following Web sites may also be of general use in familiarizing the lawyer with actual cases, governing rules, and other relevant information:

- ABA Model Rules of Professional Conduct (*www2.law.cornell.edu/cgi-bin/foliocgi.exe/ModelRules*);

- ABA Model Code of Professional Responsibility (*www2.law.cornell.edu/cgi-bin/foliocgi.exe/Mdlcpr*);

- ABA Center for Professional Responsibility (*www.abanet.org/cpr/home.html*);

- Professional Responsibility Codes in Each State (*www.legalethics.com/states.htm*); (*www.law.cornell.edu/ethics/index.html*)

(These sites contain links to the professional responsibility codes of every state and the District of Columbia, and indicate whether each state's code tracks the Model Code, the Model Rules, represents either a major modification to the Model Rules, or is the state's own code);

- National Organization of Bar Counsel (NOBC) (*http://nobc.org*) (NOBC offers a current developments page containing summaries of recent cases involving attorney discipline);

- FindLaw.com

 (*www.findlaw.com/01topics/14ethics/index.html*); and

- The EOIR, which posts a list of suspended and expelled lawyers on its Web site at (*www.usdoj.gov/eoir/profcond/chart.htm*).

---

an Overview," in *Ethics and Your Immigration Practice*, supra note 4, at 1 and 30, respectively.

[42] 72 *Interpreter Releases* 757, 761 (June 5, 1995).

[43] *Id.* at 764.

[44] AILA Ethics Conference, New York, Nov. 6, 1998. Presentation made by Sarah D. McShea, Esq., an attorney who represents indicted attorneys.

UTILIZING IMMIGRATION PARAPROFESSIONALS: THE ETHICAL CONSIDERATIONS

by Mark J. Newman and Russell C. Ford[*]

INTRODUCTION

To meet their tremendous responsibilities, modern immigration attorneys heavily rely on non-attorney assistants. Appropriate utilization of these paraprofessionals carries the responsibility of supervising the delivery of competent legal services, preserving client confidentiality and deterring the unauthorized practice of law.

Immigration paralegals come from a variety of backgrounds and are now used in innumerable roles. They may have been experienced secretaries, have paralegal certificates, have baccalaureate or law degrees from the United States or abroad, some are licensed attorneys in foreign jurisdictions, have language and cultural affinities, or are former INS/DHS, Department of Labor, or State Department employees. These key support personnel can exert an immense influence over clients and shoulder substantial day-to-day responsibilities for cases. Immigration practices tend to use paralegals to a greater extent than attorneys in many other practice areas. This ranges from general practitioners, who—not limiting their practice to immigration rely to a great extent on their paralegals—to immigration attorneys utilizing immigration dedicated paralegals, to in-house paralegals at Fortune 100 companies.

This article surveys the regulatory landscape and addresses some of the common pitfalls that an immigration practitioner encounters when utilizing paraprofessionals.

DEFINITION OF TERMS

Legal Assistant/Paralegal—General Definition

American Bar Association (ABA) Definition: A legal assistant or paralegal is a person, qualified through education, training or work experience, who is employed or retained by a lawyer, law office, corporation, governmental agency, or other entity and who performs specifically delegated substantive legal work *for which the lawyer is responsible.*[1]

The National Association of Legal Assistants (NALA[2]*) Definition*: NALA does not differentiate between "legal assistant" and "paralegal" and defines both as a distinguishable group of persons who assist attorneys in the delivery of legal services. Through formal education, training and experience, legal assistants have knowledge and expertise regarding the legal system and substantive and proce-

---

[*] Mark J. Newman is the immigration law partner at Troutman Sanders. Newman's practice ranges from the transfer of international business executives to the defense of corporations charged with employer sanction violations. He continues his practice in immigration litigation and appellate work before various administrative agencies and in the federal courts. Newman practiced immigration and trial law in Florida for 10 years before moving to Atlanta and joining Troutman Sanders in 1989. He served as lead counsel in the federal class action proceedings to acquire lawful permanent residence for the more than 100,000 Mariel Cubans. Newman served as chairman of AILA's Atlanta District Director's Liaison Committee and co-chaired the ABA/Prentice Hall Seminar on the 1990 Immigration Act in Atlanta. He co-authored *Immigration Law and Practice in Florida*. He received his undergraduate degree in 1976 from Princeton University and his law degree in 1979 from the University of Miami School of Law.

Russell C. Ford is an associate in the Immigration law practice at Troutman Sanders LLP. Prior to joining the firm in January 2004, Ford practiced Immigration Law in New York and Atlanta for four years. Ford's practice focuses on employment-based immigration for multinational corporations, universities and colleges, and sports organizations. He works with companies to obtain work authorization on behalf of graduates, trainees, new hires, and transferees. He also advises companies on employment-based immigration issues and employment documentation issues. Ford is a member of AILA and has presented at several seminars regarding immigration issues, problems, and techniques. Ford received his undergraduate degree in 1995 from Stonehill College, a master's degree in 1996 from Boston University, and his law degree in 1999 from Tulane University School of Law.

---

[1] Article 21.12 of the ABA By-Laws (as amended, August 1997).

[2] NALA is a leading professional association for legal assistants and paralegals and provides continuing education, professional development programs, and voluntary certification programs. Information on NALA can be found at *www.nala.org*.

dural law which qualify them to do work of a legal nature *under the supervision of an attorney.*

The National Federation of Paralegal Associations, Inc. (NFPA[3]) Definition: A paralegal is a person qualified through education, training or work experience to perform substantive legal work that requires knowledge of legal concepts and is customarily, but not exclusively, performed by a lawyer. This person may be retained or employed by a lawyer, law office, governmental agency or other entity or may be authorized by administrative, statutory or court authority to perform this work. NFPA does not differentiate between "paralegal" or "legal assistant."

Legal Assistant/Paralegal—State-by-State (non-inclusive) Definition Survey:

Arizona: through case law, has adopted the ABA definition and utilizes the terms, paralegal, legal assistant, and law clerk interchangeably[4];

California: California Business & Professions Code Secs. 6450, *et seq.* defines who can use the term "paralegal," education and experience requirements, and mandatory ethical requirements. "'Paralegal' means a person who either contracts with or is employed by an attorney, law firm, corporation, governmental agency, or other entity and who performs substantial legal work under the direction and supervision of an active member of the State Bar of California, as defined in Section 6060, an attorney practicing law in the federal courts of this state, that has been specifically delegated by the attorney to him or her."

Colorado: Legal Assistants (and/or paralegals) are a distinguishable group of persons who assist attorneys in the delivery of legal services. Through education, training and experience, legal assistants have knowledge and expertise regarding the legal system and substantive and procedural law which will qualify them to do work of a legal nature under the direction and supervision of a licensed attorney.

Connecticut: Legal assistants or paralegals are persons employed by law offices who are not admitted to practice law but a major part of whose work is performing tasks commonly performed by lawyers and who are under the general supervision and control of lawyers. Paralegals may be salaried employees or independent contractors such as freelance paralegals utilized on occasion by lawyers for special assignments.[5]

Florida: Legal assistant means a person, who, under the supervision and direction of a licensed attorney, engages in legal research, and case development and planning in relation to modifications, initial proceedings, services, processes, or applications, or who prepares or interprets legal documents or selects, compiles, and uses technical information from references such as digests, encyclopedias, or practice manual and analyzes and follows procedural problems that involve independent decisions.[6]

Illinois: "Paralegal" means a person who is qualified through education, training, or work experience and is employed by a lawyer, law office, governmental agency, or other entity to work under the direction of an attorney in a capacity that involves the performance of substantive legal work that usually requires a sufficient knowledge of legal concepts and would be performed by the attorney in the absence of the paralegal."[7]

Indiana: State Supreme Court has enacted the Rules of Professional Conduct: Guidelines on the Use of Paralegals states that all lawyers must utilize paralegals according to certain guidelines pursuant to an attorney's duty to supervise in Rule 5.3. The Indiana Code at Section 1-1-4.6 defines "paralegal" as a "person who is (1) qualified through education, training, or work experience; and (2) employed by a lawyer, law office, governmental agency, or other entity, to work under the direction of an attorney in a capacity that involves the performance of substantive legal work that usually requires a sufficient knowledge of legal concepts and would be performed by the attorney in the absence of the paralegal."

---

[3] NFPA is a nonprofit, professional organization comprising state and local paralegal associations throughout the United States and Canada. NFPA affirms the paralegal profession as an independent, self-directed profession which supports increased quality, efficiency, and accessibility in the delivery of legal services. NFPA promotes the growth, development and recognition of the profession as an integral partner in the delivery of legal services. Information on NFPA can be found at *www.paralegals.org*.

[4] *See Continental Townhomes East Unit One Association v. Brockbank*, 152 Ariz. 537, 545 n. 9 (1986).

[5] Special Inter-Committee Group to Study the Role of Paralegals, December 1985, Connecticut State Bar Association.

[6] Florida Statutes Annotated Section 57.104.

[7] Illinois State Statutes, 5 ILCS 70/1.35.

Iowa: The Iowa legislature adopted a detailed set of guidelines outlining when an attorney could delegate to a non-lawyer, but did not specifically define paralegal, legal assistant or otherwise.

Kentucky: The Kentucky State Supreme Court in Rule 3.700 defines "paralegals" as persons under the supervision and direction of a licensed lawyer, who may apply knowledge of law and legal procedures in rendering direct assistance to lawyers engaged in legal research, preparing or interpreting legal documents and writing detailed procedures for practicing in certain fields of law; select, compile and use technical information from such references as digests, encyclopedias or practice manuals, and analyze and follow procedural problems that involve independent decisions.

Maine: "Paralegal" or "legal assistant" means a person who is qualified by education, training or work experience, who is employed or retained by an attorney, law office, corporation, governmental agency or other entity and who performs specifically delegated substantive legal work for which an attorney is responsible.[8]

Michigan: A "paralegal" is any person currently employed or retained by a lawyer, law office, governmental agency, or other entity engaged in the practice of law, in a capacity or function which involves the performance under the direction and supervision of an attorney of specifically delegated substantive legal work, which work, for the most part, requires a sufficient knowledge of legal concepts such that absent that legal assistant, the attorney would perform the tasks and which is not primarily clerical or secretarial in nature.[9]

Missouri: The Missouri State Bar adopted guidelines for using paralegals and defined "paralegal" as a person qualified through education, training or work experience, employed or retained by an attorney, law firm, government agency, corporation, or other entity to perform substantive and procedural legal work under the ultimate direction and supervision of an attorney or as authorized by administrative, statutory, or court authority.

Montana: "Paralegal" or "legal assistant" means a person qualified through education, training, or work experience to perform substantive legal work that requires knowledge of legal concepts and that is customarily but not exclusively performed by a lawyer and who may be retained or employed by one or more lawyers or law offices, or pursuant to administrative, statutory, or court authority to perform this work.[10]

Nevada: Nevada State Bar Association, Division of Legal Assistants, defines a legal assistant (or paralegal) as a person, qualified through education, training or work experience, who is employed or retained by a lawyer, law office, governmental agency, or other entity, in a capacity or function which involves the performance, under the ultimate direction and supervision of an attorney, of specifically delegated substantive legal work which work for the most part, requires a sufficient knowledge of legal concepts that, absent such assistant, the attorney would perform the task.

New Hampshire: State Supreme Court issued Administrative Rule 3, which defines "paralegals" as a person not admitted to the practice of law in N.H. who is an employee of or an assistant to an active member of the N.H. Bar, a partnership comprised of active members of the N.H. Bar, a professional association within the meaning of RSA Chapter 294-A, and, who, under the control and supervision of an active member of the N.H. Bar renders services related to but not constituting the practice of law.

New Mexico: State Supreme Court issued a definition of "legal assistant" as a person not admitted to the practice of law who provides assistance to a licensed lawyer and for whose work that licensed lawyer is ultimately responsible.

North Carolina: State Bar Association adopted requirements for "legal assistants" to be eligible to join the "Legal Assistant Section." These requirements defined a "legal assistant" as a person, qualified through education and work experience, who is employed as an employee and not as an independent contractor, on a full-time basis (at least 800 hours), by either one attorney, a single law firm, one governmental agency, or one other business entity in a capacity or function which involves the performance of a substantial amount of specifically delegated substantive legal work, which work, for the most part, requires a sufficient knowledge of legal concepts that, absent such person doing the work, the attorney would perform the task; the performance of legal work to be under the actual direction and su-

---

[8] Maine Revised Statutes Annotated, Title 4, Section 921.

[9] Michigan State Bar, Bylaws, Article 1.

[10] Montana Code 37-60-101.

pervision of an attorney who is licensed to practice law in the state of N.C. and who has ultimate responsibility and accountability for such person's work—the supervising attorney to be the attorney who employs such person.

[*Editor's Note*: According to the North Carolina Academy of Trial Lawyers, on July 16, 2004, statutory changes to NCGS 84-23 and 84-37 were enacted. If signed by the Governor, the changes become effective on October 1, 2004. The statutes authorize the North Carolina State Bar to regulate NC certified paralegals and seek injunctive relief for the improper use of the titles.

On July 16, 2004, the North Carolina State Bar Council voted to approve the Plan for Paralegal Certification contingent upon the Governor signing it. Once signed, the Plan for Paralegal Certification will be sent to the NC Supreme Court for approval.

The NC State Bar Council anticipates appointing the initial Board of Paralegal Certification during its October Council meeting.]

North Dakota: State Supreme Court adopted Rule 1.5, which defines "legal assistant (or paralegal)" as a person who assists lawyers in the delivery of legal services, and who through formal education, training, or experience, has knowledge and expertise regarding the legal system and substantive and procedural law which qualifies the person to do work of a legal nature under the direct supervision of a licensed lawyer.[11]

Oklahoma: State Bar Association defines "legal assistant" or "paralegal" as a person qualified by education, training or work experience who is employed or retained by a lawyer, law office, corporation, governmental agency or other entity who performs specifically delegated substantive legal work for which a lawyer is responsible, and absent such assistant, the lawyer would perform the task.

Rhode Island: State Supreme Court adopted Rule 5.5, which sets guidelines for the use of "legal assistants" and defines these non-lawyers as one who, under the supervision of a lawyer, applies knowledge of law and legal procedures rendering direct assistance to lawyers, clients and courts.[12]

South Dakota: State Legislature has passed several laws regarding paralegals. "Legal assistants" are a distinguishable group of persons who assist licensed attorneys in the delivery of legal services. Through formal education, training, and experience, legal assistants have knowledge and expertise regarding the legal system, substantive and procedural law, the ethical considerations of the legal profession, and the Rules of Professional Conduct as stated in Chapters 16-18, which qualify them to do work of a legal nature under the employment and direct supervision of a licensed attorney.[13] South Dakota also requires that legal assistants be certified by successfully completing the Certified Legal Assistant examination issued by NALA or through other means enunciated in Chapter 16-18-34.1 and 16-18-34.2, which will be discussed in further detail in Section II, Duty of Attorney to Supervise Paralegal.

Texas: State Bar issued "General Guidelines for the Utilization of the Services of Legal Assistants by Attorneys," which defined "legal assistant" as a person who must work under the supervision of an attorney and not provide legal advice or engage in the unauthorized practice of law. Legal assistants may perform delegated services so long as (1) the client understands the legal assistant is not an attorney, (2) the attorney maintains direct relationship with the client, (3) the attorney directs and supervises the legal assistant, and (4) the attorney remains professionally responsible for the client and the client's legal matters.

Virginia: State Bar Committee on the Unauthorized Practice of Law adopted the following definition of "paralegal/legal assistant:" one who is a specially trained individual who performs substantive legal work that requires a knowledge of legal concepts and who either works under the supervision of an attorney who assumes professional responsibility for the final work product, or works in areas where lay individuals are explicitly authorized by statute or regulation to assume certain law-related responsibilities.

Washington: State Court of Appeals defined "legal assistant" as one who is qualified through education, training, or work experience, is employed or retained by a lawyer, law office, governmental agency or other entity in a capacity or function which involves a performance under the ultimate direction and supervision of an attorney, of specifically delegated legal work, which work for the most part requires a sufficient knowledge of legal con-

---

[11] North Dakota Rules of Professional Conduct, Rule 1.5.
[12] Rhode Island Rules of Professional Conduct, Rule 5.5.
[13] South Dakota Rules of Professional Conduct 16-18-34.

cepts that, absent such assistant, the attorney would perform the task.[14]

West Virginia: State Bar Association defined "legal assistant" as a person, qualified through education, training, or work experience, who is employed or retained by a lawyer, law office, governmental agency, or other entity, in a capacity or function which involves the performance, under the ultimate direction and supervision of an attorney of delegated substantive legal work, which work, for the most part, requires sufficient knowledge of legal concepts that, absent such assistance, the attorney would perform the task.

Wisconsin: State Bar Paralegal Task Force defined "paralegal" as a person, qualified through education and training, who supervised by a lawyer licensed to practice law in WI, to perform substantive legal work requiring sufficient knowledge of legal concepts that, absent the paralegal, the attorney would perform the work.

Common Theme—"Under the supervision of an attorney"

Nearly all states, organizations representing lawyers and paralegals, and courts, have stated that a paralegal should not perform any substantive legal work *unless* that work is *properly* supervised by an attorney. We will discuss the attorney's duty to supervise a paralegal among other ethical considerations that lawyers face in the employment of and reliance upon paralegals within their practice.

THE TWO MAJOR PARALEGAL ORGANIZATIONS

National Association of Legal Assistants:

Introduction

NALA is a leading professional association for legal assistants and paralegals and was incorporated in 1975. Currently, NALA has more than 18,000 members and 92 state and local affiliated associations. NALA was formed to increase the professional standing of legal assistants, provide uniformity among the states in the utilization of legal assistants, and establish national standards of professional competence. NALA's contact information is 1516 S. Boston, #200, Tulsa, OK 74119, (918) 587-6828.

NALA has introduced Model Standards and Guidelines for the Utilization of Legal Assistants as "the proper utilization of legal assistants contributes to the delivery of cost-effective, high-quality legal services" and to provide an educational document to legal professionals.[15]

Standards

Legal assistants should meet one of the following minimum standards to demonstrate professional abilities:

- Successful completion of the Certified Legal Assistant certifying examination of NALA (discussed below[16]);
- Graduation from an ABA-approved program of study for legal assistants;
- Graduation from a course of study for legal assistants, which is institutionally accredited but not ABA approved, and which requires not less than the equivalent of 60 semester hours of classroom study;
- Graduation from a course of study for legal assistants other than set forth above and not less than six months of in-house training as a legal assistant;
- A baccalaureate degree in any field plus not less than six months of in-house training as a legal assistant;
- A minimum of three years of law-related experience under the supervision of an attorney including at least six months of in-house training as a legal assistant; or
- Two years of training as a legal assistant.[17]

Guidelines Relating to Standards of Performance and Professional Responsibility

In general, under ABA Model Rules of Professional Conduct, Rule 5.3, a legal assistant is allowed to perform any task that is properly delegated and *supervised* by an attorney, *as long as the attorney is*

---

[14] See *Absher Construction Co. v. Kent School District*, 9 P.2d 1086 (1995).

[15] NALA's Model Standards and Guidelines for Utilization of Legal Assistants, Preamble.

[16] The Certified Legal Assistant examination established by NALA in 1976 is a voluntary nationwide certification program for legal assistants.

[17] NALA's Model Standards and Guidelines for Utilization of Legal Assistants, Section III, Standards.

ultimately responsible to the client and assumes complete professional responsibility for the work product (emphasis added).[18]

NALA Guidelines

Legal Assistants should:

- Disclose their status as legal assistant at the outset of any professional relationship;
- Preserve attorney-client privilege; and
- Understand the attorney's Rules of Professional Conduct and avoid any action which would involve the attorney in violation of the Rules or give the appearance of professional impropriety.[19]

Legal Assistants should NOT:

- Establish attorney-client relationships, set legal fees, give legal opinions or advice, or represent a client before a court, unless authorized to do so by said court; or
- Engage in, encourage, or contribute to any act which would constitute the unauthorized practice of law.[20]

Legal assistants may perform services for an attorney in the representation of a client, provided:

- The services performed do not require the exercise of independent professional legal judgment;
- The attorney maintains a direct relationship with the client and maintains control of all client matters;
- The attorney supervises the legal assistant;
- The attorney remains professionally responsible for all work on behalf of the client including any actions taken by the legal assistant in connection therewith; and
- The services performed supplement, merge with and become the attorney's work product.[21]

In supervising the legal assistant, consideration should be given to:

- Designating work assignments that correspond to the legal assistant's abilities, knowledge, training and experience;
- Educating and training the legal assistant with respect to professional responsibility, local rules and practices, and firm policies;
- Monitoring the work and professional conduct of the legal assistant to ensure that the work is substantively correct and timely performed;
- Providing continuing education for the legal assistant in substantive matters through courses, institutes, workshops, seminars and in-house training; and
- Encouraging and supporting membership and active participation in professional organizations.[22]

Certified Legal Assistant (CLA) Certifying Examination

Facts:

- Currently, 11,801 legal assistants maintain a CLA credential;
- Two-day examination divided into five sections:
  - Communications;
  - Ethics;
  - Legal Research;
  - Judgment and Analytical Ability; and
  - Substantive Law.

---

[18] NALA's Model Standards and Guidelines for Utilization of Legal Assistants, Section IV, Guidelines. ABA Model Rules of Professional Conduct, Rule 5.3 states "With respect to a nonlawyer employed or retained by or associated with a lawyer: (a) a partner in a law firm shall make reasonable efforts to ensure that the firm has in effect measures giving reasonable assurance that the person's conduct is compatible with the professional obligations of the lawyer; (b) a lawyer having direct supervisory authority over the nonlawyer shall make reasonable efforts to ensure that the person's conduct is compatible with the professional obligations of the lawyer; and (c) a lawyer shall be responsible for conduct of such a person that would be a violation of the rules of professional conduct if engaged in by a lawyer if: (1) the lawyer orders or, with the knowledge of the specific conduct, ratifies the conduct involved; or (2) the lawyer is a partner in the law firm in which the person is employed, or has direct supervisory authority over the person, and knows of the conduct at a time when its consequences can be avoided or mitigated but fails to take remedial action.

[19] NALA's Model Standards and Guidelines for Utilization of Legal Assistants, Section V, Guideline 1.

[20] NALA's Model Standards and Guidelines for Utilization of Legal Assistants, Section V, Guideline 2.

[21] NALA's Model Standards and Guidelines for Utilization of Legal Assistants, Section V, Guideline 3.

[22] NALA's Model Standards and Guidelines for Utilization of Legal Assistants, Section V, Guideline 4.

The examination is voluntary and is not required by any state in order to be employed as a legal assistant.

To qualify for the CLA, a candidate must meet *one* of the following criteria:

- Graduation from a legal assistant program that is:
  - Approved by the ABA;
  - Associate degree program;
  - Post-baccalaureate certificate program in legal assistant studies;
  - Bachelor degree program in legal studies; or
  - Legal assistant program which consists of a minimum of 60 semester hours of classroom study of which 15 semester hours are substantive legal courses.
- A bachelor degree in any field plus one year of experience as a legal assistant.
- High school diploma or equivalent plus seven years of experience as a legal assistant under the supervision of a member of the Bar plus evidence of a minimum of 20 hours of continuing legal education credit within the two-year period preceding the exam date.[23]

CLA credential is valid for five years and can be renewed only with submission of evidence demonstrating completion of at least 50 hours of continuing legal education credit.

National Federation of Paralegal Associations

Formed in 1974, the National Federation of Paralegal Associations, Inc. (NFPA) is the largest and oldest national paralegal association. Created as a non-profit federation, NFPA is an issues-oriented, policy-driven professional association, directed by its membership. The NFPA contact information is: 2517 Eastlake Avenue East, Suite 200, Seattle, WA 98102. (206) 652-4120 or *info@paralegals.org*.

NFPA is comprised of local and state paralegal associations, as well as individual members. NFPA has grown from eight charter members to more than 60 associations located throughout the United States. This membership includes more than 15,000 paralegal professionals working in traditional and non-traditional roles at law firms, corporations, government agencies, legal service agencies, and other law-related entities.

NFPA was formed to:

- Foster, promote and develop the profession;
- Monitor legislation, case law and ethics' opinions affecting the profession;
- Maintain a nationwide communications network;
- Advance the educational standards of the profession; and
- Conduct seminars, research issues and engage in other matters relating to the profession.

Mission Statement

NFPA is a nonprofit professional organization comprised of state and local paralegal associations throughout the United States and Canada. NFPA affirms the paralegal profession as a self-directed profession which supports increased quality, efficiency and accessibility in the delivery of legal services. NFPA promotes growth, development and recognition of the profession as an integral partner in the delivery of legal services.[24]

According to the NFPA, paralegals perform the same functions as an attorney except those prohibited by unauthorized practice of law statutes. Therefore, NFPA is in favor of professional regulation to protect the public and a Model Code of Ethics and Professional Responsibility and Guidelines for Enforcement (adopted in 1993, revised in 1997):

- A paralegal shall maintain and achieve a high level of competence through education, training and work experience to include at least 12 hours of continuing legal education every two years;[25]
- A paralegal shall maintain a high level of personal and professional integrity including maintaining client confidences and refraining from engaging in any activity that could be perceived as an unauthorized practice of law;[26]
- A paralegal's title shall be fully disclosed in all business and professional communications in-

---

[23] National Association of Legal Assistants Certified Legal Assistant Program – Fact Sheet, June 2003.

[24] National Federation of Paralegal Associations: *www.paralegals.org*.

[25] NFPA Model Disciplinary Rules and Ethical Considerations, Section 1-1.1.

[26] NFPA Model Disciplinary Rules and Ethical Considerations, Section 1-1.2, 1-1.5, and 1-1.8.

cluding business cards, brochures, directories, and promotional materials;[27]

- Paralegals shall be subject to discipline under the Model Code.[28]

NFPA endorses the regulation of paralegals through the following plan:

- Two-tiered licensing plan, which constitutes mandatory regulation;
- Second form of regulation through certification and/or registration;
- Standards for ethics;
- Standards for discipline including a disciplinary process;
- Standards for education;
- Method for assessing the competency of paralegals;
- Defining "unauthorized practice of law" through allowable tasks for paralegals in different substantive subject areas.[29]

Paralegal Advanced Competency Exam (PACE)

Instituted in 1996 by NFPA to be consistent with two-tier licensing program discussed above. Voluntary credentialing program that is not currently required by any State to practice as a paralegal.

Tier One would test thinking and problem solving skills including general legal questions. Criteria to sit for Tier One:

- Associate's Degree in paralegal studies obtained from an institutionally accredited and/or ABA-approved paralegal education program, and six years of substantive paralegal experience; or
- Bachelor's Degree and completion of a paralegal program from an institutionally accredited school, and three years of substantive experience as a paralegal; or
- Bachelor's Degree and completion of a paralegal program with an institutionally accredited school, and two years of substantive paralegal experience; or
- Four years of experience as a paralegal before 12/31/2000.[30]

Tier Two would test knowledge of specific legal practice areas.

CERTIFICATION? LICENSURE?

What, if anything, is required, and what, if anything, are states doing to regulate the paralegal profession?

Generally, most states "regulate" paralegals through unauthorized practice of law statutes and through the State Bar's regulation of attorneys charged with supervising the paralegal. These general concepts will be discussed in more detail below.

Currently, *no* state licenses or certifies paralegals and only California has adopted educational and/or work experience requirements for individuals who wish to utilize the title "paralegal."

The American Bar Association (ABA) has issued Model Guidelines for the Utilization of Legal Assistant Services designed to provide attorneys with safeguards to employing and supervising paralegals in the course of their daily duties. These Guidelines were adopted by the ABA House of Delegates in 1991 and are generally governed by Rule 5.3 of the ABA Model Rules of Professional Conduct:

- A lawyer is responsible for all of the professional actions of a legal assistant performing legal assistant services at the lawyer's direction and should take reasonable measures to ensure that the legal assistant's conduct is consistent with the lawyer's obligations under the ABA Model Rules of Professional Conduct;[31]
- A lawyer must maintain responsibility for the work product of the legal assistant and cannot permit the legal assistant to conduct any activities prohibited by statute, court rule, administrative rule or regulation, or controlling authority;[32]

---

[27] NFPA Model Disciplinary Rules and Ethical Considerations, Section 1.1-6.

[28] NFPA Model Disciplinary Rules and Ethical Considerations, Section 2 *et seq*.

[29] NFPA Statement on Issues Affecting the Paralegal Profession, Paralegal Regulation.

[30] NFPA Statement on Issues Affecting the Paralegal Profession, Paralegal Advanced Competency Exam.

[31] ABA Model Guidelines for the Utilization of Legal Assistant Services, Guideline 1.

[32] ABA Model Guidelines for the Utilization of Legal Assistant Services, Guideline 2.

- A lawyer may not delegate to a legal assistant the ability to establish the attorney-client relationship, establishment of fees, or legal opinions;[33]
- A lawyer must ensure that the legal assistant makes all parties involved in the process (client, court, etc.) aware that the legal assistant is not licensed to practice law;[34]
- The lawyer must ensure that the legal assistant maintains all client confidences;[35]
- The lawyer may include a charge for the work performed by a legal assistant in charging legal services;[36] and
- The lawyer may not split legal fees with a legal assistant nor pay a legal assistant for the referral of legal business, nor can the legal assistant's compensation be contingent, by advance agreement, upon the profitability of the lawyer's practice.[37]

Should paralegals be licensed?

Issues to Consider

While attorneys are licensed to practice law, paralegals, notwithstanding the expansion of paralegal duties, are not required to obtain a license to practice in any state.

Licensing would require all paralegals to meet minimum education and/or work experience requirements.

NFPA is in favor of a state determined regulation process that would benefit the public by maintaining minimum standards for the profession.

NALA supports voluntary certification and self-regulation, and opposes licensing requirements for paralegals.

Currently, although several states define the term in statute or State Bar Codes of Conduct, no state has mandatory licensing or certification requirements. Only California has codified "minimum" standards that an individual must meet in order to utilize the term "paralegal." Licensing and/or certification legislation has been discussed and debated in New Jersey, North Carolina, Wisconsin, Colorado, Utah, South Dakota, Washington, and Hawaii, but has not been passed.

California—"the leader of the pack": California Business and Professions Code Sections 6450-6456: Defining "Paralegal" and setting industry standards:

'Paralegal' means a person who either contracts with or is employed by an attorney, law firm, corporation, governmental agency, or other entity and who performs substantial legal work under the direction and supervision of an active member of the State Bar of California, as defined in Section 6060, an attorney practicing law in the federal courts of this state, that has been specifically delegated by the attorney to him or her.[38]

A paralegal shall possess one of the following:

- A certificate of completion of a paralegal program approved by the ABA;
- A certificate of completion of a paralegal program at, or a degree from, a postsecondary institution that requires the successful completion of a minimum of 24 semester, or equivalent, units in law-related courses and that has been accredited by a national or regional accrediting organization or approved by the Bureau for Private Secondary and Vocational Education;
- A baccalaureate degree or an advanced degree in any subject, a minimum of one-year of law-related experience under the supervision of an attorney who has been an active member of the State Bar of California for at least the preceding three years or who has practiced in the federal courts of this state for at least the preceding three years, and a written declaration from this attorney stating that the person is qualified to perform paralegal tasks;
- A high school diploma or G.E.D., a minimum of three years of law-related experience under the supervision of an attorney who has been an active member of the State Bar of California for at least the preceding three years or who has practiced in the federal courts of this state for at least the preceding three years, and a written declaration from this attorney stating that the person is qualified to perform paralegal tasks. This experi-

---

[33] ABA Model Guidelines for the Utilization of Legal Assistant Services, Guideline 3.

[34] ABA Model Guidelines for the Utilization of Legal Assistant Services, Guideline 4.

[35] ABA Model Guidelines for the Utilization of Legal Assistant Services, Guideline 6.

[36] ABA Model Guidelines for the Utilization of Legal Assistant Services, Guideline 7.

[37] ABA Model Guidelines for the Utilization of Legal Assistant Services, Guideline 9.

[38] California Business and Professions Code Section 6450 (a).

ence and training shall be completed no later than December 31, 2003.[39]

All paralegals shall be required to certify completion every three years of four hours of mandatory continuing legal education in legal ethics as well as four hours in general law.[40]

A paralegal may not perform any services for a consumer except under the direction and supervision of an attorney, law firm, corporation, government agency, or other entity that employs or contracts with the paralegal, or unless otherwise allowed by statute, case law, court rule, or federal or state administrative rule or regulation.[41]

A paralegal can only identify himself or herself as such if he or she has met the requirements of Section 6450 (c).[42]

New Jersey: New Jersey Supreme Court formed a committee that studied the paralegal industry for five years. The committee recommended to the New Jersey Supreme Court that the New Jersey Supreme Court should adopt required licensing for paralegals. To date, New Jersey has not adopted a licensing requirement for paralegals.

Utah: The Utah State Bar Legal Assistant's Division's Licensing of Legal Assistants Committee issued a report to the Utah Board of Bar Commissioners recommending licensing requirements for paralegals. To date, the Utah State Bar does not require a paralegal to be certified or obtain a license.

Hawaii: Hawaii State Bar Association's Task Force on Paralegal Certification approved two proposals imposing regulation of paralegal use and certification requirements for paralegals. The certification program did not win the State Bar Association's approval and is before the Hawaii Supreme Court.

Indiana: As part of the Indiana Rules of Professional Conduct, the Indiana Supreme Court adopted Guidelines on the Use of Legal Assistants. Although not requiring certification or licensure, it does provide attorneys with more coherent guiding principles in the supervision of non-lawyers.

Maine: Paralegal or legal assistant mean a person, qualified by education, training or work experience, who is employed or retained by an attorney, law office, corporation, governmental agency or other entity and who performs specifically delegated substantive legal work for which an attorney is responsible.[43] A person may not use the title paralegal or legal assistant unless the person meets the definition in section 921.[44]

Pennsylvania: Pennsylvania Consolidated Statutes, Title 42, Section 2524(a) prohibits a paralegal from providing legal services unless supervised by an attorney.

Although many states define the term, provide guidelines for the use of legal assistants, and have unauthorized practice of law statutes, no state currently "regulates" the paralegal profession through certification or licensure requirements. As such, attorneys must be sure to maintain proper supervision of paralegals so as to ensure that the attorney avoids any possible bar misconduct as a result of a non-attorney's actions.

ETHICAL CONSIDERATIONS IN EMPLOYING NONLAWYER ASSISTANTS

Supervision of Paralegals

Paralegals have become essential for any immigration practitioner who wishes to remain competitive in today's legal market. The U.S. Bureau of Labor Statistics predicts that the paralegal job market will double in size from its current level of more than 100,000 nationwide in the next decade.[45] In many immigration practices, paralegals outnumber the attorneys three to one.[46] Just 20 years ago, the majority of paralegals tasks were limited to administrative office tasks and the occasional research project. Fueled by a combination of factors, the role of the paralegal has been steadily increasing and today's paralegals represent a diversity of education, experience, and backgrounds. The tasks paralegals perform, especially in an immigration practice, are limited only by creativity, legal authority, and the established parameters of the supervising attorney.

---

[39] California Business and Professions Code Section 6450 (c)(1)–(4).

[40] California Business and Professions Code Section 6450(d).

[41] California Business and Professions Code Section 6451.

[42] California Business and Professions Code Section 6452.

[43] Maine Revised Statutes, Title 4, Chapter 18, Section 921.

[44] Maine Revised Statutes, Title 4, Chapter 18, Section 922.

[45] Bureau of Labor Statistics, *Occupational Outlook Handbook*, 2002, "Paralegals and legal assistants."

[46] Although not a "scientific" survey, an informal poll of several immigration practices reveals the average ratio to be more than three paralegals for every attorney.

What are the three keys for a paralegal?

- The paralegal must be aware of the ethical and legal responsibilities arising from the attorney-client relationship, why they exist, and how they affect the paralegal;
- The paralegal must be aware that the ethical duties imposed on attorneys by state law affect paralegals; and
- Paralegals are indirectly regulated by attorney ethical codes and by state laws that prohibit non-lawyers from practicing law.

Attorneys Practicing with Paralegals—Practical Concerns

The Duty of Competence: an attorney owes his client a degree of competence including maintaining a system to monitor, track, and "hit" deadlines for submission of documents. This duty extends from the attorney through the paralegal in the representation of a client and the attorney must be aware of all cases being worked on by the paralegal and any deadlines pertinent to that matter. Competent representation requires the legal knowledge, skill, thoroughness, and preparation reasonably necessary for the representation – this duty flows through the attorney to the paralegals working directly under the attorney's supervision on a given matter.

Duty to Supervise: All Model Rules and "paralegal" definitions listed above state that an attorney must supervise a paralegal in the course of his or her daily duties. *Webster's Dictionary* defines "supervise" in the following manner: "To oversee for direction; to superintend; to inspect with authority."[47] Generally, case law seems to indicate that the attorney must supervise the manner in which the work is produced including its efficiency and effectiveness. A paralegal should not provide any communication or conduct any activity which could be construed as "legal activity" unless under the direct supervision of the attorney and with the attorneys full consent and knowledge.

Confidentiality of Information: All information relating to the representation of a client must be kept confidential unless the client consents to disclosure. Paralegals must understand that the attorney-client privilege extends to them and that they have an affirmative duty to uphold this privilege.

---

[47] *Webster's Unabridged Dictionary* (1913).

As discussed above, paralegals may perform virtually any legal task so long as the work is supervised by an attorney, the attorney assumes responsibility for the paralegal's work, and the work does not constitute the unauthorized practice of law. Therefore, attorneys must be aware of the blurred line between "authorized" and "unauthorized" practices for their support staff.

Lawyers Aiding Unauthorized Practice of Law

A lawyer is subject to discipline if he or she assists a nonlawyer in engaging in the unauthorized practice of law. For purposes of this prohibition, nonlawyers include not only those without legal training, but also disbarred, suspended, or out-of-state lawyers not licensed in the jurisdiction.

Lawyers may violate the prohibition against assisting in others' unauthorized practice by:

- Improperly delegating duties to nonlawyer staff or inadequately supervising their work;
- Offering legal services to or accepting referrals from businesses whose nonlawyer employees provide legal service to customers; or
- Working with disbarred, suspended, or out-of-state lawyers who are improperly practicing law.

Source: ABA/BNA Lawyers Manual on Professional Conduct

Practice Pointers

- Hold periodic meetings with your paralegal preferably on a weekly basis to review law changes, office procedures and client matters.
- Encourage your paralegals to update their skills and take advantage of training opportunities, including attending legal seminars.
- Provide close supervision and give your paralegals complete access to you as their supervising attorney.
- Utilize the paralegals in nontraditional roles such as maintaining the library/research materials, monitoring AILA InfoNet, and/or working on special projects such as marketing, computer support, or outbound visas.
- Do not allow paralegals to sign correspondence or applications sent to or filed with any government agencies—only counsel should sign.
- Do not allow paralegals to set legal fees with clients; however, they may provide information that

is set forth in a published price list, or, for example, they can indicate the hourly rates charged by the firm for attorneys or paralegals.

- It is highly recommended that the attorney conduct the initial interview, although you may wish to have your paralegals phone-screen potential clients. When the client initially comes to the office, it is critical the client meet with the attorney and that any fee agreement be signed by the client and the attorney, even though the paralegal may be present during those activities.

- Cross-train your paralegals in order to protect them in a down-sizing market so that they have proper skills to be able to handle various kinds of immigration matters. While some practices use a model of compartmentalizing paralegals into various specialties, it is important to continually cross-train your paralegals in various aspects and allow them to move about within your immigration practice.

- Promote the broadening of the paralegal's horizons, including attending EOIR hearings, visiting the local DHS offices, attending AILA functions including luncheons when appropriate, seminars, and conferences. Additionally, encourage your paralegals to complete their bachelor's degree, a paralegal certificate program, or apply to and attend law school.

The Unauthorized Practice of Law: Although it is convenient, economical, and often essential for the immigration practitioner to use the services of a paralegal or other "nonlawyer" assistant, the immigration practitioner cannot lose sight that the paralegal is the ultimate responsibility of the attorney and the attorney is responsible for ensuring that the paralegal performs the work in a manner consistent with the state rules on unauthorized practice of law as well as the lawyer's own ethical obligations. Furthermore, in several states, paralegals are governed by the unauthorized practice of law statutes, which sanction individuals for engaging in the practice of law without a license.

Case Study: Georgia

Background: There are no certification or licensure requirements for paralegals working in Georgia, individual certification is only a voluntary process, and there are no formal education requirements to become a paralegal in the state of Georgia.[48]

The State Bar of Georgia expressly prohibits a lawyer from assisting a nonlawyer in the performance of activities that would constitute the unauthorized practice of law. The unauthorized practice of law statute in Georgia is found at OCGA sec 15-19-50, *et seq.*

The practice of law is defined as: (1) representing litigants in court and preparing pleadings and other papers incident to any action or special proceedings in any court or other judicial body; (2) Conveyancing; (3) *Preparation of legal instruments of all kinds whereby a legal right is secured* (emphasis added); (4) Rendering of opinions as to the validity or invalidity of titles to real or personal property; (5) Giving of legal advice; and (6) Any action taken for others in any matter connected with the law.[49]

It shall be unlawful for any person other than a duly licensed attorney at law: (1) To practice or appear as an attorney at law for any person other than himself in any court of this state or before any judicial body; (2) To make it a business to practice as an attorney at law for any person other than himself in such courts; (3) To hold himself out to the public or otherwise to any person as being entitled to practice law; (4) To render or furnish legal services or advice; (5) To furnish attorneys or counsel; (6) To render legal services of any kind in actions or proceedings of any nature; and (7) To advertise that either alone or together with, by, or through any person, whether a duly or regularly admitted attorney at law or not, he has, owns, conducts, or maintains as an office for the practice of law or for furnishing legal advice, services or counsel.[50]

State Bar of Georgia's Rules of Professional Conduct provides specific guidance to lawyers who employ paralegals. For example, Georgia Rules of Professional Conduct 5.3 provides that "with respect to a nonlawyer employed or retained by or associated with a lawyer:

- A partner in a law firm shall make reasonable efforts to ensure that the firm has in effect measures giving reasonable assurance that the per-

---

[48] *See generally,* State Bar of Georgia, Rules of Professional Conduct.

[49] Unannotated Georgia Code 15-19-50.

[50] Unannotated Georgia Code 15-19-51.

son's conduct is compatible with the professional obligations of the lawyer;

- A lawyer having direct supervisory authority over the nonlawyer shall make reasonable efforts to ensure that the person's conduct is compatible with the professional obligations of the lawyer; and

- A lawyer shall be responsible for conduct of such a person that would be a violation of the Georgia Rules of Professional Conduct if engaged in by a lawyer if: (1) the lawyer orders or, with the knowledge of the specific conduct, ratifies the conduct involved; or (2) the lawyer is a partner in the law firm in which the person is employed, or has direct supervisory authority over the person, and knows of the conduct at a time when its consequences can be avoided or mitigated but fails to take reasonable remedial action.[51]

Delegation is allowed only if the lawyer supervises the nonlawyer and retains responsibility for the work.[52] Failure to provide adequate supervision also could create a situation permitting the paralegal to overstep proper bounds and commence giving legal advice. For example, in an advisory opinion issued by the State Bar of Georgia on February 11, 2000, the State Bar noted that a lawyer could be found to have aided a nonlawyer in the unauthorized practice of law in allowing the nonlawyer to "prepare and sign correspondence which threatens legal action *or provides legal advice* or both ... a lawyer should never place a non-lawyer in situations in which he or she is called upon to exercise what would amount to independent professional judgment for the lawyer's client (emphasis added)."[53] With the advent of the Internet and e-mail, the gray line of "providing legal advice" is blurred even further. Immigration practitioners must adequately supervise all e-mail correspondence to ensure that any e-mail from a paralegal contains language that reflects the opinion of the attorney or firm, *i.e.,* "the attorney with whom I [paralegal] work indicates that ..." or "it is the policy of our firm ..."

CONCLUSION

What is the moral to be learned from the above discussion? Ethical training for paralegals, adequate supervision, and consistent review of a paralegal's work are tasks that an immigration practitioner cannot ignore. Clear office procedures and job descriptions provided to the paralegal, in writing, with comprehensive and continuous training, can greatly assist the immigration practitioner in demonstrating that the attorney has made a reasonable effort to ensure compliance by paralegals with the Rules of Professional Conduct and the attorney's own ethical standards. Additionally, the immigration practitioner should have written supervision guidelines requiring that a lawyer review, approve, and personally sign all legal documents and correspondence.

---

[51] State Bar of Georgia, Rules of Professional Conduct, Rule 5.3.
[52] *Id.* rule 5.5.
[53] Formal Advisory Opinion No. 00-2, State Bar of Georgia, February 11, 2000.

DUAL REPRESENTATION IN IMMIGRATION PRACTICE
by Bruce A. Hake[*]

INTRODUCTION

Dual representation is the most important area of legal ethics for immigration practice. The paradigm of legal representation is a relationship between one lawyer and one client. Sometimes a lawyer represents more than one client in the same matter. Such representations are called "dual" or "multiple" or "joint" representations, and the clients are called "co-clients." Multiple representations in immigration practice typically involve two clients, and hence the standard label is "dual" representation.

In most areas of American law, dual representations are discouraged. In some contexts they are even specifically prohibited. In some states, for example, a lawyer is specifically prohibited, whether by statute or by legal ethics rule, from representing both a husband and a wife in a divorce matter, because of the overwhelming risk of irreconcilable conflict. In contrast, immigration practice is a unique area of American law in that the great majority of cases are dual representations, because the majority of cases involve a petitioner (typically a U.S. citizen, in family immigration cases, or a U.S. employer, in employment-based immigration cases) who petitions the government on behalf of a foreign beneficiary.

Based on study and debate for over 10 years, this author believes that in all immigration cases involving a petitioner and a beneficiary, the lawyer has a lawyer-client relationship with both the petitioner and the beneficiary, with only one exception. The only exception are situations where the petitioner and the beneficiary are each represented by a different lawyer. The law may evolve to carve out exceptions and nuances. At the moment, however, this principle stands, no matter who started the relationship with the lawyer, no matter who pays the fee, no matter how attenuated the lawyer's contact may be with petitioner or beneficiary, and even no matter if the lawyer has attempted to exact a disclaimer of representation from either petitioner or beneficiary.

This rule is uncomfortable and some lawyers reject it, adopting the "Simple Solution" of believing they represent solely the petitioner or the beneficiary. There are many variations, and the principle applies in both family-based and employment-based cases. The paradigmatic situation, however, involves a lawyer preparing immigration papers on behalf of a corporate client for one of the corporation's employees.

It can be expensive to ignore the dual representation rules. Recently, in a case in which this author served as an expert witness, this lesson was learned the hard way by a prominent immigration lawyer who advised a corporate client about the mechanics and immigration implications of laying off an adjustment of status applicant co-client: the lawyer agreed to pay $250,000 in damages after initially denying that the corporate client's employee was his client as well.

Even those new to the practice of immigration law know that conflicts of interest often arise between petitioners and beneficiaries in both employment and family-based cases. Lawyers may represent two parties simultaneously, if so authorized, unless their interests conflict irreconcilably. In all cases, it is crucial to make clear to all concerned that the case involves dual representation and what that means.

All parties should be advised in writing regarding the nature of the representation, what will happen in the event of conflicts, and what is expected regarding confidential information. In particular, it should be explained in writing that representing two parties simultaneously in one matter requires the lawyer to disclose information and to be equally loyal to both parties.

---

[*] **Bruce A. Hake**, *www.hake.com/pc*, is a lawyer in Damascus, Maryland. From 1988 to 1993, he was editor of *Immigration Briefings* and consulting editor to *Interpreter Releases*. He has served as chairman of the Ethics Committee of the AILA Washington, D.C., chapter, and he has frequently lectured on legal ethics. This is a revised version of Hake's article, "Dual Representation in Immigration Practice," 2 *Bender's Immigr. Bull.* 568 (July 15, 1997). (Reprint permission granted by *Bender's Immigration Bulletin*.) That, in turn, was a condensed version of his landmark article, "Dual Representation in Immigration Practice: The Simple Solution Is the Wrong Solution," 5 Geo. Immigr. L.J. 581–639 (Fall 1991). Michael Maggio and Randy Auerbach provided helpful edits to this version.

The "portability" provisions of the American Competitiveness in the 21st Century Act (AC21)[1] have created analytical headaches for any lawyer trying responsibly to acknowledge and follow the dual representation rules, to the point where the law seems to scream for change. Nonetheless, AC21's difficulties do not destroy the principles that determine the formation of lawyer-client relationships. An employer's plans to lay off a co-client, a co-client's expressed desire to "port" under AC21 or otherwise leave the employer, or a spouse's expressed dissatisfactions with his or her marriage are as common in the practice of immigration law as they are in the rest of life.

When a conflict of interest develops, the lawyer cannot take sides or pretend the conflict does not exist. Instead, the lawyer must try to resolve the conflict, and if that is impossible, must withdraw from representing both parties in that particular matter.

Lawyers who let both parties know what dual representation entails will minimize the risk that their clients will disclose information that creates a potential conflict. This, however, is not necessarily easy. It can be surprising for a corporate client to learn that its lawyer also represents its would-be employee. Likewise, it can be difficult to explain to a foreign worker who has just hired his or her first lawyer that the lawyer also represents the boss, that the lawyer must be loyal to the boss, too, and that despite the attorney-client privilege, there are some things the lawyer does not want to hear. In family-based cases the problem can be even more pronounced. Occasionally immigration lawyers develop a closer relationship with the spouse of a foreigner who hired them, and that spouse tells of abuses by the other client—abuses that can give rise to rights under immigration law, such as a battered spouse petition—that conflict with the interest of the other client who could face criminal prosecution.

It is understandable and correct that immigration lawyers are eager to avoid conflicts of interest. Too many immigration lawyers incorrectly embrace the so-called "Simple Solution" to avoid conflicts. In essence, the Simple Solution says that the party who pays is the only client. Advocates of the Simple Solution argue that it is simple and clean, that it minimizes dual representation risks, and that it accurately reflects the lawyers' loyalties. Some lawyers say they have adopted the Simple Solution in reliance on advice heard at legal conferences. Such advice probably was founded, under the rubric of "identifying the client," on an understandable but mistaken interpretation of the corporate and other representation rules.

The Simple Solution, however, is clearly unethical and may create malpractice risks. This conclusion is supported by an apparent majority of the immigration bar and by bar ethics authorities that have addressed the issue.[2]

This article emphasizes the basic issue of how lawyer-client relationships are formed. Most issues discussed are generally applicable across all areas of immigration practice, although the focus is on the Simple Solution in the context of corporate representation involving pursuit of employment-related immigration status, where the practice is most common and most sharply defined. However, the concept can have a much broader scope, e.g., in most family immigration cases. It applies as well as to employment-based cases where the lawyer is hired by a foreigner to file an employment-based application and the employer and employee both incorrectly believe that the lawyer is only the foreigner's lawyer.

Lawyers who adopt the Simple Solution regard themselves as counsel solely to a corporate client or to an individual foreign client in situations where they actually are conducting a dual representation of the corporation and an alien. These lawyers believe a duty of loyalty is owed only to the "real client," and that the key issue in employer-employee representations is identifying the real client—usually the first to engage the lawyer, the one who pays the fees, the one who directs the representation, and the one more likely to continue to employ the lawyer. This Simple Solution is an attempt to avoid lawyer-client relationships with aliens who appear to be, and are, clients. This is not the right way to represent immigration clients because it conflicts with ethics rules governing dual representation.

An alien is either a client—in which case the lawyer is subject to the obligations of that relationship—or the alien is not a client, in which case the lawyer may not give the alien legal advice. Whether the alien is a client depends more on what the lawyer does, and what the alien believes, than on what the lawyer says. Rather than minimizing risks, the Sim-

---

[1] Pub. L. No. 106-313, 114 Stat. 1251 (2000).

[2] *See, e.g.*, Los Angeles County Bar Ass'n Ethics Comm. Formal Op. No. 465 (Apr. 15, 1991).

ple Solution *increases* the risk of ethical sanctions and malpractice liability. It also increases the risk of not providing professional service to all actual clients.

BASIC PRINCIPLES

Dual (or multiple) representation occurs when a lawyer represents two (or more) co-clients in a single matter. In most areas of law practice, dual representation is relatively uncommon. In immigration practice, however, it is very common, because many immigration benefits, such as family-based or work-related immigration status, involve joint action by an alien beneficiary and an employer-petitioner or a U.S. citizen (or permanent resident). Although most immigration practice areas usually involve dual representations, some, such as deportation defense, usually do not.[3]

Dual representation is ethical and standard practice, when conducted in accord with the legal ethics rules. When a lawyer represents two parties, the lawyer is usually understood to have a lawyer-client relationship with both. If a conflict of interest arises, the lawyer must consult further with the clients and may have to withdraw from representation of both clients in that matter if either client will not or cannot consent to waive the conflict.

A lawyer can be engaged in a dual representation unknowingly. There is a clear trend in the law toward the recognition of implied lawyer-client relationships. A lawyer-client relationship does not require an express contract if there are good reasons to find that a lawyer was acting as a person's lawyer. Further, an obvious client may be a client for reasons that might not be obvious. For example, whether an individual or institution is a client does not depend on who pays the lawyer's fee. The critical question is whether the lawyer gives the person or institution legal advice or accepts confidential information. This means that lawyers may overlook client-lawyer relationships that have arisen in their practice, especially in dual representations.

CONFLICTS AND LOYALTIES

Although any number of problems can arise in dual representations, these problems generally fall into two classes: conflicts issues, and what can be called "other loyalty issues." Most dual representation problems involve conflicts. There are other problems as well, such as the extra demands placed on a lawyer who has to deal with more than one client: duties to communicate with each co-client, to involve each co-client in decisions, to continually consider the interests of each, and so forth. These problems are based on the duty to accord each co-client the same level of professional loyalty that any client should be accorded. The Simple Solution is an attempt to avoid both kinds of problems and the responsibilities they entail.

In considering dual representation issues, lawyers tend to think exclusively in terms of conflicts of interest. That is natural, because the essence of the dual representation rules is resolving conflicts. However, criticism of the Simple Solution is ultimately not based on a concern about conflicts; it is based on the more basic issue of loyalty to clients.

For example, when asked whether an overseas alien beneficiary of a citizen client's preference petition is ever regarded as a dually represented co-client, several experienced practitioners' first instinct was to note that the issue seldom arises, because conflicts of interest are rare in such cases. That is generally true. Conflicts are relatively rare in practice, and they are usually resolvable, especially in family cases, where essential interests are usually closely aligned. However, these practitioners' instinct amounts, in a way, to putting the cart before the horse; whether an alien is a client does not depend on whether a conflict is likely if the alien is a client. Analogously, whether a couple is married does not depend on whether they are likely to divorce. To the contrary, whether an alien is a client is a separate and more basic issue than the issue of potential conflicts.

This is a significant distinction, because a lawyer-client relationship affects many aspects of a lawyer's conduct beyond conflicts concerns. If conflicts concerns were the critical factor in deciding whether an alien is a client, then that would be an unimportant issue in situations where conflicts are rare. But whether an alien is a client is always an important issue, because, beyond conflict-related obligations, lawyers owe many duties to clients that are not owed to nonclients.

Lawyers' duties to clients are not platitudes. They are specific legal duties, violations of which are punishable by ethics sanctions, malpractice liability, and oversight by the Justice Department and

---

[3] *But see Lopez v. INS,* 775 F.2d 1015 (9th Cir. 1985) (lawyer's representation of multiple respondents in deportation proceeding was appropriate).

the Department of Homeland Security. Outside the sphere of conflicts, the Simple Solution can lead to other ethical violations, such as breaches of the duties of confidentiality and communication. Therefore, it is prudent for a practitioner to err on the side of regarding as clients the foreigners who benefit from his or her legal advice and services, as well as the institutions and individuals who petition for them.

FORMATION OF A LAWYER-CLIENT RELATIONSHIP

There is a very clear trend toward recognition of implied lawyer-client relationships based on the lawyer's conduct and the putative client's expectation. A lawyer-client relationship does not require an express contract if there are good reasons to find that a lawyer was acting as a person's lawyer. Therefore, the Simple Solution's disclaimer of a client relationship with the alien is ineffective.

The legal ethics rules somewhat duck the issue of who is a client. The definition has been left to common law, which draws a black-and-white distinction between clients and nonclients. Those deemed clients are owed the full range of the lawyer's professional duties, while nonclients are owed almost no professional duties. Current law draws no distinction between categories of clients, nor does it recognize the fact that in the real world lawyers must and do make distinctions about how they treat different categories of nonclients.

The Simple Solution reflects the practical reality that lawyers feel closer ties to a long-term, paying client than to the co-client with whom they have fleeting contacts. The courts and bar authorities, however, apply an amalgam of contract, agency, and tort law, tending toward great expansion of the circumstances that signal the formation of a lawyer-client relationship.[4]

A lawyer-client relationship exists under a tort theory, even absent an express contract, whenever a person seeks and receives legal advice under circumstances in which a reasonable person would rely on the advice. An implied lawyer-client relationship exists whenever the lay party submits confidential information to an attorney whom he reasonably believes is acting to further his interests. This certainly says that the lawyer is the lawyer for all concerned in employment- and family-based cases.

A "client" is a person on whose behalf a lawyer acts. Performing legal services for another, which may include simply providing advice and information under circumstances indicating an lawyer-client relationship, is evidence of a lawyer-client relationship. A lawyer-client relationship can be inferred from conduct; it is sufficiently established if it is shown the putative client seeks and receives advice on legal consequences of past or contemplated actions. This, too, confirms that it is foolish for an immigration lawyer to claim that either the petitioner or the beneficiary is not the "real" client because attorney's fees were paid by the other client.

One court found a lawyer-client relationship, implied from the lawyer's conduct, between a lawyer and Canadian nationals the lawyer had assisted in seeking permanent resident status.[5] The lawyer asserted he was not the aliens' lawyer but a "co-venturer" in an investment scheme designed to gain them permanent residence. In addition to the aliens' subjective understanding of their relationship with the lawyer, the court relied on the facts that the lawyer had contacted the INS and the Social Security Administration on their behalf; had mentioned green cards in letters to them; had written to them on his lawyer letterhead; and had made himself available to answer INS questions when the aliens crossed the border. The court imposed a four-month suspension.

The fiduciary relationship between lawyer and client is not dependent on the lawyer's acceptance of employment, orally or in writing. The existence of a lawyer-client relationship may be established by the client's "reasonable perception."

Although a third party may pay a client's legal fees, a lawyer's relationship of trust and confidence and the obligation to protect confidential information will, however, be with the client—the person or entity whose legal interests the lawyer is retained to protect."[6]

A law firm's belief was held to be irrelevant to the issue of whether a lawyer-client relationship ex-

---

[4] *See, e.g., Togstad v. Vesely, Otto, Miller & Keefe,* 291 N.W.2d 686 (Minn. 1980) (imposing an estoppel against a lawyer denying an attorney-client relationship where there was only a brief consultation and the lawyer claimed he had declined to accept the case).

[5] *In re O'Byrne,* 694 P.2d 955 (Or. 1985).

[6] Wolfram, *Modern Legal Ethics,* 502 (1986)

isted; the policy of avoiding the appearance of impropriety is a key concern in deciding the issue.[7]

Summary of Factors

The following factors, alone or in combination, have been held to create an implied lawyer-client relationship, or to be irrelevant to the issue of its creation:

Lawyer's conduct

- gives legal advice, including information about the law as well as advice regarding a course of conduct
- accepts confidential information and acts to further person's interests
- represents a person's interests, regardless of who pays the fee
- acts on a person's behalf
- performs legal services
- signs an acknowledgment of service on behalf of an alleged client
- represents a person in judicial or semi-judicial proceedings
- enters an appearance on behalf of a person
- files labor certification application in which lawyer appears as employer's counsel
- contacts government agencies, *e.g.*, USCIS or Social Security Administration, on a person's behalf
- mentions green cards in letter to alleged clients
- writes to putative clients on law firm letterhead
- makes him- or herself available to answer DHS questions when aliens cross the border
- fiduciary relationship between lawyer and client is not dependent on the lawyer's acceptance of employment, orally or in writing
- irrelevant whether law firm believes it has embarked on lawyer-client relationship

Putative client's conduct and expectation

- seeks, receives, and reasonably relies upon legal advice
- submits confidential information to lawyer, who is reasonably believed to be acting to further person's interests
- reasonably believes the lawyer is acting as his or her lawyer
- irrelevant whether putative client pays the fees.

THE APPEARANCE OF IMPROPRIETY

Although tarnished because of ambiguity and difficulty of application, the rule that lawyers should bend over backwards to avoid even the appearance of impropriety, because of the discredit it brings to the profession, has long been a cardinal principle of legal ethics. The Third Circuit inquires whether an "average layman" in the position of an objecting party would perceive an impropriety.[8] It can scarcely be doubted that an average layman would think it improper for a lawyer to give legal advice to a person, file forms and otherwise represent the person in administrative forums in proceedings leading to changes in the person's legal rights and duties, and mediate the person's relationship with an employer (or others) as well, while disclaiming the role of a lawyer.

CORPORATE REPRESENTATION RULES

Legal ethics reference materials nearly always devote more space to conflicts of interest than to any other topic. Much of this space is devoted to the corporate representation rules. Those rules involve the tricky issue of "identifying the client" when a lawyer retained by a corporation is asked to consider issues in which the legal rights of the corporation are entangled with the legal rights of persons connected with the corporation, such as directors, shareholders, or employees. Some legal justifications for the Simple Solution reflect an understandable misunderstanding of the corporate representation rules. Indeed, misunderstanding of these rules may be the primary source of the Simple Solution.

Rule 1.13 of the District of Columbia Rules of Professional Responsibility[9] ("D.C. Rules") provides:

---

[7] *Jack Eckerd Corp. v. Dart Group Corp.*, 621 F. Supp. 725, 731 (D. Del. 1985).

[8] *Pantry Pride, Inc. v. Finley, Kumble, Wagner, Heine, Underberg & Casey*, 697 F.2d 524, 530 (3d Cir. 1982).

[9] While this article specifically cites to the D.C. Rules, the principles addressed in those citations are generally applicable across the United States.

(a) A lawyer employed or retained by an organization represents the organization acting through its duly authorized constituents.

(b) In dealing with an organization's directors, officers, employees, members, shareholders or other constituents, a lawyer shall explain the identity of the client when it is apparent that the organization's interests may be adverse to those of the constituents with whom the lawyer is dealing.

(c) A lawyer representing an organization may also represent any of its ... employees ..., subject to the provisions of Rule 1.7 [Conflicts]....

This rule is the source of a common statement in legal ethics materials: a corporate lawyer represents the corporation, not the employees. The rule, however, has little to do with the Simple Solution (except that subsection (c) indicates that employer-employee dual representations are permissible and subject to the usual conflicts rules). The general philosophy of the rule is that a corporate lawyer ordinarily represents the organization as an entity, not the individuals comprising the entity.

That general rule, however, is subject to many exceptions. "[I]t is not appropriate to regard the entity as the client in every situation involving an entity, for individual constituents of the organization may be entitled to legal representation in their own right." [10] One situation where the corporation is not the only client is where the corporation "provide[s] legal representation ... for employees." "It is important to recognize ... that when an entity lawyer also represents individuals within the entity, he is taking on new clients." "[W]hen a corporation retains a lawyer specifically to represent certain employees, the corporation is not considered to be the client." The Simple Solution, a complete inversion of that principle, is plainly not justifiable under the corporate representation rules.

PROHIBITION AGAINST ADVISING NONCLIENTS

Whatever the force of the previous arguments, the Simple Solution is destroyed by the prohibition against giving legal advice to nonclients. D.C. Rule 4.3 provides:

In dealing on behalf of a client with a person who is not represented by counsel, a lawyer shall not:

(a) give advice to the unrepresented person other than the advice to secure counsel, if the interests of such person are or have a reasonable possibility of being in conflict with the interests of the lawyer's client;

(b) state or imply to unrepresented persons whose interests are not in conflict with the interests of the lawyer's client that the lawyer is disinterested. When the lawyer knows or reasonably should know that the unrepresented person misunderstands the lawyer's role in the matter, the lawyer shall make reasonable efforts to correct the misunderstanding.

The comment to Rule 4.3 provides:

The Rule distinguishes between situations involving unrepresented third parties whose interests may be adverse to those of the lawyer's client and those in which the third party's interests are not in conflict with the client's. *In the former situation, the possibility of the lawyer's compromising the unrepresented person's interest is so great that the rule prohibits the giving of any advice, apart from the advice that the unrepresented person obtain counsel* (emphasis added).

If an employee is not a client, the employer's lawyer may not give the employee any kind of personal legal advice other than the recommendation to seek independent counsel.[11]

These prohibitions against giving legal advice to a nonclient probably constitute a dispositive refutation of the Simple Solution. An advocate of the Simple Solution might object to this analysis on the ground that soliciting information from an alien employee to fill out forms, on behalf of the employer, does not constitute "giving legal advice." This objection is unsound for many reasons. Immigration lawyers are not data entry clerks. Moreover, the bar's position on the unauthorized practice of law is inconsistent with the objection. It is hard to imagine that a lawyer could diligently and competently undertake the complexities of something like a labor certification application without, in substance if not in form, advising the beneficiary about legal requirements and legal consequences. What is more, a competent lawyer must obtain at the outset from the foreigner information, such as whether any of the grounds of inadmissibility may apply, that the for-

---

[10] Hazard & Hodes, *The Law of Lawyering*, 57 (1985).

[11] See *W.T. Grant Co. v. Haines*, 531 F.2d 671, 675–76 (2d Cir. 1976).

eigner would expect to held in confidence Indeed, asserting that a person's complex legal interests could be responsibly handled in such a way could also present an appearance of impropriety.

POTENTIAL MALPRACTICE LIABILITY

To establish legal malpractice, a plaintiff must show: (1) the existence of a lawyer-client relationship; (2) that the lawyer neglected a reasonable duty; and (3) that the lawyer's negligence was the proximate cause of a loss to the plaintiff. The Simple Solution is a functional attempt to limit malpractice liability, because it denies a lawyer-client relationship. This attempt is likely to fail in a malpractice action, because the definition of "client" is expanding, especially in tort cases. Further, the attempt to limit malpractice liability may itself be professional misconduct. D.C. Rule 1.8(g)(1) provides flatly: "A lawyer shall not make an agreement prospectively limiting the lawyer's liability to a client for malpractice."

LIMITING THE SCOPE OF REPRESENTATION

"An agreement concerning the scope of the representation must accord with the legal ethics rules and other law. Thus, the client may not be asked to agree to representation so limited in scope as to violate Rule 1.1 [competence], or to surrender the right to terminate the lawyer's services or the right to settle litigation that the lawyer might wish to continue."[12] Disclosure and consent are not mere formalities—they must be tailored to a client's actual circumstances.

Due to the strength of the authorities regarding the establishment of a lawyer-client relationship by conduct and expectation, and in light of other principles, including the rule against giving legal advice to nonclients, it seems unnecessary to analyze systematically whether the Simple Solution can be sustained—and a lawyer-client relationship thus denied—in the face of the lawyer's disclaimer of a lawyer-client relationship or the alien's signature on an engagement letter or other document purporting to consent to such an arrangement. In some states the traditional agency law and express contract law analysis that once defined the scope of lawyer-client relationships is still more common in opinions than the tort and implied contract principles discussed in this article. Nonetheless, on the facts of the Simple Solution, no court or bar authority is likely to hold that an alien could make a meaningful and valid consent to such an arrangement.

A lawyer's ethical duties must be tailored to a client's actual circumstances. A disclaimer, such as an advance waiver of conflicts, that might escape impropriety if exacted from a large company represented by independent legal counsel, might be unconscionable if imposed on certain individuals. It is clear from the cases that powerful parties, such as some corporations, must bear tender regard for the rights of vulnerable parties, such as some alien employees. However, this article's conclusions do not depend on an assumption that corporations are strong and aliens are weak. There are all kinds of corporations and all kinds of aliens. In immigration cases employers and alien employees sometimes but infrequently are commensurate in resources and sophistication, such as when a small consulting company seeks to hire a foreign professional. These criticisms of the Simple Solution apply in such cases, but even more so when the parties are notably unequal in bargaining power.

UNAUTHORIZED PRACTICE OF LAW

The Simple Solution also gets whipsawed by the bar's position on unauthorized practice. The Simple Solution asserts in effect that a lawyer's filling out forms and performing other actions in pursuit of an immigration benefit for an alien on behalf of an employer is not practicing law. Meanwhile, the bar argues that filling out forms and other actions in pursuit of immigration benefits for aliens constitute the unauthorized practice of law when performed by nonlawyers. If those actions constitute practicing law when performed by nonlawyers, how can they be regarded as not practicing law when performed by lawyers?

THE DUTY OF LOYALTY AND THE LAW OF AGENCY

After giving respect to a lawyer's duties to the administration of justice, the legal ethics rules boil down to the duty of loyalty to the client.[13] The lawyer's many duties of loyalty derive from the com-

---

[12] D.C. Rules, Comment to Rule 1.2, ¶ 5.

[13] *See* "Ethical Issues in Immigration Practice," 90-8 *Immigration Briefings* (Aug. 1990).

mon and statutory law of agency, which generally prohibits agents from taking actions disloyal to the interests of a principal, or from exploiting a principal's confidences for self-gain or the gain of third parties. Even if legal ethics rules did not exist, lawyers would still be subject to civil actions for breaches of the duty of loyalty. A lawyer's duties of loyalty include the duties of zealous representation, communication, shared decisionmaking, confidentiality, and avoidance of conflicts, to name some of the more important duties.

THE CO-CLIENT RULE

If a lawyer jointly represents two or more clients with respect to the same matter, the clients ordinarily have no expectation that their communications with the lawyer, with respect to the joint matter, will be kept from each other.[14] This so-called "co-client rule" is very important. A lawyer has a duty to warn clients about limits on confidentiality, and the lawyer needs to be aware of the possible ramifications of the co-client rule. Again, advising all concerned about this in writing at the start of the case, and especially in employment-based cases, makes for fewer conflicts, happier clients, and less anxiety.[15]

CONCLUSION

Loyalty to clients is the foundation of legal ethics. The Simple Solution, a strategy for evading that principle, is clearly unethical. In the employer and employee context, the prudent and proper course is to regard the alien and the employer as co-clients and follow the established rules regarding conflicts of interest. The same applies to family-based immigration cases. If a serious conflict arises, it may be possible to resolve the conflict and obtain consent to continued dual representation, or it may be necessary to withdraw. Educating clients about these issues is an important responsibility for all immigration lawyers.

---

[14] Wolfram, *supra* n. 6, §6.4.8 at 274. *But see* D.C. Bar Legal Ethics Committee Op. No. 296 (Feb. 15, 2000) (mere fact of joint representation, without more, does not provide a basis for implied authorization to disclose one client's confidences to another). This decision is consistent with this article's conclusions, except that it adopts the view that co-clients in an employer/employee immigration context are ordinarily not entitled to confidential information of the other unless they have specifically consented in advance. This makes it especially important for Washington, D.C. practitioners to anticipate in writing in advance how confidential information will be treated in all dual representations.

[15] "Where express consent to share client confidences has not been obtained and one client shares in confidence relevant information that the lawyer should report to the non-disclosing client in order to keep that client reasonably informed, to satisfy his duty to the non-disclosing client the lawyer should seek consent of the disclosing client to share the information or ask the client to disclose the information directly to the other client. If the lawyer cannot achieve disclosure, a conflict of interest is created that requires withdrawal." *Id.*

RISK MANAGEMENT FOR THE IMMIGRATION PRACTITIONER

*by John L. Pinnix**

INTRODUCTION

The way we were ... The way we are

Four years, and half a lifetime ago, this author wrote:

> During the professional career of the majority of the members of AILA, the practice emphasis of many immigration attorneys has shifted from a general immigration practice, which often included a mix of family, refugee/asylum, trial and business cases, to principally—if not exclusively—business cases.
>
> Several factors have contributed to this shift. A dynamic, technology driven, full employment economy has led employers to utilize the increased business visas and labor certification-exempt programs created by IMMACT90.[1]
>
> As with any area of law, immigration attorneys are attracted to their area of interest for a myriad of reasons. Undoubtedly, during the 1990s, some new practitioners, or their firms, perceived business immigration law as an under-served or emerging specialty niche. The practice emphasis of some of the more seasoned practitioners also shifted in the 1990s, both as a conscious reaction to the draconian restrictions in areas such as asylum and immigration defense and in anticipation of constriction in family law occasioned by the imposition of the three- and ten-year bars, mandatory affidavits of support, and the sunsetting of INA §245(i). Their shift in emphasis was also in response to the siren song of a potentially remunerative area that might ameliorate the decline predicted for other areas of immigration practice. In a realization that the complexities of modern immigration law invites if not compels sub-specialization, seasoned attorneys in growing firms also limited their immigration practices to a few areas—such as business.[2]

Fortunately, that snapshot did not inspire this author to attempt to peer into the future and offer any prophesy. Today, a perfect storm, consisting of a shallow economic recovery, post-9/11 national security concerns, and re-invigorated restrictionists, has transformed our practices; the world of many immigration attorneys has revolved almost 180 degrees. More and more lawyers are serving fewer and fewer business clients. Now, as old hands are rediscovering their family practice roots, attorneys are encountering unconscionable delays never intended by the legislators of yore who created our pitifully antiqued family quota system. The new practice frontiers are in areas such as border issues, national security, and, as of this writing, the now late and unlamented Special Registration program. Long in the wilderness, litigation is on the verge of becoming fashionable. PERM[3] is coming on stage.

Every stage of a case has the potential to frustrate the most otherwise reasonable and virtuous client seeking nothing more than lawful status and family reunification. Even without the quota backlogs, governmental processing delays can destroy families. No less formidable and demanding is the human resources director, whose own job is on the line because no one anticipated there would be six-month lag in securing an advance parole for a key scientist, who has a desperate need to travel abroad—tomorrow.

In identifying basic rules for *Risk Aversion*, there are some constants—whether an attorney's area of practice emphasis is business, family, or defense. The fact patterns giving rise to ethical dilemmas vary: the family practitioner may belatedly learn that a marriage is dubious; the attorney trying a removal

---

* **John L. Pinnix** is a past president of the American Immigration Lawyers Association (2002–2003) and a founding member of AILA's Carolinas Chapter. He attained B.A. and M.A. degrees in History at the University of North Carolina at Greensboro and his J.D. at the Wake Forest University School of Law. He has served as an adjunct professor at North Carolina Central University School of Law and as a Senior Lecturing Fellow at Duke University School of Law. Pinnix is a principal in the Raleigh law firm, Allen and Pinnix, P.A., and is a North Carolina Board-Certified Immigration Specialist.

[1] Immigration Act of 1990, Pub. L. No. 101-649, 104 Stat. 4978 (Nov. 29, 1990).

[2] John L. Pinnix, "Risk Management for the Business Practitioner," 2 *Immigration & Nationality Law Handbook* 78 (2000–01 ed.).

[3] Program Electronic Review Management.

case may learn that the testimony on which he was hinging his case is suspect; and the business immigration attorney learns that the employee has a criminal conviction undisclosed to the employer. Though mindful of Mark Twain's warning against all generalities, including this one, there are nevertheless basic, fundamental precautions every immigration attorney can implement that will vastly reduce his or her exposure.

As in other practice areas, there are distinctions between questionable ethical conduct, malpractice, conflicts of interest, and issues of professionalism and confidentiality that face attorneys handling immigration issues.[4] From obstruction of justice, to subordination of perjury, to harboring, immigration attorneys' exposure has never been limited to civil liability or professional sanctions; but over the last decade, from IIRAIRA[5] to the USA PATRIOT Act[6] the bars have been raised. For instance, §213 of IIRAIRA removes any doubt that it is unlawful for any individual to knowingly and willfully fail to disclose, conceal or cover up the fact that he or she has, on behalf of any person and for a fee or other remuneration, prepared or assisted in preparing an application for immigration benefits that was falsely made.

While the distinctions between malpractice and other conduct are easily made by malpractice carriers and are of understandably keen interest to the would-be claimant (who wants to be known as the "insured") upon learning that the suit he or she is facing may be actionable, but is not at least for the purpose of the malpractice coverage, the actual distinction may be more academic to the attorney than the issues at hand. A negligence suit, bar grievance, criminal indictment, or loss of a single client can impact the attorney's firm, other clients, and family for the remainder of his or her professional career.

The tactics for risk prevention suggested by this article go beyond modifying conduct that will allow an underwriter a better night's sleep and address practices that may avoid an uncovered suit, professional grievance, or the wrath of a disgruntled client. They are not intended to be in any way exhaustive but are rather a professional reality check.

FIVE "EASY" PIECES

The real world practice of immigration law is fraught with situational ethical dilemmas.

Consider this: Either the petitioner or beneficiary may initiate contact with an attorney for assistance in securing a family-based "green card" for the beneficiary; it is rare indeed for a husband and wife to have independent representation at the outset of an immediate relative case. When there is a falling out among the relatives, the sponsoring uncle regrets signing an I-864 for the troubled teenage niece he has never met. Or, on the eve of the 90-day window to remove conditional status, the husband and wife whom you have represented for years separately call you and blurt out confidences that make your continued representation of either virtually impossible.

And in the business area in regard to who selects and meets with counsel, who signs the retainer agreement, or who pays the fees, an immigration attorney often *defacto* represents both the petitioning employer and the beneficiary employee. By extension, this representation often includes derivative beneficiaries.

Although the employer may initially think of the attorney as the worker's representative, or the worker may think of the attorney solely as the company's lawyer, the parties will soon be sharing confidences with the attorney necessary to process the application or petition. And the course of action the attorney charts will necessarily have legal implications for all of the parties.

As desirable as independent representation for each party may be (for both family and business based cases), it is usually not sought by the client, not only for financial reasons, but also to facilitate processing.

Further consider the following, altogether possible, scenarios:

---

[4] The Illegal Immigration Reform and Immigrant Responsibility Act of 1996 (IIRAIRA) Division C of the Departments of Commerce, Justice, and State, and the Judiciary Appropriations Act of 1997, Pub. L. No. 104-208, 110 Stat. 3009 (Sept. 30, 1996); *See*, for instance, §213 of IIRAIRA, which pertains to the preparation of an application, and §214, which amends 18 USC §1546(a).

[5] The Illegal Immigration Reform and Immigrant Responsibility Act of 1996 (IIRAIRA) Division C of the Departments of Commerce, Justice, and State, and the Judiciary Appropriations Act of 1997, Pub. L. No. 104-208, 110 Stat. 3009 (Sept. 30, 1996).

[6] Uniting and Strengthening America by Providing Appropriate Tools Required to Intercept and Obstruct Terrorism Act of 2001, Pub. L. No. 107-56, 115 Stat. 272; *see* "International Security, Civil Liberties, and Human Rights After 9/11—An Outline," by Robert E. Juceam (with selected materials prepared by Dian R. Gray) in this volume.

1. Fred Mertz, a Canadian entrepreneur, consults with you regarding a possible investment. Fred tells you, "Forget about filing anything for my wife Ethel. She has worked in the Boston office of Consolidated Aluminum Toothpicks for years and they think she is an American." The following day the Maple Leaf plunges and you do not hear from Fred again. Six weeks later, Consolidated Aluminum Toothpicks contacts you and asks you to represent the company. Your first task will be to supervise the audit of their 2,500 employees' I-9s.

2. José Melez entered the United States without inspection on July 4, 1997. He came to join Rosa, his childhood sweetheart; they married and now have four U.S. citizen children—the youngest, George, has a serious heart defect. Soon after he arrived, José's priest found him a "sponsor" and you timely file a labor certification that grandfathered José under §245(i). When the I-140/I-485 is ripe for adjudication, the service center transfers the file to your district office to schedule an interview. Although you occasionally speak by phone, you haven't actually seen José in a couple of years. Because José has been out of town, you arrange to meet the couple for final preparation outside the district office an hour before the scheduled interview. "This is the happiest day of my life," José exclaims. "I only wished my mother had lived to see it." You respond, that you are sorry, "I didn't know she had died." "Yes," says José, "I just got back from her funeral in Juaréz." "I was so afraid for him every moment he was away," Rosa added, "it's harder and harder to come in without papers." "Now what do we need to do to get ready for the interview?" they asked, together.

3. You have represented Bret Bolivar for years, beginning with his NACARA application. At long last, you accompany him to his naturalization interview. When he is given a date for the swearing-in ceremony, he says his brother, Bart, is coming in from a neighboring state for the happy occasion and the family wants you to represent Bart, since his "identical" NACARA case seems to be languishing. Bart makes an appointment to meet with you the day before Bret's ceremony. Your new legal assistant does an intake and reports that much of the case appears to be similar since Bret and Bart are identical twins. But she says Bart is awaiting his birth certificate, all he brought with him is a Matricula Consular and Mexican military card. He isn't sure how to get his birth certificate from the authorities in Monterrey.

4. Your oldest and most valued client is World Wide Widgets. Three months ago, an I-140/I-485 was filed at the California Service Center on behalf of Widget employee, Walter Worker. Last week, Walter's wife, Wanda, calls you at your home demanding to know when the adjustment will be completed "because Walter wants to leave the employment of World-Wide Widgets and accept a position with their competitor Norfolk and Western Widgets." Later the same evening, Walter calls you, apologizes for Wanda's "insolence," and begs you not to mention the call to World-Wide's human resources department; but "by the way, do you think the adjustment will occur before my divorce from Wanda becomes final?" The next day the director of human resources at World-Wide Widgets instructs you to *quietly* delay all immigration work pending a decision regarding a buy-out offer. A possible Canadian purchaser wants to move "corporate" to Winnipeg, manufacturing to Oaxaca, and reacting to the failure of Congress to meet the need for H-1Bs, high-tech functions will be fulfilled through virtual offices abroad. You are told, "We may need to re-file a couple of labor certifications for a few jobs that will be transferred to West Virginia; we should know where we stand within three to four months." That evening, Walter Worker, knowing nothing about the director's call, e-mails you to remind you that his daughter, Wyonia, turns 21 in eight months.

5. Walnut Cove Assisted Living, which you have never represented, has an approved I-140 for a professional nurse. The original beneficiary was in TN status and after determining he would never pass the CFGNS, he returned to Canada. Walnut Cove offers the position to Mary Worth who is visiting the United States. In completing the information required for the I-485, Mary becomes concerned about the question regarding arrests and convictions. In the late 1960s, early in her career, she thinks she was "charged" in Winnipeg for a (nonmarijuana) controlled substance violation. The record has been "expunged" and does not appear on any police checks. Mary hopes that this will not be a problem because she is the sole support of her 93-year-old mother who is in a rest home and the salary offered is substantially more than she earns in Canada. Mary

comes to you for advice and you indicate that serious issues are involved that will require some research. Minutes after your initial consultation with Mary, you receive a call from your old client, World-Wide Widgets, with "great news": "We have just purchased all 50 Walnut Cove Assisted Living facilities."

WARNING SIGNS

"Danger, Danger, Will Robinson!"

As they say, "it doesn't take a rocket scientist ..." There are often early warning signs that foreshadow later melt-downs in business cases. Every attorney has legitimate reasons to sometimes give him or herself a pass for lack of 20/20 hindsight, but the seasoned practitioner can often avoid heartburn by taking the time to face and address troubling issues or facts as soon as they are identified. The following examples include the business immigration attorney's equivalent to the family immigration attorney's classic "bed-check" problems:

Your Contact is Limited to the Employee

At the least, this situation creates the potential that the parties are not reading from the same page of music; if problems arise later in the case, they may be harder to resolve. Is the employer willing to raise the offered wage if dictated by the wage survey? Is the employer willing and able to hold the job open until the start of the next fiscal year? Does the employer understand when a new or amended petition is required? And, in one critical area of the business immigration practice, limiting contact to the employee is entirely impermissible: labor certifications.

The Employer is Willing to "Sponsor" the Worker; "I'll Sign Whatever You Prepare for Me"

In going down this road, the practitioner must distinguish between the appropriate role of counseling and assisting the employer in the preparation of a petition within the purview and intent of the applicable law that will facilitate an approval based on a legitimate job, and impermissibly assisting in the creation of an accommodation position or characterizing the position in a way that bears faint resemblance to the actual terms and conditions of employment.

The Beneficiary Awaiting Employment Authorization Can Never be Reached at Home During the Day

Scenarios such as your staff encountering the worker at the "future" job site prior to the approval of the petition suggest several issues and ethical dilemmas. Tempting though it may be, "Don't Ask, Don't Tell" does not discharge the attorney's responsibility to the client nor may it satisfy the attorney's duty to U.S. Citizenship and Immigration Services (USCIS). You must confront the issue and you can only do this by knowing the facts. Were false documents used to secure the employment? Did the employment begin before or after the filing of a change or extension of nonimmigrant status or before or after the filing of the ETA-750 or I-485? Can the matter be cured by exiting the United States and re-entering; of course, without resuming unauthorized employment? Will the I-485 be covered by §245(i) or (k)? Has the employee lied to you, and, if so, are you willing to continue the representation?

Opportunities to Expand Your Client Base or Profit Center

You receive the following e-mail:

Dear Sir: We are an international professional concern with offices in Rangoon, Nairobi, Milan, and Bratislava. We are looking for U.S. counsel to assist us in providing immigration assistance for up to 250 professionals during the upcoming year. Please provide your fee schedule for qualified referrals. Initially, we have several pre-screened computer programmers who need to come to the United States for final placement interviews. To qualify for B visas, they need a sponsor who is a U.S. citizen stating that they will be visiting him or her. Air tickets, hotel accommodation, food, and any other expenses will be solely on the workers' account. Kindly contact us if you can help with these cases.

The author trusts that passing on this opportunity is a no brainer. But what about a U.S.-based solicitation promising you a very substantial fee for referring your client for some opportunity. Even if referral fees are permitted by your bar, is your due diligence to your client compromised or co-opted by the fee, especially if you do little, if any, legal work?

The Hired Gun Syndrome

Something about your couple doesn't seem exactly right; but what the heck, they want to retain you right now. After all, you tell yourself, "everyone is entitled to representation and integral to America's greatness is that we are a pluralistic society." Besides, you are loath to have some USCIS examiner expect your clients to conform to a 1950s Ozzie and Harriet stereotype. So, maybe there is a good reason this couple hasn't told their parents about their marriage ... maybe there is a good reason neither the husband or wife have a bank account ... maybe there is a good reason that some Ph.D candidate with a fundamentalist religious background married a 19-year-old U.S. citizen high school dropout with two felony drug convictions ... maybe there is a good reason that the 42-year-old wife's six and nine-year-olds haven't met their 26-year-old stepdad. But if there is a good reason, and there may well be one, you should satisfy yourself about the legitimacy of the relationship before even thinking about sending the file over the government's transom. Who are you to judge? It's only your license.

Servicing and Maintaining Clients: Know When to Hold Them, Know When to Fold Them

Never lose sight of the basics. This begins with an absolute duty to have and maintain the professional competence required to handle your client's case. Model Rule 1.1 requires that: "a lawyer shall provide competent representation for a client. Competent representation requires legal knowledge, skill, thoroughness, and preparation reasonably necessary for the representation."[7]

Everyone has to begin somewhere and any licensed attorney can lawfully accept an immigration case. But immigration law is a complex area of practice, not a field for the dabbler. Over two decades ago John P. Boyd, a former INS District Director and then a Seattle attorney, told a West Coast symposium, "... the general practitioner, unfamiliar with immigration procedures, confronted with an immigration problem for the first time, may not realize the potential danger and far-reaching consequences inherent in what appears to be a simple matter. It is only after a practitioner has experienced firsthand a debacle affecting the lives of his clients that he fully realizes the necessity for a specialist."[8] This is even more true today.

The Basics 101

In addition to the duty to possess the requisite professional competence, the other basics are: (1) you have the duty to diligently and timely pursue the case; (2) your client is entitled to your full and undivided loyalty; conflicts of interests are impermissible, and the client's confidences are sacrosanct; (3) the acts and omissions of your staff are inseparable from you; and (4) if you are scratching your head and formulating exceptions to the preceding tenets, you are outside of the basics and may already have a problem.

To minimally comply with the basic requirements of professionalism and ethics, you must comply with the following: maintain and use an up-to-date professional library; track deadlines through multiple tickler systems; routinely do conflict checks; have a written retainer agreement or engagement letter for every client; train your staff and oversee their work product at every stage of the case; maintain professional liability insurance; and oversee appropriate termination of representation including maintenance, or disposing, of the client's records pursuant to the governing bar rules.

An Ounce of Prevention

There are no "silver bullets," but a high percentage of problems can be avoided or minimized by the attorney who routinely follows basic procedures that should be second nature to an entry-level lawyer. Unfortunately, the harried professional may suppress his better, natural instincts or delegate without adequate supervision to the paraprofessional staff. The actual capital outlay for these procedures is usually minimal; and while their administration can at times be time consuming, this, too, is nominal in comparison with defending a suit or bar grievance.

According to Lawyers Mutual Liability Insurance Company, a North Carolina professional liability insurer, in order of frequency, the most common complaints about attorneys are:

- Did not return the client's telephone calls;
- Did not attend to the client's case;
- Did not explain the process to the client;
- Did not predict the outcome of the case correctly;
- Did not do what the client asked; and
- Had a conflict of interest.

Only a tiny fraction of Lawyers Mutual's policyholders are immigration attorneys but these complaints have clear resonance to the practitioner han-

---

[7] ABA/BNA Lawyers' Manual on Professional Conduct (ABA Manual); "ABA Model Rules of Professional Conduct" at Rule 1:1 (Feb., 21, 1996).

[8] "Immigration and Nationality Law: The Client Who Seeks Permanent Residency Status," *Campbell Law Observer*, p. 5 (Dec. 26, 1980).

dling immigration issues. Some of the complaints are remediable by discipline and common courtesy.

Each of the following complaints is addressed by the Model Rules:[9]

Returning Telephone Calls

Returning telephone calls often goes along with explaining the process. Both the attorney and the staff should promptly return telephone calls.[10] The perception that the attorney has failed to explain the process is a related problem that can be met by maintaining lines of communication, *i.e.*, returning the client's calls. Of course, the attorney should clearly explain the case before accepting representation and throughout the process as mid-course corrections are required, or when governmental delays impact the original timetable of the client's case.[11]

Today's client is inundated by provocative anecdotes in the media. There is almost endless material on the internet regarding virtually every subject, including immigration. Clients often do not understand that this material can be posted by anyone and much of it is speculation and otherwise lacks critical analysis. Even accurate information is dangerous if it is not correctly interpreted in the context of an individual's case. Absent clairvoyance, it is not always possible to know if even a well-educated and seemingly sophisticated client understands your explanation of processes that even most nonimmigration attorneys find hard to grasp. Invariably, the attorney will make judgment calls. Those who service clients on a flat-fee basis will, on occasion, be accused of streamlining the process so that the attorney is free to proceed to handle another matter; while those charging by the hour will be accused of "churning" the account to add to their billable hours.

There is no universal answer to address this area of professional risk; but clearly the better you and your staff know the individual client, the better position you are in to gauge his or her understanding of the process or at least the client's comfort level or informed consent *vis a vis* your course of action.

Attending to the Case

According to the American Bar Association, failure to "attend to a case" is one of the most frequent reasons for complaints to lawyer discipline tribunals.[12]

Correctly Predicting the Outcome of the Case

The dynamics of immigration law have made the "prediction" of the outcome of a matter sometimes problematical even for the seasoned practitioner. Since 1986, there have been more than a half-dozen major immigration statutes enacted.[13] In many instances, the implementing regulations have not been promulgated and the attorney has been fortunate if the agency provided any policy guidance, however informal. USCIS service centers are in meltdown, the appellate boards are years overdue in issuing decisions, the agencies are underfunded and the Department of Labor is suffering apparent permanent paralysis. Under these conditions, the attorney who attempts to predict the outcome of a case is on a fool's errand.

This is, of course, intolerable, given that the course of the client's life and fortune may often literally depend on the attorney's advice. Under these conditions, the attorney who guarantees results or makes predications regarding processing times without qualification and periodic professional re-

---

[9] *See* article entitled, "Ethical Issues for Immigration Lawyers," in this volume.

[10] "A lawyer shall keep a client reasonably informed about the status of a matter and promptly comply with reasonable requests for information." Model Rule 1.4.

[11] "A lawyer shall explain the matter to the extent reasonably necessary to permit the client to make informed decisions," Model Rule 1.4.

[12] ABA Manual, "Lawyer Client Relationship," at 31: 402 (Nov. 26, 1996). Model Rule 1.3 requires that "a lawyer shall act with reasonable diligence and promptness in representing a client." And the attorney has the ethical obligation of diligence to "carry through to conclusion all matters undertaken for a client." ABA Manual at 01:109.

[13] These include: Immigration Reform and Control Act of 1986 (IRCA), Pub. L. No. 99-603, 100 Stat. 3359 (Nov. 6, 1986); Immigration Marriage Fraud Amendments Act of 1986, Pub. L. No. 99-639, 100 Stat. 3537; Immigration Act of 1990 (IMMACT90), Pub. L. No. 101-649, 104 Stat. 4978 (Nov. 29, 1990); Chinese Student Protection Act of 1992, Pub. L. No. 102-404, 106 Stat. 1969; Violent Crime Control and Law Enforcement Act of 1994, Pub. L. No. 103-322, 108 Stat. 1953, 2024; 1994 U.S. Code Cong. & Admin. News p. 1801; Anti-Terrorism and Effective Death Penalty Act of 1996 ("AEDPA") Pub. L. No. 104-132, 110 Stat. 279; Personal Responsibility and Work Opportunity Reconciliation Act of 1996, Pub. L. No. 104-193, 110 Stat. 2105 (Aug. 22, 1996); The Illegal Immigration Reform and Immigrant Responsibility Act of 1996 (IIRAIRA) Division C of the Departments of Commerce, Justice, and State, and the Judiciary Appropriations Act of 1997, Pub. L. No. 104-208, 110 Stat. 30.

evaluation has abdicated his ethical and professional duty to the client.

Did Not Do What the Client Asked

Sometimes there may be no panacea to complaints that the attorney "did not do what I asked." If the complaint is substantive rather than a matter of perception, the attorney may only be able to explain to the client why he or she cannot, or will not, do what the client asked. Perhaps it is unlawful, unethical, or just unwise. A legal sage once observed that "sometimes the best advice you can give your client is not to make a damn fool of himself." Even if you can lawfully and ethically proceed, a course of action may in your professional estimation be tactically inappropriate. When the client insists on substituting his or her judgment for yours, you need to evaluate whether you want to terminate your relationship with that client. You need not only consult your own retainer agreement, but the applicable rules of professional conduct. In some jurisdictions, withdrawal has not been permitted without "good cause."

Some rules now expressly allow withdrawal without cause or without client consent, subject to the authority of courts to require continued representation and provided the withdrawal can be accomplished without material prejudice to the client. In addition to "good cause" and the requirement that withdrawal can be accomplished without material prejudice to the client, Model Rule 1.16 lists situations under which an attorney may withdraw. These circumstances include: the client persists in actions the lawyer reasonably believes are criminal or fraudulent; the client has used the lawyer's services to perpetrate fraud; the client insists on an objective that the lawyer considers repugnant or imprudent; or the representation has been rendered unreasonably difficult by the client.

The retainer agreement of the author's firm requires the client to acknowledge that "it is essential that [the] Client advise [the] Attorneys of the true facts pertaining to this case, that the information provided on the Questionnaire submitted to [the] Attorneys is true and accurate to the best of [the] Client's knowledge and that [the] Client promptly notify [the] Attorneys of any changes or corrections." Breach of this provision permits immediate termination of representation by the firm, and the firm rarely fails to exercise this option.

Had a Conflict of Interest

Applicable Rules of Professional Conduct often address conflict situations arising in the context of litigation or scenarios uncommon to an immigration practice. But common sense and good practice policy dictate that representation should be declined at the outset if there is a conflict of interest; if a conflict is later identified, the client should be promptly notified and the issue of continued representation should be immediately resolved.

The New York City Bar Association recently found the following to be the *minimum* components of an effective conflicts of interest checking system:[14]

- All law firms, even solo practitioners, must maintain "records," whether written or electronic.
- The records should be maintained in a way that allows them to be quickly and easily checked for conflicts.

To qualify as a "record", the law firm must be able to systematically and accurately check for information when it is considering a new engagement.

- The records of prior engagements must be made at or near the time of the engagement.
- The records should be made within days, not weeks of the initial engagement, so that they may be checked before commencing a new engagement.
- The records should be updated periodically as additional parties or other relevant information is acquired that might create a conflict of interest.
- The records should be organized in a way that permits efficient access to the information contained therein.
- List clients and former clients alphabetically and list engagements undertaken for each client in chronological order under each name.
- Maintain a list of adverse parties cross-referenced to the client and matter in which the adverse parties were involved.

Certain information, at a minimum, should be maintained in the system:

- Client names
- Adverse party names
- Description of engagement

---

[14] NYC Bar Ass'n Formal Op. 2003–03.

HELP IN TIME OF TROUBLE

The regulations only partially address discipline of attorneys and nonattorney representatives; they do not provide guidance on some of the most serious ethical issues, such as conflicts of interest. Generally, the ethics rules applicable to immigration attorneys are the rules of ethics for the state in which the lawyer is licensed to practice. In addition, most states have statutes regulating businesses and professions. State and federal laws regarding fraud apply to all lawyers, irrespective of their area of practice."

The attorney encounters a legal or ethical issue that cannot be resolved after diligent research (and, if applicable, after consultation with other firm members). A filing deadline is at hand, or sometimes more intimidating, the Vice President for Human Resources absolutely needs to know an answer before the start of the next business day in Bonn. Where do you turn?

The Bar

Many state bars have counselors who will advise attorneys on ethical issues. Because these bar counselors may not be familiar with immigration issues, the querying attorney will have to carefully explain the areas of concern. A less than full understanding of the problem could hopelessly skew the opinion, thereby rendering it worthless.

Note: Before utilizing this resource, the attorney should be familiar with the parameters of the service and be sure that the query will not have any unintended collateral consequence.

Attorneys will normally seek an opinion from the bar in their home state. Attorneys needing assistance in other jurisdictions can start with the state's court or bar Web page. A description profiling the services provided by each state bar is contained in the *Martindale-Hubbell Law Directory*; a directory of state bar associations is published in the American Bar Association's annual "Leadership Directory"; and referrals also may be obtained through the National Organization of Bar Counsel, Inc., 515 Fifth Street, N.W., Building A, Room 127, Washington, D.C. 20001; (202) 638-1501; fax: (202) 638-0862; or online: *www.nobc.org*.

The American Bar Association's "ETHICSearch" permits attorneys to call, write, fax, or e-mail descriptions of situations posing ethical problems. They will receive citations to the authorities including: applicable ABA ethics rules, ethics opinions issued by the ABA as well as state and local bar opinions, and other relevant research materials; *e.g.*, case law, law review articles, and treatise materials. Most inquiries are handled on a same-day basis.

Most ETHICSearch searches are free of charge. If additional research is requested, there is an hourly charge of $30 for members of the Center for Professional Responsibility, $45 for other ABA members, and $60 for nonmembers. The minimum charge is $15. Expedited services as well as fax and mailing services also can be arranged. Call (800) 285-2221, fax ethics questions to (312) 988-5491, or send an e-mail to *ethicsearch@staff.abanet.org*. You can write to ETHICSearch at ABA Center for Professional Responsibility, 321 North Clark Street, Chicago, IL 60610.

Professional Liability Insurers

Many professional liability insurers have proactive risk management programs to assist their policy holders. Just as with bar counselors, the policy holder may have to carefully explain the areas of concern if the company does not specialize in the immigration coverage area. Even if the carrier cannot resolve the problem at hand, prompt consultation with the company may be necessary under the terms of the policy.

Practice Pointer: The author encourages every attorney to maintain adequate professional liability coverage and encourages the attorney to periodically review the terms of the policy keeping in mind any changed circumstances and understanding that not every potentially actionable occurrence is covered.

The Government

AILA's formal liaison and other initiatives directed toward the State Department, Department of Labor, the EOIR, USICE, USCBP, USCIS, and the Social Security Administration at every level are extraordinarily valuable tools in ascertaining and influencing immigration policy for our clients. This aside, to paraphrase the venerable punch line, "the government is here to help you," is all too often true in the real world, at the "retail level." With sincere respect to the thousands of dedicated public servants and leaving issues of motive and intent aside, the agencies charged with the administration of U.S. immigration laws are neither competent nor equipped to give advice on which you can rely.

Whatever advice is available is necessarily myopic: consuls do not know or understand the regulations the USCIS service centers follow; whatever understanding a state workforce agency (SWA) has of nonimmigrant programs is limited to the areas it is charged to administer. USCIS "consumer" publications and Web site are replete with errors and USCIS hotlines constantly give erroneous advice, some of which if followed could actually render the recipient inadmissible or removable. If you get an answer you like, how can you ensure that USCIS will later honor it; if you receive an answer you do not like, do you follow it? If you do not follow it, after you have notice of the government's position, you may have incurred additional exposure.

If our immigration laws were in any way user-friendly and if the advice of the government could be readily obtained or confidentially relied on, the business community, with its eye on the bottom line, would not be utilizing the services of immigration attorneys.

The American Immigration Lawyers Association

By virtue of their membership, AILA attorneys have access to the AILA Mentor Program. This is an invaluable resource for evaluating and coping with ethical issues.

The AILA mentor is a practicing immigration attorney with at least five years of experience in the area of practice. There are mentors for the specific area designated as "Ethics and Professional Responsibility," as well as for virtually every area of immigration practice.

The mentor does not charge any fee for a brief consultation, not to exceed 15 minutes. The attorney seeking consultation must ask the AILA mentor for assistance directly. Use of this system by legal assistants and secretaries is not permitted; the calling attorney should research the issue before calling the mentor. Current mentors and the guidelines for the program may be found on the AILA InfoNet site.

Practice Pointer: Invaluable though a volunteer mentor can be, some issues will necessitate formal association of outside counsel. When this occurs, the practitioner will need to decide from the outset whether the outside counsel is representing the original client or the attorney.

The World Wide Web

Check out *www.legalethics.com*; assume that your client is looking at it, too.

CONCLUSION

Always do right.
This will gratify some people,
And astonish the rest.—Mark Twain

Representing foreign nationals has always posed potential ethical challenges to the attorney. These have included cultural, educational, and linguistical barriers, as well as a misunderstanding of the role lawyers play in the immigration process and the American legal system. Sometimes just as challenging is the U.S. petitioner who expects legal counsel to be creative and resourceful and may not care about or understand the constraints the law places on an immigration practitioner.

It is the immigration attorney's calling and responsibility to reconcile these differences and balance the interest of each client. An immigration practice requires identifying and drawing on a commonality of professionalism and ethical precepts, the same precepts that ideally are part of the professional fiber of every person practicing our profession. These precepts should be nurtured, cultivated, and preserved. Now more than ever, immigration attorneys have the unique responsibility not only to further the interest of their clients but to educate the public as to the contributions of all immigrants to our nation, and to lead the fight to protect the fundamental due process rights guaranteed by our Constitution.

It is said that Carroll W. Weathers, who practiced real estate law in Raleigh, North Carolina, for 17 years before serving as the Dean of the Wake Forest University School of Law for another 20 years, wished for his students that "to the end, their lives may be lived in the service of others, and they may find the satisfaction that comes from a noble purpose, high ideals and exemplary living."[15] Dean Weathers, blind and retired, continued to teach legal ethics at Wake Forest until his death at age 82. It is doubtful that Carroll Weathers ever handled an immigration matter, but he fervently believed in legal ethics and that an attorney "occupies a preferred station of leadership, possesses exceptional influence, and it not only is his privilege but his duty to use his influence and position on behalf of a better social order, and live as a worthy example to others." Such should be the highest aspiration of an immigration attorney.

---

[15] "What Would Dean Weathers Do?" *North Carolina Lawyer*, September/October 1999.

UTILIZING A RECORDS RETENTION PROGRAM TO PROTECT THE CLIENTS' INTERESTS, TOO!

by Donald S. Skupsky[*]

Editor's Caveat: Donald S. Skupsky's groundbreaking article is not expressly written for immigration attorneys. In implementing a document retention policy, prudence may dictate that an immigration practitioner consider issues uncommon to lawyers who practice in other areas. During the course of a career, it is not unusual for the members of an immigration firm to encounter the same client on multiple occasions: as an overstay, an EWI, a short-term visitor, a student with duration of status, a nonimmigrant worker, the beneficiary of a family or employment-based adjustment application, and/or as an applicant for citizenship. Nor is it unusual for multiple files for the same individual, under different names, to be created within a firm. And this may be compounded exponentially by the principal beneficiary's derivatives. Don't you want, and need to, know if the history the client presents to you as you prepare his or her N-400 in 2004 is consistent with the 1988 amnesty filing? Was there once unauthorized employment that now necessitates consular processing? Was there a false claim to citizenship made on an I-9 completed in 1998?

At a minimum, having the benefit of old files can facilitate the preparation of an application. More seriously, in the post-9/11 world, there have been suggestions that adjudications will be delayed until all of the beneficiary's files are reconciled and reviewed. FOIAs are backlogged and do not always result in the production of every file. Among an immigration attorney's worst nightmares should be that of an adjustment derailed—or worse—because of inconsistencies contained in an earlier filing, also submitted by his or her firm.

---

[*] **Donald S. Skupsky**, JD, CRM, FAI, MIT, is President of Information Requirements Clearinghouse (Denver, Colorado). He is the author of *Recordkeeping Requirements, Records Retention Procedures*, and *Legal Requirements for Microfilm, Computer and Optical Disk Records*; the co-author of *Law, Records and Information Management: The Court Cases*; the developer of **RetentionManager™** software; and the editor of *Legal Requirements for Business Records: The Electronic Edition*.

Skupsky is also a Records and Information Management Consultant, and a noted national speaker and writer on law, records, and information management issues. He received the Juris Doctor degree from the University of Michigan Law School and has been admitted to the bar in Colorado and Michigan. He is also a Certified Record Manager (CRM). Skupsky received the prestigious Emmett Leahy Award in 1994 from the Institute of Certified Records Managers for outstanding contributions to the information and records management profession. In 1995, he was admitted to the Company of Fellows, the highest honor bestowed by the Association of Records Managers and Administrators (ARMA, Inc.). In 1999, he received the Masters of Information Technology award from the Association of Information and Image Management (AIIM).

Readers may contact Skupsky at Information Requirements Clearinghouse, 5600 S. Quebec Street, Suite 250C, Greenwood Village, CO 80111; (303) 721-7500, (303) 721-8849 fax; or *dskupsky@irch.com*. See also www.irch.com.

INTRODUCTION

Attorneys recognize the benefits of proper management of records. Records must be well organized and accessible. Otherwise, they waste valuable staff time looking for records, or worse, misfile or lose valuable client information.

However, most records lose value over time. Even the most important client records may never be needed or used in the future.

Timely destruction of valueless records offers a low-cost way to reduce the amount of space used for record storage. A records retention program provides a "back door" for your records by eliminating the accumulation of valueless records. It also improves your ability to handle important information. By getting rid of the junk, you reduce the chances of filing errors and speed the retrieval of important information.

DUTIES RELATED TO CLIENT FILES

The Problem with Destroying Client Files

But attorneys often refrain from developing records retention programs or even destroying records under an existing retention program citing several reasons:

- The process of destroying records is "nonbillable time" and administrative overhead.

- The attorneys are too busy to review the files prior to destruction.
- The clients may need these records some time in the future.
- Attorneys believe that the client file belongs to the client and cannot be destroyed without the client's permission.

This article focuses on the last point. While some of the supporting research is presented, other research has necessarily been omitted for brevity.

The Role of Files and Records in a Client Engagement

A client engages an attorney to pursue the client's interest in a legal matter. The goal of the engagement is the litigation, settlement, preparation of legal document, obtaining legal advice, etc.

The "client file" is the file used by attorneys to store all the material created by the attorneys and received from the client as part of an engagement with a client. Clearly, the goal of an engagement is NOT to create a client file. The client file is merely a byproduct of the engagement—part of the means used by the attorney to manage the engagement.

The Duty to Create Client Files

The Rules of Professional Conduct and bar association ethical opinions do not address any duties or requirements for maintaining the client files including form of records, content of files and filing methods. These issues are left totally to the professional judgment of the attorney.

The ethical opinions do not require an attorney to maintain client records in the first place. Yet, some opinions then attempt to establish duties and requirements related to the retention and destruction of the client files.

The Duty to Retain Client Files

The L.A. Country Bar Association,[1] the American Bar Association,[2] the New York State Bar Association[3] and other bar associations have issued ethical opinions related to the retention of client files by attorney. These opinions unanimously support the establishment of a records retention program and the ultimate destruction of client files.

The American Bar Association, for example, states the following:

- The Rules of Professional Conduct does not set forth particular rules or guidelines on the subject. This Committee had not previously issued an opinion that deals directly with the subject.
- We cannot say that there is a specific time during which a lawyer must preserve all files and beyond which he is free to destroy all files.
- Good common sense should provide answers to most questions that arise.

With the foregoing limitations in mind, we suggest the considerations set forth below.

1. Unless the client consents, a lawyer should not destroy or discard items that clearly or probably belong to the client. Such items include those furnished to the lawyer by or in behalf of the client, the return of which could reasonably be expected by the client, and original documents (especially when not filed or recorded in the public records).

2. A lawyer should use care not to destroy or discard information that the lawyer knows or should know may still be necessary or useful in the assertion or defense of the client's position in a matter for which the applicable statutory limitations period has not expired.

3. A lawyer should use care not to destroy or discard information that the client may need, has not previously been given to the client, and is not otherwise readily available to the client, and which the client may reasonably expect will be preserved by the lawyer.

4. In determining the length of time for retention of disposition of a file, a lawyer should exercise discretion. The nature and contents of some files may indicate a need for longer retention than do the nature and contents of other files, based upon their obvious relevance and materiality to matters that can be expected to arise.

5. A lawyer should take special care to preserve, indefinitely, accurate and complete records of the lawyer's receipt and disbursement of trust funds.

6. In disposing of a file, a lawyer should protect the confidentiality of the contents.

---

[1] Los Angeles Bar Association, Opinion 420, October 5, 1983.

[2] American Bar Association, Informal Opinion 1384, "Disposition of a Lawyer's Closed or Dormant Files Relating to Representation of or Services to Clients," May 14, 1977.

[3] New York State Bar Association, Opinion 623, November 7, 1991.

7. A lawyer should not destroy or dispose of a file without screening it in order to determine that consideration has been given to the matters discussed above.

8. A lawyer should preserve, perhaps for an extended time, an index or identification of the files that the lawyer has destroyed or disposed of.

Although the ABA opinion is "informal" and not binding, this opinion and others place severe procedural burdens on the retention program including:

- The duty to inspect and screen the client files before destruction.
- The duty to client property prior to destruction.
- The duty to protect client confidences.
- The duty to maintain an index of destroyed files.
- The duty to notify clients prior to destruction.

These duties would create significant additional work to attorneys desiring to destroy old client files. For example, if notice was provided to clients prior to destruction of records, some clients would request the opportunity to review the files. The attorneys would then have to review the files, purge extraneous material, organize the material and perhaps remove some attorney notes and related documents that may not be client property. The costs and burdens of these tasks may appear to outweigh the benefits of even undertaking a retention program for client files in the first place.

This article focuses on how attorneys can understand the various ethical opinions related to records retention in a new light. The goal is not to ignore or violate these opinions, but to show how a retention program can be implemented without the restrictions of these opinions, and, yet, not constitute a violation of the Rules of Professional Responsibility.

Protection of client interests is a paramount ethical duty for attorneys. But, this duty is not compromised by the outright destruction of valueless client files after a reasonably long period of time. While there is always some risk associated with any records retention program, there is no reason to believe that the risk is any greater for attorneys electing a retention procedure that is calculated to protect the client interested, but deviates somewhat from the mainstream of advisory opinions. In fact, research has not uncovered instances when attorneys have been sanctioned for following reasonable records destruction practices.

WHO OWNS THE CLIENT FILES?

The Source of the Belief that the Client Files Belong to the Clients

The ABA opinion cited above correctly states that the Rules of Professional Conduct do not address retention of client files. Here's a sampling of the provisions from the ABA and California opinions that address the issue:

ABA Rule 1.16 supports this position:

(d) Upon termination of representation, a lawyer shall take steps to the extent reasonably practicable to protect a client's interests, such as . . . surrendering papers and property to which the client is entitled . . . The lawyer may retain papers relating to the client to the extent permitted by other law.

Ca. Rule 3-700(D)(1) requires lawyers whose representation has terminated to:

. . . promptly release to the client, at the request of the client, all the client papers and property. "Client papers and property" include . . . items reasonably necessary to the client's representation.

The Rules of Professional Responsibility create a duty upon termination for the attorneys to provide clients with materials from the client file on request. Thus, if the client wants the files, they can request them and the attorney has a duty to turn over the records.

What is the basis for this duty? When the representation terminates[4] before the matter is complete, the client will not have yet reaped the benefits intended by the representation. The fees paid to the attorney went toward the "work in progress." Since the representation is terminated, the client will need to hire and pay another attorney to complete the matter.

Since the work in progress is the only tangible product available for the fees paid by the client, the Rules of Professional Conduct and ethical opinions establish a duty for the attorney to release to the client the work in progress in the client file. The attorney may also retain a right to the same information, and maintain a copy of the client file, based on ethical duties and general business responsibility.

_____

[4] Regardless of whether termination was for cause, firing of the attorney or withdrawal by the attorney.

During the representation, the client receives the products and services resulting from the representation. If not, the client can pursue appropriate channel—*e.g.*, request for work in progress, suit related to professional malpractice, etc.

After the representation is completed, the client files then serve as a remnant of the representation, but is not the representation itself. The material may be useful for subsequent matters, protecting client interests in case the subject of the representation is disputed or for answering questions. Both logically and legally, the client does not have a property right to the client file after the representation—the client already received the products of the representation.

The Ownership of the Attorney Work Product

Some of the later ethics opinions addressed the issue of an attorney placing a lien on the client file or refusing to it turn over to the client until appropriate fees were paid.[5] A key opinion appears in L.A. Op. 330 (1972) where the ethics committee reviewed again the question of releasing files to the client or succeeding attorney and provided additional guidance.

L.A. Op. 330 concludes that the client has a right to make copies of the client file, including the attorney "work product," but that the client should bear the cost. But, the committee took a different opinion for "documents for which the client has already paid":

> ... *The costs of reproducing the entire attorney's office file, including so-called "work product," should be borne by the client, but the former attorney should certainly not profit from such copying....*
>
> *If the documents being sought by the client are documents for which the client has already paid—excluding fees for the attorney's professional services—(e.g., deposition transcripts, photocopies of documents obtained from opposing counsel and already paid for by the client, reports by experts which have been billed directly to the client, etc.), the attorney should turn those documents over to the client without further charge.*

In the Committee's opinion, "work product" for which the client may be billed, belongs to the client.

This opinion is significant for three reasons:

- It infers that the client does not own the client file by stating that the client should pay for copying costs. Clearly, the client does not own the client file as property — the client just has a right to the information.

- It states that the client does not have to pay the copying costs for the documents for which he has already paid. The opinion then indicates examples of the type of documents for which a client would normally be billed: transcription, copies from opposing counsel, reports from experts, etc. This "work product" consists of documents for which there normally is a separate charge. And, since the client already paid a separate fee for these documents, this "work product ... belongs to the client."

- It clarifies the ownership of the "work product" in the client file. The "work product" for which the client has been charged a separate fee "belongs to the client." But the "work product" produced by the attorney and billed as "attorney's professional services" does not belong to the client. The client therefore must pay the copying costs to get a copy of this portion of the file.

The Rules of Professional Responsibility establish the duty of the attorney to properly represent a client's interest during and after the engagement. The "representation" interest is what some ethical opinions may have misconstrued as a client property right in the client file. The Rules do not stand for a position that the client files belongs to the client—just that the client has a right to access documents in the client file as part of representation.

L.A. Op. 330 is one of the most significant opinions in determining whether attorneys may destroy client files under a records retention program and what procedures should be included in the program.[6] The significance of this opinion for records retention purposes is: *the client does not own the client file*, but merely has a right to a copy of the material. Therefore, the attorney must *own* the file since only the attorney has both rights to access and possession.

The widespread belief that the client owns the client files can be traced to the subsequent misinterpretations and misstatements of L.A. Op. 330, repeated again and again in ethical opinions and court

---

[5] L.A. Country Bar Ethics Opinion No. 48, 103, 197, 253.

[6] The other two are L.A. Op. 475 and ABA Informal Opinion 1384 (1977).

cases. Here is a sampling of the erroneous restatements of L.A. Op. 330 and the incorrect conclusions reached by courts and bar associations:

- In *Weiss v. Marcus*[7] we find: "The 'work product' of an attorney belongs to the client, whether or not the attorney has been paid for his services." (Cite to L.A. Op. 330.)
- In *Kellen v. Delug*[8], we find: ". . . It is a breach of the duty imposed by rule 2-111(A)(2) to retain a client's case files after discharge, in that an attorney's work product belongs absolutely to the client whether or not the attorney has been paid for his services." The opinion further incorrectly cites *Weiss v. Marcus*[9], a secondary source, as the real source.
- L.A. Op. 405 (1982) expands the misinterpretation by quoting both L.A. Op. 330 and *Weiss v. Marcus* as the definitive source of a new conclusion: ". . . virtually everything in a client's file is the property of the client, because it either has been copied at client expense, or the time utilized to create it has been at client expense."
- L.A. Op. 420 (1983) further expands the misinterpretation by quoting L.A. Op. 330 and 405 as standing for a similar conclusion: "In opinions 330, 362[10], and 405, this Committee has consistently taken the position that the file, including "work product," is the property of the client." Again, the committee ignored what L.A. Op. 330 really said.

From a simple duty stated in L.A. Op. 330 to permit clients to copy the client file, the various ethics committees have granted the client a property right—a gross misinterpretation of the original opinion. Certainly, an ethics committee could make an independent interpretation that the client file is the property of the client. Instead, they assert that L.A. Op. 330 stands for that principle and provides no other support for the property conclusion. In the end, the property conclusion is based on *nothing*—not L.A. Op. 330, not the court cases, and not the Rules of Professional Conduct.

---

[7] *Weiss v. Marcus*, 124 Cal. Rptr. 297 (Cal. Ct. App. 1975).
[8] *Keller v. DeLug*, 203 Cal. Rptr. 879 (Cal. Ct. App. 1984).
[9] *Weiss v. Marcus*, 124 Cal. Rptr. 297 (Cal. Ct. App. 1975).
[10] L.A. Op. 362 actually correctly interprets L.A. Op. 330 to mean that a withdrawing attorney has the duty to release documents to the client that have been paid for by the client and make available to the client only office files.

The Status of the Client File Under Property Law

The ethics opinions themselves also confirm that the client does not have a property interest in the client files.

L.A. Op. 103 confirms that the ethics committee only focuses on ethics issues and has uniformly avoided addressing issues of legal rights of the parties:

Query 1: Is the attorney obligated to deliver his entire office file to client without restriction? . . .
Query 3: Must the attorney deliver to client or his agent copies of any part or all of the file?
As to query 1 and query 3, the Committee is of the opinion that they each involve a question as to the legal rights of the party rather than ethics. The committee has uniformly taken the position that it should not undertake to answer questions of that character.

ABA Informal Opinion 1384 confirms the same position:

Questions can arise as to ownership of or proprietary interests in the contents of a lawyer's file. These are usually questions of law, and this Committee has no jurisdiction to determine or give opinions on questions of law.

N.Y. State Opinion 623 (1991) confirms the uncertainty regarding the ownership of the client files:

Which documents may be deemed to belong to the lawyer is not always easy to ascertain; in certain instances, the lawyer's ownership of such documents may be a complex issue of both law and fact.

Therefore, the ownership of the client file should *not* be a question decided by an ethics committee. Instead, it should be a question of law decided, if necessary, by the judicial system. Obviously, some ethics committees have overstepped their authority.

Even when a client gives an attorney property, such as documents, during the representation, there is some reasonable expectation that attaches to the property:

- If it is important to the client or the client needs it immediately, the client will ask for it back after the representation concludes.
- If the client has a later need for the property, the client will ask for it back within some reasonable period after the representation conclusion.

- If the client does not ask for it back within some reasonable period, the client demonstrates that the property is not needed.
- If the attorney maintains property of another for some long period of time, and the client does not request it back, the client has probably forgotten about the property or has abandoned it.

Even the law assumes that the property is abandoned if not claimed within some specified period. L.A. Op. 475 addresses the question of documents with intrinsic value that may have been abandoned:

Even after five years has elapsed, the lawyer may not destroy documents that have intrinsic value without the consent of the former client. Intrinsically valuable documents are those materials, such as money orders, travelers checks, stocks, bonds, wills, original deeds, original notes, judgments and the like, which have value, or may have value, in and of themselves, or which themselves create or extinguish legal rights or obligations.

Under California Unclaimed Property Law, C.C.P. §§1500, et seq., certain intrinsically valuable unclaimed property escheats to the State after seven years. What constitutes "unclaimed" property in the context of closed client files is a question beyond the scope of this opinion.

So while the ethics committee recognizes the importance of preserving documents that have intrinsic value, it also recognizes that the documents may be considered abandoned or unclaimed property after a number of years. Under property law, once the property is abandoned, it no longer belongs to the party, although it may be later claimed if still in existence and the party can prove ownership. Under state escheat law, the unclaimed property should be turned over to the state.

But, ABA Rules of Prof. Conduct EC 4-6 requires that attorneys protect client confidences and not reveal any information about the client:

The obligation of a lawyer to preserve the confidences and secrets of his client continues after the termination of his employment.

When confronted with the dual obligation of giving client property to the state under escheat laws and protecting client confidences, an attorney faces a legal and ethical quandary. The only action that meets both requirements is to either return the documents to the client or destroy them.

The Status of the Client File Under Contract Law

Under contract law, unless otherwise specified in an engagement agreement, the client has no particular right to the work papers and documents in the client file. The client contracts for a result or a specific unit of work. If the work is completed and documents required by the agreement are provided to the client or other designated parties, the appropriate fee is to be paid. If the work is not completed, the client may bring legal action.

But when the engagement is successfully completed, the client has no right to the client file and cannot compel the attorney to turn over the client file, unless the agreement specifically gave the client the right to the file.

The Client File Belongs to the Attorney

Clients may have a right to the client file under the Rules of Professional Conduct, contract law, and property law, if the representation is terminated prior to the conclusion of the matter. After the representation or the subject matter of the representation (*e.g.*, trusts, monetary instruments, etc. exist after the representation ends) have both concluded, the client may have right to subpoena the file in legal malpractice litigation. Otherwise, the client has not right to the client file after the representation ends.

The Rules of Professional Responsibility and the early ethics opinions support only one conclusion— the client file is the property of the attorney and the client has a right to copy material from the file. L.A. Op. 197 (1952) supports this conclusion:

It would appear that an attorney is under no legal duty to deliver his office file to the former client. Copies of pleadings and of briefs are made by an attorney for his own use and convenience in the action. They are the attorney's property and not the client's. Such correspondence likewise would seem to be the property of the attorney.

Other jurisdictions specifically support this conclusion:

Fl. Op. 88-11 (5/93) states that the material in the client file belongs to the lawyer, not the client.

N.Y. State Op. 623 (11/91):

When a file has been closed, except to the extent that the law may require otherwise, all documents belonging to the lawyer may be destroyed without consultation or notice to the client in the absence of extraordinary circumstances manifesting a client's clear and present need for such documents. *Cf., e.g., N.Y State 398 (1975); N.Y. City 1986-4 (1986).* Absent a legal requirement to such extraordinary circumstances, the lawyer's only obligation with respect to such documents is to preserve confidentiality.

The Rights of Lawyers to Destroy Client Files

Ethics opinions recognize that client files need not be kept forever:

ABA Informal Opinion 1384 states:

All lawyers are aware of the continuing economic burden of storing retired and inactive files. . . . A lawyer does not have a general duty to preserve all of his files permanently. Mounting and substantial storage costs can affect the cost of legal services, and the public interest is not served by unnecessary and avoidable additions to the cost of legal services.

L.A. Opinion 475 (1993) concurs that an attorney "is not required to maintain the files in storage forever."

N.Y. Opinion 460 (1977) states:

The ethics of our profession do not cast upon lawyers the unreasonable burden of maintaining all files and records relating to their client. Indeed, the Rules of Professional Conduct is remarkably silent on this subject.

N.Y. Opinion 623 (1991) states:

Where a file has been closed, except to the extent that the law may require otherwise, all documents belonging to the lawyer may be destroyed without consultation or notice to the client in the absence of extraordinary circumstances manifesting a client's clear and present need for the documents.

WHY DEVELOP A RECORDS RETENTION PROGRAM FOR CLIENT FILES

A properly designed records retention program provides you significant benefits:

- **Reduce record storage costs each year.** A records retention program saves money through space, staff and equipment savings, initially, and then through cost avoidance in future years.

- **Conflict with client records retention programs.** Many corporate clients have now established records retention programs. In some cases, the corporate client may have already destroyed its versions of the records under its own records retention program. Rules of Professional Responsibility X of the American Bar Association Rules of Professional Responsibility specifies the legal duty of a lawyer to protect the interests of its clients. An attorney compromises its clients' interests by maintaining records longer than the period specified by the client's records retention program. Timely destruction of client files would eliminate the potential embarrassment and risk of legal liability, and also enable the attorney to recognize the other benefits for a records retention program.

- **Liability due to materials found in client files.** Separate from the differences in retention periods, an attorney could face liability based upon documents maintained in client files. Some attorneys have also utilized material developed for other clients for the benefit of a follow-on client. Copies of these records may also be maintained in the other client's file. If discovered inadvertently, this could result in an action for breach of confidentiality or privacy should the documents related to one client be reviewed by another client.

  The American Bar Association Rules of Professional Conduct specify that "the obligation of a lawyer to preserve the confidences and secrets of his client continues after the termination of his employment".[11] The longer client records remain in existence the greater the chance this obligation may be compromised.

- **Problems related to conflicts checking.** An attorney must check for conflicts before accepting new engagements. If the files continue to exist a long time, these old files may have to be reviewed. If the files have been destroyed, no review is possible and a conflict becomes improbable.

- **Problems with abandoned property.** After a while, the client forgets about material in the client files or legally the client material must be classified as abandoned. Under state law, abandoned property must be give to the state under escheat law. However, the Rules of Professional Conduct prohibit revealing client confidences. The only solution to resolving this dilemma is to destroy the client file in a timely manner.

- **Problems with commingling attorney and client property.** ABA R.P.C. 1.15 prohibits attorneys from commingling attorney and client property. Even if the attorney assumes that the client file

---

[11] ABA EC 4-6 for the Code of Professional Responsibility.

contains some client property, than the attorney must also assume that it contains some attorney property—*e.g.*, notes, drafts, copies, reference material from other cases, research, etc. Ethics opinions do not claim that the *entire* client files is the client's property (although some comments indicate that the client may have a right to access the entire file). By maintaining the client file with no clear identification of which part belongs to the client, the attorney perpetually violates the ethical prohibition against commingling property.

- *Improved access to valuable information.* A records retention program and an improved filing system improve the access to valuable information.
- *Legal compliance.* A good records retention program also ensures compliance with the multitude of laws affecting your records.
- *Protection during litigation, government investigation, or audit.* A good records retention program also protects the organization during litigation, government investigation or audit. The program ensures that designated records exist and that other designated records do not exist.
- *Practice opportunities.* When attorneys implement their own records retention program, they gain valuable expertise that can be marketed to clients.

THE PROBLEMS AND RISKS OF DESTROYING CLIENT FILES

When Attorneys Believe the Files Belong to the Clients

Since some ethical opinions conclude that the client file belong to the client. In that case, the client file may be destroyed after stated procedures have been followed—notice to client, review of file content, etc. But, there are risk when following this alternative:

- The attorney must obtain the last know address of the clients and sent them traceable letters (*e.g.*, registered, certified, Federal Express, etc.) offering them the files. Even so, clients may later claim that the attorneys did not send the letter or failed to make a reasonable effort to get a current address.
- When provided notice, clients may request their files. Attorneys will then have to spend the time and money inspecting the file prior to turning it over.

- These burden may persuade many attorneys to just "keep everything forever" and accept the costs and problems of permanent retention. Long term retention of the client files may work to the client's detriment—and violate the Rules of Professional Conduct.

Therefore, even adherence to published ethical opinions—correct or not—creates significant risks for attorneys.

When Attorneys Believe the Files Do Not Belong to the Clients

Even when attorneys accept that the files do not belong to the client, they may fear repercussions based on the published ethical opinions. Here are some issues that may alleviate these fears:

- *Status of ethical opinions.* Ethics opinions are merely the opinion of a local or state bar association committee or ABA committee empowered to issue such opinions in response to real or hypothetical issues raised by bar association member. Ethics opinions are not binding and do not have the power of law. But, grievance boards and courts may elect to treat the opinion as either a definitive statement of the legal profession regarding the issue or as additional evidence of appropriate ethical conduct.
- *Ethical opinions are in conflict with the Rules of Professional Conduct.* The Rules of Professional Conduct do indicate that client files belong to the client, do not requirement attorneys to keep records forever, and do not require any procedures before destroying client files.
- *Ethical opinions are based on inappropriate assumptions.* The ethical opinion related to ownership and destruction of client files are based on incorrect or indefensible assumptions, and try to establish duties and requirements that extend far beyond the pronouncements in the Rules of Professional Responsibility. Based on the analysis above, the client file does not belong to the client and an attorney has no legal duty to keep the client file forever or even offer it back to the client prior to destruction.
- *Ethics opinions consistently permit attorneys to destroy their records.* Destroying client files that only contained attorney property and contained no property belonging to the client without notice to the client or inspection of the files would comply with requirements of the ethical opinions.

Since the ethical opinions defer to the attorney's judgment in determining the ownership of property in the client files, an attorney acts reasonably by reviewing the ethical opinions and concluding that none of the material in the client file belongs to the client. Similarly, an attorney acts reasonably by inspecting a sampling of client files which would be candidates for destruction under the proposed records retention schedule and actually confirms that the files do not contain client property, contain only abandoned client property, or contain client property of such a minor nature that the property has no current value. An attorney could also verify that client property with intrinsic value—*e.g.*, wills, trusts, stock certificates, bonds, etc.—have either been returned to the clients or are maintained in a safe area other than in the client file.

- *An ethical review or grievance proceeding would likely never be undertaken*. A proceeding will probably never occur due to the weaknesses in the ethical opinions, the unenforceable nature of the opinions and the professional judgment exercised by the attorney in reaching these conclusions.

If an ethical review or grievance proceeding still was instituted, the attorney would likely prevail for the reasons stated above. In the unlikely event that the attorney loses, the likely sanctions would be minimal since there would only be a minor technical violations of the ethics opinion, no violations of the Rules of Professional Conduct, and no harm done to the client.

CONCLUSION

- The ethical opinions addressing the retention of client files are seriously flawed in both logic and law.

- An attorney may elect to destroy client files in a reasonable period after the conclusion of the representation, without notice to the client. The retention period should not commence until the subject matter of the representation has concluded.

- The attorney should document the destruction under the records retention program for review and audit purposes.

- For all past engagements, the attorneys should place clients on notice by stating the records retention policy in a newsletter or letter sent to all past and current clients.

- For all future engagements, the engagement letter should state the records retention policy.

THE MALPRACTICE INSURANCE "GODS" ARE MORE LIKELY TO HELP THOSE WHO HAVE HELPED THEMSELVES: RISK MANAGEMENT SUGGESTIONS FOR THE IMMIGRATION LAWYER

by David E. Walker[*]

The rapid increase in civil litigation in the United States over the last few decades has been both boon and bane to the practicing attorney. The boon is evident; the bane has been an increase in the frequency of attorney malpractice lawsuits brought by disgruntled clients. The increased threat of attorney malpractice lawsuits deserves special attention and must be considered by all attorneys in the administration of their practice.

As an initial matter, practicing attorneys in all areas of specialization should evaluate their professional liability exposures and procure professional liability insurance to cover those exposures. This exercise is best undertaken with the assistance of an insurance broker with experience in the area of professional liability risks. However, simply procuring professional liability insurance is not the final solution. Nearly all professional liability insuring agreements impose not insignificant deductible obligations which continue to expose the attorney to financial loss. Indeed, in many instances this is the insurer's first step toward loss control—providing incentive to the insured to regulate his or her practice so as to minimize the likelihood of claims. In addition, many professional liability insurers require their insureds to implement risk management measures to assist with loss prevention under their policies.

The following suggestions incorporate many of those loss prevention techniques:

Should I have the client execute a formal agreement for retention?

Understanding the scope of representation is of paramount importance in ensuring that both the attorney and the client understand the services to be provided and the fee to be assessed for the service. There are a significant number of attorney malpractice claims that can be traced directly to misunderstandings created at the outset of the attorney-client relationship. In many instances, those claims could have been prevented or at least minimized in scope by a clear agreement executed or countersigned by the client explicitly defining the scope of the attorney's representation.

The retention agreement should expressly identify the client for whom services are to be provided. This can be particularly critical in the immigration law arena where the client may be seeking a change in status which as an end result will effect the status of dependents or relatives residing outside of the United States. The agreement should expressly acknowledge or disavow any duties or benefits running to those relatives or dependents, depending upon the unique circumstances of each case. In addition, the precise immigration law service being provided should be identified and the attorney's activities limited solely to that service unless the contract is subsequently amended in a writing agreed by all parties to the agreement.

Finally, the immigration lawyer should ensure that linguistic barriers are addressed so that the client understands the agreement and is able to execute it. If a translator is present, either a professional translator or a relative who speaks the attorney's and the client's native language, consideration should be given to having the retention agreement transcribed to the client's native language for his signature. While burdensome at the front end, this type of activity could prove greatly beneficial should a client later claim ignorance to the lawyer's initial cautions.

What steps can and should be taken in the initial meeting with a client to ensure the client is properly informed of the contingencies in the legal process?

The initial meeting between a prospective client and a lawyer is in many instances the client's first exposure to the legal world. The lawyer should therefore take the opportunity to begin educating the client on the contingencies inherent in the process. First of all, the lawyer should advise the client orally

---

[*] **David E. Walker** is a partner with the Chicago law firm of Lord, Bissell & Brook LLP and frequently represents professional liability insurers. The views expressed herein are not necessarily the views of Lord, Bissell & Brook LLP or its clients. Walker previously worked as a representative for a professional liability insurance company.

and also in writing that success simply cannot be guaranteed. This maxim is basic to the lawyer, and, consequently, one that is easily forgotten. Thus perhaps the easiest technique is to incorporate a statement in the written retention agreement that informs the client that guarantees on the outcome of a case cannot be given, either with respect to success in the endeavor or the time within which an outcome can be achieved.

The latter point is sometimes the most critical point to make in the immigration law context. The federal and state bureaucracies involved in the immigration arena simply prohibit in many instances the ability to guarantee a client that immigration relief or changes in status can be obtained within a specified period. The lawyer, therefore, must clearly and unequivocally inform the client that while she will do all in her power to achieve the result in a timely fashion, the precise timing of the outcome cannot be secured.

Proper attention again must also be given to overcoming language barriers which might prevent the client from understanding these considerations or which might allow the client to distance himself or herself at a later time from the cautions which the lawyer has conveyed.

Once the client is retained, how do I ensure that he or she remains closely advised about the status of the case?

It is generally accepted that the client who is kept informed during the legal process and who is provided with full and candid disclosures is less likely at the end of the day to pursue litigation against his attorney for an adverse outcome. The easiest and most efficient way of accomplishing this goal is simply to copy the client on all letters which the attorney sends out and to forward to the client copies of all documents received regarding the client's case. An additional technique is simply to dictate letters to the client each time the immigration lawyer conducts a regular review of the status of his or her case load. The letter generally can be prepared in a short amount of time and provides the client with a brief update on the status of the case and the activity which remains to be accomplished. This type of letter may be particularly beneficial where the lawyer is experiencing difficulties with the client's employer or prospective employer in obtaining the materials necessary to complete employment-based applications.

What steps can be taken to ensure that deadlines are followed?

Meeting deadlines is perhaps the most critical task in managing professional liability risks. For example, the failure to file a lawsuit in the civil litigation arena prior to expiration of the statute of limitations is probably the clearest breach of an attorney's duty of care. The failure to file within deadlines imposed by statute or regulations applications for relief from deportation or labor certification applications can have similar ramifications. There are many methods available to ensure that an attorney adheres to limitations and filing deadlines.

First, there are numerous computer software packages available which are tailored to assisting attorneys with complying with deadlines, some of which are targeted solely at the immigration law practice. Next, manual systems are plentiful and in many instances can and indeed should be used in conjunction with computer-assisted docket control. These systems can range from the simple but often burdensome task of reviewing each client's file on a weekly or monthly basis to a global office calendar which lists all deadlines for each client's case. The flaw in these systems is obvious: the failure to write down deadlines in a religious fashion can lead to gaps. Thus backup systems should be employed, such as having each attorney maintain a personal calendar with all possible deadlines listed in addition to having a legal assistant knowledgeable of the deadlines maintain a separate calendar. Finally, a solo practitioner should identify and obtain agreement from another lawyer to assist her with her docket in the event personal illness, emergencies or other exigencies prevent the lawyer from attending hearings or timely filing documents.

The methods available to monitor compliance with deadlines can be endless. The important aspect of docket control, however, is universal: strict adherence to a regimen of inputting deadlines and an equally strict adherence to reviewing the deadlines for each client's case on a regular basis.

How do I stay abreast of developments in the law?

With the monumental changes in immigration law recently, remaining knowledgeable in an attorney's practice area can literally consume all time available to service a client's needs. The following are possible solutions:

(1) Remain active in bar associations and immigration law associations, such as AILA, to obtain educational materials not only from the association

itself but also from individuals in those associations with whom professional relationships are developed;

(2) Avoid accepting cases in areas of the law in which your knowledge is limited. A little knowledge can be a dangerous thing, and in many instances it is difficult for the practicing attorney to acknowledge that he is not prepared to take on a paying client's case which is outside his area of expertise. If a case is rejected, the rejection should be in writing and should inform the client that time limitations exist which might impact the availability of relief;

(3) Participate in seminars provided by national organizations and local bar associations. Many times, this is the only way for the practicing attorney to participate in a focused, intensive discussion of changes in the law. In addition, it is common for Administrative Law Judges or governmental lawyers to participate in these seminars and provide insight into the specific areas on which a particular agency is focusing or where it is encountering frequent difficulties; and,

(4) With the prevalence of personal computers, programs exist through services such as Westlaw which can automatically alert the practitioner to recent developments of importance in the particular area of immigration law in which the practitioner specializes.

How do I ensure that a client has received all the assistance he or she needs?

The simple answer is to write the client a letter in which the client is informed that he or she has obtained the relief sought or, conversely, his or her request for relief has been denied. If the relief sought was obtained, advise the client in unequivocal terms that you are ending the attorney-client relationship and will no longer provide him or her with legal assistance unless he or she expressly requests it. If the relief sought was denied, advise the client that there are no further avenues of relief or, alternatively, advise the client of other available avenues and request the client to inform you whether he or she wishes you to proceed with his or her representation. A written rider to the attorney-client retention agreement should memorialize any agreement to provide additional services.

What should be done when I realize a mistake has been made?

Of critical importance is to notify your professional liability insurer in writing as early as possible and obtain its input in dealing with the problem. Almost every insurance policy currently available has strict requirements for providing notice when an attorney becomes aware of circumstances which could give rise to a claim. Failure to abide by the notice condition can result in a loss of coverage. Moreover, and perhaps equally as important, the insurer will generally have experienced claims technicians who may be able to provide assistance either in minimizing the damage caused or in working with the client to undo the mistake and eliminate any damages which otherwise might have been sustained.

Ethical obligations imposed by Codes of Professional Conduct are widely construed as requiring an attorney to disclose fully problems or mistakes made in the handling of a client's case. So long as the applicable ethical rules allow it, consultation with the attorney's professional liability insurer should be the rule of the day prior to discussing the matter with the client so as to avoid violations of any policy conditions which forbid admissions of liability.

What do I do if I am named in a formal lawsuit for malpractice or am threatened with such a lawsuit?

Not unlike the situation in which an attorney learns of circumstances potentially giving rise to a claim, the attorney should immediately notify his insurer in writing of the threat or the lawsuit and forward all necessary papers to the insurer. An insurer's duty to defend its insured against lawsuits for damages can be the overriding benefit in many professional liability policies. Notice to the insurer in compliance with policy conditions is a prerequisite to obtaining that benefit. Once notice is provided to the insurer, all future contacts with the client should be referred to the insurer for handling in accordance with its practices unless the insurer advises otherwise. If the client is a current client, close contact should be maintained with the insurer to ensure compliance with policy conditions while also ensuring that additional grounds for malpractice are not created pending withdrawal from the client's case.

The foregoing suggestions are directed to practicing attorneys for management of their professional liability risks. The suggestions should not be treated as formal legal advice and are not offered in that capacity. Rather, each attorney should undertake an independent evaluation of the techniques likely to assist him or her in controlling the possibility of attorney malpractice lawsuits unique to his or her practice.

SAFEGUARDING AGAINST CRIMINAL PROSECUTION AND MALPRACTICE IN IMMIGRATION LAW —AN OUTLINE OF KEY TOPICS

by Robert E. Juceam[*]

As immigration lawyers, we frequently represent clients unsophisticated in almost every way—with the English language, understanding of our legal system and our laws, dealing with lawyers and law offices, trusting us with full disclosure of background and material facts, or even telling us their complete objectives in the representation. Some clients come from a governmental system where administrative bribes and lies are the grist of success. Others have escaped persecution only by stealth and falsehood. Often, clients have limited or no funds and even a reasonable fee is beyond their means. Lawyers have an obligation to recognize these factors, to reject cases where they are not competent or committed to serve as counselors or zealous advocates, and to strive to ensure that clients seek only what they have a legitimate basis to achieve. In some cases, lawyers must say "no."

This outline identifies selected topics of current interest to the immigration law lawyer with a focus on exposure to criminal prosecution and civil malpractice claims for alleged wrongdoing. It touches on numerous issues affecting how we perceive ourselves, structure our services, recognize our limits, and honor our being entrusted officers of the court. Usually, ethical matters and outcomes are jurisdiction-specific, since rules of professional conduct and discipline are rooted in the lawyer's state of licensure and jurisdictions where the attorney is admitted or permitted to practice. Sometimes, more than one jurisdiction's code or rules of professional responsibility will apply, with conflicts or tensions between or among their prescriptions.

Additionally, the underlying requirements of civil and criminal law may promote additional uncertainty, since professional codes and rules presume compliance with the law. This is notably so in the field of immigration law, with all of its regulatory structure, gray areas of entitlement, discretionary relief, often drastic remedies for the alien and quixotic, informal practice. Rapid-fire statutory and regulatory changes, including broadly stated federal crimes newly applied in recent years, and public perceptions of lawyers generally in a post 9/11 world as facilitators of fraud and illegality, have heightened concern for those seeking ethical certainty and bullet-proof defenses to civil charges, penalties, damage claims and criminal prosecution.

At bottom, we should recognize that we are regulated professionals enveloped in a broad range of disciplinary jurisdictions, with multiple sources of rules governing behavior and adjudicatory processes. The sensible lawyer structures legal practice defensively—by behaving well during the representation, knowing the law and practice, sizing up properly each client and being able to demonstrate in hindsight legal and ethical compliance in a convincing testimonial and evidentiary manner.

Without losing perspective, even a zealous advocate should arrange to practice and manage the law office on the assumption that law enforcement or professional discipline authorities may scrutinize behavior, and clients or third parties may question or challenge professional conduct.[1]

I. THE LAWYER AS A REGULATED PROFESSIONAL

A. Licensed Professional

1. State law and codes of licensing authorities—*e.g.*, N.Y. Judiciary Law §90 (McKinney 2002); N.Y. Comp. Codes R. & Regs. tit. 22, §1200.[2]

   a. Mandated Codes of Professional Responsibility.

      i. Disciplinary rules affecting license.

      ii. Ethical precepts and exhortations.

      iii. Pro bono services.

      iv. Mandatory CLE.

      v. Mandated registration—*e.g.*, N.Y. Comp. Codes R. & Regs. tit. 22, §118 (2003).

      vi. Individual court rules—*e.g.*, New York Appellate Division Rules—N.Y. Comp. Codes R. & Regs. tit. 22, §§603, 605, 606, 609, 806, 691.

B. Voluntary Codes of Professional Conduct

1. Specialty bars—Ethical Guidelines.

---

[*] © Copyright **Robert E. Juceam**, 2000; 2002; 2004. All rights reserved. The assistance of the following individuals at Fried, Frank, Harris, Shriver & Jacobson LLP in the preparation of this outline is gratefully acknowledged: associate Dian R. Gray; summer associates Jeremy Goldman, Marc Romanoff, and Victor Suthammanont; and intern Raquel Aragon.

[1] As a general bibliography, please see: ABA/BNA Lawyers' Manual on Professional Conduct (2003 and Monthly Reports) and American Law Institute, Restatement (Third) of The Law Governing Lawyers and the sources cited therein.

[2] While many references herein concentrate on New York cases, statutes, rules, etc., the principles stated are national in scope.

2. ABA Section of Litigation—Code of Civility; N.Y. Comp. Codes R. & Regs. tit. 22, §1200.
3. Codes adopted by industry associations.
4. Ethics opinions of bar associations.

C. Rules of Practice of the Forum
1. Federal Courts—Local Rules incorporating state ethical rules; Federal Courts—Rule 11; ABA Standards on Imposing Lawyer Sanctions.
2. State Courts—Local Rules—N.Y. Comp. Codes R. & Regs. tit. 22, §130 (2003) (Costs and Sanctions) State Courts—Rule 11 analogs.
3. Immigration Court Rules—*see* Rules Governing Practice before the Immigration Court (EOIR) and DHS under 8 CFR §1003.101 to §1003.107

   a. A rule promulgated on June 27, 2000 governing the conduct of attorneys practicing before the INS/DHS and the Executive Office for Immigration Review (EOIR), which administers the Immigration Courts and the Board of Immigration Appeals (BIA), provides the EOIR with the authority to investigate complaints and to impose a wide range of disciplinary sanctions, ranging from private censure to expulsion from practice before the DHS or EOIR.

     i. Pursuant to 8 CFR §1003.103, the EOIR can sanction attorneys who have been found guilty or who have pleaded guilty or *nolo contendere* to a serious crime or who have been disciplined in other jurisdictions.

     ii. If such a conviction or disciplinary action occurred on or after August 28, 2000, the rule also imposes a duty on the attorney to notify the EOIR voluntarily. 8 CFR §1003.103(c).

     iii. The second ground under which the EOIR can sanction attorneys is 8 CFR §1003.104, which provides that the EOIR can sanction attorneys who have been the subject of a complaint filed with the Office of the General Counsel of the EOIR.

     iv. 8 CFR §292 (2003) (and other agency rules of practice). Lists 14 non-exclusive categories when an Immigration Judge, the BIA or the Attorney General may suspend or bar an attorney from further practice. (Does not cover government trial attorneys.)

   Inherent powers of the BIA. See *In re Jean Jean Charlemagne,* A 29351845 (2/8/94).

D. The Limits of Law

1. Civil Law.
   a. Liability in contract.
   b. Malpractice and tort liability rules.
   c. 8 USC (Aliens and Nationality).
   d. Consumer agencies.
     i. *Aponte v. Raychuk,* 575 N.Y.S.2d 272 (1991) ($206,000 in fines for false advertising).
     ii. See Randall Scott Hetrick, Unfair Trade Practices Applied to Attorney Conduct: A National Review, 18 J. Legal Prob. 329 (1993).

2. Criminal Law.
   a. 8 USC (Aliens and Nationality) crimes.
   b. 18 USC (Crimes and Criminal Procedure), especially:
     i. §1001 (False statement to agency).
     ii. §2 (Aid and Abet) [("assist"), ("counsel"), or ("encourage")].
     iii.
     iv. §4 (Misprision of felony) (Active concealment).
     v. §1503 *et seq.* (Obstruction of Justice).
     vi. §1341 (Mail and Wire Fraud).

3. Malpractice Insurance.
   a. Risk management assessments and peer reviews.
   b. Premium ratings.
   c. Availability of insurance at all.
   d. Claims made form.
   e. Limitations on scope of coverage and coverage limits.
   f. Prior acts.
   g. Exclusions—self dealing; intentional misconduct; fraud.

4. The "Market" Discipline.
   a. Reputation and referrals.
   b. Client acceptance.
   c. The "Media" coverage.
   d. Advertising.

II. THE ROLE OF THE LAWYER
A. Advocate in adversary proceedings and for benefits.
B. Counselor—analysis and advice.
C. Negotiator—getting third parties to "yes."
D. Friend.
E. If in-house or in-government—role as officer, employee, or subordinate, usually involved in organic policy and business, not just "legal advice."
F. Roles blur and risks increase where lawyer also:
   1. Is director of the client's business.
   2. Is an investor in or business partner of the client.
   3. Has business dealings with client.
   4. Has policy or operational business responsibilities.
   5. Acts for more than one client with actual or potential conflicting interests.

III. DUTIES OF THE LAWYER
A. To Client
1. Contractual—in engagement letter, by oral contract or implied in law.
2. Under Code of Professional Responsibility.
3. In tort—as a "fiduciary."
4. Under statutes.
5. State's "Bill of Client Rights."

B. To Third Parties Who Pay the Bill or Are Affected By Lawyer Behavior, Including Counter-Parties and Adversaries of the Client

1. In tort and contract.
2. Under Code of Professional Responsibility.
3. Under statutes.

IV. THE MECHANISMS OF ENFORCEMENT

A. Lawyer or Law Firm Self Assessment and Restraint

B. Angry Client or Affiliate of Client (*e.g.*, Family Members, Parent Corporation)

1. Bar referral.
2. Agency referral.
3. Suit.
4. Publicity.

C. Angry Adversary or Counter-party

1. Bar referral.
2. Agency referral.
3. Suit.
4. Publicity.

D. An Affected or Interested Unit of Government or Tribunal Before Which Lawyer Appears or Is Authorized to Practice

E. Local, State and Federal Civil and Criminal Law Prosecutors and Regulators

F. Consumer Affairs Agencies

1. False advertising.
2. Consumer fraud.
3. Cease and Desist Orders.
4. Fines and penalties.

G. Bar Counsel and Licensure Authorities

1. Inquiry.
2. Proceedings.
3. Discipline and disbarment.

H. The Media

I. Insurers—Denial of, or Substandard Rating for, Coverage

V. LAW OFFICE MANAGEMENT AND RISK

A. The Intake Process

1. Do you want this client?
2. Can you competently and lawfully assist the client?
3. Have you delegated intake to nonlawyers?
4. Is there full disclosure about, and agreement on, fee arrangements and scope of services?
5. Does the client understand any limitations on your services and have reasonable expectations about your role and the certainty or uncertainty of outcome?
6. Have you explained the rules of confidence and attorney client privilege and their different limitations, and how privilege or confidences can be lost?
7. Was there a conflict check and a record made of it? Was a record made of the basis for judgments in resolving potential conflicts?
8. Have you done a "full" background interview that would give sufficient information to analyze alternatives to achieve client objectives?
9. Have you made disclosure of relevant facts about referral and any referral fees?
10. Have you done due diligence on the client—prior lawyers, a government informant, litigation history?

B. The Engagement Letter

1. Mandatory in many jurisdictions and now required for New York.
2. Not a selling document. You and the client already have determined to have the engagement.
3. Ambiguities will be construed against the lawyer.
4. Evidences aspects of "the contract;" currently, in New York, lawyers cannot negate professional duties or have client indemnify the lawyer.

C. Files and Records/Attorneys' Liens

1. Conflicts and control docket for appointments and filing, court and appeal dates.
2. Client documents in your custody do not become your documents.
3. Do you have a protocol for advising the client and dealing with a subpoena or CID for your client files?
4. When can you dispose of your files?
   a. Most jurisdictions have a five year Code-mandated retention period.
   b. As to the lawyer's documents, retain long enough to meet, (i) statutory record keeping requirements, (ii) statute of limitations periods, (iii) needs for office precedent, and (iv) defense against potential claims.
   c. As to client documents, return at end of representation to:
      i. Avoid cost of maintaining.
      ii. Minimize liability for breach of trust or contract if documents lost or destroyed.
5. Meet Code obligations to return. Look at state attorneys' lien laws about withholding "client files" and "client records."
   a. Cannot prejudice former client.
   b. Factual and characterization issues.

D. The Nonengagement Letter

1. Increasingly recommended by insurers to put potential client on notice that lawyer regards contact as not resulting in engagement (and that any client belief there was an engagement is in error).
2. Generally, ends tolling of malpractice limitations period.
3. Lawyer should have proof of delivery.

4. Should be sent even if potential engagement not accepted after initial interview.

   a. *See* David J. Meiselman, *Attorney Malpractice: Law & Procedure* §1.2 (1980; 1998 Supp.).

   b. Absence of fee does not control whether relationship came into existence or ended. *See In re McGlothlen*, 99 Wash. 2d 575, 66 F.2d 1330 (1983).

E. The Disengagement or Termination Letter. Withdrawal or Ending of Engagement Triggers Duties. Model Code DR 2-110; Model Rules 1-16(d)

1. Return of unearned fees.
2. Return of client properties and papers.
3. Cooperation with successor counsel.
4. Protect client interests for reasonable period to permit locating new counsel and transitioning work.

   a. Give client reasonable notice of withdrawal.

   b. *See* Restatement of the Law Governing Lawyers §45(2)(c).

   c. Secure any required court or tribunal permission to be relieved of appearance. Nonpayment of fees may not be sufficient.

5. Retaining Liens. *See* Thomas G. Fischer, Attorney's Assertion of Retaining Lien as Violation of Ethical Code or Rules Governing Professional Conduct, 69 A.L.R. 4th 974 (1989).

   a. Ethical rules neither endorse nor condemn.

   b. Arise at common law. Do not exist under federal common law.

   c. But Supremacy Clause may trump state lien. *See RTC v. Elman*, 949 F.2d 624 (2d Cir. 1991).

   d. Lien overcome by client's inability to pay. *See, e.g.*, D.C. Code of Professional Responsibility Rule 1.8(i).

   e. In most jurisdictions, lien never applies or deemed lapsed where withdrawal was triggered by fee dispute. *See, e.g., Acad. of Cal. Optometrists Inc. v. Superior Court*, 124 Cal Reptr. 668 (Cal. Ct. App. 1978).

F. Maintaining Competence

1. CLE.
2. Bar association membership and participation in committee work.
3. Adequate library or library access.

G. Staff and Partner Intake Procedures

1. Scrutinize prior employment for potential conflicts.
2. Review restrictions on practice of former government employees.

H. Staff and Partner Exits

1. Have an exit procedure.
2. Ensure transition of client work.
3. Screen client documents and other firm records so confidences remain in the firm.
4. Review firm agreements to avoid disputes over post departure "competition" and unlawful forfeiture of earned benefits.
5. Establish ground rules for notice to and other communications with existing clients.
6. Anticipate conflicts and their resolution when departing lawyer practices elsewhere.

I. "Sale" of Practices

1. Many jurisdictions still prohibit the "sale" of a legal practice.
2. In these jurisdictions, cases can be transferred with client consent after full disclosure, and fees are apportioned based on contribution to the case.

VI. SPECIFIC ISSUES

A. Is There a, and Who Is the, "Client?"

1. Not defined in Codes or Rules.
2. Usually a matter of fact evaluated under principles of agency and contract law.

   a. *See* Ronald Friedman, "The Creation of the Attorney Client Relationship: An Emerging View," 22 Cal. W.L. Rep. 209 (1986).

   b. Usually implied from circumstances and "client's" reasonable reliance on existence of engagement.

     i. Preliminary consultation usually triggers fiduciary duties of lawyer, especially as to confidentiality. *Westinghouse Elec. Corp. v. Ken-McGee Corp.*, 580 F.2d 1311 (7th Cir. 1978).

     ii. Actual employment need not be undertaken.

B. Arbitration in Engagement Agreement

1. Can arbitration of disputes be a condition of engagement? *See* Rule 3.4(f)(2)(v).
2. Courts are split:

   a. Absolutely not. Ohio Ethics Op. 96-9 (1996).

   b. Clearly yes. Maine Prof. Ethics Op. 170 (1999).

   c. Maybe. DC Ethics Op. 211 (1990); Arizona Ethics Op. 94–5 (1994).

   d. New York gives client right to arbitrate most fee disputes. DR §2-106(E), N.Y. Comp. Codes R. & Regs. tit. 22, §1215 (2002).

C. Compulsory Disclosure of Client Identity

1. Generally can be compelled.
2. Exception: Last Link Doctrine where the government knows all material facts to establish element of offense except identity. *See In re Grand Jury*, 11th Cir. 91-8305, 10/24/91, (GJ 90-2); *In re Grand Jury (Cheney)*, 898 F.2d 565 (7th Cir. 1990).

D. Compulsory Disclosure of Client Whereabouts

1. In bail jumping context, lawyer can be called as witness to testify in federal court as to what he told client about required court date. *See* Modern Federal Jury Instructions §§55.01.

2. But absent crime-fraud exception to privilege or communication relating to ongoing flight or obstruction charge, whereabouts is a protected confidence. *See* D.C. Ethical Op. 206 (6/19/96). Lawyer obliged not to disclose whereabouts [*see* Rules 1.6, 1.16 and 3.4(c) of DC Code] even if he thereby cannot withdraw as representative of record in immigration proceedings.

E. Birds and Bees

1. Increasingly for most of the last decade, jurisdictions expressly made it unethical for a lawyer to have sexual relations with a client during representation in a matrimonial matter.

2. New York in DR 5-111 now proscribes any demand for sexual relations as incident to or a condition of representation. Also proscribed are coercion, intimidation and undue influence to gain sexual relations with a client.

3. But, a lawyer in a law firm is not prohibited from sexual relations with a firm client if the lawyer is not personally involved in the representation. Moreover, all lawyers are ethically free to continue consensual relations predating the representation.

4. Lawyer suspended who proposed to a client in existing matrimonial and unrelated auto accident cases that she pay off a fee balance by oral sex. The lawyer was taped with police assistance at a negotiating meeting where the amount of debt would be reduced by specific acts, each to be separately valued. In the absence of ultimate agreement, the meeting ended and the police would not prosecute. A grievance and civil suit followed. The Ohio Supreme Court suspended the lawyer for 18 months. *In re Feneli*, Ohio, No. 98-2664, 7/7/99). He settled the civil claim for $25,000.

F. Special Problems of E-mail and the Internet

1. Ethical issues are featured on *www.legalethics.com*, may be accessed through *www.visalaw.com/memphis* containing other useful material and links as well.

2. In setting up or participating in Internet chats, do lawyers develop a "client" relationship? Are they giving "legal advice?" Do disclaimers work? State bar ethics committees are currently groping with the adaptation of traditional rules to the new technologies.

3. Unencrypted Internet e-mail.

   a. Does it violate Rule 1.6(a) because it fails adequately to protect client confidences, or evidences an intent that there be no confidence?

   b. *See* ABA Standing Committee on Ethics and Professional Responsibility Formal Op. 99-413. Argues for treating unencrypted e-mail with the same expectation of privacy as telephone calls.

   c. *See* Micalyn Harris, *E-mail Ethics for Attorney-Client Communications: Comments on ABA Opinion Regarding Unencrypted Internet E-mail*, The Professional Lawyer (Vol. 10, No. 3, Spring 1999), for analysis and critique of the ABA Opinion, the need for review of local Codes, and suggesting it is appropriate for the lawyer to discuss with the client *in advance* the risks of using e-mail for communications and obtaining the client's informed consent.

G. Taping Conversations with Clients, Adversaries and the Court

1. Check federal, state and local law for criminal law violations. *See, e.g.*, 18 USC §2515 (prohibiting intentional interception of wire communications and prohibiting the introduction into evidence of any information obtained from a wiretap). *See United States v. Wuliger*, 981 F.2d 1497 (6th Cir. 1997) (finding no impeachment exception to the exclusionary rule of §2515 in civil proceedings despite other circuit decisions to contrary).

2. Traditionally a violation of ethical/disciplinary rules without express consent of all on call, based on the theory that the proscriptions against lawyer "dishonesty, fraud, deceit or misrepresentation" warranted or compelled that result.

3. Recently, the prior "majority" bar association views have been called unreasoned and without foundation in the Codes. *See* Maine Bar Ethics Op. 168 (3/99) (concluding it is "not nice" but not proscribed).

4. On June 24, 2001, the American Bar Association issued Formal Opinion 01-422 on "Electronic Recordings by Lawyers Without the Knowledge of all Participants." It withdrew a 1974 ABA opinion, and determined that such a recording "does not necessarily violate the Model Rules."

5. While "the better practice may be . . . to obtain consent prior to recording," the conclusion of an increasing number of commentators and bar committees is that "attorneys are not per se prohibited from ever recording conversations without the express permission of all other parties to the conversation." Alaska Bar Association Ethics Op. 2003-1.

6. New York's Association of the Bar of the City of New York recently concluded that "a lawyer may . . . engage in the undisclosed taping of a conversation if the lawyer has a reasonable basis for believing that disclosure of the taping would [not] impair pursuit of a generally accepted societal good." Digest, Formal Op. 2003-02.

   a. The opinion reflects the Ethics' Committee strong distaste for taping and its implications of trickery.

   b. Taping as a "routine practice" remains "unethical" in the Committee's opinion.

   c. The Opinion particularizes circumstances where undisclosed taping is more likely to be generally acceptable.

H. Can Nonlawyers Share in Firm Profits?

1. Still prohibited in most jurisdictions. Flat rule "guards" against unethical fee splitting, paying nonlawyers "feeders" and "ambulance chasing."

2. New York adopted DR 3-102(A)(3) in July, 1999 to permit sharing. Rule change reflected business nature of profession and the contribution of paralegals and other support staff; employer firm responsible for controlling its profit allocation.

I. Retainers

1. Ambiguity in meaning and usage of term "retainer."

   a. Is it an advance against future services?

   b. Is it securing availability apart from other fees to be earned for future services?

   c. If (a), remains client "property" until earned. If (b), the lawyer owns it.

2. Lawyer as a fiduciary.

   a. A lawyer should hold property of others with care. Model Rules of Prof'l Conduct R. 1.15, cmt [1] (2001).

   b. Lawyers should hold client's money with a fiduciary duty to safeguard and account for every penny of it until all disbursed.

3. Lawyer, on termination, must take reasonable steps to protect client interests, including "refunding any advance payment of fee that has not been earned." Model Rules of Prof'l Conduct R. 1.16 (2001).

   a. Fee must be "reasonable." Model Rules of Prof'l Conduct R. 1.5(a) (2001).

   b. Duty under Rule 1.16(d) to account for even a "non-refundable" retainer.

4. Local disciplinary rules regarding requiring deposit of "advance" retainers in trust accounts absent client's informed consent in writing otherwise.

   a. "Advance fee deposits" are funds given to a lawyer for providing future services. Such funds belong to the client until the lawyer has earned them. *See Baranowski v. State Bar*, 154 Cal. Rptr. 752, 593 P.2d 613, fn. 4 (1979).

   b. "Retainers" are funds paid by a client to secure a lawyer's availability over a given period of time. The funds are considered earned at the time of payment. Provided that the client agrees to such an arrangement, the funds are not refundable and the lawyer is entitled to the funds regardless of whether any services are actually performed for the client. *See Id.*

   c. In *Matter of Cooperman*, 83 N.Y.2d 465, 471 (N.Y. 1994), the New York Court of Appeals held that an agreement that "compromise[s] the client's absolute right to terminate the unique fiduciary attorney-client relationship" is void as against public policy and violative of the Code of Professional Responsibility, especially DR 2-110(A)(3) (requiring withdrawing attorneys to "refund promptly any part of a fee paid in advance that has not been earned"), DR 2-110(B)(4) (mandating withdrawal if an attorney is discharged by the client) and DR 2-106(A) (prohibiting a lawyer from entering into an agreement for, charging or collecting an illegal or excessive fee).

5. Because fee disputes are so large an area of bar counsel's dockets, there is a focus on fee arrangements. Increasingly, states have required written letters of engagement and labeled "nonrefundable" retainers as unethical "per se." *See* DR 2-106 (N.Y. Comp. Codes R. & Regs. tit. 22, §1200-11); *In re Cooperman*, 591 N.Y.S.2d 855 (2d Dept 1993). Case outcomes seem to consider the sophistication of the client, whether the jurisdiction has anticommingling rule on client deposits and whether the client was advised by independent counsel on the fee arrangements.

J. Federal Subpoenas on Lawyer Files

1. McDade Act—28 USC §530B.

   a. Provides that federal attorneys generally must comply with state rules, and local federal court rules, regarding issuing subpoenas to attorneys.

   b. Some federal district courts and states require prior judicial approval before directing a subpoena to a lawyer.

      i. A number of states are deleting this general ethical requirement in face of continued governmental opposition as it relates to U.S. Attorneys' grand jury practices.

      ii. See *United States v. Colorado Supreme Court*, 189 F.3d 1281 (10th Cir. 1999) (holding that Rule 3.8(f)(2) of the Colorado Rules of Professional Conduct, which requires prior judicial approval of subpoenas by federal attorneys in non-grand jury criminal proceedings, is a rule of ethics applicable to federal prosecutors by the McDade Act).

2. Proposed Legislation. In September 2001, Senators Patrick Leahy, Orrin Hatch and Ron Wyden introduced S.1437, the Professional Standards for Government Attorneys Act of 2001, which would have, among other things, required the Judicial Conference of the United States to make recommendations to the Chief Justice of the United States regarding amending the Federal Rules of Criminal Procedure to provide for a uniform national rule for government attorneys that would govern communications with represented persons and parties. The bill failed to win support, however, and has not been reintroduced to date.

K. Lawyer's Advice to "Shut-Up" as Basis for Suspending License

1. *See In re of Martin L. Blatt*, 324 A.2d 15 (N.J. Sup. Ct. 1974):

   During a grand jury investigation before a subpoena was issued to client, Lawyer suggested that his client alter a document to be given to a potential witness to clarify meaning by adding a word. *Witness testified*: "[The lawyer] indicated if . . . our records were subpoenaed, . . . we should keep our mouths shut" and in the likely event authorities would question [us] we should be uncooperative and say as little as possible.

   Court concluded: Both the alteration of the document and the urging of the potential witnesses to cooperate as little as possible "each . . . constituted a violation of the ethical standards governing the conduct of attorneys." The attempt to deny evidence to law enforcement authorities "constituted conduct prejudicial to the administration of justice in violation of DR 1-102(5)." *Result*: Attorney suspended.

2. *See* DR 2-110(B)(2): "A lawyer . . . shall withdraw from employment, if . . . it is obvious that . . . continued employment will result in violation of a Disciplinary

Rule." DR2-110(B)(2). *In re Hopkins*, 687 A2d 983 (D.C. Ct. App. 1996).

3. *See* 42 USC §1985(2): Provides a private cause of action against those who conspire to deter a party or witness from attending or testifying in a court of the United States. *See, e.g., Brewer v. Rockwell Int'l Corp.*, 40 F.3d 1119 (10th Cir. 1994) (target of conspiracy has standing to bring civil damage action under §1985).

L. Conflict of Interest and Disqualification

1. Model Rule 1.7; Model Code 5-105(A).
2. Conflicts arise from:
   a. Lawyer interests adverse to client.
   b. Lawyer business transactions with client.
   c. Lawyer gifts from client.
   d. Lawyer financial assistance to client.
   e. Lawyer fees paid by third party.
   f. Representation adverse to interests of existing client.
   g. Representation adverse to interest of former client.
   h. Lawyer possession of confidential information.
   i. Multiple representations.
   j. Fee arrangements—*e.g.*, literary or media rights.
3. Possible consequences:
   a. Bar discipline.
   b. Disqualification by tribunal.
   c. Malpractice and other civil liability to damaged client.
   d. Possible inability to act for any of the conflicted interests.

M. Lawyer Obligations to Third Parties

1. DR7-102(A); 7-106(C)(2); 7-108(D); Model Rule 4.4.
2. Legal Opinions prepared for release to third parties.
3. Limitation on communications with persons represented by counsel.
4. Threatening "adversary" with criminal prosecution.
5. Lawyer compliance with fair debt collection practice acts and fines and penalties for lack of compliance.
6. Limitation on communications with unrepresented persons.
7. Obligation to be truthful in statements to others.
8. Common law and statutory tort liability.

N. Lawyer Obligations to the Tribunal

1. Frivolity.
   a. Fed. R. Civ. P. 11; 28 USC §1927; Fed. R. App. P. 38 and 28 USC §1912; inherent power of tribunals; state analogs.
   b. Model Rule 3.1; Code DR 7-102.
2. Failure to make reasonable efforts to expedite litigation consistent with interests of client.
   a. Model Rule 3.2 (expediting litigation).
   b. Code DR7-101 (duty of zealousness not violated by punctuality in commitments).
3. Client Perjury.
   a. Model Rules 3.3, 1.6 and 1.16 (requires actual knowledge to disclose).
   b. Code DR7-102; 2-110; 4-101.
   c. Lawyer obligation to discourage if prospective or recant if completed.
   d. Civil cases.
      i. Withdrawal.
      ii. A few jurisdictions require disclosure.
   e. Criminal cases.
      i. Withdrawal [*see Nix v. Whiteside*, 475 U.S. 157 (1986)].
      ii. If withdrawal prevented by tribunal, alternative requirements in different jurisdictions:
         a. Disclose.
         b. Use narrative for eliciting client testimony and make no reference in closing.
         c. Ignore and zealously advocate.
      iii. The lawyer obligation arises when the lawyer "knows" of the past or anticipated perjury. Differences abound over what is the standard of "knowledge"—suspects, reasonably infers, certainty. *See* Donald Liskov, *Criminal Defendant Perjury: A Lawyer's Choice Between Ethics, the Constitution, and the Truth*, 28 New Eng. L. Rev. 881 (Spring 1994); John Wesley Hall, Jr., *Handling Client Perjury After Nix v. Whiteside, A Criminal Defense Lawyers View*, 42 Mercer L. Rev. 769, 794 (1991).
4. Candor to Tribunal.
   a. Model Rule 3.3.
   b. Code DR 7-102; 7-106.
   c. Duty to disclose adverse legal authority not disclosed by opposing counsel and material facts.
   d. Duty to not knowingly make false statements of material facts or offer false evidence.
   e. Lawyer as witness.
      i. Model Rule 3.7.
      ii. Code DR5-101(B); DR5-102.
   f. Communications with jurors or judge.
      i. Model Rule 3.5.
      ii. Code DR7-108; 7-110.
   g. Fairness to opposing party.
      i. Model Rule 3.4 (destruction of evidence, falsifying evidence).
      ii. Code DR7-102; 7-106; 7-109.
   h. Courtroom conduct.
      i. Model Rule 3.5 (no disruption).
      ii. Code DR7-106 (no degrading).
   i. Special obligations of prosecutors.
      i. Model Rule 3.8.
      ii. Code DR7-103.
   j. Trial publicity.
      i. Model Rule 3.6

ii. Code DR7-107
k. Fashioning witness testimony.
  i. Role of lawyer.
    a. "Implanted or supplied recollection."
    b. Suggesting actual language of testimony.
    c. Opinion 79 (District of Columbia Bar—Legal Ethics Committee) December 18, 1979 ("[A] lawyer may not prepare, or assist in preparing, testimony that he or she knows, or ought to know, is false or misleading.").
    d. New York and Model Rules jurisdictions require "actual knowledge of the fact in question" before a lawyer can conclude there is sufficient information that evidence is false. "Actual knowledge" can be inferred. Conscious avoidance of falsity does not prevent a finding of actual knowledge. Charles W. Wolfram, *Modern Legal Ethics*, 12.5.3 at 655 (1986); Restatement (Third) of The Law Governing Lawyers; *United States v. Hanlon*, 548 F.2d 1096 (2d Cir. 1977) (false statement conviction sustained under conscious avoidance doctrine).
    e. DR 7-102(A)(4), (6) and (7); EC 7-26.
    f. *Genders v. United States*, 425 U.S. 80, 90 n.3 (1976) (noting distinction between discussing testimony and seeking improperly to influence it).
    g. *United States v. DeZarn*, 157 F.3d 1042 (6th Cir. 1998) (sustaining sentence enhancement for obstruction of justice following perjury conviction based on exculpatory categorical answers to questions with a partially mistaken premise; distinguishes non-responsive or partially responsive answers from categorically complete questions).
    h. See Bruce A. Green, *Lying Clients: An Age Old Problem*, 26 Litigation No. 1, (Fall 1999) (American Bar Association, Section on Litigation); Norman Lefstein, *Client Perjury in Criminal Cases: Still in Search of an Answer*, 1 Geo. J. Legal Ethics 521 (1988); *but see* Monroe H. Freedman, *But Only If You Know in Uphoff*, Ethical Problems Facing The Criminal Defense Lawyer 135 (1995).
    i. *Wilson v. Sundstrand Corp.*, 2003 U.S. Dist. LEXIS 14356 (N.D. Ill. 2003) (defendants were penalized lawyers fees and other sanctions for leading witness testimony by way of "speaking" objections).
    j. *In re Geoghan*, 686 N.Y.S. 2d 839 (N.Y. App. Div. 1999) (lawyer offered to have client testify falsely in criminal matter in exchange for settlement of civil matter); *Goodsell v. Mississippi Bar*, 667 So.2d 7 (Miss. 1996) (lawyer knowingly allowed witness to testify untruthfully); *In re Storment*, 873 S.W.2d 227 (Mo. 1994) (lawyer counseled and assisted client to testify untruthfully); *In re Edson*, 530 A.2d 1246 (N.J. 1987) (same).
    k. *Cf. In the Matter of Howard D. Deutsch*, 730 N.Y.S.2d 503 (N.Y. App. Div. First Dept. 2001) (disbarring a former senior partner in an immigration law firm who was found guilty in federal court of, among other things, witness tampering in violation of 18 USC §§1512(b)(1) and (b)(3) for removing certain physical evidence from, and inserting fabricated exculpatory evidence into, the files of a client then the subject of an INS criminal investigation).
l. Spoliation of evidence and e-mail discovery failures.
  i. *See* Barbara S. Gillers, Spoliation of Evidence—What are the Ethics Issues? The New York Professional Responsibility Report, at 7ff (November 1999), *available at www.nycrr.com* (members only). *See also* John M. Fedders & Lauryn H. Guttenplan, Document Retention and Destruction: Practical, Legal and Ethical Considerations, 56 Notre Dame L. Rev. 1 (1980). *See also* Margaret M. Koesel, *et al.*, Spoliation of Evidence: Sanctions and Remedies for Destruction of Evidence in Civil Litigation (2000).
  ii. E-mail discovery failures
    a. *See generally Digital Discovery & e-Evidence, Best Practices & Evolving Law*, Vol. 4, No. 8 (August 2004) (summarizing and analyzing recent cases, and describing best practices).
    b. In *Zubulake v. UBS Warburg LLC*, 02 Civ. 1243, 2004 U.S. Dist. LEXIS 13574 (S.D.N.Y. July 20, 2004), Judge Shira Sheindlin found that UBS failed to preserve and produce relevant e-mails, and produced certain other e-mails two years late.
      1. In discussing counsel's obligations, the court said: "Counsel must oversee compliance with the litigation hold, monitoring the party's efforts to retain and produce the relevant documents" and that to do this, "counsel must be become fully familiar with her client's document retention policies, as well as the client's data retention architecture. This will invariably involve speaking with information technology personnel, who can explain system-wide backup procedures and the actual (as opposed to theoretical) implementation of the firm's recycling policy." *Id.* at *32–33. The court concluded, "It is *not* sufficient to notify all employees of a litigation hold and expect that the party will then retain and produce all relevant information. Counsel must take affirmative steps to monitor compliance so that all sources of discoverable information are identified and searched." *Id.* at *35.
      2. There were four previous opinions by the District Court in this case relating to the discovery of electronic documents. *See* 217 F.R.D. 309, 312 (S.D.N.Y. 2003) (addressing the legal standards for determining the cost allocation for producing e-mails contained on backup tapes); 2003 U.S. Dist. LEXIS 7940, No. 02 Civ. 1243, 2003 WL 21087136 (S.D.N.Y. May 13, 2003) (deny-

ing plaintiff's motion to release the transcript of a certain deposition to securities regulators); 216 F.R.D. 280 (S.D.N.Y. 2003) (allocating costs for backup tape restoration between plaintiff and defendant); 220 F.R.D. 212 (S.D.N.Y. 2003) (ordering sanctions against defendant for violating its duty to preserve evidence).

c. In *United States v. Philip Morris*, 2004 WL 1627252 (D.D.C. July 21, 2004), the court imposed sanctions of $2.75 million on Philip Morris for the willful destruction of e-mails by 11 high-ranking Philip Morris officers and supervisors in violation of the company's document retention policy and a court order. *Id.* at *4. The court also precluded the testimony of the 11 individuals at trial. *Id.* In explaining the large monetary sanction, the court stated, "it is essential that such conduct be deterred, that the corporate and legal community understand that such conduct will not be tolerated, and that the amount of the monetary sanction fully reflect the reckless disregard and gross indifference display by [the defendants] toward their discover and document preservation obligations." *Id.* at *3.

m. SEC proceedings.

i. Lucent agreed to pay a $25 million civil penalty as part of its settlement of securities fraud charges brought by the SEC. According to an SEC press release, Lucent was penalized for, among other things, "incomplete document production, producing key documents after the testimony of relevant witnesses, and fail[ure] to ensure that a relevant document was preserved and produced pursuant to a subpoena." See Lucent Settles SEC Enforcement Action Charging the Company with $1.1 Billion Accounting Fraud, at *www.sec.gov/news/press/2004-67.htm*.

ii. Banc of America consented to a $10 million civil penalty for its failure to produce certain e-mails in response to the SEC's discovery requests and for the destruction of certain e-mails before production. *See* SEC Release No. 49386 (March 10, 2004) at *www.sec.gov/litigation/admin/34-49386.htm*.

O. Confidentiality

1. Confidences have limited protections. Model Rules 1.6 and 1.13. Code DR4-101.
2. Broader than communications protected by attorney client privilege.
   a. Belong to the client.
   b. Does not end with end of representation. *Kilpatrick v. Wiley*, 37 P.3d 1130 (Utah 2002).
3. May not be disclosed to third parties by a lawyer without client consent or certain public policy grounds.
   a. Implied consent.
   b. If would aid or further crimes and frauds.
   c. If not intended as or kept confidential by client.
   d. To benefit lawyer (in fee dispute or in defense of lawyer conduct).
   e. When lawyer is obliged otherwise to comply with law.
      i. Code would permit disclosure.
      ii. Rules do not provide for this ground of disclosure.
   f. ABA Model Rules adopted in 2003 broadened the permissible scope of disclosure; Rule 1.6(b) now provides:
   "(b) A lawyer may reveal information relating to the representation of a client to the extent the lawyer reasonably believes necessary:
   (1) to prevent reasonably certain death or substantial bodily harm;
   (2) to prevent the client from committing a crime or fraud that is reasonably certain to result in substantial injury to the financial interests or property of another and in furtherance of which the client has used or is using the lawyer's services;
   (3) to prevent, mitigate or rectify substantial injury to the financial interests or property of another that is reasonably certain to result or has resulted from the client's commission of a crime or fraud in furtherance of which the client has used the lawyer's services;
   (4) to secure legal advice about the lawyer's compliance with these Rules;
   (5) to establish a claim or defense on behalf of the lawyer in a controversy between the lawyer and the client, to establish a defense to a criminal charge or civil claim against the lawyer based upon conduct in which the client was involved, or to respond to allegations in any proceeding concerning the lawyer's representation of the client; or
   (6) to comply with other law or a court order."
   Model Rule 1.6(b).
   g. In addition, ABA Model Rule 1.13 provides:
   (a) A lawyer employed or retained by an organization represents the organization acting through its duly authorized constituents.
   (b) If a lawyer for an organization knows that an officer, employee or other person associated with the organization is engaged in action, intends to act or refuses to act in a matter related to the representation that is a violation of a legal obligation to the organization, or a violation of law that reasonably might be imputed to the organization, and that is likely to result in substantial injury to the organization, then the lawyer shall proceed as is reasonably necessary in the best interest of the organization. Unless the lawyer reasonably believes that it is not necessary in the best interest of the organization to do so, the lawyer shall refer the matter to higher authority in the organization, including, if warranted by the circumstances to the highest authority that can act on behalf of the organization as determined by applicable law.
   (c) Except as provided in paragraph (d), if
      (1) despite the lawyer's efforts in accordance with paragraph (b) the highest authority that can act on behalf of the organization insists upon or fails to

address in a timely and appropriate manner an action, or a refusal to act, that is clearly a violation of law, and

(2) the lawyer reasonably believes that the violation is reasonably certain to result in substantial injury to the organization, then the lawyer may reveal information relating to the representation whether or not Rule 1.6 permits such disclosure, but only if and to the extent the lawyer reasonably believes necessary to prevent substantial injury to the organization.

(d) Paragraph (c) shall not apply with respect to information relating to a lawyer's representation of an organization to investigate an alleged violation of law, or to defend the organization or an officer, employee or other constituent associated with the organization against a claim arising out of an alleged violation of law.

(e) A lawyer who reasonably believes that he or she has been discharged because of the lawyer's actions taken pursuant to paragraphs (b) or (c), or who withdraws under circumstances that require or permit the lawyer to take action under either of those paragraphs, shall proceed as the lawyer reasonably believes necessary to assure that the organization's highest authority is informed of the lawyer's discharge or withdrawal.

(f) In dealing with an organization's directors, officers, employees, members, shareholders or other constituents, a lawyer shall explain the identity of the client when the lawyer knows or reasonably should know that the organization's interests are adverse to those of the constituents with whom the lawyer is dealing.

(g) A lawyer representing an organization may also represent any of its directors, officers, employees, members, shareholders or other constituents, subject to the provisions of Rule 1.7. If the organization's consent to the dual representation is required by Rule 1.7, the consent shall be given by an appropriate official of the organization other than the individual who is to be represented, or by the shareholders.

Model Rule 1.13.

g. *Azriliant v. Oppenheim*, 457 N.Y.S.2d 80 (N.Y. App. Div. 1982) (former partners in law firm not disqualified because partners did not owe duty of confidentiality to each other).

h. *People v. DePallo*, 754 N.E.2d 751 (N.Y. 2001) (attorney did not violate duty of confidentiality when he disclosed client's perjury because intent to commit a crime is not protected by privilege and client has right to testify, but not to perjure).

i. *In re Piatt*, 2002 Ariz. LEXIS 192 (Sup. Ct. Ariz. 2002) (attorney violated duty of confidentiality by disclosing name and location of client in Witness Protection Program, impugning the reputation of client in filings, and other conduct damaging to client).

j. *Lawyer Disciplinary Bd. v. McGraw*, 461 S.E.2d 850 (W.V. 1995) (state Attorney General disciplined for disclosure of public agency's litigation position to concerned citizens, when disclosure violated duty of confidentiality).

VII. CAUSES OF ACTION FOR DAMAGES

A. Breach of Contract

1. Written or oral.
2. Consider carefully making "promises" in engagement letters.
3. Cannot limit liability.

B. Tort Liability to Client and Third Parties—Elements of Attorney Malpractice Action in New York. See 76 N.Y. Jur. 2d 1363

1. Negligence, *i.e.*, failure to exercise that degree of skill, care and diligence commonly possessed by a lawyer.
2. Proximate cause (see N.Y. Pattern Jury Instructions PJI 2:70, 2004).
3. Actual damages.
4. *See Prudential Ins. Co. v. Dewey, Ballentine, Bushby, Palmer & Wood*, 170 A.D.2d 108, 573 N.Y.S.2d 981 (Sup. Ct.), aff'd, 80 N.Y.2d 377, 590 N.Y.2d 831, 605 N.E.2d 318 (1st Dept. 1991) (opinion letter).
5. Plaintiff must show there would have been favorable outcome "but for" the attorney's negligence to meet proximate cause test in a malpractice case. *Carmel v. Lunney*, 70 N.Y.2d 169, 578 N.Y.S.2d 605, 511 N.E.2d 1126 (N.Y. 1987) ("but for" test under pressure from expansion of liability for breach of fiduciary duty and negligent misrepresentation); *Weil, Gotshal & Manges, LLP v. Fashion Boutique of Short Hills, Inc.*, 2004 WL 1746349 (N.Y. App. Div. First Dept. Aug. 5, 2004) (reinstating a legal malpractice claim and noting that under New York law, there is only one standard of causation for both a legal malpractice claim and a claim for breach of fiduciary duty: the client must demonstrate that "but for" the attorney's conduct, "the client would have prevailed in the underlying matter or would not have sustained any ascertainable damages") (citation omitted).
6. Attorney is not a guarantor of outcome. N.Y. Pattern Jury Instructions 2:152 (2004).
7. N.Y. malpractice cases do not adopt a "locality" standard of care—they reference the "legal community" as a whole.
8. Expert Testimony. See D.E. Ytreberg, Admissibility and Necessity Of Expert Evidence As To Standards Of Practice And Negligence In Attorney Malpractice Actions, 17 A.L.R.3d 1442 (1968).
9. No reported malpractice cases in N.Y. have turned on a lawyer's claim to "specialization" or "specialty practice." *See* DR 2-105 (restrictions on use of "specialization"). In other jurisdictions however a lawyer hired as such has been held to standard of performance of the average specialist of that type. *See* Restatement (Third), The Law Governing Lawyers, Section 52, cmt. d; *Walker v. Bangs*, 92 Wash.2d 854, 601 P.2d 1279 (1979).

10. Client's culpable conduct may negate proximate cause. It also may serve as an affirmative defense in malpractice cases mitigating the lawyer's negligence. *Arnau Indus. Inc. Ret. Trust v. Brown, Raysman, Millstein, Felder, L.L.P.*, 96 N.Y.2d 300, 727 N.Y.S.2d 688 (N.Y. 2001).

11. After 1996, three year statute of limitations. N.Y.C.P.L.R. §9214(6).

12. "Overbilling" or "excessive fee" claims are not malpractice.

13. Attorneys may be vicariously liable for negligence of agent hired on behalf of client. *Kleeman v. Reingold*, 81 N.Y.2d 270, 614 N.E.2d 712, 598 N.Y.S.2d 149 (1993) (process server).

14. Prejudgment interest is available in New York for attorney malpractice claims. N.Y.C.P.L.R. §5001.

VIII. SELECTED MALPRACTICE AND DISCIPLINARY PLEADINGS AND CASES[3]

A. "Rude" and "Frivolous" Behavior to Clients and Adversaries

1. A 12-lawyer immigration law firm became the first to be subject to public censure, a discipline sanction usually applied only to individuals. Its conduct from 1998 to 2002 was held to reflect a "pattern . . . involving rude and discourteous behavior to clients—conduct that strikes at the very heart of a lawyer's or law-firm's relation to the public." *Matter of Wilens and Baker*, 2004 NY Slip.Op. 04077 (N.Y. App. Div. 1st Dept. 2004) available at www.courts.state.ny.us/reporter/3dseries/2004/2004_04077.htm (July 21, 2004). Conduct included:

   a. Refusal to discuss cases unless additional fees paid.

   b. Treating clients in a rude and demeaning manner, including yelling at them and ordering them to leave the office.

2. An attorney was sanctioned for "frivolous" conduct ranging from attempts to harass opponents and barking like a dog at a witness (after the witness, in answer to a deposition question, described the lawyer's threatening letter as a "mad dog" letter). The opposition counsel calmly said "Mr. Fink, please refrain from barking." The offending lawyer, who claimed he was just clearing his throat, was fined $8,500. *See* N.Y.L.J. May 14, 2004.

3. Lawyer who, while questioning witness in a deposition, allegedly flew into "a total rage" and flung his fist in order to punch his way past the witness to attack adversary, was the subject of an application for an arrest warrant. *See* www.law.com/jsp/article.jsp?id=1084316053680 (May 18, 2004).

B. Complaints for Damages—Conflicts of Interest[4]

1. E-2 visa denied and opportunity lost by plaintiff who, with dependents, filed complaint against lawyer, law firm and E-2 "sponsors" in California. *Kim v. Lee*, May 19, 2004, Case BC 315792, Los Angeles Superior Court.

   a. Causes of Action—Malpractice, Breach of Contract, Intentional Misrepresentation, Negligent Misrepresentation, Promise Made Without Intention to Perform, Breach of Covenant of Good Faith and Loss of Consortium.

   b. Alleged failure to use reasonable care as shown by:

      i. Conflicting representation of plaintiffs, defendants and third party purchaser of business.

      ii. Failure to disclose conflicts.

      iii. Incompetence in that transaction did not qualify for E-2 visa for plaintiff.

      iv. Failure to advise plaintiff that transaction was going to fail if plaintiff did not pay overdue sums.

   c. Essential facts alleged:

      i. Beginning in September 2002 and until December 2003, Plaintiff Kim, a Los Angeles resident, was told orally by his uncle KS Lee that, by working with Lee's business partners and some of his attorneys, Lee could obtain an E-2 visa for Kim and his family by investing in or buying businesses and real estate. Shortly after Lee made those representations, Kim gave Lee and Lee's partner the total sum of about $580,000, which they used to purchase several properties and business under the disguise of investing for Kim.

      ii. On or about October 2002, Kim had retained the defendant lawyers Thomas Lee and Theodore Lee to represent him in obtaining an E-2 visa and in structuring his purchase of a video store. These lawyers were also the lawyers for KS Lee, his partners and the third-party purchaser of the video store.

      iii. After giving the money, Kim was told by Lee that Kim had purchased a video store and as a result would surely receive his E-2 visa. Unbeknownst to Kim, Lee and his partners cancelled the escrow on the video store on their own and concealed from Kim that in August 2003, the INS conclusively had rejected Kim's E-2 visa application, on the grounds that the purchase price was outside of the escrow, and that proof of purchase was therefore inadequate. The video store was eventually sold to a third-party, which transaction was effected using an escrow, and the third-party was accordingly granted an E-2 visa.

---

[3] Reference is made to court-filed complaints to illustrate allegations actually made and the circumstances out of which claims may arise. The allegations are just that—not facts—and this section does not undertake to analyze or reference answers, counterclaims, motions or dispositions of the cases on the merits.

[4] Reference to a complaint or its allegations does not suggest the allegations are true and the complaints are designed to illustrate nature of allegations made, not merits of the claim. No documents or analysis is provided as to any response to the cited complaint or as to the ultimate outcome of the cases, and none should be implied.

2. Breach of contract, intentional infliction of emotional distress, conspiracy and negligent malpractice claims filed by employee allegedly wrongfully terminated against employer and law firm. Employer had paid for employee to consult as to immigration matters. *See Robson v. Hewlett-Packard Co.; Fragoman (sic), Del Rey, Bernsen & Loewy, P.C. & John Does*, Complaint, 103 CVO 05526 filed Sept. 22, 2003 in Santa Clara California Superior Court.

   a. Law firm allegedly failed to advise employee of applicable regulations.

   b. Law firm allegedly refused to provide employee with INS-issued document as to him preventing travel.

   c. Law firm allegedly misrepresented employee's status to INS.

   d. Law firm inflicted emotion distress by allegedly wrongfully advising employee he was accumulating "unlawful presence" time.

   e. Damages sought for front and back pay, loss of career earnings and reputation, emotional distress, defamation, and multiple and punitive damages.

3. Malpractice allegedly led to imprisonment. Complaint alleging claims for damages due to incarceration, personal injury (fright and mental anguish) and for attorneys' fees based on negligence, breach of contract and misrepresentation was filed February 19, 2004 in *Galdamez v. Kraeger*, Superior Court of Maricopa County, Arizona, Docket CV 2004-003304.

   a. Plaintiff's alien husband and U.S. citizen wife allegedly retained the services of defendant attorney Kraeger and his firm to represent them in obtaining permanent residence for husband through an adjustment of status based upon his marriage to wife. They allegedly informed the attorney of husband's prior immigration proceedings, including his rejected residence application based on a request for political asylum and an ensuing alternative order of voluntary departure with which he did not comply.

   b. Kraeger informed them of an INS rule or regulation that permitted husband to remain in the country pending the application for adjustment of status but not of consequences of the VD order (as to which Kraeger presumably will claim that he had no information). Kraeger then filed the requisite documents. An I-130 interview was held at which the husband told the INS that he had not left the country. The interviewer told husband that because he failed to comply with the order of voluntary deportation, the order was still in effect. Thus, he would need to file a motion to reopen the deportation proceedings before any adjustment could occur. Promptly, husband was jailed pending INS executing the prior deportation order.

   c. Wife eventually convinced the INS under *Lozada* not to deport her husband based on an ineffective assistance of counsel claim.

   d. Plaintiffs now sue the attorney for damages claiming that, as a result of his malpractice, husband was imprisoned for nearly two months.

C. Causation Required for Malpractice Claim Damages

Defendant immigration attorneys moved for summary judgment on plaintiff alien's claims alleging legal malpractice and breach of contract for counsel's failure to properly handle plaintiff's petition for permanent residency. Specifically, plaintiff alleges that the lawyers failed to 1) submit employment contracts with the H-1B application, 2) process an application for extension of plaintiff's H-1B visa, and 3) take the necessary steps to obtain working status for plaintiff so he could begin work on time. The court dismissed the breach of contract claim as duplicative and granted the attorneys' motion for summary judgment on the malpractice claim because the plaintiff could not "establish a causal connection between defendants' actions or inactions and the damages plaintiff claims he has suffered." *Borsuk v. Jeffries*, No. 98 Civ. 4088, 2000 U.S. Dist. LEXIS 9795 (S.D.N.Y. July 14, 2000).

IX. CRIMES AND CIVIL PENALTIES

A. Penalties for Document Fraud (8 USC §1324c)

1. Criminalizes the unlawful attempted use or the providing of any forged, counterfeit, altered or falsely made document to obtain a benefit under 8 USC.

2. Criminalizes the unlawful preparing, filing or assisting another in preparing or filing any application for benefits under 8 USC or filing any document in connection with such application "with knowledge or in reckless disregard of the fact that such application or document was falsely made or . . . does not relate to the person on whose behalf it was . . . submitted . . . ."

3. Provides criminal penalties for the felony of "knowingly and willfully" failing to disclose or covering up the fact the person prepared or assisted another in preparing a falsely made application for benefits under 8 USC.

4. The foregoing crimes are in addition to the penalties available under Title 18.

   a. An immigration lawyer who represented Nigerians and Ethiopians in proceedings before the INS was convicted as codefendant under 8 USC §1324(a)(1)(A)(iv) for falsifying documents for the aliens' citizenship applications. The lawyer and the other codefendant, one Oloyede, ran a scheme in which Oloyede would sell false documents to illegal aliens and would then refer the clients to the attorney, who would use the documents to prepare the INS applications. *United States v. Oloyede*, 982 F.2d 133 (4th Cir. 1992).

   b. In a state ethics case, *Boyle v. People*, 2004 Colo. Discipl. LEXIS 31 (Sup. Ct. Colo. May 12, 2004), a lawyer falsified labor certification for two clients, whom he knew did not have the requisite experience or jobs.

   c. *In re Chu*, 369 N.E.2d 1 (N.Y. 1977) (lawyer disbarred for conviction of making false and fraudulent submissions to the INS and arranging of marriages for immigrants to gain visas).

d. *In re Gautam*, 660 N.Y.S.2d 106 (N.Y. App. Div. 1997) (attorney disbarred for filing false asylum applications); *In re Pandit*, 655 N.Y.S.2d 467 (N.Y. App. Div. 1997) (same).

e. *In re Baljit Singh*, 607 N.Y.S.2d 250 (N.Y. App. Div. 1994) (attorney counseled client, a New York resident, to obtain California documents and file for asylum as a resident of California).

B. When Document Destruction Becomes Justice Obstruction

1. *See generally*, Abramowitz and Bohrer, *New York Law Journal*, March 5, 2002 (explaining that the destruction of documents may constitute obstruction of justice even before a proceeding is commenced where destruction is with intent to make documents unavailable). *See also* Ann Davis, "UBS Is Sanctioned for Withholding E-mails," *The Wall Street Journal*, July 21, 2004 (describing how a U.S. District Judge in the S.D.N.Y. laid out a new standard for the preservation of evidence, specifically, that company lawyers must warn employees not to destroy evidence relevant to a lawsuit, and that they must actively supervise the process).

2. *Kronish v. United States*, 150 F.3d 112, 126-30 (2d Cir. 1998) (discussing the principle of law that a party's intentional destruction of evidence can, under certain circumstances, support an inference that the evidence would have been unfavorable to the party responsible for its destruction).

3. *United States v. Lundwall*, 1 F. Supp.2d 249 (S.D.N.Y. 1998) (holding that 18 USC §1503, the general or "omnibus" obstruction of justice statute, reaches deliberate destruction of documents in civil litigation between private parties).

C. Obstruction of Justice in the Course of Representation

1. Obstruction of justice provisions, equally applicable to attorneys, are found in 18 USC §§1503, 1505, 1512, and 1513. *See* Mary C. Spearing, *Obstruction Of Justice and Attorneys Who Work On Civil Fraud Cases, Qui Tam: Beyond Government Contracts*, 456 PLI/LIT, 521 (1993); *see also* Kathleen F. Brickey, *Corporate Criminal Liability* §12:01—§12:29 (2d ed. 1992).

2. 18 USC §1503 forbids corruptly influencing any grand or petit juror or officer of the court by threats or force, or by letter or communication. It also proscribes endeavoring to influence, obstruct, or impede "the due administration of justice." (Omnibus Clause, 18 USC §1503 et seq.)

a. "[A]ny corrupt endeavor whatsoever, to 'influence or impede any . . . witness . . . 'whether successful or not, is proscribed by the obstruction of justice statute." *United States v. Cintolo*, 818 F.2d 980, 991 (1st Cir. 1987) (citations omitted).

b. "[M]eans, though lawful in themselves, can cross the line of illegality if (i) employed with a corrupt motive, (ii) to hinder the due administration of justice, so long as (iii) the means have the capacity to obstruct." *Id.* at 992.

c. The Supreme Court's reading of §1503 "makes conduct punishable where the defendant acts with an intent to obstruct justice, and in a manner that is likely to obstruct justice, but is foiled in some way." *United States v. Aguilar*, 515 U.S. 593, 601–602 (1995).

3. The U.S. Supreme Court set limits on the Omnibus Clause of §1503.

a. In *United States v. Aguilar*, the court affirmed the reversal of the defendant judge's conviction for endeavoring to obstruct justice in violation of §1503 where the government failed to show that the agent to whom the judge lied was an arm of the grand jury. The Supreme Court held that it did "not believe that uttering false statements to an investigating agent . . . who might or might not testify before a grand jury is sufficient to make out a violation of the catch-all provision of §1503." *Id.* at 600.

b. The court further held that "the endeavor must have the 'natural and probable effect' of interfering with the due administration of justice . . . and a person lacking knowledge that his actions are likely to affect a pending proceeding necessarily lacks the requisite intent to obstruct." *Id.* at 594.

D. Elements of a §1503 Offense

1. A §1503 offense requires:

a. A nexus with a pending federal judicial proceeding;

b. That the defendant knew of or had notice about the proceeding; and

c. That the defendant acted corruptly with intent to obstruct or interfere with the proceeding or due administration of justice.

2. Pending federal judicial proceeding.

a. There is some dispute among Circuits as to what constitutes a pending judicial proceeding for purposes of §1503. *See* Keith Palfin & Sandhya Prabhu, *Obstruction of Justice*, 40 AM. CRIM. L. REV. 873, 888 (2003).

i. Most Circuits hold that there must be an investigation in contemplation of or before the grand jury. *See United States v. Monus*, 128 F.3d 376, 389 (6th Cir. 1997) (a judicial proceeding is pending "'where a subpoena is issued in furtherance of an actual grand jury investigation, *i.e.*, to secure a presently contemplated presentation of evidence before the grand jury.'" [quoting *United States v. Tackett*, 113 F.3d 603, 612 n.6 (6th Cir. 1997)]; *United States v. Davis*, 183 F.3d 231, 240–41 (3d Cir. 1999) (a wiretap order cannot be considered a judicial proceeding under §1503); *United States v. Cueto*, 151 F.3d 620, 634 (7th Cir. 1998) ("It is well established that investigations undertaken with the intention of presenting evidence before a grand jury are sufficient to constitute 'the due administration of justice under §1503.'") (quoting *United States v. Maloney*, 71 F.3d 645, 657 (7th Cir. 1995)); *United States v. Brady*, 168 F.3d

574, 577–78 (1st Cir. 1999) (purposely depriving the grand jury of information is sufficient to make out a conviction under §1503); *United States v. Grubb*, 11 F.3d 426, 438 (4th Cir. 1993) ("Interrupting the grand jury in its pursuit of information" is punishable under §1503); *United States v. Wood*, 6 F.3d 692, 696 (10th Cir. 1993) (holding that a grand jury investigation qualifies as "pending judicial proceeding" for the purpose of §1503); *United States v. Biaggi*, 853 F.2d 89, 104 (2d Cir. 1988) (declining to overturn a conviction under §1503 where the defendant encouraged another to testify falsely after he had ample notice that a grand jury proceeding was pending); *United States v. Vesich*, 724 F.2d 451, 455 (5th Cir. 1984) (a proceeding is pending for purpose of §1503 where grand jury had been impaneled).

    a. The Ninth Circuit holds that a proceeding is pending after an indictment is issued. *United States v. Wash. Water Power Co.*, 793 F.2d 1079, 1085 (9th Cir. 1986) ("It is clear that a federal proceeding is 'pending' for purposes of section 1503 once an indictment has been issued.").

    b. The Eighth and Eleventh Circuits have found no need for a pending judicial proceeding for a conviction under §1503. *See United States v. Novak*, 217 F.3d 566, 571 (8th Cir. 2000) ("There is nothing on the face of §1503 requiring a pending judicial proceeding."); *United States v. Veal*, 153 F.3d 1233, 1250 n.24 (11th Cir. 1998) ("In the second and third clauses of §1503, the federal interest originates from the status of the targeted person, a federal juror, but no judicial proceeding is required.").

  ii. The possibility of filing a post-trial motion can still be considered part of a "pending proceeding." *See United States v. Baum*, 32 F. Supp. 2d 642, 649 (S.D.N.Y. 1999) (declining to dismiss the §1503 obstruction of justice charge in the indictment of a criminal attorney, who allegedly devised a plan whereby his client would lure an alleged drug trafficker to the United States in an attempt to induce a federal prosecutor to file a post-sentence reduction motion for him). *See also United States v. Fleming*, 215 F.3d 930, 937 (9th Cir. 2000) (holding that there is sufficient evidence of a pending proceeding even if the defendant's appeal had little chances of success); *United States v. Fernandez*, 837 F.2d 1031, 1034 (11th Cir. 1988) (rejecting defendant's contention that proceeding was no longer pending at conclusion of sentencing hearing when obstruction occurred, since post-sentence appeal could still be filed and noting pending proceeding is not required under §1503).

3. Knowledge or notice of pending proceeding.

  a. In circuits that require a pending proceeding, the defendant must have knowledge of a pending judicial proceeding. *Pettibone v. United States*, 148 U.S. 197, 205 (1893).

    i. "Knowledge" does not require that defendant know that proceeding was federal in nature. *United States v. Ardito*, 782 F.2d 358 (2d Cir. 1986). *See also United States v. Aragon*, 983 F.2d 1306 (4th Cir. 1993).

    ii. In *United States v. Aguilar*, 515 U.S. 593, 599 (1995), the Supreme Court stated that if the "defendant lacks knowledge that his actions are likely to affect the judicial proceeding, he lacks the requisite intent to obstruct."

    iii. In *United States v. Washington Water Power Co.*, 793 F.2d 1079 (9th Cir. 1986), the Ninth Circuit held likelihood that conversation included news of an indictment, based on one party's likely status as a witness, was enough to prove knowledge of pending federal proceeding.

    iv. The Second Circuit has held that one who makes statements to a federal investigator not knowing that they would be repeated during the grand jury investigation cannot be convicted under §1503. *United States v. Schwarz*, 283 F.3d 76, 109 (2d Cir. 2002).

4. Corrupt intent to obstruct or interfere.

  a. The Circuits differ in their interpretation of the intent requirement. The First Circuit aptly points out the source of the conflict: confusion over the "the scienter element in the obstruction statute . . . in part, results from the promiscuous use in the cases of the ambiguous word 'intent,' which can mean either knowledge (of consequences) or purpose (to achieve them)." *Brady*, 168 F.3d at 578.

  b. In interpreting the corrupt intent requirement in 1893, the Supreme Court had held that "specific intent to violate the statute must exist to justify a conviction." *Pettibone*, 148 U.S. at 207. Many years later, in *Neiswender v. United States*, the Fourth Circuit held that an attorney can be held guilty of obstructing justice without proving he had or could have had a direct involvement with the judicial proceedings. 590 F.2d 1269 (4th Cir. 1979). In that case, soon after the criminal trial of the former governor of Maryland, the defendant offered to guarantee an acquittal in exchange for the right price. *Id.* at 1270. The Court upheld his conviction under §1503 stating, "In our view, the defendant need only have had knowledge or notice that success in his fraud would have likely resulted in an obstruction of justice. Notice is provided by the reasonable foreseeability of the natural and probable consequences of one's acts." *Id.* at 1273. The Court continued: "The defendant's design is irrelevant; if the natural result of his plan is to interfere with judicial processes, justice will be obstructed whether he hopes it is or not." *Id.* at 1274. The Second, Eleventh, Seventh, and Sixth Circuits adhere to this approach. *United States v. Buffalano*, 727 F.2d 50, 54 (2d Cir. 1984); *United States v. Silverman*, 745 F.2d 1386, 1393 (11th Cir. 1984); *United States v.*

Bucey, 876 F.2d 1297, 1314 (7th Cir. 1989); *United States v. Atkin*, 107 F.3d 1213, 1219 (6th Cir. 1997).[5]

c. In the application of this foreseeability approach, Courts have convicted attorneys for acting in furtherance of schemes to defraud. *Atkin*, 107 F.3d at 1219; *Machi*, 811 F.2d at 998; *Silverman*, 745 F.2d at 1396; *Buffalano*, 727 F.2d at 54. In fact, the conduct, in the language of the statute—an endeavor, sufficient for a conviction—is less than that required for a criminal attempt and can be simply solicitation. *Buffalano*, 727 F.2d at 53

d. There is an argument that the Fourth Circuit misapplied the "natural and probable consequences" language in *Pettibone* to the intent requirement of the statute, thus lowering the necessary level of proof and creating a new and uncodified crime. *See* Joseph V. De Marco, *Note: A Funny Thing Happened On the Way to the Courthouse: Mens Rea, Document Destruction, and the Federal Obstruction of Justice Statue*, 67 N.Y.U L. REV 570, 588 (1992). According to this argument, the *Neisweneder* approach could be used to criminalize recklessness or negligence as in the case of an attorney who inadvertently destroys or fails to adequately safeguard documents that have been subpoenaed. *Id.* at 598-605. However, in practice, prosecutorial discretion has minimized the chances of this occurring. *Id.* at 605–08.

e. Generally, the intent requirement is satisfied if the government shows that the defendant knowingly and intentionally undertook an action from which an obstruction of justice was a reasonably foreseeable result. *See United States v. Cueto*, 151 F.3d 620, 630–31 (7th Cir. 1998), *cert. denied*, 526 U.S. 1016 (1999) (upheld lawyer's conviction for conspiracy and obstruction of justice for using court processes to interfere with a federal investigation of the illegal gambling operations); *Silverman*, 745 F.2d 1386, 1393 (attempt by attorney to solicit $25,000 from his client under pretext of using it as bribe to guarantee client would receive probation upon pleading guilty is "endeavor" to obstruct justice justifying attorney's conviction for violating §1503.).

5. Acts proscribed under §1503. Conviction under §1503 can result from "subtle suggestions." In *United States v. Tranakos*, 911 F.2d 1422 (10th Cir. 1990), the court affirmed the conviction of an attorney for obstructing a witness' grand jury testimony for smiling and saying suggestively to the witness (in a case in which the ownership of trusts was at issue), "Well, you don't own any trusts, do you?" followed by, "You don't have any bank accounts in Montana, do you?" *Id.* at 1431. The court held that "One who proposes to another that the other lie in a judicial proceeding is guilty of obstructing justice . . . The statute prohibits elliptical suggestions as much as it does direct com-

mands . . . A reasonable finder of fact could have decided on this evidence that [defendant's attorney] suggested to [the witness] that [the witness] falsely tell the grand jury that he had no Montana bank accounts." *Id.* at 1432.

6. Evidence must be preserved, not destroyed, concealed, or fabricated.

In *United States v. Vesich*, 724 F.2d 451 (5th Cir. 1984), the court held that §§1503 and 1505 apply to the destruction of documents prior to issuance of a subpoena. The court said, "We have long held that the issuance of a subpoena is not necessary to trigger application of the obstruction of justice statute." *Id.* at 455. Similarly, the Sixth Circuit, in *United States v. Craft*, 105 F.3d 1123 (6th Cir. 1997), stated, "Acts that distort the evidence to be presented or otherwise impede the administration of justice are violations of 18 USC §1503. The act of altering or fabricating documents used or to be used in a judicial proceeding would fall within the obstruction of justice statute if the intent is to deceive the court." *Id.* at 1128.

The Eleventh Circuit had previously held, "It is clear that the knowing destruction or concealment of documentary evidence can constitute a violation of §1503." *United States v. Banks*, 942 F.2d 1576, 1578 (11th Cir. 1991) (*citations omitted*). *See also United States of America v. Schwartz*, SI 98 Cr. 404, 1999 U.S. Dist. LEXIS 33 (S.D.N.Y. Jan. 5, 1999) (holding that the protections of the Fifth Amendment, attorney client privilege, and "professional judgment" are no defense to intentionally withholding evidence duly subpoenaed).

7. Statute not limited to obstruction through force or intimidation.

a. In *United States v. Schaffner*, 715 F.2d 1099, 1103 (6th Cir. 1983), the Sixth Circuit stated that an attorney would violate §1503 by knowingly hiding or advising a corporation to hide an employee who gave written statements to the government incriminating the corporation in order that the employee would not be subpoenaed and would not testify at a trial.

b. In *United States v. Savoy*, 38 F. Supp.2d 406, 417 (D. Md. 1998), the court held that the retraction of defendant's perjurious affidavit was no defense to defendant's violation of §1503.

8. Defenses.

a. In *United States v. Cintolo*, 818 F.2d 980, 990 (1st Cir. 1987), the court affirmed the conviction of an attorney for conspiracy to obstruct justice where the attorney attempted to hinder the grand jury investigation of an organized crime operation by using his position as attorney for the grand jury witness to acquire information about the investigation and inhibit the witness from testifying or cooperating by urging the witness to take the Fifth Amendment.

i. The court said, "An attorney who spurns the interests of his own client and conspires to subject him to a prison term for the benefit of a third party is not performing the traditional functions of defense coun-

---

[5] Due to similar reasoning, the defense of impossibility can rarely be raised by defendants charged with violating §1503. *See* Keith Palfin & Sandhya Prabhu, *Obstruction of Justice*, 40 Am. Crim. L. Rev. 873, 888 (Spring 2003).

sel. Such an attorney is not, on any view of the matter, entitled to special perquisites and privileges." *Id.* at 995.

b. In *United States v. Cioffi*, 493 F.2d 1111, 1119 (2nd Cir. 1974), the court affirmed a conviction for endeavoring to influence a grand jury witness to invoke the Fifth Amendment privilege rather than testify regarding an extortionate loan made by defendant's associate, in violation of §1503.

c. The Second Circuit rejected the argument that advising a witness to do that which he possessed a constitutional right to do could not be criminalized. The court said, "while a witness violates no law by claiming the Fifth Amendment privilege against self-incrimination in a grand jury, one who bribes, threatens, coerces a witness to claim it or advises with corrupt motive a witness to take it, can and does obstruct the administration of justice." *Id.* "The lawful behavior of the person invoking the [Fifth] Amendment cannot be used to protect the criminal behavior of the inducer." *Id.*

d. Inducing or threatening a witness to testify falsely is proscribed (witness tampering is primarily enforced under §1512).[6]

9. Zealous representation doctrine provides no immunity to obstruction of justice charge.

a. In *United States v. Cueto*, 151 F.3d at 631, the court found that the defendant's role as an attorney was no defense to prosecution under §1503. "As a lawyer, [Cueto] possessed a heightened awareness of the law and its scope and he cannot claim lack of fair notice as to what is proscribed by [section] 1503 ... More so than an ordinary individual, an attorney, in particular a criminal defense attorney has a sophisticated understanding of the type of conduct that constitutes criminal violations of the law." *Id.* at 631–32.

The lawyer, in an effort to forestall investigation of his client's business, had complained to State's Attorney, filed motions attacking the FBI, sought the judge's disqualification, and filed pleadings in a district court action as well as a subsequent appellate brief and petition for certiorari. "[T]he contours of the line between traditional lawyering and criminal conduct ... must inevitably be drawn case-by-case. We refuse to accept the notion that lawyers may do anything, including violating the law, to zealously advocate their clients' interests and then avoid criminal prosecution by claiming that they were 'just doing their job.' As the First Circuit stated in *Cintolo*, 'we refuse to chip some sort of special exception for lawyers into the brickwork of §1503.'" *Id.* at 634.

b. The court in *Cueto* cited with approval *United States v. Cintolo*, 818 F.2d 980. In *Cintolo*, the court stated, "We emphatically reject the notion that a law degree, like some sorcerer's amulet, can ward off the rigors of the criminal law... By our reckoning, attorneys cannot be relieved of obligations of lawfulness imposed on the citizenry at large ... As sworn officers of the court, lawyers should not seek to avail themselves of relaxed rules of conduct. To the exact contrary, they should be held to the highest standards in promoting the cause of justice." *Id.* at 996. "The fact that [attorney's] participation was clothed, at least in part, in the mantle of superficially 'professional' conduct does not exonerate the lawyer from culpability." *Id.* at 990. The court went so far to say that "even were we inclined to credit the claim that [the witness] voluntarily acceded to actions by [the attorney] aimed at sending him to jail in order to protect [the third party], no effective defense avails to [the attorney] as a result." *Id.*

E. Conspiracy

1. Elements of conspiracy under federal law.

Conspiracy is an agreement between two or more persons to commit an unlawful act by knowingly engaging in the conspiracy, intending to commit those offenses that were the objects of the conspiracy, and commission of an "overt act" by one or more members of the conspiracy. *See* 2 Kevin O'Malley, Jay Grenig & Hon. William Lee, Federal Jury Practice and Instructions: Criminal §31.02 (5th ed. 2000); Committee on Pattern Jury Instructions District Judges Association, Fifth Circuit Pattern Jury Instructions: Criminal (2001).

2. Supreme Court revives broad definition of conspiracy.

a. In *United States v. Recio*, 537 U.S. 270 (2003), the issue was whether the government could charge suspects with conspiracy when the alleged crime had already been discovered and prevented from occurring. The Supreme Court held that a conspiracy does not automatically terminate simply because the Government defeated the conspiracy's objective.

b. Writing for the majority, Justice Breyer emphasized that "[t]he Court has repeatedly said that the essence of a conspiracy is 'an agreement to commit an unlawful act.' That agreement is 'a distinct evil,' which 'may exist and be punished whether or not the substantive crime ensues.' The conspiracy poses a 'threat to the

---

[6] *See United States v. Vesich*, 724 F.2d 451 (5th Cir.), *reh'g denied*, 726 F.2d 168 (5th Cir. 1984), *superseded by statute on other grounds as stated in United States v. Gonzalez*, 922 F.2d 1044, (2d Cir. 1991) (upholding conviction of an attorney for endeavoring to obstruct justice in violation of §1503, by urging a potential grand jury witness and former client to testify falsely before a grand jury investigating narcotics trafficking; attorney later perjured himself in denying that gave such advice in his own grand jury testimony).The attorney advised the witness to lie by giving the grand jury phony names of his contacts in the narcotics business. *Id.* at 459. The court noted that the attorney "explained to [the witness] at length how [the witness] could successfully lie to the grand jury if he were called to testify. Upon listening to the recording of [the attorney's] language and tone of voice during that conversation, the jury was plainly justified in concluding that [the attorney] was not merely a disinterested party explaining the workings of the grand jury system, but meant his words to encourage and advise [the witness] to lie to the grand jury." *Id.*

public' over and above the threat of the commission of the relevant substantive crime—both because the 'combination in crime makes more likely the commission of [other] crimes' and because it 'decreases the probability that the individuals involved will depart from their path of criminality.'" 537 U.S. at 275. (Internal citations omitted.)

c. In light of *Recio*, an individual charged with conspiracy and linked to the conspiracy, such as Zacarias Moussaoui, will have difficulty arguing that it was factually impossible for him to carry out the conspiracy to hijack a plane on September 11 because he was jail at the time. *See* David G. Savage, *A Trio of Cases Could Determine How the Government Probes Security Threats*, ABA Journal, Dec. 20, 2002

3. Doctrine of conscious avoidance.

a. "Conscious avoidance occurs when a person deliberately closes his eyes to avoid having knowledge of what would otherwise be obvious to him. But such deliberate ignorance . . . does not establish that person's innocence." *United States v. Reyes*, 302 F.3d 48 (2d Cir. 2002); *see also United States v. Abreu*, 342 F.3d 183, 188 (2d Cir. 2003). "[T]he doctrine may be invoked to prove defendant had knowledge of the unlawful conspiracy. But . . . [the doctrine may not] be used to prove intent to participate in a conspiracy... Yet once defendant's participation in a conspiracy has been proved, conscious avoidance may properly be used to prove his knowledge of its unlawful objectives." *Reyes*, 302 F.3d at 54–55. *See also United States v. Hollender*, No. 02-1720(L); 03-1196, 2004 U.S. App. LEXIS 498, *6-7 (2d Cir. Jan. 14, 2004).

In reversing the decision of the lower court to set aside the guilty verdict, Judge Cardamone reinstated Reyes' conviction of engaging in a stolen automobile air bag conspiracy, finding that Reyes demonstrated a conscious avoidance of guilt in the context of a conspiracy. Following Reyes' arrest, an FBI agent had asked him whether he knew the business associate from whom he received checks for brokering the sale of airbags dealt in stolen airbags. Reyes had responded, "with an analogy to drug use and when you see a friend using drugs you see what's happening, but you turn the other way." *Reyes*, 302 F.3d. at 52.

b. In *United States v. Svoboda*, 347 F. 3d 471, 477 (2d Cir. 2003), the Second Circuit further clarified the permissible use of the conscious avoidance doctrine. The defendant in that case was convicted of conspiracy to commit securities fraud, but claimed that he did not know that the person from whom he received insider information had obtained it illegally. *Id.* at 475. He challenged his conviction based on language in *Reyes*. The Court, however, rejected his argument, holding: "We do not permit the [conscious avoidance] doctrine to be used to prove intent in a conspiracy." *Id.* at. 478

4. Example of conspiracy by immigration lawyer.

In *United States v. Jacques Dessange, Inc.*, an immigration lawyer was convicted as co-defendant and co-conspirator under 18 USC §1546, which prohibits knowingly submitting visa applications containing material false statements. The attorney was charged with assisting his client in falsifying visa applications for workers at the client's American subsidiary and its franchisees of a French hair salon company. Over the course of three years, the attorney and his partner obtained scores of L-1A visas by representing that the applicants were assuming managerial positions in the subsidiary headquarters, when in fact the majority of them were placed as hairstylists at franchise locations, and therefore not qualified to obtain L-1A status. *United States v. Jacques Dessange, Inc.*, 103 F. Supp.2d 701 (S.D.N.Y. 2000).

F. Wire and Mail Fraud

1. In *United States v. Rybicki*, 354 F.3d 124 (2d Cir. 2003), the Second Circuit held that, in the private sector, there are four elements to the crime of a §1346 scheme or artifice to deprive another of the intangible right of honest services:

a. A scheme or artifice to defraud;

b. For the purpose of knowingly and intentionally depriving another of the intangible right of honest services as thus defined;

c. Where the misrepresentations (or omissions) made by the defendants are material in that they have the natural tendency to influence or are capable of influencing the employer to change its behavior; and

d. Use of the mails or wires in furtherance of the scheme.

2. 18 USC §§1341 and 1343 respectively penalize the use of mail or wires to perpetrate a "scheme or artifice to defraud." Section 1346 provides that "the term 'scheme or artifice to defraud' includes a scheme or artifice to deprive another of the intangible right of honest services." In *Rybicki*, the defendant lawyers were found guilty of violating each element of §1346. Specializing in personal injury cases, the lawyers devised a scheme in which they would, "acting through intermediaries, arrange for payments to be made to claims adjustors employed by insurance companies that had insured against injuries sustained by the defendants' clients." The scheme was intended to induce the adjustors to settle the lawyers' clients' claims more expeditiously. Although each insurance company had a written policy forbidding adjustors from receiving any gifts or fees and to report any such offers, the adjustors did not report the payments.

3. The federal mail and wire fraud statutes, 18 USC §§1341, 1343, attach criminal liability to a broad range of fraudulent conduct. The mail fraud statute, §1341, "proscribes use of the mails in furtherance of 'any scheme or artifice to defraud, or for obtaining money or property by means of false or fraudulent pretenses, representations, or promises.'" *Cleveland v. United States*, 531 U.S. 12, 15 (2003). In fact, each use of the mail constitutes a separate

offense and can constitute a separate count under the indictment. *See* Nirav Shah, *Mail and Wire Fraud*, 40 AM. CRIM. L. REV. at 825, 829 (2003).

The wire fraud statute requires interstate communication, but has identical language and is interpreted in the same manner as the mail fraud statute. *See United States v. Fountain*, 357 F.3d 250, 253 (2d Cir. 2004). The broad language of the statute has allowed prosecutors to charge defendants for a broad range of conduct, including stock fraud, commodity frauds, blackmail, counterfeiting, election fraud, and bribery. *See* 40 AM. CRIM. L. REV. at 825.

4. The elements of mail fraud in the Second Circuit are: "(1) a scheme to defraud, (2) money or property [as the object to the scheme], (3) use of the mails. . . to further the scheme." *Fountain*, 357 F.3d at 255 [quoting *United States v. Dinome*, 86 F.3d 227, 283 (2d Cir. 1996)]. To prove the first element of mail fraud, the government must establish beyond a reasonable doubt that a scheme existed in which use of the mails was reasonably foreseeable and that an actual mailing occurred in furtherance of that scheme. *See* 40 AM. CRIM. L. REV. at 830. Imbedded in this first element is a materiality requirement. *United States v. Neder*, 527 U.S. at 25 (1999) (holding that the common law understanding of fraudulent conduct included materiality and should be applied in the interpretation of this statute).

5. *Rybicki* particularizes the property requirement in the statutory language. Courts have disagreed over the definition of "property" in this statute, and specifically if it should include intangible property rights. *See* 40 AM. CRIM. L. REV. at 833. In February 2004, the Second Circuit upheld defendant John Fountain's conviction under the mail and wire fraud statutes for his involvement in a scheme in which he transported cigarettes from Canada to a Native American Reservation and back to Canada where they were then sold on the black market. *Fountain*, 357 F.3d at 252. He challenged his conviction in light of the Supreme Court's ruling in *Cleveland v. United States*. *See id*. at 256–57. In *Cleveland*, the Court held that unissued state video poker licenses did not qualify as "property" under mail and wire fraud statutes because there must be symmetry in the meaning of the term—the implement used in the alleged mail fraud scheme must be transferable in both the defendants' and victims' hands. *See Cleveland*, 531 U.S. at 15. The Second Circuit held that taxes still qualify as property after *Cleveland* and that, since the Canadian government had been defrauded of them, Fountain's conviction would stand. *Fountain*, 357 F.3d at 260.

6. The property requirement was also analyzed in *United States v. Hausmann*, 345 F.3d 952 (7th Cir. 2003), a case similar in many respects to *Rybicki*. Attorney Hausmann was convicted for his involvement in a kickback scheme with a chiropractor to whom he referred his clients who had been injured in car accidents. *Id*. at 958. Hausmann challenged his conviction claiming that the statute was overly vague and therefore unconstitutional and, moreover, it invited arbitrary policing of private business conduct. *Id*. The Seventh Circuit rejected these arguments, holding that prior case law put the defendant on notice of the fact that the misuse of one's fiduciary duty for personal gain leads to criminal liability under the mail and wire fraud statutes under the intangible rights doctrine. *Id*.

7. Intent to defraud.

The government must also prove that the defendant had specific intent to defraud. However, since "direct proof of harm is often unavailable, courts have long permitted fact finders to rely of a variety of circumstantial evidence, including evidence of actual or contemplated harm, to infer such intent." *United States v. Welch*, 327 F.3d 1081, 1105 (10th Cir. 2003). Further, a "defendant's reckless indifference to the truth of a representation may [also] establish the intent to defraud under §1341." *See id*.

8. Mailing in the furtherance of a scheme to defraud.

Finally, the government must prove that the defendant used, or caused to be used, the United States Postal Service or a private interstate carrier. *See* 18 USC §1341. However, the mailing need not be complete or integral to the scheme. *See United States v. Segal*, No. 02 CR 112, 2004 U.S. Dist. LEXIS 407, at *22 (N.D. Ill. Jan. 12, 2004). In a recent case, an indictment where the defendants were alleged to cause to be mailed blank license renewal forms "in furtherance of a fraudulent scheme" were sufficient for an indictment for mail fraud under section 1341. *Id*.

G. The "Immigration Law" Crimes—8 USC §1323 *et seq.*

1. Understanding the elements of the immigration crimes is a prerequisite to effective client intake and case planning and analysis.

2. Lawyers can be implicated in the associational crimes (*e.g.*, aiding and abetting, conspiracy, harboring, false statement, record keeping failure) and misprision of felony in connection with the immigration and nationality law crimes. *See* www.usdoj.gov/usao/eousa/foia_reading_room/usam/title9/73mcrm.htm, DOJ, U.S. Attorney Manual, 9-73.010–9-73.801.

a. 8 USC §1323—Unlawful bringing of aliens into the United States: Authorizes civil penalties on carriers (ships, planes, etc.) who bring unauthorized aliens to the United States.

b. 8 USC §1324—Bringing in and harboring certain aliens: Distilled into a legal test, the five elements of the crime of transporting illegal aliens are: (1) the defendant transported an alien within the United States; (2) the alien was in the United States in violation of law; (3) this was known to the defendant; (4) the defendant knew or had reasonable grounds to believe that the alien's last entry into the United States was within the last three years; and (5) defendant acted willfully in furtherance of the alien's violation of the law. *United States v. Shaddix*, 693 F.2d 1135 (5th Cir. 1982).

c. Harboring: The term "harboring" means "to afford shelter to" and is not limited to clandestine sheltering, as in a smuggling operation. *United States v. Acosta De Evans*, 531 F.2d 428 (9th Cir. 1976).

3. Criminal prosecution of lawyers.

a. In a 23 count superseding indictment, the U.S. charged Maqsood Hamid Mir, an immigration attorney practicing in Maryland, with racketeering, conspiring to harbor aliens, and submitting false labor certification applications for those harbored aliens which permitted the illegal aliens to enter and remain in the United States as permanent resident aliens. Thomas M. DiBiagio, the U.S. Attorney said, "This indictment should send a message to those who take advantage of the immigration laws—particularly immigration attorneys and businessmen who exploit their small businesses and law practices to sponsor aliens illegally—that they will be prosecuted aggressively and to the full extent of the law." *See* Press Release, U.S. Department of Justice, U.S. Attorney, District of Maryland, "Immigration Lawyer and Others Charged In Racketeering Scheme," (Mar. 2, 2004) available at *www.usdoj.gov/usao/md/press_releases/press04/MirRackettIndict.pdf*; *see also* Ruben Castaneda, "5 Charged in Work Visa Fraud", *Washington Post*, March 3, 2004, at B02.

b. 8 USC §1324a—Unlawful employment of aliens.

c. 8 USC §1324c—Penalties for document fraud. A civil penalty under this statute does not violate Double Jeopardy Clause when assessed after a criminal conviction for same conduct. *Noriega-Perez v. United States*, 179 F.3d 1166 (9th Cir. 1999).

d. 8 USC §1325—Improper entry by alien; marriage fraud; immigration-related entrepreneurship fraud. *See Boyle v. People*, 2004 Colo. Discipl. LEXIS 31 (Sup. Ct. Colo. May 12, 2004)—immigration attorney disbarred for improperly instructing his client to enter country on B-1 visitor's visa, knowing client intended to obtain employment, thus ineligible for B-1 visa and falsifying labor certifications on behalf of clients was reinstated.

e. 8 USC §1326—unlawful reentry after deportation or removal. To obtain a conviction under 8 USC §1326, the government must show (1) that the defendant is an alien who was previously arrested and deported, (2) that he re-entered the United States voluntarily, and (3) that he failed to secure the express permission of the Attorney General to return. *United States v. Joya-Martinez*, 947 F.2d 1141 (4th Cir. 1991).

f. 8 USC §1327—Aiding entry of certain criminal or subversive aliens.

g. 8 USC §1328—Importation of aliens for immoral purpose; willful failure or refusal to depart.

H. Money Laundering—18 USC §1956

1. Recent developments.

a. The Homeland Security Act of 2002 created the Bureau of Immigration and Customs Enforcement (ICE), bringing together the enforcement and investigative arms of the Customs Service, the former Immigration and Naturalization Service (INS), and the Federal Protective Service (FPS) under the Department of Homeland Security.

b. A May 13, 2003 Memorandum of Agreement between Homeland Security Secretary Ridge and Attorney General Ashcroft assigned the FBI the lead role in investigating terrorist financing.

c. Title III of the USA PATRIOT Act enlists, for the first time, securities brokers and dealers, insurance companies and money-transfer services in detecting money laundering.

2. Immigration lawyers.

a. In May 2004, Mohamed Alamgir, a Washington D.C. immigration lawyer, pleaded guilty to money laundering (among other crimes) after filing more than 200 fraudulent visa applications. *See* Immigration Attorney Guilty of Fraud and Conspiracy (May 13, 2004) *www.visalaw.com/04may1/12may104.html*.

b. In March 2003, Samuel G. Kooritzky, a Virginia attorney, was sentenced to 10 years' imprisonment and ordered to pay $2.3 million in restitution after being convicted in 2002 of one count of money laundering (among numerous other crimes). The charges stemmed from his efforts to file fraudulent applications for alien employment certification with the U.S. Department of Labor on behalf of Northern Virginia businesses and local immigrants. *See* Immigration Lawyer in Virginia Sentenced in Immigration Fraud Case (March 12, 2003) at *www.garmo.com/archive/00000081*.

FILING IMMIGRATION APPLICATIONS AND PETITIONS: ETHICAL RESPONSIBILITIES AND CRIMINAL PENALTIES

*by Edwin R. Rubin**

This article is based on an article by the author originally published in the April 2004 issue of the New Jersey Lawyer Magazine, a publication of the New Jersey State Bar Association. Each state has its own version of disciplinary rules and they vary significantly. The reader must review the rules applicable to the relevant jurisdiction(s) regarding the issues presented.

INTRODUCTION

This article addresses ethical and criminal issues that may arise in completing and filing immigration related petitions and applications before the U.S. Citizenship and Immigration Services (USCIS), the Department of Labor (DOL), and the Executive Office for Immigration Review (EOIR). This exercise is intended to demonstrate the interplay between often competing requirements; to that end, the author analyzes the New Jersey Rules of Professional Conduct (NJRPC), and, as appropriate, makes comparisons to the ABA Model Rules of Professional Conduct and the New York Lawyers Code of Professional Responsibility.

The primary focus is on the responsibility of the attorney practicing immigration law to assure submitted information is accurate, but many aspects of the discussion are directly applicable to non-attorneys involved in the process. Individuals preparing family based petitions, employer representatives preparing employment based applications and petitions and accredited representatives are subject to many of the provisions discussed. There appears to be little doubt that these executive adjudicative agencies meet the definition of "tribunal" for all purposes discussed below.[1]

The duty of competence is the cornerstone for the rest of the rules of professional conduct and competent handling of a matter "includes inquiry into and analysis of the factual and legal elements of the problem" [citations omitted].[2] Most clients provide complete and accurate information after proper questioning by counsel. Obtaining the information necessary to make an informed decision necessarily requires knowledge of the applicable law. The complexity and uncertainty of many provisions of the Immigration and Nationality Act, regulations and other interpretations complicate the task of providing effective and ethical representation.

Therefore, immigration practitioners are increasingly confronted with a variety of ethical issues and potential criminal responsibility in everyday practice situations.[3] Perhaps the best way to avoid potential problems is to thoroughly explore the material and determinative facts with the potential client before agreeing to undertake representation.

The challenges counsel faces in immigration matters include understanding the balance between confidentiality[4] and candor toward the tribunal,[5] a

---

* **Edwin R. Rubin** is a partner in the Newark, NJ, firm of Rubin & Dornbaum with practice limited to immigration and nationality matters. Rubin is past national president of the American Immigration Lawyers Association and can be reached by phone at (973) 623-4444 or e-mail: erubin@rdimmlaw.com.

[1] New Jersey Rules of Professional Conduct (hereafter NJRPC) 1.0(n), "Tribunal" denotes a court...administrative agency or other body acting in an adjudicative capacity. A[n] *continued*

... administrative agency ... acts in an adjudicative capacity when a neutral official, after the presentation of evidence or legal argument by a party or parties, will render a binding legal judgment directly affecting the party's interest in a particular matter". See NJ Advisory Committee on Professional Ethics Opinion 677, 138 N.J.L.J. 590 (Oct 10, 1994), 3 N.J.L. 2015 (Oct 17, 1994).

[2] Michaels, *New Jersey Attorney Ethics*, 2004 ed., p. 243.

[3] *See* Bruce A. Hake, "Attorney Misconduct – A Rebuttal," 4 Geo. L. Immigr L.J. 727 (1990), Bruce A. Hake, "Dual Representation in Immigration Practice: The Simple Solution is the Wrong Solution," 5 Geo. L. Immigr L.J. 727 (581), Panetha Abdollah, The Labor Certification Process: Complex Ethical Issues for Immigration Lawyers," 17 Geo. L. Immigr L.J. 707 (2003).

[4] NJRPC 1.6 "Confidentiality of Information." *See also* ABA Model Rules of Professional Conduct (hereafter Model Rules) 1.6., discussed *infra*. Note the significant difference between New Jersey and the ABA Model Rules in the wording of the provision as to what information is covered and whether it must be revealed. NJPRC 1.6(b) states the lawyer "shall" reveal the designated information to appropriate authority while the Model Rules state the lawyer "may" reveal *continued*

particularly thorny issue. Counsel is faced with rules of conduct by the state, the agencies involved and a number of criminal provisions relating to fraud or material misrepresentation[6] that can be triggered by the submission of applications prepared without proper care. At the initial consultation or during the course of representation, the attorney may become aware of facts affecting the applicant's eligibility. When, if ever, does the law require disclosure to the tribunal? May counsel withdraw without disclosure? How far must counsel go in ascertaining facts that might affect a client's eligibility? This article will attempt to provide a basic framework for analyzing these questions.

Confidentiality versus Candor Toward the Tribunal

On January 1, 2004, the NJRPC were amended by an order of the New Jersey Supreme Court issued on November 17, 2003.[7] Although the recent amendments to the NJRPC make at least one apparently important change, the New Jersey rules relating to Confidentiality of Information still require the disclosure of confidential information to prevent the client "... from committing a criminal, illegal or fraudulent act that the lawyer reasonably believes is likely to perpetrate a fraud upon a tribunal."[8] On the other hand, "A lawyer may reveal such information to the extent the lawyer reasonably believes necessary ... to rectify the consequences of a client's criminal, illegal or fraudulent act in furtherance of which the lawyer's services had been used."[9] This last provision permitting rather than mandating disclosure appears to relate to past conduct that has already resulted in consequences while the mandatory disclosure provision relates to adjudications not yet issued.

"Reasonable belief" for the purpose of NJRPC 1.6 is the belief or conclusion of a reasonable lawyer that is based on information that has some foundation in fact and constitutes prima facie evidence of the matters referred to in subsections (b), (c) or (d)".[10] NJRPC 1.0 contains slightly different definitions for the terms "reasonable" or "reasonably," "reasonable belief," and "reasonable should know."[11]

The corollary rule regarding candor toward the tribunal was changed in New Jersey in a way that arguably eases the burden of candor versus confidentiality. The rules concerning candor toward the tribunal, of course, prohibit a lawyer from knowingly making false statements or knowingly allowing false statement to be made by the client to a tribunal and also require disclosure in specified circumstances.[12]

The change made by the New Jersey Supreme Court, effective January 1, 2004,[13] eases to some degree the burden placed on counsel. While the prior rule required disclosure to the tribunal of a material fact where counsel had "knowledge that the tribunal

---

under the conditions stated. The conditions are also stated in significantly different terms. New Jersey generally has been thought to have gone as far as any state in favoring candor toward the tribunal over confidentiality. The New York rules are organized significantly differently than the Model Rules or NJRPC making direct comparison difficult. New York Disciplinary Rule (hereafter NYDR) 4-101 uses the term "may" rather than shall in discussing client confidences and their revelation.

[5] NJRPC 3.3 and Model Rules 3.3 "Candor Toward the Tribunal". Both rules, as now constituted appear to require certain disclosures. See discussion *infra*. NYDR 7-103 requires disclosure where a fraud has been committed but only where it is not protected "as a confidence or secret."

[6] Under Immigration and Nationality Act [hereafter INA] §212(a)(6)(C), 8 USC §1182(a)(6)(C), "Any alien who, by fraud or willfully misrepresenting a material fact, seeks to procure (or has sought to procure or has procured) a visa, other documentation, or admission into the United States or other benefit provided under this Act is inadmissible." See the discussion of fraud and misrepresentation – at 9 *Foreign Affairs Manual* 40.63, Notes. Discussion of the issues of "materiality" and "willfulness" are beyond the scope of this article. See notes 31–36 and accompanying text. *See also Matter of Tijam*, 22 I&N Dec. 408 (BIA 1998) for a discussion of these terms.

[7] Michaels, *supra*, n.2. and 1075.

[8] NJRPC 1.6(b)(2).
[9] NJRPC 1.6(d)(1).
[10] NJRPC 1.6(e).
[11] NJRPC 1.0(i) states, "'Reasonable' or 'reasonably' when used in relation to conduct by a lawyer denotes the conduct of a reasonably prudent and competent lawyer." NJRPC 1.0(j) states, "'Reasonable belief' or 'reasonably believes' when used in reference to a lawyer denotes that the lawyer believes the matter in question and that the circumstances are such that the belief is reasonable." NJRPC 1.0(k) states, "'Reasonably should know' when used in reference to a lawyer denotes that a lawyer of reasonable prudence and competence would ascertain the matter in question." The Model rules are identical.
[12] NJRPC 3.3(a)(1).
[13] *Supra*, n.2.

may tend to be misled by such failure" [emphasis added], the new rule says, "A lawyer shall not knowingly[14] ... fail to disclose to the tribunal a material fact knowing that the omission is reasonably certain to mislead the tribunal, except that it shall not be a breach of this rule if disclosure is protected by a recognized privilege or is otherwise prohibited by law" [emphasis added].[15]

It is relatively clear that the exception for a recognized privilege does not mean there is a blanket privilege of confidentiality for information received from a client for, as discussed above, NJRPC 3.3 mandates disclosure to prevent a fraud on the tribunal.[16] However, one learned author has stated that the "courts in New Jersey had never invoked the rule to mandate the disclosure of information learned from a client."[17] Nevertheless, the NJRPC together with other provisions governing practice discussed below require those preparing immigration filings to use care in completing forms and setting forth the facts of the case.

NJRPC 3.3(c) permits a lawyer to refuse to offer evidence that the lawyer reasonably believes to be false despite a client's instructions to the lawyer to introduce such evidence. From a practical perspective, it is probably best under this situation to withdraw from the matter. Note the difference between evidence the lawyer knows to be false in NJRPC 3.3(a) and reasonably believes to be false in NJRPC 3.3(c).

Most state rules favor confidentiality over this mandate of candor to the tribunal, although the pendulum may be slowly swinging toward the concept that candor toward the tribunal is more important than confidentiality. Although each state's rules must be consulted, no jurisdiction permits an attorney to knowingly provide false information to the tribunal.[18]

The prudent attorney should distinguish between putting the government to its proof where the government has the burden and affirmatively presenting information to the tribunal that the attorney knows or should have known was false, as in an application to USCIS, where the burden rests with the applicant.

For example, one may know that a client is deportable but insist that the government prove the ground(s) for deportation by clear, convincing and unequivocal evidence. The attorney may not present evidence to USCIS that the attorney knows is false (or reasonable should know is false) under the belief that the knowledge of its falsity is covered by the attorney client privilege or that it is the government's responsibility to determine whether it is false

---

[14] NJRPC 1.0(f) states, " 'Knowingly,' 'known," or 'knows' denotes actual knowledge of the fact in question. A person's knowledge may be inferred from the circumstances." Accord Model Rules 1.0(f).

[15] NJRPC 3.3(a)(5).

[16] NJRPC 3.3 Candor Toward the Tribunal states,

"(a) A lawyer shall not knowingly:

(1) make a false statement of material fact or law to a tribunal;

(2) fail to disclose a material fact to a tribunal when disclosure is necessary to avoid assisting an illegal, criminal or fraudulent act by the client;

(3) fail to disclose to the tribunal legal authority in the controlling jurisdiction known to the lawyer to be directly adverse to the position of the client and not disclosed by opposing counsel;

(4) offer evidence that the lawyer knows to be false. If a lawyer has offered material evidence and comes to know of its falsity, the lawyer shall take reasonable remedial measures; or

(5) fail to disclose to the tribunal a material fact with knowledge that the tribunal may tend to be misled by such failure.

(b) The duties stated in paragraph (a) continue to the conclusion of the proceeding, and apply even if compliance requires disclosure of information otherwise protected by NJRPC 1.6.

(c) A lawyer may refuse to offer evidence that the lawyer reasonably believes is false.

(d) In an ex parte proceeding, a lawyer shall inform the tribunal of all relevant facts known to the lawyer that should be disclosed to permit the tribunal to make an informed decision, whether or not the facts are adverse."

[17] Michaels, *supra* at p. 633.

[18] *See www.abanet.org/legresources/ethics.html*—the American Bar Association Web site relating to Ethics; *www.law.cornell.edu/ethics/index.html*—an excellent site with many links to state ethics, rules, opinions, etc.; Kevin H. Michaels, New Jersey Attorney Ethics, (2004); Geoffrey C. Hazard, Jr. & S. Koniak, The Law and Ethics of Lawyering, (1990); C. Wolfram, Modern Legal Ethics, (1986); American Bar Association/The Bureau of National Affairs, Inc., Lawyer's Manual on Professional Conduct; "Model Rules of Professional Conduct", ABA Center for Professional Responsibility. New Jersey Rules of Professional Conduct and Opinions of the N.J. Advisory Committee on Professional Ethics maybe accessed through *www.judiciary.state.nj.us/oae/links.htm*.

or that the attorney is only meeting the obligation to represent the client zealously.

The Duty to Inquire

In New Jersey, which has opted for a strict rule concerning candor toward the tribunal, NJRPC 3.3 requires certain disclosures. Counsel should review the applicable jurisdiction's disciplinary rules to determine the applicable standard. In New Jersey, the questions then becomes what did the attorney know and what should the attorney have known. "It is a complicated question whether ... willful blindness rises to the level of knowledge. According to one expert: 'For the most part, a lawyer is not under an obligation to seek out information.' But, as in the criminal law, a lawyer's studied ignorance of a readily accessible fact by consciously avoiding finding the fact is the functional equivalent of knowledge of the fact."[19]

The concept of conscious avoidance has been used to determine whether one has knowledge of an element necessary for conviction in the criminal law context. An illustrative immigration fraud prosecution against an attorney involved the issue of whether the attorney actually knew the statements in applications submitted to immigration were false. In affirming the conviction, the Second Circuit held that "a conscious avoidance instruction is appropriate when a defendant claims to lack some specific aspect of knowledge necessary to conviction where the evidence may be construed as deliberate ignorance" [citations omitted].[20]

IMMIGRATION DISCIPLINARY REGULATIONS

On June 27, 2000, the U.S. Department of Justice (DOJ) published new regulations relating to Professional Conduct for Practitioners, which became effective July 27, 2000.[21] The new regulations amended both the EOIR regulations concerning practice before the immigration courts, the Board of Immigration Appeals,[22] and the Immigration Service.[23] The rules provide for appropriate disciplinary action where a practitioner:

"(c) Knowingly or with reckless disregard makes a false statement of material fact or law, or willfully misleads, misinforms, threatens, or deceives any person (including a party to a case or an officer or employee of the Department of Justice), concerning any material and relevant matter relating to a case, including knowingly or with reckless disregard offering false evidence. If a practitioner has offered material evidence and comes to know of its falsity, the practitioner shall take appropriate remedial measures;"[24]

In response to comments to the proposed rule that this provision was too vague and that DOJ should provide more guidance, the promulgation concluded, "The language in this provision closely resembles the language in the current regulation, combined with language from ABA Model Rule 3.3 ... This problem includes the submission of once valid documents that have been altered (*e.g.*, foreign birth certificates), falsely created documents (*e.g.*, visas or letters from religious or political groups), and valid documents that contain false information (*e.g.*, asylum applications). This provision as written is broad enough to deal with these types of fraud."[25]

The NJRPC 3.3, as indicated, leans more toward candor than confidentiality but the immigration regulation adds the element of reckless disregard prompting the question whether the NJRPC differs from the immigration regulation. Is there a difference? What about other jurisdictions.

Criminal Provisions

There are many provisions in federal statutes with more specific descriptions of the type of misrepresentation to be punished including visa fraud,[26] marriage fraud,[27] failure to carry one's resident alien card (usually referred to as a green card),[28] and knowingly making a false statement on an application submitted to immigration.[29] Each has its own

---

[19] C. Wolfram, Modern Legal Ethics, 1986. *See also* Michaels, *supra*, in particular Chapters 15 and 30.

[20] *U.S. v. Walker*, 191 F.3d 326 (2nd Cir. 1999). [E]vidence easily supported the inference that even if Walker did not have direct knowledge of the crimes occurring in his office, he deliberately remained ignorant of them. Under these circumstances, the charge was proper.

[21] 65 Fed. Reg. 39513 *et seq.* (June 27, 2000).

[22] 8 CFR §3.102.

[23] 8 CFR §292.3(b).

[24] 8 CFR §3.102(c) incorporated by reference into 8 CFR §292.3(b).

[25] *Supra,* n. 21 at p. 39518.

[26] 18 USC §1546.

[27] 8 USC §1325 (c), INA §275 (c).

[28] 8 USC §1304(e), INA §264 (e).

[29] 18 USC §1546(a).

specific requirements and further discussion is beyond the scope of this article.

The federal law contains a "catch-all" provision regarding false statements.[30] In a prosecution for violation of 18 USC §1001, "willful blindness" may be equated with "knowingly and willfully."[31] This statute has been used frequently in the immigration context including conviction of an attorney who placed false information on an application concerning priority dates even though there was no ability to actually deceive immigration with that information.[32]

The provision covers even unsworn, oral statements.[33] The provisions in 18 USC §1001, are quite broad. Materiality is an element of the crime but the definition of materiality is expansive. A statement is material if it has the "natural tendency to influence, or was capable of influencing, the decision making body."[34] It has never been the test of materiality that the misrepresentation or concealment would *more likely than not* have produced an erroneous decision, or even that it would *more likely than not* have triggered an investigation."[35]

In addition, The Illegal Immigration Reform and Immigrant Responsibility Act of 1996 (IIRAIRA),[36] created civil liability for individuals who prepare, file or assist another person in preparing or filing an application for benefits with knowledge or in reckless disregard of the fact that such application or document was falsely made.[37] A fine of $250–$2,000 per document for first offense and $2,000–$5,000 for subsequent offenses is established.[38] A new definition of "falsely make" was added in the same statute. The definition is, "To prepare or provide an application or document, with knowledge or in reckless disregard of the fact that the application or document contains a false, fictitious or fraudulent statement or material misrepresentation or has no basis in the law or fact, or otherwise fails to state a fact which is material to the purpose for which it was submitted."[39] The provisions are retroactive.

Since this is, in part, a civil provision, it apparently creates a lower threshold for finding a violation than similar criminal provisions. Note also that a violation occurs when the preparer "fails to state a material fact". These changes may impose an even higher burden to inquire into the veracity of information provided by clients, particularly since the preparer is now responsible to assure all material facts are included. IIRAIRA also makes it a crime for a person (presumably this includes attorneys) to "knowingly and willfully" conceal or fail to disclose his role in preparing for a fee or other remuneration a false application for benefits under the INA. Imprisonment for up to five years is included in the penalty for a first violation.[40]

THE USA PATRIOT ACT

In response to the events of September 11, 2001, Congress passed an extensive legislative package known as The USA PATRIOT Act.[41] The USA PATRIOT Act contains many provisions of concern to counsel. One provision makes those who the Attorney General or a consular officer knows or has reason to believe has engaged, is engaging or seeks to enter the United States to engage in a money laundering offense[42] inadmissible to the United States.[43]

---

[30] 18 USC §1001. "Whoever, in any matter within the jurisdiction of any department or agency of the United States knowingly and willfully falsifies, conceals or covers up by any trick, scheme, or device a material fact, or makes any false, fictitious, or fraudulent statements or representations, or makes any false writing or document knowing the same contain any false, fictitious, or fraudulent statement or entry, shall be fined not more than $10,000 or imprisoned not more than five years or both.

[31] *U.S. v Singh*, 222 F.3d 6 (1st Cir. 2000).

[32] *U.S. v Lopez*, 728 F.2d 1359 (11th Cir. 1984), *reh. den.* 733 F.2d 908 (11th Cir.), *cert. denied*, 469 U.S. 828, 105 S. Ct. 112, 83 L.Ed. 2d 56.

[33] *U.S. v. Des Jardins*, 772 F.2d 578 (9th Cir 1985).

[34] *Kungys v United States*, 485 U.S. 759, 770, 99 L. Ed. 2d 839, 108 S. Ct. 1537 (1988) [citations and internal quotation marks omitted].

[35] *Kungys, supra,* at 771.

[36] The Illegal Immigration Reform Immigrant Responsibility Act of 1996 (IIRAIRA), Division C of the Department of Commerce, Justice and State and the Appropriations Act of 1997, Pub. L. No. 104-208, 110 Stat. 3009 (Sept. 30, 1996) at §531(a).

[37] 8 USC §1324c(a)(5), INA §274C(a)(5).

[38] 8 USC §1324c(d)(3), INA §274C(d)(3).

[39] 8 USC §1324c(d)(3), INA §274C(d)(3).

[40] 8 USC §1324c(e), INA §274C(e).

[41] Uniting and Strengthening America by Providing Appropriate Tools Required to Intercept and Obstruct Terrorism Act of 2001, Pub. L. No. 107-56, 115 Stat. 272 (Oct. 26, 2001).

[42] The crime of money laundering is set forth at 18 USC §§ 1956 and 1957.

[43] 8 USC §1182(a)(2)(I), INA §212(a)(2)(I).

This adds yet another area of inquiry and counseling required of an attorney in determining a potential client's eligibility to enter the United States. An expanded ground of inadmissibility was also created for terrorist related activity.[44] The definition is quite broad encompassing being part of or contributing to organizations determined to be aiding terrorism. Counsel, therefore, must use care to elicit and evaluate all information required for completion of immigration forms requesting a listing of membership in organizations or activities involving terrorism.[45]

CONCLUSION

The purpose of this article is to start readers on the road to thought and evaluation of the issues presented. Some questions are easy—it is never proper for a lawyer to knowingly mislead a tribunal. Some issues will require very careful thought, evaluation and preparation of documents designed to advise the client(s) and protect the attorney from charges of breach of confidentiality, the duty of loyalty or even criminal charges. Each attorney must evaluate the more difficult and, at best, partially answered concerns with lawyer-like analysis and preparation. The bottom line is that the license to practice law is something to be protected and may not be taken for granted. The risks of being found to have violated a duty to a client or the tribunal are real. The never ending balancing act of candor to the tribunal while zealously representing the client continues to have difficult issues to be evaluated carefully before undertaking a matter.

Experts on attorney responsibility and ethics frequently state that the first duty is to know the law. In one way or another, every state code of professional responsibility mandates that an attorney not undertake a matter that he or she is not competent to handle. Immigration law is complex, in part because of the complexity of the statute and regulations. Many believe that only the Internal Revenue Code is a more complex statute than the Immigration and Nationality Act. "We have had occasion to note the striking resemblance between some of the laws we are called upon to interpret and King Minos's labyrinth in ancient Crete. The Tax Laws and the Immigration and Nationality Acts are examples we have cited of Congress' ingenuity in passing statutes certain to accelerate the aging process of judges."[46] Practitioners are also faced with a failure of the USCIS to clarify many recurring issues. Indeed, we have no regulations concerning "unlawful presence"[47], a concept introduced in IIRAIRA in 1996[48] or "adjustment of status and H-1B portability" as introduced in 2000.[49] How can we meet our ethical responsibilities when the law remains so unsettled? What is a material fact with regard to a change of employment for an applicant for adjustment of status? The immigration practitioner must do his or her best to keep current on all developments affecting the specific areas in which he or she undertakes to represent a client or clients.

As if this complexity of statutes, regulations and ever changing procedures were not enough to make immigration practice difficult, the attorney undertaking an immigration matter has to contend with cultural differences and possible language barriers. The consequence of not representing a client properly is frequently banishment from the United States for that individual or, at least, an inability to regularize one's status. Since many who seek counsel in this area of the law are, in fact, not entitled to remain in the United States, the practitioner must be prepared to convey this information to potential clients. Attorneys must be prepared to advise clients clearly of the consequences of action or inaction. With recent changes creating ever harsher penalties for conduct in violation of the law, assuring the client or potential client understands the advice being given is more important than ever.

---

[44] 8 USC §1182(a)(3)(B), INA §212(a)(3)(B) as amended by §411(a)(1) of the PATRIOT Act, *supra*.

[45] *See* for example Form I-485, Application to Register Permanent Residence or Adjust Status, revised 2/7/00, questions at Part C, Question 3 and Question 4 on page 3; and, Form N-400, Application for Naturalization, revised 7/23/02, at Part 10.B, Questions 8 and 9.c.

[46] *Lok v. INS*, 548 F.2d 37, 38 (2nd Cir. 1977).

[47] 8 USC §1182(a)(9)(B), INA §212(a)(9)(B).

[48] *Supra*.

[49] H-1B portability codified at 8 USC §1184(m)(1) and (2), INA §§214(m)(1) and (2). Adjustment portability for certain employment-based applicants for adjustment of status codified at 8 USC §§1154(j) and 1182(a)(5)(A)(iv), INA §§204(j) and 212(a)(5)(A)(v). Sections were added to the INA by the American Competitiveness in the 21st Century Act (AC21), Pub. L. No. 106-313, 114 Stat. 1251 (Oct. 17, 2001).

MULTI-JURISDICTIONAL DISCIPLINARY ENFORCEMENT

*by James G. Gavin**

Rules of professional conduct for attorneys have existed for decades and arose, at least in part, out of recognition that the practice of law is an honorable calling and a service to society. As Dean Roscoe Pound observed, we are "... pursuing a learned art as a common calling in the spirit of public service—no less a public service because it may incidentally be a means of livelihood."[1] At about the same time, and before his ascent to the U.S. Supreme Court, Justice William J. Brennan, Jr., articulated the importance of effective attorney discipline. In a statement now printed in the manual provided to public and attorney volunteers in the disciplinary system of the state from which he came, Brennan observed:

> [T]he confidence of people in the administration of justice is a prime requisite for free representative government. It would be tragic indeed if that confidence and respect should be lost out of public suspicion, be it ever so slight, that the profession cannot be counted upon courageously to rid its rank of those who by their serious misconduct demonstrate their contempt for the professional ideals which earn that respect and confidence for us. *In re Frankel*, 20 N.J. 588, 602 (1956) (dissenting opinion).

Not so long ago, immigration lawyers, along with other attorneys, had to look no further than the ethics rules of the states in which they were admitted to find all of the standards that would be involved in an official examination of their professional conduct. Today, though, we must also concern ourselves with the rules of any jurisdiction in which our services are provided or offered to be provided, whether in a judicial proceeding or otherwise, as well as with federal agency rules. Though we must be admitted and in good standing under but one "highest court" in order to be "authorized to practice," INA §292; 8 CFR §§1.1(f), 292.1(a)(1), 1001.1(f) and 1003.16(b), each of us may represent clients from many states and provide our services in many different jurisdictions. Unlike before, each of us now has the potential of becoming subject to the disciplinary authorities of each of the 50 states and the District of Columbia, as well as to new disciplinary powers of the Department of Justice (DOJ). Its Rules of Conduct were promulgated on June 27, 2000, 65 Fed. Reg. 39513, *et seq.*, and extend to immigration practitioners before the immigration courts and the Board of Immigration Appeals (BIA) under 8 CFR §1003.101(b) and to those before the Department of Homeland Security (DHS) under 8 CFR §292.3(a)(2).

The expansion of disciplinary authority at the state level was prompted by wide recognition preceding the 2002 amendments to the ABA Model Rules of Professional Conduct that lawyers were more and more representing clients in jurisdictions other than where they may be licensed. Consequently, Model Rule 5.5 (see exhibit) was amended to explicitly permit this in a variety of situations. At the same time, Model Rule 8.5—which is part of the focus of this article—was amended to expand the disciplinary authority applicable to lawyers engaged in practice across the boundaries of traditional ethics enforcement, and now provides as follows:

Rule 8.5—Disciplinary Authority; Choice of Law

(a) Disciplinary Authority. A lawyer admitted to practice in this jurisdiction is subject to the disciplinary authority of this jurisdiction, regardless of where the lawyer's conduct occurs. A lawyer not admitted in this jurisdiction is also subject to the disciplinary authority of this jurisdiction if the lawyer provides or offers to provide any legal services in this jurisdiction. A lawyer may be subject to the disciplinary authority of both this jurisdiction and another jurisdiction for the same conduct.

(b) Choice of Law. In any exercise of the disciplinary authority of this jurisdiction, the rules of professional conduct to be applied shall be as follows: (1) for conduct in connection with a matter pending before a tribunal, the rules of the jurisdiction in which the tribu-

---

* **James G. Gavin** practices immigration law in Burlington, New Jersey, and is a graduate of the University of Scranton and of the Rutgers-Camden School of Law. He is a past chair of the AILA New Jersey Chapter, a former New Jersey District Ethics Committee member, and also has advocated and litigated cases involving conditions of confinement and provision of community-based human services.

[1] *The Lawyer from Antiquity to Modern Times* (St. Paul: West Pub. Co., 1953), p.5.

nal sits, unless the rules of the tribunal provide otherwise; and (2) for any other conduct, the rules of the jurisdiction in which the lawyer's conduct occurred, or, if the predominant effect of the conduct is in a different jurisdiction, the rules of that jurisdiction shall be applied to the conduct. A lawyer shall not be subject to discipline if the lawyer's conduct conforms to the rules of a jurisdiction in which the lawyer reasonably believes the predominant effect of the lawyer's conduct will occur.

As the various U.S. jurisdictions go about adopting some form of the new Model Rules, variations between the jurisdictions remain significant. A Model Rule may or may not be adopted intact, and even when it is, the ABA Comments, which form an integral element of each Model Rule, may not be included in the adoption. Not surprisingly, the variations found in the quiltwork of state ethics systems extend to the basic principles and definitions found in the "Preamble, Scope and Terminology" section. As with the ABA Comments, this element of the Model Rules may be modified in the format of a jurisdiction's ethics provisions, or may be entirely excluded.

If the differences among the jurisdictions were simply matters of style of expression or organization, the multi-jurisdictional application of ethics rules to practicing attorneys might not be of great importance. They are not, however, and extend even so far as the application of the rules, in their various formulations, for resolving the core conflicts that inevitably arise from time to time in legal practice. As recognized at paragraph 8 of the Preamble to the Model Rules, "[v]irtually all difficult ethical problems arise from conflict between a lawyer's responsibilities to clients, to the legal system and to the lawyer's own interest in remaining an ethical person while earning a satisfactory living."

For immigration lawyers, variation in ethics standards and enforcement is further complicated, and complicated significantly, by the federal rules for practitioners. Numerous objections to the implementation of this system had been raised during the comment period. The final rule observed that:

A chief concern of many commenters was that this rule would have a chilling effect on an immigration practitioner's ability to advocate zealously for his or her client, suggesting that both the First Amendment right to freedom of speech and the Sixth Amendment right to counsel were implicated by such a rule. A similar majority argued that it is not the function of EOIR or the Service to control the conduct of attorneys who have been admitted to the practice of law by state courts.[2]

Commenters were also concerned about the way the system would be utilized by federal authorities, it being noted that:

A large number of commenters were concerned that the disciplinary process may be used to intimidate, retaliate, or otherwise harass practitioners who are successful in advocating against the government in immigration proceedings. One commenter suggested that this rule might be used to "intimidate and control any lawyer who might be so bold as to file a motion to recuse a judge (or) seek to enter an objection upon the record."[3]

The ABA itself suggested that the state systems for attorney discipline (which are largely based on its Model Rules) were adequate for handling allegations of misconduct arising in immigration proceedings. 65 Fed. Reg. 39524. It was not alone in this opinion:

Several commenters suggested that the rules for sanctions are too vague and do not contain the level of detail, specificity, and explanation provided by the American Bar Association Model Rules of Professional Conduct.

65 Fed. Reg. 39517.

The government defended its right to establish its Rules for Practitioners by asserting that "Congress vested implied authority with the Attorney General" to do so. 65 Fed. Reg. 39514. It found this as arising out of its general rule-making authority under INA §103(a)(3) and the provision that individuals have the "privilege" of being represented in proceedings at INA §292. *Id.* Referring later to these provisions as "enabling language," the government also claimed support in what it called "Congress' ... public interest purposes." 65 Fed. Reg. 39522. While suggesting there to be multiple purposes, the only one named at this point was "the public interest in deciding whether to admit or exclude aliens." *Id.* Consequently, the government declared its disciplinary regulations valid and, therefore, preemptive over state rules under the authority of *Sperry v. Florida*, 373 U.S. 379 (1963). 65 Fed. Reg. 39524. It

---

[2] 65 Fed. Reg. 39515.
[3] 65 Fed. Reg. 39520.

attempted to assuage fears of misuse of the system by observing that only the Offices of General Counsel would be responsible for conducting preliminary inquiries and issuing charging documents for disciplinary proceedings, which would then be heard by immigration judges and the BIA. 65 Fed. Reg. 39521.

Despite this and other statements meant to placate concerns—including the observation that "the revised grounds for disciplinary sanctions include language, whenever possible, that is similar, if not identical to, the ABA Model Rules" (65 Fed. Reg. 39517)—it is clear that this executive agency discipline is vastly different from that administered in the states. Of the 13 grounds found at 8 CFR §1003.102, 10 define particular forms of misconduct that might be determined in a disciplinary proceeding to have occurred in an immigration context. Five of these are similar, though in no instance identical, to an ABA Model Rule provision, and may be summarized as follows:

8 CFR §1003.102

(a) Charging grossly excessive fees (see Model Rule 1.5).

(c) Knowing or reckless false statements; deception or offering of false evidence (see Model Rule 3.3, though this does not refer to "reckless" conduct.

(d) Solicitation of professional employment (see Model Rule 7.3).

(f) False or misleading statement of qualifications (see Model Rule 7.4, though this focuses on statements where specialty certification is utilized).

(j) Frivolous behavior (see Model Rule 3.1, though this is much less suggestive of broad applicability).

The other five grounds proscribing particular forms of misconduct and summarized here do not have corresponding provisions in the Model Rules:

8 CFR §1003.102

(b) Bribery and coercion.

(g) Contumelious or otherwise obnoxious conduct.

(i) Knowing or reckless false certification of copies.

(l) Repeated lateness for hearings.

(m) Assisting the unauthorized practice of law.

While these 10 grounds may be particularized, they are also, in some instances, exceedingly vague. At least as to the ground of "contumelious or otherwise obnoxious conduct," this seems to have been recognized by the government, as well, at the time of its June 27, 2000, promulgation:

A finding of contempt will become a prerequisite to the imposition of disciplinary action pursuant to this subsection. Therefore, the current language will be retained in the final rule, pending amendment by the contempt regulations, which will be published in the near future.[4]

The original language remains, however, with broader government concerns or difficulties as to its particularized grounds being suggested by its reticence in their regard, the reports of discipline that we have seen so far fall under the remaining three subsections. In each of these, discipline may be administered following a determination in an earlier proceeding which had the collateral consequence of establishing a basis for discipline under one of the following summarized grounds:

8 CFR §1003.102

(e) Being subject to a final order of disbarment or suspension by any court or government agency.

(h) Being found guilty of a serious crime.

(k) Being determined by the BIA or an immigration judge to have engaged in conduct that constitutes the ineffective assistance of counsel.

In defending its system against what it termed the ABA's "general objection to federal oversight of the professional conduct of those who appear before federal agencies," the government asserted the paramount importance of uniformity and consistency. It was "imperative," it said, that the agencies "administer a uniform disciplinary system." Furthermore, "the problems" required "national uniformity" and a "national standard" to avoid leaving "immigration attorneys in one state subject to discipline, while possibly exempting immigration attorneys in another state."[5]

In spite of these federal government ideals and intentions, however, inconsistency relative to its disciplinary system is already apparent. Two areas of

---

[4] 65 Fed. Reg. 39519.

[5] 65 Fed. Reg. 39524.

early concern are application of Department of Justice policy regarding "ineffective assistance of counsel," and the imposition of discipline upon attorneys who have been suspended or disbarred under state systems.

The former arises out of DOJ's position in *Matter of Assaad*, 23 I&N Dec. 553 (BIA, 2003). Citing *Coleman v. Thompson*, 501 U.S. 722 (1991), the government requested reconsideration of *Matter of Lozada*, 19 I&N Dec. 637 (BIA, 1988), suggesting that "where there is no constitutional right to the appointment of counsel at government expense, there is no constitutional basis for a claim of ineffective assistance of counsel." *Matter of Assaad*, *supra*, 23 I&N Dec. at 554. This suggestion was rejected by the *en banc* Board on the weight of circuit court precedent which "consistently continued to recognize that ... a respondent has a Fifth Amendment due process right to a fair immigration hearing and may be denied that right if counsel prevents the respondent from meaningfully presenting his or her case." *Id.* at 558. However, a vigorous dissent would have put aside this principle and lined up with the government on the theory that any right to the effective assistance of an attorney is limited to the extent of the government's constitutional obligation to supply one. *Id.* at 563.

While the government would deny a victimized respondent relief, however, its announcement of disciplinary actions dated July 26, 2004, and posted on the EOIR Web site contains the names of two attorneys found to have provided ineffective assistance in removal cases, one for failing to file a brief as promised, and the other for unspecified reasons. In addition, under 8 CFR §1003.106(d), this public discipline is reported to the ABA National Lawyer Regulatory Data Bank and to every jurisdiction in which each attorney is admitted.

If the government may have such serious recourse against attorneys found to have provided ineffective assistance, it seems incongruous for government policy not to recognize that serious recourse also should be available to the recognized victims, however the representation upon which they relied became available to them.

Appreciation of the inconsistency endemic in a system that imposes additional discipline based on the results of ethics proceedings in the several states requires an understanding of how examination of identical conduct may well produce different results arising from variations in the rules from state to state. The following hypothetical, modeled on an actual case, is presented to aid such understanding and is based on a situation wherein the tension which often arises involving the duties of loyalty to the client and candor to the tribunal is implicated. Its consideration under New Jersey ethics provisions and those of another state, Maryland being chosen, should also help to clarify what the implementation by the several states of some form of Model Rule 8.5, as recently amended, may hold in store:

- On March 1, 2003, attorney is retained to represent defendant involved that day in a motor vehicle accident in which two people were killed. He left the scene but surrendered later and was arraigned in the local municipal court and charged with aggravated manslaughter and death by auto as to each fatality. He faced a possible prison sentence of 60 years with the further possibility of 85 percent parole ineligibility. Bail was set at a high amount, and the defendant remained incarcerated.

- On March 15, 2003, motor vehicle summonses were issued charging defendant with reckless driving, leaving the scene of an accident and failure to report an accident. A municipal court date of April 15, 2003, was set, at which time the criminal charges remained pending in state court.

- Several years earlier, a directive had been sent to all municipal court administrators, judges and prosecutors advising them of a Supreme Court decision barring subsequent prosecution of indictable offenses after disposition of the motor vehicle charges in a local court and arising out of the same incident. These officials were directed to have procedures in place for detecting situations where this might occur, and to suspend proceedings on the motor vehicle charges and communicate with the county prosecutor in these situations. Though the directive remained in effect, the local court did not have the required procedures and none of the local officials involved was apparently aware of it, though defense counsel was.

- On April 15, 2003, the prosecutor, who had not reviewed the court list for that day, was busy outside the courtroom with other matters. Defendant's case proceeded, however, and the judge, who on March 1 had arraigned the same defendant who, with counsel, now appeared before him, was taking his guilty pleas. Though required by court rules to take a factual basis from the defendant, the judge failed to do so before sentencing the defendant to pay fines, which were satisfied that same day. At no point did Counsel address the criminal charges or the prospective debarment of further prosecution.

- Shortly thereafter, when these events and their consequences came to light, defense counsel was charged with a violation under Rule of Professional Conduct (RPC) 3.3, "Candor Toward the Tribunal."

In the prosecution of this charge of ethical violation, it can be argued that although the attorney owes a client the duty of fidelity, the tribunal before which he or she practices is concomitantly owed the duty of good faith and honorable dealing. Further, that allegiance owed to a client can never override the professional loyalty owed to the justice system, and that it is an impermissible deception upon a court to keep from it relevant and decisive facts of which the attorney has knowledge; in such situations, silence is no less a misrepresentation than words.

Conversely, in answering such a charge, the attorney may argue that competently representing a criminal defendant is a crucial component to the fair working of the adversarial system and within the best traditions of the administration of justice. Further, that defense counsel has no obligation to do the prosecutor's job or to bring attention to imminent pitfalls, and that to do otherwise would violate a defendant's Sixth Amendment right to the effective assistance of counsel, as well as counsel's duty of diligence under NJRPC 1.3.

Notwithstanding these competing considerations, the most decisive factor for the ethics proceeding decision-maker may well be the particular version of the rule concerning candor to be applied. For instance, as of the date of the events in the hypothetical, NJRPC 3.3 included the following explicit proscription, which was an addition to those set forth in the Model Rule:

(a) a lawyer shall not knowingly ...

(5) fail to disclose to the tribunal a material fact with knowledge that the tribunal may tend to be misled by such failure.

The New Jersey Comments to this version of the rule go on to provide that "[t]his applies both to facts that are at issue in the case as well as facts relating to the management of the case." However, deeper research would also reveal Opinion 643 of the New Jersey Advisory Committee on Professional Ethics, which concerned an inquiry from an attorney in a family law proceeding. This Opinion suggested that in spite of the use of "shall" in NJRPC 3.3(a)(5), some balancing of the interests may be possible and necessary in the lawyer's exercise of professional judgment where requiring disclosure in the circumstances may have especially harsh consequences.

In Maryland, on the other hand, a provision such as NJRPC 3.3(a)(5) did not exist on the dates in the hypothetical. Moreover, and at further variance with New Jersey, Maryland Rule 3.3 contained the following addition to the Model Rule:

(e) Notwithstanding paragraphs (a) through (d), a lawyer for an accused in a criminal case need not disclose that the accused intends to testify falsely or has testified falsely if the lawyer reasonably believes that the disclosure would jeopardize any constitutional right of the accused.

Given these variations in the RPCs, what if the attorney in the hypothetical had his or her ethical conscience and habits of practice formed under the Maryland rules and was specially admitted in New Jersey to represent the defendant? Should a good faith belief that the attorney's actions were consistent with the highest traditions of the legal profession provide insulation from being determined to have been unethical? Should it make a difference whether he or she was aware of the difference in the states' rules? Indeed, should a New Jersey attorney, acting with a keen appreciation of the constitutional rights of the client and with a good faith belief that his or her actions were consistent with the legal profession's highest standards be found unethical in the circumstances? And how might the disciplinary proceedings be influenced if they occur (or to go a step further, if they and all of the actionable events occur) after January 1, 2004? As of this date, NJRPC 3.3(a)(5) was amended to read:

(a) A lawyer shall not knowingly ...

(5) fail to disclose to the tribunal a material fact knowing that the omission is reasonably certain to mislead the tribunal, except that it shall not be a breach of this rule if the disclosure is protected by a recognized privilege or is otherwise prohibited by law.

Attorneys practicing at points of conflict such as represented above would do well to remember that a state's rules of conduct are in place to support legal practice that conforms with professional ideals and also aim to earn the people's respect and their confidence in the administration of justice. Attorneys should also realize that each jurisdiction's rules of professional conduct are, at least in part, a reflection of local values, policy choices, expectations and concerns. These local factors are reinforced over time, both by the teaching effect flowing from their very existence and by the practical application of the rules. They may find expression not only in the manner in which the rules are applied to particular cases, but also in decisions as to whether complaints are filed in the first place. For instance, might not an ethical charge under RPC 1.1 ("Competence") against the prosecutor in the hypothetical seem as appropriate, at least in an analytical sense, as the charge under Rule 3.3 leveled against defense counsel?

In addition to the elements of local culture at play, might variations in the facts of the underlying case, extraneous to the inherent qualities of counsel's conduct, also make a difference in the decision to prosecute either of the attorney participants?

For instance, what if the accident victims had been injured rather than killed and the criminal charges not so severe? Or what if the local court disposition had been set aside and the more severe charges allowed to proceed? As with defense counsel, however, a key element in any possible disciplinary proceeding as to the prosecutor may well be the particular version of the RPC to be applied. Again looking to the New Jersey and Maryland rules, it appears that in the former "gross negligence" or a "pattern of negligence or neglect" would have to be proven. In Maryland, on the other hand, discipline could attach upon a showing that the representation was short of "the legal knowledge, skill, thoroughness and preparation reasonably necessary."

Even an attorney who might provide services in only two states and does not practice before a federal agency will have much more to consider with the advent of multi-jurisdictional disciplinary enforcement. For immigration lawyers, the changes taking place not only require that we be sensitive to differences between the ethics rules of the states, but also that we pay close attention to the very different approach to discipline which has been introduced by the federal government. The aims of the system now implemented for the discipline of practitioners before DOJ and DHS go deeper than simply ensuring that particular forms of our conduct conform with agency expectations. This was brought into sharp focus by the Department of Justice rebuttal to the wide opposition, reflected in the comments section of its June 27, 2000, Final Rule, to any federal government regulation of professional conduct:

> However, as we have tried to emphasize in this final rule, the Department's imperatives, including preserving the integrity of the Board, the Immigration Courts, and the Service, ensuring the important and proper discharge of statutory duties under the immigration laws of the United States, and safeguarding a vulnerable client population, support continuing and improving the reasonable and fair regulation of such conduct.[6]

Certainly, "safeguarding a vulnerable client population" is something that immigration lawyers know a great deal about. It is also something that the rules concerning the lawyer-client relationship in the state systems, which have been developed over many years and may be based on the extensive provisions of Model Rules 1.1 through 1.18, are well positioned to address. The federal rules for practitioners, on the other hand, do not deal nearly so much with conduct offensive to individuals as they do with conduct offensive to the government. Consequently, referrals to state ethics authorities, now provided for under 8 CFR §1003.106(d), should remain the norm for prompting disciplinary action in those regrettable instances where mistreatment of clients may have occurred.

The references to preserving the integrity of administrative entities and to ensuring the proper discharge of statutory duties in defending regulation of the professional conduct of those who have a professional responsibility to oppose, sometimes, federal government policy and conduct are, in the final analysis, puzzling and worrisome. If anything concrete is suggested by the statement of these imperatives, it is that vigilance over the workings of the federal executive disciplinary system for immigration practitioners is surely in order.

With the onset of the new world of multi-jurisdictional disciplinary enforcement, it seems especially important also to re-concentrate our focus on the public part, which it is our honor to perform as immigration lawyers. By continuing to represent zealously and well the persons who have entrusted to us their interests, and by doing what we are able to promote the fair operation of the systems of justice in which we participate, we perform a role as vital as that of any government agency, both for our clients and for the public-at-large.

---

[6] 65 Fed. Reg. 39524.

EXHIBIT

ABA MODEL RULE 5.5

LAW FIRMS AND ASSOCIATIONS
UNAUTHORIZED PRACTICE OF LAW;
MULTIJURISDICTIONAL PRACTICE OF LAW

In considering multi-jurisdictional practice in today's society, practitioners must consider the latest amended version of ABA Model Rule 5.5, the text of which follows:

(a) A lawyer shall not practice law in a jurisdiction in violation of the regulation of the legal profession in that jurisdiction, or assist another in doing so.

(b) A lawyer who is not admitted to practice in this jurisdiction shall not:

(1) except as authorized by these Rules or other law, establish an office or other systematic and continuous presence in this jurisdiction for the practice of law; or

(2) hold out to the public or otherwise represent that the lawyer is admitted to practice law in this jurisdiction.

(c) A lawyer admitted in another United States jurisdiction, and not disbarred or suspended from practice in any jurisdiction, may provide legal services on a temporary basis in this jurisdiction that:

(1) are undertaken in association with a lawyer who is admitted to practice in this jurisdiction and who actively participates in the matter;

(2) are in or reasonably related to a pending or potential proceeding before a tribunal in this or another jurisdiction, if the lawyer, or a person the lawyer is assisting, is authorized by law or order to appear in such proceeding or reasonably expects to be so authorized;

(3) are in or reasonably related to a pending or potential arbitration, mediation, or other alternative dispute resolution proceeding in this or another jurisdiction, if the services arise out of or are reasonably related to the lawyer's practice in a jurisdiction in which the lawyer is admitted to practice and are not services for which the forum requires pro hac vice admission; or

(4) are not within paragraphs (c)(2) or (c)(3) and arise out of or are reasonably related to the lawyer's practice in a jurisdiction in which the lawyer is admitted to practice.

(d) A lawyer admitted in another United States jurisdiction, and not disbarred or suspended from practice in any jurisdiction, may provide legal services in this jurisdiction that:

(1) are provided to the lawyer's employer or its organizational affiliates and are not services for which the forum requires pro hac vice admission; or

(2) are services that the lawyer is authorized to provide by federal law or other law of this jurisdiction.

See ABA Center for Professional Responsibility at www.abanet.org/cpr/mrpc/rule_5_5.html.

Examples: In-house counsel (but shall not provide personal service to company employees); federal prosecutors; law professors in charge of clinics.

See www.law.washington.edu/courses/andrews/B510_Su04/Documents/sum04pr_ABA_Model_Rules_Overview_Complete.htm.

AN IMMIGRATION PRACTITIONER'S GUIDE TO THE RULES AND PROCEDURES OF PROFESSIONAL CONDUCT WHEN REPRESENTING CLIENTS BEFORE THE EOIR, BIA, AND DHS

by Royal F. Berg and Moises Hernandez[*]

INTRODUCTORY COMMENTS

On June 27, 2000, the U.S. Department of Justice published the Final Rules and Procedures of Professional Conduct for Immigration Practitioners (the Rules), 65 Fed. Reg. 39513–34.[1] The Rules, which became effective one month after publication, applies to all attorneys and other representatives who practice before the Executive Office of Immigration Review (EOIR), the Board of Immigration Appeals (BIA), and the Department of Homeland Security (formerly DOJ-INS). The Rule outlines the authority of the EOIR and DHS to investigate complaints of misconduct by practitioners who conduct business before each of these bodies, and provides for the EOIR to impose sanctions. It outlines various grounds for imposing sanctions and details the manner for conducting disciplinary procedures. It also reinstates the authority of the BIA as reviewing body of disciplinary decisions (instead of a Disciplinary Commission as set forth in the proposed rule, published in 1998). Among the reasons noted by DOJ-EOIR for the amendment to the rules and procedures are the following[2]:

1. To protect the public.
2. To preserve the integrity of immigration procedures and adjudications.
3. To maintain high professional standards among immigration practitioners.
4. To clarify the standard of professional conduct.
5. To provide for an effective process for dealing with alleged violations of the standards.

Among the significant elements contained in the Rules are various provisions that some have challenged as sharply punitive of advocates who practice before the immigration court and DHS.[3] This article attempts to highlight some of the key provisions attorneys need to be mindful of in the course of their advocacy and to offer recommendations for attorneys who regularly practice before the EOIR, the BIA, and DHS.

While the final Rules attempt to reply to some of the concerns voiced by practitioners during the commenting period of the Proposed Rules, the Rules still contain many provisions that can be viewed as needlessly severe. Some practitioners have expressed concerns that these Rules may have the possible effect of chilling an attorney's zealous advocacy of each client he or she represents before the EOIR, the BIA, or DHS. As attorneys, it is incumbent upon us to always be vigilant of regulatory provisions that restrict or threaten to hamper our ability to exercise our fundamental role as advocates for our clients. This is especially true when these regula-

---

[*] **Royal F. Berg** is a sole practitioner who has served as chair of the AILA Chicago Chapter and as chair of the AILA-EOIR Liaison Committee from 1997–2000. He currently serves on the AILA Board of Governors. He has also served as chair of the Immigration and Nationality Law Committee of the Chicago Bar Association. Berg has been a member of AILA since 1985. Berg is a frequent writer and lecturer and concentrates his practice in the areas of family, asylum, removal defense, and administrative and judicial review.

Moises Hernandez is an immigration attorney with The Midwest Immigrant and Human Rights Center in Chicago and an AILA member. He graduated from Loyola School of Law in Chicago in 2002, where he was a Child Law Fellow in the Civitas Program. A native of San Luis Potosi Mexico, Hernandez immigrated to the United States with his parents and siblings in 1976 at the age of seven. He majored in English Literature in college and worked as a child welfare social worker for five years before attending law school.

[1] *Also see* AILA InfoNet at Doc. No. 00062701 (June 27, 2001).

[2] *See* DOJ-EOIR Press Release of June 27, 2000, and DOJ-EOIR Fact Sheet, June 27, 2000.

[3] When the Proposed Rules where published in 1998, organizations such as AILA and the ABA—as well as private practitioners—submitted critical comments. AILA members also submitted objections to specific provisions of the Proposed rules and requested that the period to submit comments be extended. This request was denied.

tions are designed and enforced by the very government agencies whose decisions we regularly challenge in court.

CONCERNS AND CRITICISMS OF THE RULES

The Rules do not apply to the trial attorneys who appear before the EOIR and the BIA. A nongovernment attorney needs to be aware, when practicing before the EOIR or the BIA, that he or she is not on equal footing with regard to possible sanctions. While the government attorneys are subject to DOJ regulations and disciplinary proceedings, the government attorneys are not subject to some of the shaming provisions provided for under the Rules.[4]

The very fact that we know so little about these DOJ rules and procedures says a great deal about which attorneys the government has made a priority to sanction. Where can you find the names of sanctioned government trial attorneys that practice before the EOIR and BIA? Good question. By contrast, the names of sanctioned nongovernment attorneys are featured on the World Wide Web and posted on the bulletin boards at the various branches of the EOIR. Are government attorneys who are sanctioned by a state or federal bar subject to immediate suspension and cut off from their livelihoods? We don't know the answer to this because it is not publicized.

The Rules provide for a procedure in which authorizes both the EOIR and the DHS to conduct investigations of complaints of misconduct by attorneys that conduct business before each of these bodies, and the BIA has authority to impose sanctions. The BIA also has authority over appeals of disciplinary decisions. It is a legitimate criticism of this procedure to raise concerns over the independence of the trier of fact. The BIA is the same agency whose decisions the private attorneys routinely challenge in federal court in the course of their regular advocacy. Whether the BIA will issue decisions without an opinion in disciplinary cases is another matter that has not been made clear. This could have serious implications for the appeal of a disciplinary decision to the federal court.

Also raising questions of the independence of the Rules is the fact that they were drafted by the EOIR with extensive input from the INS (now DHS). Again, this is the very agency that we regularly oppose and whose decisions we challenge before the immigration court in the course of our regular advocacy.

The Rules outline not only the grounds for which an attorney can be disciplined but also the procedures for investigating complaints of misconduct and for imposing sanctions. However, these systems and procedures are largely duplicative because all attorneys who practice before the immigration court or DHS are already subject to the rules of professional conduct and investigation and sanction procedures of the respective state and or federal bars of which they are members.[5]

Failure to respond within 30 days to a Notice of Intent to Discipline (NID) "shall constitute an admission of the allegations in the Notice of Intent to Discipline and no further evidence with respect to such allegations need be adduced."[6] Note that failure to reply to an NID does not result in the proceeding going forward with a complaining party still bearing the burden of making a factual showing regarding the alleged wrongdoing before a trier of fact. Rather, this failure to comply with a deadline is paramount to a conclusive finding on the facts.

The overall tone of the grounds for sanctions and some of the shortcut procedural provisions have a distinctly punitive tone and slant against private practitioners. It is difficult to see how the particular tone and bent of the Rules help further the stated purpose of the rules as amended (*i.e.*, to protect the public, preserve the integrity of immigration proceedings and adjudications, and maintain a high professional standard among practitioners), and they may very well have a chilling effect on the advocacy of attorneys.

THE GROUNDS

The following is a section-by-section review of each of the 13 different grounds listed in 8 CFR

---

[4] DOJ-EOIR Fact Sheet of June 27, 2000. For detailed discussion of comments regarding this provision, see 65 Fed. Reg. 39522, Sections 3.109 and 292.3-Discipline of Government Attorneys/Immigration Judges.

[5] According to Jennifer Barns, EOIR Bar Counsel, as many as 70 percent to 80 percent of sanctions imposed under the Rules have been reciprocal sanctions, that is, sanctions imposed as a direct result of the attorney first being sanctioned by a state or federal bar.

[6] 8 CFR §1003.105(d).

§1003.102. Note that this list of grounds is not exclusive.

The introductory paragraph of §1003.102 states:

It is deemed in the public interest for an adjudicating official or the Board to impose disciplinary sanctions against any practitioner who falls within one or more of the categories enumerated in this section but these categories do not constitute the exclusive grounds for which disciplinary sanctions may be imposed in the public interest. Nothing in this regulation should be read to denigrate the practitioner's duty to represent zealously his or her client within the bounds of law.

In 8 CFR §1003.102, the rules list 13 separate "categories" for which a practitioner "shall be subject to disciplinary sanctions in the public interest":

8 CFR §1003.102(a)

Prohibits charging or receiving either directly or indirectly, any fee or compensation, which "shall be deemed to be grossly excessive."

The factors to be considered include the time and labor required; the novelty and difficulty of the questions involved and the skill required to perform the legal services properly; the likelihood if apparent to the client that the acceptance of the particular employment will preclude other employment by the attorney; the fee customarily charged in the locality for similar legal services; the amount involved and the results obtained; the time limitations imposed by the client or the circumstances; the nature and length of the professional relationship with the client; and the experience, reputation, and ability of the attorney or attorneys performing the service.

The explanation of this provision in the Preamble to the rules, published in the *Federal Register* states that the primary purpose is to protect clients not to interfere with attorney-client fee arrangements, adding that the "grossly excessive" standard is higher than the reasonable fees" standard of the ABA Model Rules.

The Preamble goes on to state that the "expert jurists" in immigration law who command higher fees for their services than other immigration practitioners would not be in violation based solely on their fee.

8 CFR §1003.102(b)

Prohibits bribing, attempting to bribe, coercing, or attempting to do so, "by any means whatsoever, any person ... to commit any act or to refrain from performing any act in connection with any case." This provision is simple, straightforward, and all encompassing!

8 CFR §1003.102(c)

Prohibits knowing or with reckless disregard making a false statement of material fact or law, or willfully misleading, misinforming, threatening, or deceiving any person concerning any material and relevant matter relating to a case.

The rule also provides that if a practitioner has offered material evidence and comes to know of its falsity, the practitioner "shall take appropriate remedial measures," but does not describe what those measures are, or how to handle the ethical dilemma of not betraying a client's confidence.

The Preamble states that subsection (c) would not preclude "pursuing a practitioner who prepares false or misleading unsigned documents, although the ability to prove who prepared such documents might be difficult." The Preamble further notes that, "Immigration Judges across the country have indicated that the filing of false or fraudulent documents is a growing problem."

8 CFR §1003.102(d)

Prohibits soliciting "professional employment through in-person or live telephone contact or through the use of runners, from a prospective client with whom the practitioner has no family or prior professional relationship, when a significant motive for doing so is the practitioner's pecuniary gain." (Apparently, solicitation would be allowed if we are going to do any cases obtained pro bono.)

The rule allows for mailing advertisement material, unsolicited, if it includes the words "Advertising Material" on the outside of the envelope of any written communication and at the beginning and ending of any recorded communication.

However, such advertising material or a similar solicitation document may not be distributed by "any person in or around the premises of any building in which an immigration court is located." The Preamble asserts that this rule closely resembles a related ABA Model Rule and an IRS regulation.

8 CFR §1003.102(e)

Reads, "is subject to a final order of disbarment or suspension, or has resigned with an admission of misconduct," in the jurisdiction of any state, territory, commonwealth, the District of Columbia, any federal court, or before any executive department, board, commission, or other governmental unit. It is under this category, that the EOIR already has disbarred 11 lawyers.

8 CFR §1003.102(f)

Prohibits knowing or with reckless disregard, making a false or misleading "communication" about one's qualifications or services. This category makes a communication false or misleading if, (1) it "contains a material misrepresentation of fact or law, or omits a fact necessary to make the statement considered as a whole not materially misleading, or, (2) contains an assertion about the practitioner on his or her qualifications or services that cannot be substantiated."

Subsection (f) also prohibits an attorney from stating or implying that he or she has been recognized or certified as a specialist in immigration and/or nationality law, unless such certification is granted by the appropriate state regulatory authority, or by an organization that has been approved by the appropriate state regulatory authority to grant such certification.

In other words, a practitioner cannot say he or she is a specialist in immigration law, unless the practitioner's state allows him or her to say so. It is the authors' understanding that only Texas and California do so. Can an attorney say his or her practice is limited to or concentrated in immigration law? The Rules don't specifically address that language.

8 CFR §1003.102(g)

Subsection (g) is the authors' favorite. It prohibits engaging in "contumelious or otherwise obnoxious conduct." *Black's Law Dictionary* defines "contumelious" as "willfully stubborn and disobedient conduct, commonly punishable as contempt of court."

The Preamble adds:

Nothing in this provision is intended to impinge upon a practitioner's zealous representation of his or her client. However, even zealous representation does not entitle a practitioner to engage in contumelious or obnoxious conduct. Immigration Judges were recently given contempt authority in section 304 of IIRAIRA. (Emphasis added.)

However, the Preamble notes, this authority will be exercised only after the Department issues regulations, which "will be published in the near future." If these agencies consider something that began four years ago to be a recent event, it is anyone's guess what "near future" means.

The Preamble does state that the contempt regulations are expected to provide that a practitioner can be disciplined under the Rules of Professional Conduct when that practitioner has been sanctioned for contemptuous conduct by an immigration judge under the judge's contempt power under INA §240(b)(1).

Many have speculated that INS has been fighting the contempt powers regulations for the last four years, and was responsible for precluding the trial attorneys from being included in the Rules of Professional Responsibility.

8 CFR §1003.102(h)

Includes having been found "guilty of, or pleaded guilty or nolo contendere to, a serious crime, ... [which] includes any felony and any lesser crime ... that involves interference with the administration of justice, false swearing, misrepresentation fraud, willful failure to file income tax returns, deceit, dishonesty, bribery, extortion, misappropriation, theft, or an attempt, or a conspiracy or solicitation of another, to commit a serious crime."

8 CFR §1003.102(i)

Includes knowingly or with reckless disregard, falsely certifying a copy of a document as being a true and complete copy of an original. **Note: Be careful about what you certify!!**

8 CFR §1003.102(j)

Includes engaging in "frivolous behavior in a procedure before an immigration court, the Board, or any other administrative appellate body." The rule describes this in broad terms, stating that a practitioner engages in frivolous behavior when "he or she knows or reasonably should have known that his or her actions lack an arguable basis in law or fact, or are taken for an improper purpose, such as to harass or to cause unnecessary delay."

The practitioner's signature on any "file, application, motion, appeal, brief, or other document constitutes certification by the signer that the signer has read the filing, application, motion, appeal, brief, or other document, and that to the best of his knowledge, information, and belief formed after inquiry reasonable under the circumstances, the document is well-grounded in fact and is warranted by existing law or by a good faith argument for the extension, modification, or reversal of existing law or the establishment of new law, and is not interposed for any improper purpose."

8 CFR §1003.102(k)

Includes engaging in conduct that constitutes ineffective assistance of counsel, as previously determined in a finding by the Board or immigration judge in an immigration proceeding, and a disciplinary complaint is filed within one year of the finding.

In other words, if a practitioner is found to have been ineffective for something he or she did or did not do 10 years ago, that practitioner can be disciplined if a complaint is filed within one year of the finding, not within one year of what the practitioner did or did not do.

This is particularly troubling, in that, often we have to allege ineffective assistance to get a case reopened, and state why we have not filed a complaint with the state disciplinary authority. *See Matter of Lozada*, 19 I&N Dec. 637 (BIA 1988). Now, a finding of ineffective assistance will also lead to discipline by EOIR, if a complaint is filed within one year of the finding.

8 CFR §1003.102(l)

Includes repeatedly failing to appear for scheduled hearings in a timely manner and without good cause. The Preamble notes that the provision does not define the number of occasions that will amount to "repeated" failures to appear, and notes the "good cause element" is more than what is provided in a similar rule that the Social Security Administration has issued.

8 CFR §1003.102(m)

Includes assisting any person, other than a practitioner as defined in §1003.101(b) in the performance of activity that constitutes the unauthorized practice of law.

The Preamble adds that:

This ground is necessary ... in order to protect the public from the mistakes of untrained and unqualified individuals, as well as the schemes of unscrupulous immigration practitioners, and reflects the concerns of a number of commenters.

THE PROCEDURE

Provides that the General Counsel of EOIR, "shall file" a petition to suspend immediately from practice before the Board and the immigration courts, any practitioner who has pled guilty, or nolo contendere to a "serious crime" as defined in §1003.102(h).

That section includes "any felony" and "lesser crimes" involving a laundry list of activities and offenses. It is very inclusive. Section 1003.103 also provides that EOIR General Counsel shall petition the Board for immediate suspension of "any practitioner who has been disbarred or suspended on an interim or final basis by, or has resigned with an admission of misconduct, from the highest court of any state, possession, territory, D.C., or any Federal Court."

DHS General Counsel also may petition the Board to include practice before DHS in any suspension order.

8 CFR §1003.103(a)(2)

Provides that upon the filing of the petition, with a certified copy of a court record of conviction or discipline, the Board "shall forthwith enter an order immediately suspending the practitioner" from practice before the Board, the immigration courts, and/or DHS, "notwithstanding" any pending appeal!

The suspension continues until the imposition of a final administrative decision. Therefore, our ability to earn a livelihood, support our families, and represent our clients is taken away, even though we may win a reversal of a discipline order by our state bar!

The Rules do provide that the Board may set aside an immediate suspension order "upon good cause shown," when it is in the "interest of justice to do so," without an explanation of what that means. Perhaps it means, when it is in the interests of the Department of Justice to do so.

8 CFR §1003.103(b)

Provides that the Office of General Counsel of the EOIR "shall promptly initiate summary disciplinary proceedings against any practitioner" who is subject to immediate suspension. These summary disciplinary proceedings are commenced with the issuance of a Notice of Intent to Discipline, "accompanied by a certified copy of the order, judgment, and/or record evidencing the underlying criminal conviction, discipline, or registration."

8 CFR §1003.103(c)

Provides that any practitioner who has been convicted, or has pleaded guilty or nolo contendere, or who has been disbarred, suspended, or resigned, must notify the Office of the General Counsel of

EOIR within 30 days. This duty to notify applies only to convictions and orders of discipline entered on or after August 28, 2000. Failure to notify may result in immediate suspension and "other final discipline."

8 CFR §1003.104

Provides that "any individual" may file complaints. Though complaints must be filed in writing, complainants do not have to use the new Form EOIR-44. Complaints involving behavior before the Board or the immigration courts are filed with the EOIR General Counsel. Complaints concerning actions before DHS are filed with the General Counsel of that agency and are dealt with pursuant to the procedures outlined at §292.3(d).

The Rules provide that the General Counsel for EOIR "shall notify" the General Counsel of DHS of any complaint that pertains in "whole or in part" to a matter involving the Immigration Service. No doubt, the EOIR will broadly interpret this provision.

8 CFR §1003.104(b)

Provides that either upon receipt of a complaint or on its own initiative, the Office of the General Counsel of the EOIR "will initiate" a "preliminary inquiry." A client or former client waives any "attorney-client privilege" and any other applicable privilege to the extent necessary to conduct the inquiry and any subsequent proceedings.

8 CFR §1003.104(c)

Provides that the Office of the General Counsel of the EOIR "prior to the issuance of the Notice to Discipline, in its discretion, may issue warning letters, admonitions, and enter into agreements."

8 CFR §1003.104(d)

Provides that the Office of the General Counsel of the EOIR shall refer allegations or information regarding criminal conduct to the "Inspector General, and if appropriate" the FBI. This section further requires EOIR's Office of General Counsel to "coordinate in advance" with the appropriate investigative and prosecutorial authorities within the Department "to ensure that neither the disciplinary process nor criminal prosecutions are jeopardized."

8 CFR §1003.105

Perhaps the most important of the new sections, entitled, "Notice of Intent to Discipline," it details the formal commencement of proceedings. It provides that if upon completion of the preliminary inquiry, the Office of the General Counsel of the EOIR determines that "sufficient prima facie evidence" exists to warrant charging a practitioner with "professional misconduct, … it will issue a Notice of Intent to Discipline" (NID). The NID must be personally served on the practitioner, pursuant to 8 CFR §103.5a. The NID must contain a statement of the charge(s), a copy of the preliminary inquiry report, the proposed disciplinary sanctions, the procedure for filing an answer or requesting a hearing, and the mailing address and telephone number of the Board.

8 CFR §1003.105(c)(1)

Entitled "Answer," this section gives the practitioner 30 days to file an answer with the Board. The practitioner may request an extension of time to answer, but must do so no later than three working days before the time to answer has expired. The practitioner must serve a copy of his or her answer on the Office of the General Counsel, which filed the complaint.

8 CFR §1003.105(c)(2)

Provides that the answer "shall contain" a statement of facts, which constitute the grounds of defense, and shall specifically admit or deny each allegation in the NID. Note that every allegation not denied shall be deemed to be admitted, and proven, and no further evidence concerning that allegation need be "adduced." The practitioner also may submit affidavits, documents, and supporting statements.

8 CFR §1003.105(c)(3)

Provides that the practitioner shall also state in the answer whether he or she wants a hearing. Failure to request a hearing waives the right to do so later.

8 CFR §1003.105(d)(1)

Provides that failure to file a timely answer "shall constitute an admission of the allegations in the NID, and no further evidence with respect to those allegations need be adduced."

Therefore, should you receive an NID, file a timely complete answer with the Board, with a copy to the appropriate Office of the General Counsel, and make sure that you request a hearing. It is also highly advisable that you hire your own counsel in these proceedings. Remember the adage about an attorney who represents himself ....

8 CFR §1003.105(d)(2)

Provides that upon default (apparently the failure to file a timely answer), the Office of General Counsel shall submit to the Board proof of personal service of the NID. The practitioner cannot at this point request a hearing. The Board shall issue a final order adopting the discipline recommended in the NID, with three possible exceptions. These are: (1) if doing so would foster a tendency toward inconsistent disposition for comparable conduct; (2) if it would otherwise be unwarranted; or (3) if it would not be in the interests of justice.

Any final order imposing discipline does not become effective sooner than 15 days from the date of the order to "provide the practitioner an opportunity" to comply with the order, including withdrawing from any pending "immigration matter" and notifying "immigration clients" of the imposition of any sanction.

A practitioner may file a motion to set aside a default order, provided the motion is filed within 15 days of the date of the service of the final order, and the failure to answer was due to "exceptional circumstances." That term is followed by "(such as serious illness of the practitioner or death of an immediate relative of the practitioner, but not including less compelling circumstances) beyond the control of the practitioner."

The language tracts the statutory provision for filing a motion to reopen an in absentia hearing; however, that provides for 180 days to file those motions, not the 15 days given by the Rules if we fail to file an answer to an NID.

8 CFR §1003.106

Proves that upon the filing of an answer, the Chief Immigration Judge shall appoint an immigration judge as an "adjudicating official." This section also provides that the Director of EOIR may appoint an administrative law judge as an adjudicating official. The adjudicating official cannot be the complainant in the case, or be someone who the practitioner regularly appears before.

If a hearing has been requested, the adjudicating official shall designate the time and place of the hearing. "Due regard" is to be given to the location of the practitioner's practice or residence, the convenience of the witnesses, and "other relevant factors."

This section further provides that the practitioner shall be afforded "adequate time" to prepare his or her case before the hearing. Prehearing conferences may be scheduled in the discretion of the adjudicating official, and any settlement agreements reached after the NID are subject to final approval by the adjudicating officer, and by the Board if the practitioner did not file an answer.

The Rules provide that the practitioner may be represented by counsel and shall have a reasonable opportunity to examine the evidence, present evidence, and cross-examine witnesses. Once again, don't try to represent yourself!!!

Counsel for the government shall bear the burden of proving the NID's allegations. Hearings are to be conducted like other hearings before an immigration judge, and will be open to the public, unless the adjudicating officer determines otherwise.

In the interests of protecting the witnesses, the parties, or the public interest, the adjudicating official may limit the attendance or hold a closed hearing.

8 CFR §1003.106(a)(2)

Provides that if the practitioner fails to appear at the hearing, the adjudicating official "shall then proceed and decide the case in the absence of the practitioner." Any final in absentia order, shall not take effect sooner than 15 days after the issuance of the final order. A practitioner can file a motion to set aside an in absentia order within 15 days of the issuance, provided that the practitioner's failure to appear was due to the exceptional circumstances beyond the control of the practitioner.

8 CFR §1003.106(b)

Provides that the adjudicating official is to render a decision as soon as practicable after the hearing considering the entire record. If the adjudicating official determines that one or more of the grounds enumerated in the NID have been established by "clear, convincing, and unequivocal evidence," he or she shall then adopt, modify, or amend the disciplines recommended. If the adjudicating official determines that the practitioner should be suspended, the official must specify the period of time. Any ground not proven by clear, convincing, and unequivocal evidence, "shall be dismissed."

Like a decision of an immigration judge, the decision of the adjudicating official does not become final, unless appeal is waived, or the time for filing the appeal has expired. The order is not final if a timely appeal is filed.

Upon the issuance of the adjudicating official's decision, either party may appeal to the Board to conduct a de novo review of the record. The practitioner must appeal on Form EOIR-45. Parties must comply with all pertinent provisions for appeals to the Board, as set forth in 8 CFR Part 3, with respect to fees and forms.

There is currently a filing fee of $110 and a requirement of proof of service on the General Counsel's Office, which brought the NID.

8 CFR §1003.106(c)

Provides that review by the Board is "de novo." The decision by the Board is the "final administrative order as provided in 8 CFR §1003.1(d)(2)," and "shall be served upon the practitioner by personal service" pursuant to 8 CFR §103.5a. Any final order does not become effective for 15 days from the date of the order to provide the practitioner an opportunity to comply. The Rules also provide that the final order of the Board "shall be served on the Office of the General Counsel of EOIR and INS. The Board may further require that the notice of the sanctions imposed be posted at the Board, the Immigration Courts or the Service, for "any period of time as determined by the Board."

8 CFR §1003.106(d)

Entitled, "Referral," this section provides that "in addition to, or in lieu of, initiating disciplinary proceedings, the General Counsel of the EOIR may notify any appropriate Federal and/or state disciplinary or regulatory authority of any complaint against a practitioner." Additionally, this section provides that any final action imposing sanctions "shall be reported" to every jurisdiction where the practitioner is admitted or otherwise authorized to practice.

8 CFR §1003.107

Provides a procedure to petition for reinstatement," by which the petitioner is required to prove by "clear, convincing and unequivocal evidence" that "he or she possesses the moral and professional qualifications required" to appear before the Board, the immigration courts or the Service.

The Rules do not define what the "moral and professional qualifications" are. In these days of moral relativism, isn't it great to know that the Department of Justice is the fountain of wisdom when it comes to questions of morality?

The next section entitled, "Confidentiality," provides that "information concerning complaints or preliminary inquiries is confidential, "except as otherwise provided." The practitioner may request a waiver of confidentiality, but the General Counsel may decline to permit it.

Additionally, the General Counsel may disclose the information concerning a complaint or investigation to the public when the "necessity" for disclosing outweighs the "necessity" for preserving confidentiality. And who decides when the confidentiality may be violated? You guessed it, the Office of the General Counsel.

8 CFR §1003.109

Section 8 CFR §1003.109 is identical to 8 CFR §292.3(i). Both sections are entitled, "Discipline of government attorneys," and provide that complaints regarding the conduct of "Department attorneys, Immigration Judges or Board members shall be directed to the Office of Professional Responsibility." Those sections conclude with the following: "If disciplinary action is warranted, it shall be administered pursuant to the Department's attorney discipline procedures."

8 CFR §292 tracks 8 CFR §1003 and are virtually identical, with the focus of 8 CFR §292 being on the Office of the General Counsel of INS. They have the same summary discipline procedures, the same Notice of Intent to Discipline, and the same duty of the practitioner to notify, in this case, the INS of a criminal conviction or discipline.

Like them or not, the Rules are now final. We must learn them and realize they have changed the relationship between our clients and us, and between the government and us. Just how vigorously they will be enforced, or whether they will resist a court challenge, remains to be seen.

RECOMMENDATIONS

There is simply no substitute for knowing the Rules. In the already complex and often unfavorable practice environment, attorneys need to have a firm grasp of not only the substantive law but also the regulation of the agencies and tribunals before which they practice. Be aware that the Rules apply throughout the whole arch of your representation of a client. The Rules apply to your practice from how you obtain your clients and how you assess fees to the actual legal work and representation before the immigration court, DHS, as well as communications with your client and other professionals. *Remember: anyone can file a complaint against you, not just clients, judges, and attorneys—anyone!*

In additional to knowing the Rules, attorneys also are less likely to run afoul of the rules if they are well informed, *e.g.*, by participating in regular workshops on ethics, reading publications, and maintaining mentoring relationships with veteran attorneys.

As a profession of advocates with expert knowledge and sensitivity to the importance of complete and objective procedural nuance as an essential component of our system of law, it is important that we continue to voice objections and make recommendations for changes to the Rules through appropriate forums. Whether in disciplinary proceedings (should an attorney find him or herself in that unfortunate situation), in publications and meetings with DHS and EOIR, through professional organizations such as AILA, it is important that we continue to raise our concerns.

INTERNATIONAL SECURITY, CIVIL LIBERTIES, AND HUMAN RIGHTS AFTER 9/11

*by Robert E. Juceam**

"[T]he pressing exigencies of crisis . . . [provide] the greatest temptation to dispense with fundamental constitutional guarantees which, it is feared, will inhibit government action." *Kennedy v. Mendoza-Martinez*, 372 U.S. 144, 165 (1963) (Goldberg, J.) "Our efforts have been carefully crafted to avoid infringing on constitutional rights while saving American lives"

—*Attorney General John Ashcroft, addressing the Senate Judiciary Committee*

Following the September 11, 2001, attacks in New York and Washington, D.C., and during heightened security concerns ever since, there have been shifts in the public mood and changes that increase local and federal law enforcement powers and restrict or eliminate the legal rights of many. All complicate the role of the lawyer, both government and private bar. These changes include:

- enforcing and defending new laws, many hastily drafted and ambiguous;
- moving the immigration authorities into a new Department of Homeland Security;
- a media culture that makes everyone's opinion a matter of influence, often without disclosure of bias or predisposition;
- increasing authority for delay in arraignment or release of detained persons;
- pressuring to view privileges against disclosure more narrowly;
- using associational and inchoate crimes as a basis for surveillance, arrest, or prosecution;
- broadening of the scope of warrantless searches and seizures;
- potential for trying U.S. permanent residents or citizens in military tribunals;
- placing limitations on lawyer access to detained persons and denying lawyer access to those treated as military detainees;
- increasing authority for interception of telephonic and radio transmissions;
- profiling nationals of certain countries and imposing special registration requirements;
- increasing oversight of lawyers by bar disciplinary authorities.

This paper identifies and catalogs certain major changes in U.S. law, governmental structure and public policy since 9/11 as it bears on aliens entering, remaining in and being deported from the United States, and the resulting legal and cultural impact on U.S. citizens and permanent residents. A brief overview of major initiatives in Europe follows.

I. U.S. RESPONSE TO 9/11

A. Congress Authorized President Bush to Use Necessary Force to Prevent Terrorism

On September 18, 2001, Congress authorized President Bush to use all necessary and appropriate force against nations, organizations, or persons he determined planned, authorized, committed, or aided the terrorist attacks that occurred on September 11, 2001, or harbored such organizations or persons, in order to prevent any future acts of international terrorism against the United States by such nations, organizations or persons. Pub. L. No. 107-40, 115 Stat. 224.

B. President Bush Signed Homeland Security Act of 2002, Pub. L. No. 107-296, 116 Stat. 2135

1. Created Department of Homeland Security (DHS) headed by the new Secretary of Homeland Security, former Pennsylvania Governor, Tom Ridge.

2. Migration of Immigration and Naturalization Service (INS) to DHS.

   a. Protection of the borders and inspection of arriving aliens' documents implemented by U.S. Customs and Border Patrol (CBP).

   b. Enforcement of immigration and customs laws implemented by U.S. Immigration and Customs Enforcement (ICE).

   c. Issuance and adjudication of visa and naturalization petitions, asylum applications and immigration services transitioned into U.S. Citizenship and Immigration Services (USCIS).

C. Executive Order 13224 of September 23, 2001

1. Blocked property and prohibited transactions with persons who commit, threaten to commit, or support terrorism.

2. Declared national emergency because:

   a. "the continuing and immediate threat of further attacks on United States nationals or the United States constitute an unusual and extraordinary threat to the national security, foreign policy, and economy of the United States." 66 Fed. Reg. 49079 (Sept. 23, 2001).

---

* Copyright © **Robert E. Juceam**, 2002, 2003, 2004. All rights reserved. Revised August 2004. The assistance of the following individuals at Fried, Frank, Harris, Shriver & Jacobson LLP in the preparation of this outline is gratefully acknowledged: associate Dian R. Gray, summer associates Marc Romanoff and Victor Suthammanont, and intern Raquel Aragon.

b. Froze U.S. assets of groups, corporations and individuals identified as supporters of terrorism.

D. Continuation of the National Emergency

Notice continues for another year the national emergency declared on September 23, 2001, with respect to persons who commit, threaten to commit, or support terrorism. 68 Fed. Reg. 55189 (Sept. 18, 2003).

E. Change in Consciousness/Attitude Toward Immigrants, Asylees, Refugees

1. Increased detention. Identities of detainees, basis for detention, and detention location withheld.

2. Deceleration of the refugee application process.

   a. Dramatic drop in the number of refugees admitted to the United States since September 11, 2001.

   b. Of the 70,000 authorized slots available in 2002, the United States admitted only 27,500 refugees, the lowest number in over 20 years. *See* Mae M. Chang, "Security Roadblock to Refugees: U.S. Admission Rate Looks to Remain Low," *N.Y. Newsday*, Sept. 26, 2002; George Lardner, Jr., "U.S. Welcomes Fewer Refugees: '02 Admissions Had Ripple Effect in Post-9/11 World, Report Says," *Washington Post*, May 30, 2003.

   c. In 2003, the State Department was authorized to admit 50,000 refugees, but did not meet that number. In part this is a result of Attorney General Ashcroft having ordered a review of existing refugee files for ties to terrorist groups. *See* Greg Krikorian and Patrick J. McDonnell, "Ashcroft Orders Review of Asylum Cases," *L.A. Times*, Sept. 26, 2002.

   d. The U.S. Committee for Refugees reported in its World Refugee Survey 2003 that:

   i. The United States essentially has closed its doors after 9/11; and

   ii. This has had a ripple effect on other nations, who have also chosen to follow suit by admitting fewer refugees. *See* George Lardner, Jr., "U.S. Welcomes Fewer Refugees: '02 Admissions Had Ripple Effect in Post-9/11 World, Report Says," *Washington Post*, May 30, 2003.

3. New security procedures for nationals from certain countries.

   a. In November 2001, the State Department tightened the visa approval process for young men between the ages of 16 and 45 from 26 Arab and Muslim countries. *See* Neil Lewis and Christopher Marquis, "Visa Approval Tightened for 26 Countries: FBI Scrutiny For Men From Arab, Muslim Nations," *San Francisco Chronicle*, Nov. 10, 2001.

   b. The new visa security checks procedures required up to 20 days to process but actually delays have been much longer.

   c. These procedures apply to nationals of the following countries: Afghanistan, Algeria, Bahrain, Djibouti, Egypt, Eritrea, Indonesia, Iran, Iraq, Jordan, Kuwait, Lebanon, Libya, Malaysia, Morocco, Oman, Pakistan, Qatar, Saudi Arabia, Somalia, Sudan, Syria, Tunisia, Turkey, the United Arab Emirates, and Yemen.

4. Reforms in the immigration adjudication process.

   a. New regulation revamped the structure and procedures of the Board of Immigration Appeals (BIA) after 9/11, 67 Fed. Reg. 54,878 (2002) (to be codified at 8 CFR pt. 3), *posted on* AILA InfoNet at Doc. No. 02082640 (Aug. 26, 2002).

   b. The four objectives of the rule are to:

   i. Eliminate current backlog of cases pending before the Board.

   ii. Eliminate unwarranted delay in adjudicating administrative appeals.

   iii. Utilize the resources of Board more efficiently.

   iv. Allow more resources to be allocated to resolving cases that present difficult or controversial legal questions.

   c. Key reforms of the regulation include:

   i. Improved streamlining—a single board member will decide simple cases; *see Carriche v. Aschroft*, 335 F.3d 1009 (9th Cir. 2003); a three-member panel will address difficult or novel issues.

   ii. Deference to fact-findings of immigration judges—the Board will review factual issues in appeals from immigration judges using a "clearly erroneous" standard. Decisions of DHS will continue to be reviewed under a *de novo* standard of review.

   iii. Reasonable deadlines for completing Board decisions—there will be a shortened time period for transcript production, briefing, and adjudicating appeals.

   iv. The size of the Board has been reduced from 19 members to 11 members.

   See IVC5 (Due Process Issues in the Reform).

   d. Third Circuit urge Congress and Judiciary to reform asylum process.

   In August 2004, the Third Circuit Court of Appeals "call[ed] on Congress, the Department of Justice, the Department of Homeland Security and the BIA to improve the structure and operation of the system, so that all may have the confidence that the ultimate disposition of a removal case bears a meaningful connection to the merits of the petitioner's claim(s) in light of contemporary world affairs," *Berishaj v. Ashcroft*, No. 03-1338, 2004 WL 1746299 (3d Cir. Aug. 5, 2004); see Shannon P. Duffy, "3rd Circuit Urges Congress, Executive Branch to Reform Asylum Process: Panel Labels State Department Reports 'out-of-date,'" *The Legal Intelligencer*, Aug. 9, 2004 available at *www.law.com/jsp/article.jsp?id=1090180304292*.

5. Strict penalties for immigrants' failure to submit changes of address.

   On July 22, 2002, the Department of Justice (DOJ) announced it would begin using criminal penalties against immigrants and foreign visitors who fail to notify the government within 10 days of a change of address. Although such a law has existed since 1952, its strict enforcement is a major policy shift. *See* *http://uscis.gov/graphics/lawsregs/02-32045.pdf* (official notice); *see also* U.S. to require non-citizens to report their addresses at *www.hispanicheritage.com/law/immigrantsreport_08_02.htm* (describing plight of a Palestinian father in North Carolina who was nearly deported for failing to file the required change of address form).

6. Broadening removal process to inland areas.

Effective August 11, 2004, DHS is authorized to use expedited removal procedures with aliens determined to be inadmissible under INA §212(a)(6)(C) or §212(a)(7), apprehended within 100 air miles of a U.S. land border, and who are unable to establish physical presence in the United States continuously for the 14-day period immediately prior to the date of encounter. *See* 69 FR 48877, Aug. 11, 2004, *at www.gpoaccess.gov/fr/index.html*; CBP Publishes Notice of Expansion of Expedited Removal Treatment, *posted on* AILA InfoNet at Doc. No. 04081062 (Aug. 11, 2004).

II. ANTI-TERRORISM MEASURES OF THE UNITED STATES—NEW STATUTORY AND REGULATORY PROSCRIPTIONS POST-9/11

A. Unifying and Strengthening America by Providing Appropriate Tools Required to Intercept and Obstruct Terrorism Act

1. USA PATRIOT Act, Pub. L. No. 107-56, 115 Stat. 272 (2001)

2. Creates new crime of "domestic terrorism." "The term 'domestic terrorism' means activities that—(A) involve acts dangerous to human life that are a violation of the criminal laws of the United States or any State; (B) appear to be intended—(i) to intimidate or coerce a civilian population; (ii) to influence the policy of a government by intimidation or coercion; or (iii) to affect the conduct of a government by mass destruction, assassination, or kidnapping; and (C) occur primarily within the territorial jurisdiction of the United States." USA PATRIOT Act §802 (emphasis added).

3. Establishes mandatory detention of suspected terrorists. An alien may be detained if the Attorney General certifies, based on reasonable belief, that the alien is engaged in terrorism or activity that endangers the national security of the United States. The alien must be charged with a crime within seven days of the detention, placed in removal proceedings, or released. However, if the alien's removal is unlikely in the reasonably foreseeable future, the alien may be detained for additional periods of up to six months if the release of the alien would threaten the national security of the United States or the safety of the community. USA PATRIOT Act §412(a).

4. DOJ's Overview of the USA PATRIOT Act.

    a. Improves U.S. Counter-Terrorism Efforts:

        i. By allowing investigators to use existing tools to investigate organized crime and drug trafficking.

            1. Allows law enforcement to use surveillance against more crimes of terror

            2. Allows federal agents to follow sophisticated terrorists trained to evade detection

            3. Allows law enforcement to conduct investigations without tipping off terrorists

            4. Allows federal agents to ask a court for an order to obtain business records in national security terrorism cases

        ii. Facilitates information sharing and cooperation among government agencies so that they can better "connect the dots".

        iii. Updates the law to reflect new technologies and new threats.

            1. Allows law enforcement officials to obtain a search warrant anywhere a terrorist-related activity occurs.

            2. Allows victims of computer hacking to request law enforcement assistance in monitoring the "trespassers" on their computers.

        iv. Increases the penalties for those who commit terrorist crimes.

            1. Prohibits the harboring of terrorists.

            2. Enhances maximum penalties for various crimes likely to be committed by terrorists.

            3. Enhances conspiracy penalties.

            4. Punishes terrorist attacks on mass transit systems.

            5. Punishes bioterrorists.

Eliminates the statutes of limitations for certain terrorism crimes and lengthens them for other terrorist crimes.

See DOJ, USA PATRIOT Act Overview, available at *www.lifeandliberty.gov*.

5. Several provisions of the USA PATRIOT Act enacted to track terror suspects such as eavesdropping, surveillance, and access to financial and computer records expire at the end of 2005 unless Congress and the President extend them.

In April 2004, President Bush started a campaign to persuade Congress to renew the USA PATRIOT Act, make all of its provisions permanent, expand its reach, and close legal loopholes that deny law enforcement officials tools to fight terror which they have to fight other crime. *See* Press Release, The White House, President Bush Calls for Renewing the USA PATRIOT Act: Remarks by the President on the USA PATRIOT Act, Hershey Lodge and Convention Center, Apr. 19, 2004, *at www.whitehouse.gov/news/releases/2004/04/print/20040419-4.html*.

6. Opposition to repeal sunset provisions.

    a. Concerns about increased powers.

        i. The ACLU, the Electronic Privacy Information Center (EPIC), and other free speech organizations filed a lawsuit in October 2002 under the Freedom of Information Act (FOIA) against the DOJ in an attempt to obtain documents detailing how the USA PATRIOT Act had been used to monitor suspects. *See* Complaint, at *www.aclu.org/Privacy/Privacy. cfm?ID=11040&c=130.*

ii. The suit was dismissed. However, the ACLU did obtain a highly redacted list of the DOJ surveillance orders approved under the Act between October 2001 and January 2003. *See* Bill Wallace, "Revisiting the Patriot Act: Two Years After the Attacks that Inspired the Much-Debated Surveillance Law, Controversy Over it Continues," *PCWorld.com*, Sept. 11, 2003. The text of an admitted 1,228 secret warrants, granted by Attorney General Ashcroft pursuant to the PATRIOT Act, will remain confidential, even to Congress, for the time being. *See* Tanya Weinberg, "Patriot Act, Initiatives Disturb Civil Libertarians; Broward Decree Urges 'Respect,'" *Sun-Sentinel*, May 11, 2003.

b. Secrecy of Department of Justice (DOJ)'s actions.

Almost every aspect of the case, *M.K.B. v. Warden, et al.*, No. 03-6747 (Oct. 6, 2003), was cloaked in secrecy as the matter was being litigated in the district and appellate courts. The docket merely read "In re Petition for Writ of Habeas Corpus." No further information was made available and the proceedings were sealed. The redacted petition for certiorari was the first public filing in the case. On January 2, 2004, the Reporters Committee for Freedom of the Press and several print and broadcast media companies and journalists filed a motion in the Supreme Court seeking leave to intervene in order to monitor and report on the proceedings for the benefit of the public. The motion was denied on February 23, 2004.

c. Threat to privacy and individual rights.

i. *See In re All Matters Submitted to the Foreign Intelligence Surveillance Court*, 218 F. Supp.2d 611 (Foreign Intel. Surveil. Ct. 2002) (ordering the government to comply with its minimization procedures to protect the privacy of Americans in intrusive surveillances and searches). On appeal, the government successfully evaded the Court's imposition of minimization procedures. *See In re Sealed Case No. 02-001*, 310 F.3d 717, 730–34 (Foreign Intel. Surveil. Ct. 2002) (holding that the lower court's adoption of minimization procedures was in error because these procedures were not mandated by FISA as originally enacted, or as amended by the USA PATRIOT Act).

ii. Section 215 of the USA PATRIOT Act authorizes federal agents to examine book and computer records at libraries and forbids libraries from informing patrons that the government is monitoring their reading and computer use. *See* USA PATRIOT Act §§201, 202, 206, 212, 215, 217; *see also* Rene Sanchez, "Librarians Make Some Noise Over Patriot Act; Concerns About Privacy Prompt Some to Warn Patrons, Destroy Records of Book and Computer Use," *Washington Post*, Apr. 10, 2003. The American Library Association formally denounced the USA PATRIOT Act, urging Congress to amend those sections that threaten or abridge the rights of inquiry and free expression. *See* American Library Association, "Resolution on the USA PATRIOT Act and Other Measures that Infringe on Rights of Library Users," 2003 ALA Mid-winter Meeting, available at *www.ala.org /alaorg/oif/usapatriotresolution.html.*

d. Several cities and counties have passed resolutions opposing the USA PATRIOT Act

7. Attorney General's July 2004 Field Report on the USA PATRIOT Act.

a. The USA PATRIOT Act has:

i. Facilitated the coordination and sharing of information in terrorism investigations.

1. By bringing down the wall separating intelligence from law enforcement and greatly enhancing foreign intelligence information sharing.

ii. Strengthened the criminal laws against terrorism.

1. By making it easier to prosecute those responsible for funneling money to terrorists.

2. By protecting against cyberterrorism.

3. By criminalizing attacking a mass transportation system.

iii. Removed a number of significant obstacles that prevented law enforcement from effectively investigating terrorism and related criminal activity.

iv. Modernized federal laws to reflect new technology.

1. Provides new tools to fight terrorists and criminals who use modern technologies to plot their attacks.

2. Enhances existing investigative tools.

3. Promotes cooperation of third parties, such as telecommunications companies, by expressly permitting disclosure of certain records during emergencies.

b. As of May 5, 2004, the DOJ has charged 310 defendants with terrorism-related criminal offenses; 179 of them have been convicted. *See* DOJ, Report from the Field: The USA PATRIOT Act at Work, July 2004, at *www.lifeandliberty.gov/docs/071304_report_from_the_ field.pdf.*

8. New CIA Chief Nominated.

On August 10, 2004, President Bush nominated Congressman Porter Gross (R-FL) as the next Director of the Central Intelligence Agency (CIA). Goss has chaired the House permanent Select Committee on Intelligence since 1997. The President said he would look to Goss to assist him in implementing the recommendations of the 9/11 Commission. *See* Press Release, The White House, President Bush Nominates Congressman Goss as Director of CIA, Aug. 10, 2004, *available at www.whitehouse.gov/news/releases/2004/08/20040810-*

3.html; see 9/11 Commission Report, *infra*. The nomination awaits Senate approval.

B. The 9/11 Commission Report—How Could It Be, and Revamping the Intelligence Community

1. The Commission examined more than "2.5 million pages of documents and interviewed more than 1,200 individuals in 10 countries" including "nearly every senior official from the current and previous administrations" as well as holding "19 days of hearings and [taking] public testimony from 160 witnesses."

2. The Commission found that "[a]cross the government, there were failures of imagination, policy, capabilities, and management."

    a. The hijackers did much that should have drawn the attention of law enforcement and immigration authorities prior to 9/11.

    b. Neither the Bush or Clinton administrations properly understood the magnitude of the threat of terrorism, and domestically, agencies and law enforcement were unprepared for an event like 9/11.

3. The Commission suggests realigning the various intelligence into a "joint command" model, based on the system the military uses to organize the Army, Navy, and Air Force by theaters. They also call for:

    a. The creation of a cabinet position responsible for the unified intelligence community, the National Intelligence Director.

    b. A commitment to moral leadership and diplomacy aimed at winning the ideological war.

    c. For security-related federal funding to be allocated among states according to risk, and not subject to pork-barrel politics.

    d. Integrate the U.S. border security system into a larger network of screening points including the transportation system and access to vital facilities.

    e. Complete a biometric entry-exit screening system.

    f. Raise United States and global border security standards for travel and border crossing.

See 9/11 Commission Report, available at *www.9-11 commission.gov*; *see also* "9-11 Commission Report Recommendations," available at *http://grumet.net/911/recommendations.html*.

4. Senator Kerry, the Democratic Party candidate for President, has endorsed all of the Commission's recommendations. Under pressure from Democrats to act quickly, President Bush announced that he would enact some of the 9/11 commissioners' recommendations including:

    a. the appointment of a new national intelligence director as his principal adviser on countering terrorism; and

    b. the creation of new National Counterterrorism Center to integrate foreign and domestic intelligence.

5. Congressional Hearings on 9/11 Commission Recommendations.

    a. U.S. Senate Committee on Governmental Affairs commenced hearings on "Making America Safer: Examining the Recommendations of the 9-11 Commission," on July 30, 2004, at *http://govt-aff.senate.gov/index.cfm?Fuseaction=Hearings.Detail&HearingID=195*.

    b. House Government Reform Committee commenced hearings on the 9/11 Commission Report to highlight the nexus between the impediments to information sharing and the need for government reorganization on August 3, 2004. *See* Government Reform Committee to Review 9/11 Commission Recommendation, at *http://reform.house.gov/GovReform/News/DocumentSingle.aspx?DocumentID=4697*.

C. Proposed National Security Legislation

1. Domestic Security Enhancement Act of 2003.

    a. Draft proposed legislation entitled Domestic Security Enhancement Act of 2003 dated January 9, 2003, was circulated and quickly dubbed "PATRIOT II." The proposed legislation is available at *www.pbs.org/now/politics/patriot2-hi.pdf*.

    b. The draft national security legislation detailed possible expansion of powers granted under the current USA PATRIOT Act. These powers include:

        i. Expanding the definition of terror suspect to include anyone "'whom the Attorney General or Secretary of State ... has determined that there is reason to believe' has engaged in terrorism as defined in various sections of the U.S. Code, or who falls into a number of other broad categories designated as such."

        ii. Expanding the definition of "designated terrorist organization" to include any organization as the President may designate by executive order or under the authority of the INA, International Emergency Economic Powers Act, or section 5 of the United Nations Participation Act.

        iii. Introducing presumptive pre-trial detention for those charged with the wide array of "terrorist" crimes as defined throughout the statute.

        iv. Providing for expatriation of an American citizen where that citizen is "charged with 'joining, serving in, or providing material support ... to a terrorist organization [which] is engaged in hostilities with the United States, it people, or its national security interests.'" William F. Jasper, "Trading Freedom For Security," *The New American*, May 5, 2003.

        v. The Domestic Security Enhancement Act of 2003 did not become law. However, on December 13, 2003, President Bush signed into law the "Intelligence Authorization Act for Fiscal Year 2004," H.R. 2417, which, among other things, establishes within the Department of the Treasury an Office of Intelligence and Analysis responsible for the receipt, analysis, collation, and dissemination of foreign intelligence and foreign counterintelligence information relating to Treasury department operations. *See* Pub. L. No. 108-177, 117 Stat. 2599 (2003).

2. VICTORY Act.

In August 2003, the Vital Interdiction of Criminal Terrorist Organizations Act of 2003 (VICTORY Act) was proposed. If passed, the VICTORY Act would give law enforcement officials increased subpoena powers, more leeway over wiretap evidence, and authority to classify some drug offenses as terrorism. *See* text of Act, available at www.libertythink.com/VICTORYAct.pdf.

3. STEP Act.

a. Taking the national security crusade further, Rep. Gresham Barrett (R-SC) proposed the Stop Terrorists Entry Program Act of 2003 (STEP Act), H.R. 3075, barring all individuals living in countries known to harbor terrorists from entering the United States after September 11, 2003.

b. The State Department list of these countries includes Cuba, Iran, Iraq, Libya, North Korea, the Sudan, and Syria.

c. The bill is currently before the House Judiciary Committee, which has referred it to the Subcommittee on Immigration, Border Security, and Claims.

4. Computer-Assisted Passenger Prescreening System II (CAPPS II).

a. CAPPS II is a computer-screening program that would have used commercial databases, intelligence information, a centralized terrorist watch list, and list of outstanding warrants to identify passengers for closer scrutiny or exclusion from flights. It is being fundamentally reshaped after much opposition from privacy proponents. *See* Ryan Singel, *Life After Death for CAPPS II?*, WIRED NEWS, July 16, 2004, available at www.wired.com/news/privacy/0,1848,64240,00.html?tw=wn_story_top5; *see also* Valerie Alberto & Dominique Bogaz, "Computer Assisted Passenger Prescreening System ('CAPPS II'): National Security v. Civil Liberties," at www.maxwell.syr.edu/campbell/Library%20Papers/Event%20papers/ISHS/AlbertoBogatz.pdf (presenting an overview of the CAPPS II system—the benefits and risks, including civil liberty concerns, related to the implementation and operation of CAPPS II).

b. The U.S. General Accounting Office (GAO) was asked to determine (1) the development status and plans for CAPPS II; (2) the status of CAPPS II in addressing key developmental, operational and public acceptance issues; and (3) other challenges that could impeded the successful implementation of the system.

   i. GAO found the transportation Security Administration (TSA) faces challenges that may impede the success of CAPPS II including:

      1. key activities in the development of CAPPS II have been delayed.

      2. TSA has not established a complete plan that identifies specific system functionality. *See* GAO Report to Congressional Committees, "Computer-Assisted Passenger Prescreening System Faces Significant Implementation Challenges," Feb, 2004, available at *www.gao.gov/new.items/d04385.pdf.*

D. Enhanced Border Security and Visa Entry Reform Act of 2002

1. Student Exchange Visitor Information System (SEVIS).

a. Section 501 of the Border Security Act mandates that the government establish electronic means to maintain, monitor, and verify current records on non-immigrant foreign students and exchange visitors during the course of their stay in the United States. *See* 8 USC §1761. As of August 1, 2003, all institutions and organizations that accept foreign students or exchange visitors must comply with the government's computerized data management system called Student Exchange Visitor Information System (SEVIS). *See* "Immigration: Student and Exchange Visitor Information System (SEVIS) available at *www.ice.gov/graphics/sevis/index.htm.*

b. SEVIS is an internet-based software application that transmits electronic information and event notification to ICE and the Department of State throughout the student's stay in the United States. The program requires DHS to notify institutions of higher education when aliens accepted for those institutions are admitted to the United States on student visas and requires colleges to report to ICE within 30 days of the school's registration whether or not the students registered for classes. 8 USC §1761.

c. Universities must electronically transmit current data to ICE and the Department of State on foreign students on a regular basis, such as where they live, their majors, changes of address or name, when a student falls out of status, i.e. fails to carry a full course load, working illegally, dropped out of the program, etc. 8 USC §1761. The SEVIS database is crosschecked against other government databases in order to identify possible national security threats. Institutions that fail to ensure that their foreign students register risk losing the ability to enroll foreign students.

2. Restrictions on issuance of visas to nonimmigrants from countries believed to be state sponsors of terrorism.

a. Section 306 of the Border Security Act provides that no nonimmigrant visas will be issued "to any alien from a country that is a state sponsor of international terrorism unless the Secretary of State determines, in consultation with the Attorney General and the heads other appropriate United States agencies, that such alien does not pose a threat to the safety or national security of the United States." 8 USC §1735.

3. National Security Entry-Exit Registration System (NSEERS)—Special Registration.

a. Section 302 of the Border Security Act calls for the implementation of an integrated entry and exit data system for all U.S. ports of entry. 8 USC §1731. The Act mandates that the Attorney General and Secretary of the State establish a database containing the arrival and departure data from machine-readable visas, passports, and other travel and entry documents possessed by aliens. *Id.* Additionally, all security databases relevant to making a determination of admissibility are to be made interoperable. *Id.*

  i. The requirement that all passports used by travelers from the 22 countries in the Visa Waiver Program (VWP) must be machine-readable becomes effective on October 26, 2004.

b. NSEERS Special Registration required men between 16 and 45 years old from countries with suspected terrorist ties, who temporarily reside in the United States, to register with DHS to be fingerprinted, photographed, interviewed, and have their visa documents inspected. The procedures apply to holders of student, business, or tourist visas who are believed to fit the criteria of a potential terrorist. The government would not disclose the criteria. *See* Susan Sachs, "U.S. Will Fingerprint Some Foreign Visitors," *N.Y. Times*, Sept. 9, 2002. Registrants must notify immigration authorities of changes of address, employment, or school; use specially designated ports when they leave the U.S.; and report in person to an immigration officer at the port on their departure date.

c. The first round of Special Registration began on December 16, 2002 and targeted citizens of Iran, Iraq, Libya, Syria, and Sudan. The registration procedure was chaotic and resulted in hundreds of men, many with pending applications to become permanent residents, being arrested and detained on immigration violations.

d. November 15, 2003 marked the one-year anniversary of NSEERS. During that year, approximately 175,000 aliens registered with immigration officials under NSEERS; some registered at airports as they entered the country, others already in the U.S. were required to undergo "call-in" registration. *See* ACLU of Washington "NSEERS Special Registration: Update on Federal Immigration Program" at *www.aclu-wa.org/ISSUES/otherissues/INSSpecialRegTravAlert.html.*

e. Approximately 13,800 persons registered as part of the call-in registration are in the process of being deported, due to immigration status violations, not terrorism charges. *Id.; see also* Press Release, DHS, NSEERS 30-Day and Annual Interview Requirement to Be Suspended (Dec. 1, 2003).

f. After the mass arrests following the initial phase of mandated special registration, many undocumented aliens left to Canada rather than face detention. The asylum process in Canada is more flexible; there is no mandatory registration, and the threat of deportation is less imminent. *See* Sam Stanton & Emily Bazar, "Immigrants Flee From Fear in America," *Sacramento Bee*, Sept. 23, 2003. However, under a United States-Canada accord named the Safe Third Country Agreement, refugee claimants who arrive at Canada border crossings from the United States will automatically be turned back and forced to apply for asylum in the United States. *See* "Canada and U.S. Negotiators Agree to Final Draft Text of Safe Third Country Agreement," at *www.cic.gc.ca/english/policy/safe-third.html*. Many are unaware that they will be precluded from seeking asylum in the United States if they did not file claims for asylum in the first year after their arrival in the United States. *See* Bill Frelick & Patrick Giantonio, "Trapped By the Legacy of Sept. 11," *Ottawa Citizen*, Mar. 19, 2003.

g. On December 24, 2002, a coalition of Muslim-American rights groups filed a class-action lawsuit against the Attorney General and the former-INS seeking a temporary restraining order to stop the arrests and deportation of undocumented immigrants who filed residency applications. However, Santa Ana District Court Judge Alicemarie Stolter refused to grant the TRO, citing the federal court's lack of jurisdiction in immigration matters. *See* "Calif. Judge Refuses to Bar Arrests, Deportation Of Illegal Immigrants," *Associated Press*, Jan. 10, 2003. Peter Schey, an attorney with the Center For Human Rights and Constitutional Law in Los Angeles who represents several immigrants, said, "[i]n light of the mass, warrantless arrests, which we believe to be illegal, it is difficult for us to recommend, in good faith, for people to come forward to register." *Id.*

h. In December 2003, much of NSEERS was suspended. *See* Press Release, "Fact Sheet: Changes to National Security Entry/Exit Registration System (NSEERS)," Dec. 1, 2003, at *www.dhs.gov/dhspublic/display?content=3020.*

  i. Lifts requirement that aliens must re-register after one year (or after thirty days if initially registered at a port-of-entry) of continuous presence in the United States.

  1. request extension or waiver of deadline by when 27 countries in VWP must produce 100 percent biometric passports from October 2004 to November 20, 2006.

  2. Under a new interim rule, the DHS will have discretion to notify individual nonimmigrant aliens subject to NSEERS registration to appear for one or more "continuing registration interviews" to determine whether the alien is complying with the conditions of his or her nonimmigrant visa status and admission. *See* Suspending the 30-Day and Annual Interview Requirements From the Special Registration Process for Certain Nonimmigrants, 68 Fed. Reg. 67577(Dec, 2, 2003) (to be codified at 8 CFR pt. 264).

4. Transition from NSEERS to United States Visitor and Immigrant Status Indicator Technology (US-VISIT).

a. Section 303 of the Border Security Act requires that, by no later than October 26, 2004, the Attorney General and the Secretary of State must (1) issue only machine-readable, tamper resistant visas and other travel and entry documents that use biometric identifiers; and (2) install at all ports of entry of the U.S. equipment and software to allow biometric comparison and authentication of all U.S. visas, passports, and other travel and entry documents issued to aliens. 8 USC §1732.

b. In accordance with congressional mandates requiring the DHS to create an integrated, automated entry-exit system that records the arrival and departure of aliens; that equipment be deployed at all ports of entry to allow for the verification of aliens' identities and the authentication of their travel documents through the comparison of biometric identifier; and that the entry exit system record alien arrival and departure information from these biometrically authenticated documents, the DHS established the US-VISIT. 69 Fed. Reg. 468 (Jan. 5, 2004) (to be codified at 8 CFR pt. 214, 215 and 235).

c. The law provides that the Secretary of Homeland Security or his delegate may require aliens, seeking admission to the United States by air, sea and land ports pursuant to a nonimmigrant visa, to provide fingerprint, photographs or other biometric identifiers upon arrival in or departure from the United States. *Id.* Exemptions apply to certain aliens such as those under the age of 14 or over the age of 79.

d. The DHS launched US-VISIT on January 5, 2004, at 115 airports and cruise ship terminals and 14 seaports. The biometric arrival and departure data the DHS collects from each alien are entered into an automated identification system (IDENT) to be checked against law enforcement and intelligence systems to determine whether the alien is a threat to national security or public safety, or is otherwise inadmissible. By recording more complete arrival and departure data, the law facilitates the development of better methods for identifying aliens who are inadmissible to the United States and those who overstay their lawful admission periods. *See* Siobhan Gorman, "Taking Names at the Border," *National Journal*, May 31, 2003.

e. US-VISIT faced opposition even before the program was implemented. An alliance of directors of the 30 largest airports sent a letter in September 2003 to the DHS advocating a delay in the implementation of the program because they do not know where they will build the screening machines or how airports should redesign terminals to accommodate the new equipment. *See* Bryon Okada, "Airports Ask to Stall Fingerprinting Screening, *Star-Telegram*, Sept. 17, 2003. A GAO report released September 23, 2003 found the program to be a "very risky endeavor." The investigators agreed with the goal of the program, but noted that size of the program plan raised doubts about effective management. Moreover, the report continued, the program's budget has not been sufficiently defined and many details have not been worked out. *See Associated Press*, "GAO Says Program to Track Foreign Visitors is Flawed," Sept. 24, 2003. One critic observed that "US-VISIT does not overtly discriminate against Muslims. But in combination with VWP, US-VISIT will have a predictable discriminatory effect." Shahriar Hafizi, "US-VISIT, the Program to Digitally Photograph and Fingerscan U.S. Visitors: Its Discriminatory Effect, and Its Potential For Abuse," *Findlaw.com*, Feb. 10, 2004.

f. On August 9, 2004, President Bush signed into law H.R. 4417 (Pub. L. No. 108-299) to extend by one year until October 26, 2005, the requirement for VWP countries to have biometrics included in passports. *See* Department of State Press Statement, Extension of requirement for Biometric Passport issuance by Visa Waiver Program Countries (Aug. 10, 2004) at *www.state.gov/r/pa/prs/ps/2004/35066pf.htm*. DHS will be enrolling VWP travelers through US-VISIT beginning on September 30, 2004.

5. Cap On Temporary Work Visa Petitions.

a. On February 17, 2004, USCIS, formerly INS, announced that it had reached its mandated quota of 65,000 H-1B visa petitions for new specialty workers for fiscal year 2004 and would not accept any more

b. On March 9, 2004, USCIS announced that it had reached its limit of 66,000 H-2B visas petitions for unskilled temporary non-agricultural workers for the fiscal year ending September 30, 2004. This federal cap will adversely affect the seasonal U.S. businesses that rely on seasonal foreign workers during the summer months to run their businesses, especially the Maine and New Hampshire tourist businesses.

c. On March 29, 2004, Senator Edward M. Kennedy and Representative Bill Delahunt, Democrats of Massachusetts, submitted the Save the Summer Act of 2004 (H.R. 4052/S. 2252), which would immediately raise the cap on H-2B visas to 106,000 for this year only. Although the legislation has bipartisan congressional support it has not been enacted soon enough to save the summer of 2004; query as to its ultimate prospects.

6. Border Crossing Cards

a. DHS has decided to expand the time restrictions on border crossing cards (BCCs) used by Mexicans to enter the United States for temporary visits from 72 hours to a period of 30 days. As a result, only BCC holders applying for entry for more than 30 days would be subject to processing through US-VISIT. *See* DHS Press Release, "Department Of Homeland Security Announces Expanded Border Control Plans," Aug. 10, 2004, available at *www.aila.org/infonet/fileViewer.aspx?docID=13770*.

E. Federal Initiatives to Assist/Improve the Lives of Undocumented Immigrants

1. Agricultural Job Opportunity, Benefits, and Security Act of 2003—AgJOBS (S. 1645/HR 3142).

a. The bill would allow immigrant farm workers who are already working in the United States to establish legal residency after satisfying certain employment criteria over a period of certain years—a path to legalization through documented record of field work.

i. if worked for 100 days in agriculture between March 1, 2002 and August 31, 2002, qualify for temporary work visa. Could earn legal status if continue working at least 360 days during the next 6 years.

b. The farm worker bill received strong bi-partisan support as well as the support of over 400 organizations. However the bill has stalled in Congress. Sen. Larry Craig (R-ID), one of the chief sponsors of the bill sought to get the measure onto the Senate floor before the end of the year by attaching the bill to an unrelated class action lawsuit reform bill, however Sen. Majority Leader Bill Frist (R-TN) refused to let the Senate consider the bill. The President appears reluctant to embrace the farm workers bill in this election year for fear of being perceived as granting amnesty to illegal aliens.

2. Proposed Temporary Worker Program for Undocumented Immigrants—Guest worker program.

a. On January 7, 2004, President Bush proposed a new temporary worker program that would match willing foreign workers with willing American employers, when no American can be found to fill the jobs. *See* Press Release, The White House, President Bush Proposes New Temporary Worker Program: Remarks by the President on Immigration Policy (Jan. 7, 2004); *see also* "Fact Sheet: Fair and Secure Immigration Reform" (Jan. 7, 2004), *at www.whitehouse.gov/news/releases/2004/01/print/20040107-1.html*. The program offers legal status, as temporary workers, to millions of undocumented workers currently employed in the United States and to those in foreign countries who seek to participate in the program and have been offered employment in the United States. The new legal status offered by the program will last three years and will be renewable, but not permanent; participants must return to their home countries after their employment permits expire. *See id.*

b. This program was to be part of President Bush's new immigration reforms. However the administration has not yet proposed any specific legislation and administration officials told the Senate Foreign Relations Committee in March, 2004, that the President would likely not support any other immigration bills pending in Congress. *See* Rachel L. Swarms, "White House Irks Senators by Inaction on Immigrants," *NY Times*, Mar. 24, 2004.

  i. Republican opposition has eliminated any chance of Congress acting on this proposal this year.

  ii. Critics argue that the proposal was a political ploy for the Latino vote.

3. Safe, Orderly, Legal Visa and Enforcement (SOLVE) Act.

a. Bill drafted by Senator Kennedy (D-Mass) and Representative Gutierrez (D-Ill).

b. Would provide all undocumented workers, not just farm workers, either a green card or permanent legal residence if they prove that they:

  i. Have lived in the United States for five consecutive years.

  ii. Have worked in the United States for at least two of the five years.

  iii. Paid taxes

c. Eligible workers would be required to undergo medical exams and criminal background checks and their spouses and children under the 21 would also qualify for either green cards or permanent legal residence.

4. Development, Relief and Education for Alien Minors (DREAM) Act (S.1545) Student Adjustment Act (H.R. 1684).

a. Opportunity for college-bound children of undocumented immigrants who were brought to the United States illegally to attend a public university in their home state and pay in-state tuition and to gain legal residency, if the children meet all of these criteria:

  i. were under the age of 16 when they entered the country.

  ii. lived in the state for 5 continuous years.

  iii. graduated from an American high school.

  iv. have no criminal record.

  v. have good moral character.

b. Pending in Congress—the bill passed the Senate Judiciary Committee in the Fall of 2003 but has stalled in the full Senate.

c. Proponents of the Bill argue that it gives children who are in the United States through no fault of their own a chance to better themselves and realize the American dream

d. Critics argue that the DREAM Act rewards people who come to the United States illegally; would encourage more people to come to the United States illegally; and forces U.S. citizens to compete for admission and limited tuition assistance programs with illegal aliens.

5. Efforts to facilitate the naturalization for immigrants in the U.S. military.

a. On July 3, 2002, President Bush issued Executive Order 13269 that provides for expedited naturalization for aliens and noncitizens serving in an active duty status in the Armed Forces of the United States during the period of Operation Enduring Freedom. 67 Fed. Reg. 45287 (July 8, 2002).

b. Officially, illegal immigrants cannot join the military. However, in a widely watched case, Army Private Juan Escalante enlisted in the military with a fake green card and was shipped off to Iraq. He too sought citizenship under Executive Order 13269. The military opted not to pursue disciplinary action against Escalante for illegally joining the Army and, on February 11, 2004, Escalante was sworn in as an American citizen. *See* Florangela Davila, "Army Private Receives New Rank: U.S. Citizen," *Seattle Times*, (Feb. 12, 2004); Donatella Lorch, "A Matter of Loyalty: He Joined the Army With a Fake Green Card. Now What?" *Newsweek*, Nov. 3, 2003.

c. The government awarded U.S. citizenship posthumously to 12 noncitizen soldiers who died in service to the United States in Operation Iraqi Freedom.

d. Members of Congress support immigration legislation that expedites the process for legal immigrants who returned from military service in Operation Iraqi Freedom to become U.S. citizens.

i. The House bill cut the time active duty members of the U.S. military must wait before applying for citizenship from three years to one. The Senate bill cut the time to two years. Both versions waive naturalization fees for applicants who are in the military and grant eligibility for immigration benefits to close relatives of citizens or U.S. permanent residents killed on duty in the armed services.

F. State Initiatives

1. Rules for issuance of drivers' licenses changed.

a. At least 20 states prohibit illegal immigrants from obtaining driver's licenses. Under an executive order signed by Governor Jeb Bush, foreigners applying for Florida licenses are given a 30-day temporary permit while police investigate their identification. Exec. Order No. 01-300 (Oct. 11, 2001). At Governor Bush's direction, driver's licenses issued to foreign nationals in Florida, who are in the United States temporarily, expire on the same date that their immigration status expires. This measure was intended to lead to immigration arrests, but law enforcement agencies apparently are not enforcing the measure. *See* Alfonso Chardy, "Police Not Screening For Illegal Foreigners; Officers Unaware of Program Or Don't Know How to Proceed," *Miami Herald*, Jan. 21, 2003.

i. In April 2004, Governor Jeb Bush endorsed a bill (Senate Bill 1360) allowing illegal aliens and foreign nations who reside in Florida to obtain Florida drivers' licenses, provided strict screening requirements are met (such as fingerprinting and background checks) to ensure the applicants are not terrorists. *See* Michael Vasquez & Gary Fineout, "Governor Endorses Illegal-Alien Driving Bill: Gov. Jeb Bush Favors Giving Illegal Immigrants Driver's Licenses, as Long as There are Security Measures to weed out Criminals," *Miami Herald*, Apr. 6, 2004. The bill subsequently died in the Committee on Transportation. *See www.flsenate.gov.*

ii. Congressman Tom Tancredo (R-CO), chairman of the House Immigration Reform Caucus, observed that, "A driver's license can become a 'breeder document' for other documents for establishing false identifies and gaining access to social services and voter registration. It allows you to board airplanes and is basically a domestic passport." *See editorial,* "Ambushed: Governor Joins Brother In Pandering to Illegals," *Vero Beach Press Journal*, Apr. 8, 2004.

iii. Proponents point out that the measure would improve safety on the streets and immigrants would be able to purchase insurance. Critics argue that the measure encourages illegal immigration.

iv. California repealed its law that allowed illegal immigrants to obtain driver's licenses.

1. In Florida and North Carolina, drivers no longer have the option of refusing to be photographed for religious reasons

2. In Massachusetts, the Registry of Motor Vehicles has toughened its enforcement of the law requiring immigrants to show a Social Security card to get a driver's license, effectively altering the purpose of a state-issued I.D. from a document that verified a person's knowledge of the rules of the road to a kind of internal U.S. passport. *See* Kirsten Lombardi, "Out in the Cold," *Boston Phoenix*, Sept. 5, 2002.

3. Maryland's Attorney General addressed the issue of licensing illegal immigrants by issuing an opinion concluding that the state could not make legal presence in the country a prerequisite to obtaining a driver's license, but the Motor Vehicle Administration may require applicants to prove their identity with immigration documents. *See* Nurith C. Aizenman, "Licensing Foreign Drivers Studied," *Washington Post*, Oct. 13, 2003.

4. The American Immigration Lawyers Association (AILA) opposes limiting an immigrant's access to driver's licenses based on immigration status. *See* "AILA Issue Paper: Restricting Immigrant Access to Driver's Licenses" *posted on* AILA InfoNet at Doc. No. 21IP2003, Aug. 9, 2002.

2. Prohibition on inquiring about immigration status.

On April 9, 2004, Maine Governor, John Baldacci signed an Executive Order that prohibits state employees, other than law enforcement officers, from inquiring about or disclosing a person's immigration status, unless necessary for the determination of benefit eligibility of State services, required by law or court order, or necessary to safeguard public health.

3. State law enforcement officers to have jurisdictional authority to enforce federal immigration laws.

a. CLEAR Act of 2003 (HR 2671)—bill pending in the House of Representatives would authorize local law enforcement to detain people solely for immigration violations.

i. Local law enforcement agencies feel pressure to assume the work of immigration officials. Law enforcement agencies that don't agree to enforce immigration laws or to share information about illegal immigrants they apprehend to federal officials risk cuts in their budgets and federal funding.

ii. local law enforcement argue that:

1. immigration laws are complex and they lack the knowledge and expertise in dealing with immigration issues; and

2. the move would destroy the trust/bridges they built with minority/immigrant communities, *i.e.*, immigrants will be reluctant to cooperate in terrorism investigations for fear of deportation.

3. could lead to civil liberties abuses.

iii. Supporters of the bill argue that the number of immigrants and terrorist threats have increased and federal officials need help in enforcing the immigration laws.

Florida and Alabama law enforcement departments are authorize by ICE to arrest and detain immigrants for immigration violations.

b. The Senate version of this bill, Homeland Security Enhancement (HSEA) Act, would authorize local law enforcement officers to investigate, arrest, and detain non-citizens whom they decided are "unlawfully present".

i. This proposed legislation raises similar concerns about potential for abuse: unfair arrests.

ii. mandates that states not issue driver's licenses to illegal aliens.

c. Proposed Ban on Services to Illegal Immigrants.

May be preempted by 8 USC §1601. *League of United Latin American Citizens v. Wilson*, 1998 U.S. Dist. LEXIS 3418 (N.D. Cal. 1998).

III. RESURRECTION OF MILITARY COMMISSIONS TO COMBAT TERRORISM

A. Authority for Military Commissions

1. U.S. Constitution, Article I, Section 8.
2. U.S. Constitution, Article II.
3. Uniform Code of Military Justice, Article 21.

B. History of United States Use of Military Commissions

1. *Ex Parte Quirin*, 317 U.S. 1 (1942).

a. Jurisdiction of military tribunal ordered by President Franklin Roosevelt to try eight German saboteurs who tried to enter the United States secretly during war time was upheld.

b. The Court stated, "Citizenship in the United States of an enemy belligerent does not relieve him from the consequences of a belligerency which is unlawful because in (sic) violation of the law of war. Citizens who associate themselves with the military arm of the enemy government, and with its aid, guidance and direction enter this country bent on hostile acts, are enemy belligerents within the meaning of the Hague Convention and the law of war." *Id.* at 37–38.

2. Application of *Yamashita*, 327 U.S. 1 (1946).

Jurisdiction of military tribunal to try Japanese General Yamashita for war crimes was upheld.

3. *Madsen v. Kinsella*, 343 U.S. 341 (1952).

Jurisdiction of military commission to try a U.S. citizen for murder of her husband, a U.S. serviceman, in occupied Germany in 1950 was upheld.

C. Purpose of Military Commissions

To detain and try noncitizens accused of violating the law of war.

D. Who Would be Subjected to Military Commissions under the November 13, 2001 Executive Order?

1. Order not limited to those accused of war crimes or to the 9/11 attacks or acts related to the attacks.

2. Pertains to non–U.S. citizens who are believed to be members of al Qaeda; who engaged in, aided or abetted, or conspired to commit acts of international terrorism, or acts in preparation, that have caused, threaten to cause, or have as their aim to cause injury to or adverse effects on the United States, its citizens, national security, foreign policy, or economy; or knowingly harbored such persons.

3. The November 13 Order does not preclude applicability to lawful permanent residents; neither does the Order apply to acts only outside the United States.

E. Aspects of Procedures that Military Commissions Would be Permitted to Follow under the November 13, 2001, Order

1. Full and fair trial with military commission sitting as trier of fact and law.

2. Admission of evidence that would have probative value to reasonable person in the opinion of presiding officer.

3. Conviction and sentencing by two-thirds of the members of the commission present at the time of the vote.

4. Submission of the record of the trial for review by the President or by the Secretary of Defense; an individual may not seek judicial review in any U.S. court or state court, court of any nation, or international tribunal.

F. Possible Constitutional Shortfalls

1. No juries;
2. Proceedings can be secret;
3. Evidence gathered without Fourth Amendment constraints is admissible; and
4. Unanimous vote not required for conviction.

G. Congressional Support for the November 13, 2001, Order

1. On December 12, 2001, Congresswoman Zoe Lofgren (D-CA) and Congresswoman Jane Harman (D-CA), both attorneys, introduced The Foreign Terrorist Military Tribunal Authorization Act of 2001, H.R. 3468, that provides congressional support for the November 13, 2001 Executive Order and specifies the circumstances under which military tribunals may be convened. *See* Press Release, "Harman and Lofgren Introduce Foreign Terrorist Military Tribunal Authorization Act: Bill Preserves Constitution While Providing Swift Justice For Terrorists (Dec. 13, 2001), at *www.house.gov/harman/press/releases/2001/121201PR_militarytribunals.html*.

2. The Foreign Terrorist Military Tribunal Authorization Act.

a. authorizes the use of military tribunals in response to the 9/11 attacks;

b. limits the jurisdiction of the tribunals to foreign nationals apprehended overseas; and most importantly,

c. does not suspend the constitutional right of *habeas corpus*.

3. Congresswoman Harman said, "Absent authorization from Congress, the President's order is at best hollow and at worse could be misapplied." *Id.* Congresswoman Lofgren said, "The Act provides that those responsible for the reprehensible attacks on the United States will receive swift justice. At the same time, this bill limits the scope of the tribunals to avoid constitutional pitfalls." *Id.*

H. The Case of *United States v. Moussaoui*

1. Zacarias Moussaoui was arrested for an immigration violation in August 2001. In December, following the 9/11 attacks, he was indicted on several charges of conspiracy. The government contends that Moussaoui was part of the 9/11 conspiracy, as the so-called "20th hijacker." The indictment was amended in July of 2002, charging Moussaoui with six offenses:

   a. Conspiracy to commit acts of terrorism transcending national boundaries.

   b. Conspiracy to commit aircraft piracy.

   c. Conspiracy to destroy aircraft.

   d. Conspiracy to use weapons of mass destruction.

   e. Conspiracy to commit murder.

   f. Conspiracy to destroy property.

2. The government is seeking the death penalty for four of these offenses, (a)–(d).

3. Issue is the "constitutionally guaranteed access to evidence," *i.e.*, whether the government must make available persons captured overseas, but are in U.S. control, who may have exculpatory information with respect to Moussaoui's role in the 9/11 attacks, or who may be able to provide mitigating evidence in the death penalty phase of his trial, should he be convicted. *See United States v. Moussaoui*, 365 F.3d 292, 310 (4th Cir. 2004).

4. On appeal to the Fourth Circuit, the court of appeals affirmed and reversed the district court, holding that the summaries of classified reports could be the basis for written statements to be submitted to the jury "[as] what the witnesses would say if called to testify[.]" 365 F.3d at 316.

5. The Fourth Circuit also rejected the district court's sanctions, allowing the government to seek the death penalty.

IV. DETENTION AND CIVIL LIBERTIES

A. Increased Detentions

1. Thousands of immigrants have been detained nationwide since September 11, 2001. Attorney General Ashcroft calls it "*a deliberate campaign of arrest and detention*" to disrupt terrorism and prevent further attacks. Brian Donohue, "Terror Dragnet Lands Men in Detention Limbo," *Newshouse News Service*, Jan. 7, 2002.

2. Operation Liberty Shield.

   a. Launched by DHS on March 17, 2003—national security measures designed to increase U.S. security and readiness in the event terrorists strike the United States in reprisal for the U.S. attack on Iraq.

   b. The plan includes increased security at borders; stronger transportation protections; ongoing measures to disrupt threats against the United States; greater protections for critical infrastructure and key assets; increased public health preparedness; and federal response resources positioned and ready. *See* Press Release, "Fact Sheet: Operation Liberty Shield," (Mar. 17, 2003), *available at www.whitehouse.gov/news/releases/2003/03/print/20030317-9.html*.

   c. Under the new initiative, "[a]sylum applicants from nations where al-Qaeda, al-Qaeda sympathizers, and other terrorist groups are known to have operated will be detained for the duration of their processing period." *See* Marjorie Valbrum & Jacob M. Schlesinger, "U.S. to Tighten Asylum Policy; Some Face Immediate Detention," *Wall Street Journal*, Mar. 19, 2003. Homeland Security Secretary, Tom Ridge, said that the detention policy was imposed to prevent terrorists from entering the United States by making asylum claims. *See* Philip Shenon, "Administration's New Asylum Policy Comes Under Fire," *N.Y. Times*, Mar. 18, 2003.

   d. Detained asylum seekers could be confined for six months or more and must remain in custody until an immigration judge decides their case.

3. Migration Policy Institute published the first report detailing first-hand experiences of 406 post-9/11 detainees in June 2003. *See* Migration Policy Institute, "America's Challenge: Domestic Security, Civil Liberties, and National Unity After September 11," available at *www.migrationpolicy.org/pubs/MPI_Challenges.pdf*. The report:

   a. documents claims of mistreatment of detainees previously disclosed in the reports of the DOJ's own Office of the Inspector General. *See id.* at 21.

   b. challenges the government's use of immigration law as an antiterrorism measure claiming it has not been shown to be effective and that this approach "has substantially diminished civil liberties and stigmatized Arab- and Muslim-American communities in this country." *Id.* at 12.

   c. details that 1/3 of the 406 detainees were nationals of Egypt and Pakistan and 46 percent had lived in the United States for 6 or more years.

   d. details that Muslim and Arab communities in the United States have experienced a dramatic rise in reported hate crimes (1500 percent) since September 11, 2001, and suffered an increase in employment discrimination as evidenced by 705 EEOC claims in the first 15 months after the attacks.

4. The Institute recommends: scaling back use of the USA PATRIOT Act that infringes on civil liberties; more congressional oversight of its use; increasing procedural safeguards in immigration hearings; and engaging in a dialogue which seeks to educate the country about Arab and Muslim communities.

B. Identities of Detainees, Basis for Detention, and Detention Location Withheld by DOJ

1. Few detainees are held on federal criminal charges.

   a. most are held on immigration violations, state charges, or as material witnesses.

   b. The DOJ admits the majority are not linked to the 9/11 attacks or the al-Qaeda terrorist network. *See* Russ Feingold, "Name the Detainees," *Washington Post*, Dec. 23, 2001; Brian Donohue, "Terror Dragnet Lands Men in Detention Limbo," *Newshouse New Service*, Jan. 7, 2002.

2. The Southern District of New York was split on the ambit of the material witness statute.

   a. In *United States v. Awadallah*, 202 F. Supp.2d 55, 76 (S.D.N.Y 2002), *motion to suppress granted by, dismissed by,* 202 F. Supp.2d 82 (S.D.N.Y. 2002), Judge Scheindlin ruled that the material witness statute, 18 USC §3144, did not authorize the detention of material witnesses in connection with ongoing grand jury investigations; such detentions can only occur at the pretrial phase and after.

   b. Less than three months later, in *In Re Material Witness Warrant*, 213 F. Supp.2d 287, 300 (S.D.N.Y. 2002), Judge Mukasey declined to follow the reasoning and holding in *Awadallah* and ruled that the material witness statute authorized the detention of a material witness during an ongoing grand jury investigation and such detention was not a Fourth Amendment violation.

3. The United States appealed the *Awadallah* decision and the Second Circuit Court of Appeals reversed the judgment dismissing the perjury indictment against Awadallah and remanded for reinstatement of the indictment, *U.S. v. Awadallah*, 349, F.3d 42 (2d Cir. 2003). The Court determined that §3144 allowed the arrest and detention of grand jury witnesses because a grand jury proceeding was a "criminal proceeding" for purposes of §3144. *Id.* at 55.

C. Fifth Amendment Rights

1. Since the 9/11 attacks, the government has exercised broad authority to detain immigrants without bail, many on minor immigration violations, and without regard to specific evidence of their individualized risk of flight or danger to the community.

2. In 2001, before the events of 9/11, the Supreme Court made clear that "once an alien enters the country, the legal circumstances change, for the Due Process Clause applies to all 'persons' within the United States, including aliens, whether their presence here is lawful, unlawful, temporary, or permanent." *Zadvydas v. Davis*, 533 U.S. 678, 693, 121 S.Ct. 2491, 2500 (2001).

3. In *Zadvydas*, the Supreme Court decided that the Attorney General was not authorized by a post-removal-period statute to detain a removable alien indefinitely beyond the removal period—only for a period reasonably necessary to secure the alien's removal. The Supreme Court said that government detention violates the Due Process Clause unless it is ordered in a criminal proceeding with adequate procedural safeguards or a special justification outweighs the individual's fundamental liberty interest. The Court found that the Government proffered "no sufficiently strong justification for indefinite civil detention" of *Zadvydas*. *Id.* at 690.

4. In *Demore v. Kim*, 123 S.Ct. 1708 (Apr. 29, 2003), the Supreme Court addressed the constitutionality of the mandatory detention provision of Section 236(c) of the Immigration and Nationality Act, 8 USC §1226(c), which requires immediate detention without bond for aliens in removal proceedings who have been convicted of specified criminal offenses.

   a. In the decision below, *Kim v. Ziglar*, 276 F.3d 523 (9th Cir. 2002), the U.S. Court of Appeals for the Ninth Circuit held that to detain, pending deportation, a lawful permanent resident alien without a hearing or individualized consideration, based on the person's past convictions pursuant to §236(c), is unconstitutional. *Id.* at 528.

   b. On April 29, 2003, the Supreme Court reversed the decision of the Ninth Circuit, holding that the detention of deportable criminal aliens pending their removal proceedings is constitutionally valid because detention prevents aliens from fleeing prior to or during the proceedings and the §1226(c) detention lasts for less than 90 days. The Court distinguished *Zadvydas*, emphasizing that *Zadvydas* involved aliens challenging their detention following final deportation orders whose removal was "no longer practically attainable" and the detention at issue in *Zadvydas* was "indefinite" and "potentially permanent." *Id.* at 4–6.

5. In *Carriche v. Ashcroft*, 335 F.3d 1009 (9th Cir. 2003), *rehearing denied and reprinted as amended*, 350 F.3d 845 (9th Cir. 2003), the Ninth Circuit rejected a due process challenge to the BIA's recently-adopted streamlining guidelines.

   a. Under those procedures, a single member of the BIA affirms the decision of the Immigration Judge, thus bypassing the traditional three-judge review. In such a case, the BIA affirms without opinion and the IJ's opinion becomes the final agency action.

   b. The appellate court found that the aliens received all the administrative appeals to which they were entitled by statute and that the streamlining regulation did not implicate or restrict any right of review in the court of appeals. Thus, it did not violate the Due Process clause of the Fifth Amendment for one member of the BIA to decide the aliens' administrative appeal or for the BIA to affirm the IJ's decision without issuing an opinion.

   c. The Ninth Circuit joined four other circuits in this ruling. *Id.* at 1013 (citing *Albathani v. INS*, 318 F.3d 365, 376–79 (1st Cir. 2003); *Soadjede v. Ashcroft*, 324 F.3d 830, 832–33 (5th Cir. 2003); *Georgis v. Ashcroft*, 328 F.3d 962, 967 (7th Cir. 2003); *Mendoza v. U.S. Attorney General*, 327 F.3d 1283, 1289–90 (11th Cir. 2003)).

6. In a precedent-setting administrative decision, *In re D–J–*, 23 I&N Dec. 572 (AG 2003) (Apr. 17, 2003), Attor-

ney General John Ashcroft overruled an appellate panel of immigration judges and sided with a Miami immigration judge in ruling that Haitian asylum seekers should not be released on bond while they file their claims to remain in the United States. Nineteen-year-old Haitian political asylee, David Joseph, was denied bond and now has been detained for over 20 months.

Ashcroft expressed concerns that Haiti may be used as a staging point for terrorists and observed that the national security interests implicated by encouraging further unlawful mass migrations.

7. Standard for seeking stay of deportation order—*Douglas v. Ashcroft*, 374 F.3d 230 (3rd Cir. 2004), the Court of Appeals for the Third Circuit ruled that an alien seeking a stay of a deportation order pending a judicial review must satisfy a 4-part test modeled on the standard for granting a preliminary injunction employed by the First, Second, and Sixth Circuits, *i.e.*, a petitioner requesting a stay of a deportation order "must demonstrate [1] a likelihood of success on the merits of the underlying petition; [2] that irreparable harm would occur if a stay is not granted; [3] that the potential harm to the moving party outweighs the harm to the opposing party if a stay is not granted; and [4] that the granting of the stay would serve the public interest." *Id.* at 234.

D. Sixth Amendment Rights

1. Immigrants facing deportation in a removal proceeding or criminal penalties have the statutory right to be represented by counsel, but not at the government's expense. 8 USC §1362.

a. DHS regulations require that the alien be notified of his right to representation at no expense to the government, and be provided with a list of free legal service programs. 8 CFR §§242.1(c), 242.10, 242.16(a) (1995).

b. Deportation hearings are closed to the public; there is no jury; and a single judge makes the final determination.

c. detention of immigrations awaiting deportations should be limited to six months, but indefinite detention is more common.

2. There is a grave need for pro bono attorneys: 90 percent of immigrants in DHS custody end up unrepresented at immigration proceedings. *See* Robyn E. Blumner, "Transfer Policy For Detainees Has Been Abused," *St. Petersburg Times*, Dec. 30, 2001. The complexity of deportation proceedings make legal representation especially important and a myopic insistence upon expeditiousness in the face of a justifiable request for delay can render the right to defend with counsel an empty formality.

3. Merely informing a petitioner of his statutory right to counsel is insufficient absent adequate time to counsel. *See Ignatov v. Ashcroft*, 71 Fed. Appx. 157 (3d Cir. 2003).

4. In August 2003, the Third Circuit held that, when an alien has a facially valid basis for asylum, for example, persecution on the grounds of his religious beliefs, such that the presence of counsel at the hearing could affect the outcome of the decision, an immigration judge violated the alien's right to obtain counsel and due process by permitting his counsel to withdraw on the day of his asylum hearing and denying the alien's request for a continuance to obtain new counsel. *See id.* at 162.

5. The same month, the Ninth Circuit heard the petition of an alien who was ordered deported in absentia when the alien failed to show up for his deportation hearing based on the advice of his attorney's assistant to cross the border the day before the hearing and was unable to reenter.

a. The court held that reopening the proceedings was warranted since the alien's failure to appear was based on actual and reasonable reliance on his attorney's erroneous advice, and there was no evidence to justify a finding that the alien was not credible.

b. The Court found that the alien gave effective control of his case to his attorney, and his failure to appear based on the attorney's advice constituted exceptional circumstances beyond the alien's control. Further, the attorney's declaration did not contradict or deny the alien's assertion that the assistant told the alien to cross the border. *Monjaraz-Munoz v. INS*, 327 F.3d 892, 896 (9th Cir. 2003), *amended by, rehearing denied by*, 339 F.3d 1012, *reprinted as amended at* 2003 U.S. App. LEXIS 16271 (9th Cir. Aug. 8, 2003).

E. Department of Justice Reports

1. Three reports from the Office of the Inspector General (OIG) of the DOJ detail harsh conditions, civil rights violations, and slow improvement of the practices and procedures surrounding the detention of those picked up in the post 9/11 terrorism investigation.

2. The Inspector General's June 2003 Report.

a. The Attorney General's post-9/11 actions were sharply criticized in a report by the Inspector General which details how some of the hundreds of foreign detainees were abused by guards and kept under harsh conditions, spending 23 hours a day in cells and sleeping under bright lights. The detainees were held much longer than the 90 days as required by law, and some as long as eight months. *See* Ted Bridis, "Some of Hundreds of Foreigners Held in U.S. After Sept. 11 Were Abused by Guards, Report Says," *Associated Press*, June 3, 2003. Many of the detainees who were detained for immigration violations were held without bond along with federal prisoners who had been convicted of crimes. *See id.*

b. In response to the Inspector General's report, Jeanne Butterfeld, the Executive Director of AILA, points out that the DOJ's failure to follow the rule of law requires action upon the Bush administration. She also states that "the DOJ needs to stand up, explain what they did, and take responsibility. The agency's actions threaten fundamental Constitutional guarantees and protections that set our nation apart from others. Our government must not trample in the Constitution and on those basic rights that make our democracy so unique." *Id.*

On April 13, 2004, DHS undersecretary for border and transportation security, Asa Hutchinson, announced changes to its detention procedures—*i.e.*, new rules designed to prevent recurrence of lengthy detentions of immigrants picked up in terrorism probes by the FBI. These rules include DHS review of FBI requests for detentions; and high-ranking FBI officials to formally sign off on detentions. *See* John Mintz, "New Rules Shorten Holding Time For Detained Immigrants," *Washington Post*, Apr. 14, 2004; Devlin Barrett, "Abuse of Sept. 11 Detainees Spur Changes at Homeland Security," *Associated Press*, Apr. 14, 2004.

3. Second Justice Department Report: Civil Rights and Civil Liberties.

   a. Published in July 2003—detailing the allegations of civil rights and civil liberties violations committed by federal law enforcement officials pursuant to the USA PATRIOT Act.

   i. there were 34 complaints that the department found credible on their face, including those of Arab and Muslim immigrants who claimed that they were beaten and verbally abused.

   ii. One of the substantiated claims in the report was that of a doctor who told an inmate, "if I was in charge, I would execute every one of you." *See* Philip Shenon, "Report on U.S. Antiterrorism Law Alleges Violations of Civil Rights," *N.Y. Times*, July 21, 2003.

4. Third Justice Department Report.

   a. Released in September 2003—describes how federal authorities failed to develop adequate plans to classify illegal immigrants arrested post 9/11 as terror suspects and those who were simply in breach of immigration laws.

   Specifically, federal authorities did not ensure that the latter category of detainees was processed quickly. Rather, they were ignored, and in a particularly notorious case of a Brooklyn detention center, abused both verbally and physically.

   b. This report was to be a progress report on the earlier reports, however there was little change to be noted. For example, the DHS had not created a "clear chain of command," nor ensured that interagency communication was improved. *See* Eric Lichtblau, "Plans for Terror Inquiries Still Fall Short, Report Says," *N.Y. Times*, Sept. 9, 2003.

F. Former White House adviser Richard Clarke's book, *Against All Enemies: Inside America's War on Terror* (Simon & Schuster, 2004)

1. Discusses the manner in which every administration since Reagan has handled the threat of terrorism. Specifically, it finds that the various administrations made the following mistakes:

   a. Reagan failed to respond to the barracks bombing in Lebanon, leading to the perception that the U.S. was vulnerable to such attacks;

   b. the first Bush failed to remove Saddam Hussein, which necessitated a continuing U.S. presence in Saudi Arabia;

   c. Clinton's sex scandal and political infighting prevented him from being able to effectively fight terror, despite Clinton's understanding of the threat;

   d. the current administration failed to understand before 9/11 the gravity of the threat posed by terror, and used the 9/11 attacks to rush the nation into war in Iraq.

V. CIVIL LIBERTIES, HUMAN RIGHTS, AND NATIONAL SECURITY

Is there a balance, and if so, where is it?

A. Americans Held as Enemy Combatants and Guantanamo Detainees

1. Does the President have unilateral authority to order enemy combatants seized and detained indefinitely without counsel.

2. *Hamdi v. Rumsfeld*, 296 F.3d 278 (4th Cir. 2002), *rev'd and remanded*, 316 F.3d 450 (4th Cir. Jan 8, 2003), *rehearing en banc denied*, 337 F.3d 335 (4th Cir. 2003), *cert. granted*, 124 S.Ct. 981 (Jan. 9, 2004), *vacated by and remanded*, 124 S.Ct. 2633 (2004).

   a. *Hamdi v. Rumsfeld*, 124 S. Ct. 2633 (2004)—Yaser Hamdi, a 21-year-old born in the United States to Saudi parents and raised in Saudi Arabia, was seized on the battlefield of Afghanistan allegedly fighting for the Taliban and detained. When Hamdi was discovered to be an American citizen, President Bush declared him an "enemy combatant" and transferred Hamdi from detention in Guantanamo Bay to a floating Navy brig in Norfolk, Virginia without counsel.

   b. Hamdi's father challenged Hamdi's detention, filing a petition for habeas corpus and requesting counsel for Hamdi. Ultimately the Supreme Court vacated the judgment of the Fourth Circuit and remanded.

   i. The plurality opinion, written by Justice O'Connor (and joined by Rehnquist, Kennedy, and Breyer) held that Hamdi had a right to petition for habeas corpus, and that "due process demands some system for a citizen detainee to refute his classification" as an enemy combatant.

   1. However, if he is an enemy combatant, the plurality held that the Authorization for Use of Military Force ("AUMF") would allow Hamdi's detention indefinitely.

   2. Justice Souter (joined by Ginsberg) agreed that Hamdi was entitled to his habeas petition and due process protections, but disagreed with the plurality's opinion that AUMF gave the government the power to detain Hamdi indefinitely.

   3. Justice Scalia (joined by Stevens) dissented, arguing that "our constitutional tradition has been to prosecute him in federal court for treason or some other crime" and that without suspension of habeas, Hamdi must be released.

ii. In court papers filed on August 10, 2004, the government and Mr. Hamdi's lawyer asked for 21 days to try to negotiate "terms and conditions acceptable to both parties that would allow Mr. Hamdi to be released." See Jess Bravin, "U.S. Considers Releasing Citizen Who Was Caught in Afghanistan," *The Wall Street Journal*, August 11, 2004.

3. *Padilla v. Bush*, 233 F. Supp.2d 564 (S.D.N.Y. 2002), *adhered to on consideration by, Padilla v. Rumsfeld*, 243 F. Supp.2d 42 (S.D.N.Y. 2003), *cert. granted*, 256 F. Supp.2d 218 (S.D.N.Y. 2003), *affirmed in part, reversed in part*, 352 F.3d 695 (2d. Cir. 2003), *cert. granted*, 2004 U.S. App. LEXIS (U.S. Feb. 20, 2004), *rev'd and remanded*, 124 S.Ct. 2711 (2004).

a. *Rumsfeld v. Padilla*, 124 S.Ct. 2711 (2004)—Jose Padilla, a.k.a the "dirty bomber," or Abdullah al Muhajir, is an American citizen who was arrested pursuant to a material witness warrant in Chicago, detained, and declared an "enemy combatant" by President Bush. Padilla was transferred to naval brig in South Carolina and held incommunicado for more than a year without any charge being filed against him, without access to counsel, and without any right to challenge the basis for his detention before a U.S. judge or magistrate. After he was transferred to South Carolina, his court appointed attorney, Donna Newman, petitioned for a writ of habeas corpus.

The Second Circuit, hearing an appeal of Padilla's habeas petition, held that the federal court could exercise jurisdiction, and found for Padilla on the merits, holding that the President lacked the authority to hold Padilla militarily.

b. The Supreme Court reversed, 5-4, holding that the petition for the writ was wrongly filed in the Southern District of New York, which could not exercise jurisdiction over the brig commander in South Carolina.

The majority did not reach the merits of Padilla's petition, allowing him to refile his petition in South Carolina.

c. Justice Stevens' dissent suggests that the incommunicado detention of Padilla for so long a time without access to counsel for the purpose of extracting information may be a method of torture. "At stake in this case is nothing less than the essence of a free society."

4. *Rasul v. Bush*, 124 S.Ct. 2686, 159 L. Ed. 2d 548 (June 28, 2004)—Shafiq Rasul and other foreign nationals were seized in Afghanistan during hostilities between the United States and the Taliban, and held at the Naval Base at Guantanamo Bay, Cuba.

a. Each of the petitioners filed an action in the D.C. district court in some manner contesting their detention in Guantanamo Bay.

b. The court of appeals affirmed dismissal of all the actions for lack of jurisdiction.

c. The Supreme Court, 6-3, reversed the district court and court of appeals, holding that the habeas corpus statute, 28 USC §§2241(a), (c)(3), gives federal courts the power to hear petitions for writs from territories that the U.S. controls.

d. Along with the *Hamdi* opinion, discussed *infra*, this decision seems to imply that detainees have a right to have their status as enemy combatants determined in a timely manner by a neutral decision maker.

5. In *Bush v. Gherebi*, 262 F. Supp.2d 1064 (9th Cir. 2004), the Court of Appeals for the Ninth Circuit ruled that Falen Gherebi, a Libyan captured on the battlefield in Afghanistan and imprisoned at Guantanamo Bay, should be allowed to have access to counsel and the courts. On June 30, 2004, the Supreme Court vacated the judgment, and remanded the case to the Ninth Circuit for further consideration in light of *Rumsfeld v. Padilla*, 124 S.Ct. 2711 (2004), discussed *infra*.

6. Widespread pattern of abusive detention methods in interrogating prisoners captured in the Afghanistan and Iraq conflicts.

7. ABA condemns the use of torture, and cruel, inhuman or degrading treatment and punishment upon persons within the custody or physical control of the U.S. See ABA Task Force on Treatment of Enemy Combatants & Association of the Bar of the City of New York Report and recommendation to the House of Delegates at the Annual Meeting in Atlanta.

VI. USE OF SECRECY TO COMBAT TERRORISM

A. Examples of Secret Evidence

1. Secret wiretaps allowed in foreign intelligence investigations by 50 USC §1803 upon warrant by Foreign Intelligence Surveillance Court.

§1806(k)(1) allows for coordination of secretly obtained evidence between intelligence community and law enforcement

2. 8 USC §1229a(b)(4)(B) allows "reasonable opportunity" to for an alien to examine evidence against her in a deportation proceeding, but not to examine national security information.

3. *United States v. Moussaoui*, 2002 U.S. Dist. LEXIS 16530 (E.D. Va. 2002)—denying Moussaoui access to secret evidence against him, unless he first obtained the necessary security clearance, on the basis of national security.

B. Secrecy of detention

1. Government's arguments in support of maintaining secrecy.

a. Disclosure would allow terrorist groups to ascertain the thrusts of government investigations.

b. Deportation hearings have traditionally been open only at the discretion of the government.

c. May expose witnesses to intimidation or harm.

d. Disclosure may stigmatize detainees who have no connections with terrorism.

e. Government has discretion to do as it pleases within administrative proceedings.

2. Arguments in support of open trials and disclosure of evidence.

   a. Due process protected by public scrutiny, protecting against unfairness and mistake

   b. Secrecy determination by Creppy directive is overbroad.

   c. Deportation hearings have traditionally been open to the public.

   d. Open hearings show judicial process is ongoing – the "cathartic effect" argument.

   e. There is the perception of integrity and fairness.

   f. Allows citizen participation.

C. Courts addressing the legitimacy of secret detentions

1. Michigan District Court & Sixth Circuit cases.

   a. *Detroit Free Press v. Ashcroft*, 195 F. Supp.2d 937 (E.D. Mich. 2002), *affirmed by*, 303 F.3d 681 (6th Cir. 2002), *rehearing en banc denied*, 2003 U.S. App. Lexis 1278 (6th Cir. Jan. 22 2003).

      i. The U.S. district court judge ruled that closed immigration hearings in the wake of September 11th violates the First Amendment rights of the public and press to observe the trials and issued an injunction requiring access.

      ii. The Sixth Circuit Court of Appeals affirmed the lower court decision requiring the government to open the removal hearings for Rabih Haddad, whose charity was accused of aiding terrorism. "Democracies die behind closed doors," wrote Judge Damon J. Keith for the unanimous three-judge Sixth Circuit panel. 303 F.3d at 683. "When government begins closing doors, it selectively controls information rightfully belonging to the people. Selective information is misinformation." *Id.* "In an area such as immigration, where the government has unlimited authority, the press and the public serve as perhaps the only check on abusive government practices." *Id.* at 704.

      iii. The Eastern District of Michigan granted Haddad's motion for a preliminary injunction and ordered the Government to release Haddad from detention or hold a new detention hearing that is open to the press and public before a different immigration judge. The Government appealed the order directing that either a public hearing be conducted or that he be released, and Haddad appealed the order that upheld the closure of a portion of the detention hearing.

         1. The appellate court noted that, because a final order of removal had been entered and effectuated, the conditions of Haddad's pre-removal detention were no longer at issue, determined that the appeals became moot on appeal, vacated the district court's decision, and remanded with instructions to dismiss the complaint. *See Haddad v. Ashcroft*, 221 F. Supp.2d 799, 805 (E.D. Mich. 2002), *remanded by* 2003 U.S App. Lexis 19768 (2003).

2. N.J District Court & Third Circuit.

   a. *North Jersey Media Group, Inc. v. Ashcroft*, 205 F. Supp.2d 288 (D.N.J. 2002), *stay granted*, 536 U.S. 954 (2002), *reversed by*, 308 F.3d 198 (3d Cir. 2002), *cert denied*, 155 L.Ed. 2d 1106, 123 S.Ct. 2215 (2003).

      i. New Jersey trial Judge John Bissell ordered the Justice Department to open all alien-removal hearings related to terrorism to the public, unless the government meets a high standard of necessity and argues it case by case. "The countervailing interests advanced by the government regarding the impeding of terrorism are serious and legitimate, particularly in the wake of the dastardly attacks of September 11, 2001, and the continuing threat of their repetition. However, these concerns can be well served by addressing the need to close specific proceedings regarding particular deportees." 205 F. Supp.2d at 305. The Supreme Court halted the order until all appeals were decided.

      ii. On October 8, 2002, the Third Circuit Court of Appeals disagreed with the Sixth Circuit ruling in *Detroit Free Press* and reversed the lower court's ruling, stating that the Attorney General has a right to close the deportation hearings for reasons of national security. *See* 308 F.3d 198 (3d Cir. 2002); David B. Caruso, "Deportations Hearings Can be Closed," *The Associated Press*, Oct. 8, 2002. Chief Judge Edward Becker wrote: "Our judgment is confined to the extremely narrow class of deportation cases that are determined by the Attorney General to present national security concerns. In recognition of his experience (and our lack of experience) in this field, we defer to his judgment." 308 F.3d at 220.

3. D.C. District Court & D.C. Circuit.

   a. *Ctr. For Nat'l Sec. Studies v. United States DOJ*, 215 F. Supp.2d 94 (D.D.C 2002), *stay granted*, 217 F. Supp.2d 58 (2002), *affirmed in part, remanded in part*, 356 U.S. App. DC 333 (D.C. Cir. 2003), *cert. denied*, 124 S.Ct. 1041 (U.S. Jan. 12, 2004).

      i. District of Columbia district court Judge Gladys Kessler ordered the Justice Department on August 2, 2002, to disclose the names of all those detained and their lawyers, except as to material witnesses whose identities were sealed by court orders. "Secret arrests are 'a concept odious to a democratic society' … and profoundly antithetical to the bedrock values that characterize a free and open one such as ours." 215 F. Supp.2d at 96 (*internal citation omitted*). On August 15, 2002 Judge Kessler issued a stay of her original order until the appeals court ruled on the issue.

      ii. On June 17, 2003, in a 2–1 decision, the D.C. Court of Appeals affirmed in part, reversed in part, and remanded Judge Kessler's ruling. The court held that the government could keep confidential the detainees names, attorney's names, dates and locations of arrests, detention and release of all post-9/11 detainees, which includes those held for violations of immigration law, on criminal charges, and as material witnesses. 355 331 F.3d at 932. The Court "reiterated the principle of deference to the executive in the FOIA context when national security concerns are implicated." *Id.* at 927. The Supreme Court denied review on January 12, 2004. *See* 124 S.Ct. 1041.

VII. IMPACT OF POST-9/11 ANTI-TERRORISM MEASURES ON THE ROLE OF THE LAWYER

A. Role of Lawyer in Representation of Person Accused of Terrorist Acts

Peter Margulies, *The Virtues and Vices of Solidarity: Regulating the Roles of Lawyers for Clients Accused of Terrorist Activity*, 62 Md. L. Rev. 173, 197-200 (2003) (analyzing the concept of solidarity between attorney and client especially in the context of clients accused of terrorist activity).

B. Common Problems Lawyers Face in Accessing Detainees

1. Difficulty in locating the client because clients may be repeatedly moved to different holding facilities.

   For example, Dr. Al-Badr Al Hazmi, a Saudi Arabian doctor in San Antonio, Texas, was in custody for 13 days. During that time, he was moved to three facilities and his attorney could not locate him for 6 days. There is also a particular challenge when the client's name has not been released. *See* Jim Edwards, Attorneys Face Hidden Hurdles In September 11 Detainee Cases: More Than 500 Are Detained On Immigration Charges, 116 N.J.L.J. 789, Dec. 3, 2001.

2. Denial of access to counsel.

   a. Detainees may be held for weeks or months without access to, or opportunity to communicate with, counsel.

   b. Some have no reasonable access to a telephone, sometimes being limited to one telephone call per week.

   c. Detainees may not be permitted to take personal items with them, such as phone books, attorney cards, etc.

3. Difficulties arising with interviewing witnesses.

   a. In *United States v. John Walker Lindh*, 198 F. Supp.2d 739 (E.D. Va. 2002), U.S. District Judge T.S. Ellis III ruled that attorneys for John Walker Lindh, the alleged American Taliban, were not permitted to interview al Qaeda prisoners detained at Guantanamo Bay. Rather, they must provide questions to government interrogators and rely on the interrogators to ask the questions for them. Judge Ellis warned he could change the arrangements if he found that it "ends up impairing [the defense's] right to get reasonable and decent answers." *See* Brooke A. Masters, "Lindh Defense is Denied Access to Detainees: U.S. to Relay Questions To Prisoners in Cuba," *Washington Post*, May 29, 2002 at A7. In July 2002, Lindh plead guilty to supplying services to the Taliban and was subsequently sentenced to twenty years in October 2002. *See United States v. Lindh*, 227 F. Supp.2d 565 (E.D. Va. 2002).

   b. In *First Def. Legal Aid v. City of Chicago*, 225 F. Supp.2d 870 (N.D. Ill. 2002), *reversed by* 319 F.3d 967 (7th Cir. 2003), FDLA attorneys were, on numerous occasions, refused permission to meet and speak with witnesses whom FDLA was asked to represent at Chicago police stations. Witnesses were not informed of an attorney's presence when the attorney came to the station seeking to represent the witness.

   i. U.S. District Judge Milton Shadur granted a permanent injunction requiring police to notify witnesses being held for interrogation when lawyers are present and wish to speak with them. The case established the First Amendment right of association between attorneys and persons they have been asked to represent. *Id.* at 882. "No reasonable person would knowingly volunteer to remain in a small, windowless, locked interrogation room for such extended periods of time." *Id.* at 878. "For the government willfully to preclude a conversation between an attorney and a client in such circumstances—and to do so for purposes of manipulating the individual's decision making to the government's own advantage—is unconscionable." *Id.* at 884.

   ii. The Seventh Circuit reversed Judge Shadur's order on appeal. 319 F.3d 967 (7th Cir. 2003). It rejected the District's court's characterization of the practice of not notifying cooperating witnesses of the presence of their attorneys as a violation of the attorney's right to free association, and held that the right is personal to the cooperating witness.

4. Increased government surveillance of attorney-client communications.

   a. The Justice Department has promulgated new regulations authorizing prison officials to monitor communications between lawyers and September 11 detainees without first obtaining a court order. 66 Fed. Reg. 55062 (Oct. 31, 2001), *posted on* AILA InfoNet at Doc. No. 01110635 (Nov. 6, 2001); 28 CFR Parts 500 and 501. *See* Monitoring of Attorney-Client Communications of Suspected Terrorists, *infra*.

5. Increased bond amounts by five times or more from pre-September 11 levels.

   Previously, bond for minor visa violations was about $2,500; now bonds are in the range of $9,000–$15,000. Immigration attorney Jill Nagy of Bartle, McGrane, Duffy & Jones has noticed that the "INS is much more likely to detain somebody and require extremely high bond on deportation cases, people who are not dangerous and previously would have been released on their own recognizance or on a $500 bond .... Now, they are kept and asked for a $10,000 bond." John Caher, "Government Attitude Toward Immigrants Grows More Harsh," *New York Law Journal*, September 9, 2002.

6. Refusal to release detainees even when the case has been adjudicated for the detainee.

The DHS increasingly refuses to release detainees until after the FBI has indicated to DHS counsel that it had no interest in the detainees. The protocol seems to be that DHS will not release the detainee without a post-adjudication "clearance" letter signed by seniors at the Justice Department and FBI. Additionally, an Order from Attorney General John Ashcroft, effective September 29, 2001, imposed an automatic stay of the judge's custody decision upon the former-INS' filing of a notice of intent to appeal to the Board of Immigration Appeals.

7. Diminishing authority of immigration judges

a. Attorney General Ashcroft gave DHS the right to immediately override immigration judges' orders releasing September 11 detainees on bonds. Although immigration judges have the right to close hearings on a case-by-case basis, Attorney General Ashcroft mandated that all September 11 cases be conducted in secret for national security reasons. "The courtroom must be closed for these cases—no visitors, no family and no press," wrote Chief Immigration Judge Michael Creppy in a September 21, 2001 memo to all immigration judges. *See* Chief Immigration Judge Issues Guidelines for Secret Removal Hearings, Immigrants' Rights Update, Vol. 15, No. 8, Dec. 20, 2001, available at *www.nilc.org/immlawpolicy/removpsds/removpsds072. htm*.

i. Civil rights groups and three New Jersey publications have filed suit against the federal government on behalf of detainees seeking a ban on secret court hearings. *See* Wayne Parry, "New Lawsuit Filed On Behalf Of Terrorism Investigation Detainees," *Associated Press*, Mar. 7, 2002; *North Jersey Media Group, Inc. v. Ashcroft*, 205 F. Supp.2d 288 (D.N.J. May 28, 2002).

ii. The Third Circuit subsequently reversed the lower court, holding: "a recently-created regulatory presumption of openness with significant statutory exceptions does not present the type of 'unbroken, uncontradicted history' that *Richmond Newspapers* and its progeny require to establish a First Amendment right of access." *North Jersey Media Group, Inc. v. Ashcroft*, 308 F.3d 198, 201 (3rd Cir. 2002).

C. How the Lawyer Can be Exposed to Risk in the Course of the Representation

1. Immigration Attorney Subpoenaed to Testify In Grand Jury Investigation of Client.

a. *In Re: Grand Jury Subpoena United States of America v. [Under Seal]*, 341 F. 3d 331 (4th Cir. 2003), *cert. granted*, 2004 U.S. Lexis 1839 (U.S. Mar. 8, 2004). In March 2002, FBI agents interviewed an immigrant of Middle Eastern descent (1) to determine whether he had information that might be helpful in terrorism investigations and (2) to discuss his green card application. When the agents asked the immigrant why he answered "NO" to the question dealing with past criminal arrests (the FBI had a record of a prior shoplifting conviction), the immigrant responded that he answered in the negative on the advice of counsel and gave the names of his attorneys. *Id.* at 334. During the federal grand jury investigation of the immigrant for making a false statement on his green card application in February 2003, his counsel was subpoenaed regarding her advice. She declined to answer, claiming that her answers would reveal privileged information. The government moved to compel the attorney to answer the questions and the immigrant intervened to quash the subpoena on the ground that the questions sought to reveal privileged communications. The district court granted the government's motion to compel after concluding that the immigrant's response to the FBI agents was a waiver of privilege.

b. The immigrant challenged the ruling that he waived his attorney-client privilege with respect to the information sought by the government. *Id.* While finding that the substance of the conversation was properly privileged and thereby rejecting the government's arguments, the Fourth Circuit upheld the district court's decision that the immigrant waived privilege with his response to the FBI agents. *Id.* at 336. The Court rejected his argument that his statements merely revealed his conduct, rather than disclosing the substance of the advice, therefore did not constitute a waiver of the attorney-client privilege. *Id.* at 337.

c. The U.S. Supreme Court granted the immigrant's petition for review on March 8, 2004

2. Monitoring of Attorney-Client Communications of Suspected Terrorists.

a. On October 31, 2001, Attorney General Ashcroft adopted a new rule that permits federal prison officials to listen in on conversations between selected inmates and their lawyers whenever there is a "reasonable suspicion" that inmates will "pass messages through their attorneys" that could further a terrorist plot. 66 Fed. Reg. 55062 (Oct. 31, 2001) *posted on* AILA InfoNet at Doc. No. 01110635 (Nov. 6, 2001); 28 CFR §501.3. The purpose of the rule, according to Ashcroft, is to "thwart future acts of violence or terrorism." Under the rule, privileged information heard cannot be disclosed to investigators or prosecutors without the permission of a federal judge, creating a "firewall" between the listening agents and prosecutors. Both attorney and client must be notified that the government is listening in on their conversation

Criticism of the New Rule. Robert Hirshon, then ABA President, issued a statement expressing the ABA's opposition to the rule. *Statement of Robert E. Hirshon,* President, ABA, Nov. 9, 2001. The ABA is troubled by the new rule's impingement on right to counsel as "[n]o privilege is more 'indelibly ensconced' in the American legal system than the attorney-client privilege." *Id.*

D. New Criminal Law and Professional Risks Faced by Attorneys Since 9/11

1. Providing Material Support for Terrorists.

a. In April 2002, American criminal defense attorney, Lynne Stewart, was among four people indicted on charges of passing messages regarding Islamic Group activities to and from her client, Sheik Omar Abdel-Rahman, who is serving a life sentence in the United States for conspiring to assassinate Egyptian President Hosni Mubarak and to blow up five New York City landmarks in the 1990s.

b. In July 2003, U.S. District Judge Koeltl in the Southern District of New York dismissed two counts in the indictment charging that Stewart provided "material support" for terrorist acts, as proscribed by 18 USC §2339B, on the ground that they were void for vagueness. The remaining charges are (1) conspiracy to defraud the United States government by violating the Special Administrative Measures (SAMS) imposed on the Sheik by the Bureau of Prisons to prevent him from communicating with his followers, and (2) making false statements when she signed an affirmation promising to abide by the SAMS.

c. In October 2003, the Court denied Stewart's challenge to the government's evidence against her, holding that the government's surveillance of Stewart's conversations with her client at the prison was properly conducted under the Foreign Intelligence Surveillance Act (FISA). The Court also denied a request that the government disclose the materials it provided the FISA court to obtain the secret warrant, holding that the disclosure of the materials would hurt American security interests.

d. In November 2003, the government brought a superseding indictment against Ms. Stewart, charging that she provided material support to terrorists. The government said that the new charges are based on the same underlying conduct, but have a different legal foundation. Ms. Stewart pleaded not guilty.

e. In July 2004, Judge Koeltl denied Ms. Stewart's motion to dismiss the Superceding Indictment on the grounds of selective prosecution and vagueness, finding them without merit.

f. Ms. Stewart's trial is currently underway in the United States District Court for the Southern District of New York.

E. Scope of Warrantless Searches and Seizures

1. In April 2004, the ACLU filed suit in federal court in Seattle (No. 2:04-cv-00763-TSZ), on behalf of seven plaintiffs whose names found their way onto the Transportation Security Administration's "no fly" list of suspected terrorists.

a. Plaintiffs, who have the same name as terrorist suspects or are innocent passengers, allege that the no fly list violates airline passengers' rights to due process and freedom from unreasonable search and seizure. Plaintiffs have been stopped several times and threatened with indefinite detention even though they carried U.S. passports, valid driver's license and letter from TSA. *See* Chloe Albanesius, "Anti-Discrimination Group Sues TSA Over 'No Fly' List," *National Journal*, Apr. 6, 2004.

2. Police can search without a warrant in the following circumstances:

a. Boarder search

b. Exigent circumstances

c. Automobile stop

d. Consent

e. Hot pursuit

f. Plain view

Requires that the officer viewing be acting lawfully at time of viewing, *i.e.*, not illegally on grounds.

g. Administrative arrest

h. Incident to a lawful arrest

i. Stop and Frisk—*Terry* Stop

Requires reasonable suspicion, supposed to be used to protect officer's welfare, *i.e.*, to search a "suspicious character" for a gun.

VIII. SECURITY, CIVIL LIBERTIES & HUMAN RIGHTS IN THE EUROPEAN UNION

A. Although living with the threat and consequences of terrorism was not new to the European community when the attacks of September 11, 2001 occurred in the United States, the concern over security, civil liberties and human rights around the world became a discussion topic of the highest priority. When terrorism struck the continent on March 11, 2004, European leaders accelerated implementing counter-terrorism initiatives. Some of the changes proposed or enacted between 2001 and 2004 include:

1. Establishing a European arrest warrant;

2. Creating a common definition of terrorism;

3. Signing the UN Convention for the Suppression of the Financing of Terrorism;

4. Defining goals in a European Security Strategy;

5. Cooperating with the United States to provide mutual legal assistance and passenger name records; and

6. Establishing a Visa Information System to exchange visitor visa data.

IX. MAJOR EUROPEAN RESPONSES TO 9/11

A. Extraordinary European Council Meeting on 9/21/01, Brussels

1. European Council acted quickly to demonstrate solidarity and cooperation with the U.S. after 9/11.

Nascent stages of "global coalition" against terrorism— "The European Council is totally supportive of the American people in the face of the deadly terrorist attacks .... The European Union will cooperate with the United States in bringing to justice and punishing the perpetrators, sponsors and accomplices of such barbaric acts ... Furthermore, the European Union calls for the broadest possible global coalition against terrorism..." *See* Conclusions and Plan of Action of the Extraordinary European Council Meeting on 21 September 2001, available at *http://ue.eu.int/ueDocs/cms_Data/docs/pressData/en/ec/140.en.pdf*.

2. Approved the following Plan of Action to combat terrorism:

   a. Enhancing police and judicial cooperation.

      i. Agreement to introduce European arrest warrant to supplant current system of extradition between Member States.

         1. Expedite transfer of suspected terrorists.

         2. Agreement to adopt common definition of terrorism.

         3. Directive to improve cooperation and exchange of information between all intelligence services of the European Union (EU).

         4. Mandate that Member States share all useful data regarding terrorism with Europol.

      ii. Developing international legal instruments

         Implementation of all existing international conventions on the fight against terrorism as quickly as possible.

      iii. Putting an end to the funding of terrorism

         1. Directive to take the necessary measures to combat any form of financing for terrorist activities—*i.e.*, adoption of extension of Directive on money laundering and framework Decision on freezing assets.

         2. Encourage Member States to sign and ratify as a matter of urgency United Nations Convention for the Suppression of Financing of Terrorism.

      iv. Strengthening air security.

      v. Coordinating the EU's global action.

         1. Assume the role of coordination and providing impetus in the fight against terrorism.

         2. Ensure greater consistency and coordination between EU's policies.

      vi. Increased Involvement in "the World".

      vii. Play a greater part in the efforts of the international community to prevent and stabilize regional conflicts.

See Conclusions and Plan of Action of the Extraordinary European Council Meeting on 21 September 2001, available at *http://ue.eu.int/ueDocs/cms_Data/docs/pressData/en/ec/140.en.pdf*; European Parliament resolution on the Extraordinary European Council Meeting in Brussels on 21 September 2001, available at *www3.europarl.eu.int/omk/omnsapir.so/pv2?PRG=CALDOC&FILE=011004&LANGUE=EN&TPV=PROV&SDOCTA=4&TXTLST=1&Type_Doc=FIRST&POS=1*.

B. European Council Meeting in Laeken, Belgium, December 14–14, 2001

1. European Council reaffirmed solidarity with US and international community in combating terrorism.

2. Plan of action adopted on 9/21 is being implemented.

X. COUNTER-TERRORISM MEASURES IN EUROPEAN COUNCIL'S PLAN OF ACTION

A. Common Definition of Terrorism

1. Necessary framework to establish political and legal meaning of terrorism.

2. Civil liberties groups: protest against ambiguities/breadth of the definition of terrorism.

B. Sharing Information: Mutual Legal Assistance with the United States

1. Passenger Name Records

   a. Europe's agreement to supply Passenger Name Record to Department of Homeland Security (Customs and Border Protection).

      Applies to passenger flights to or from the United States.

   b. Issues over privacy.

      i. E.U. Council consents that the agreement does not violate E.U. law.

         President of E.U. Parliament calls for a withdrawal of the agreement amidst opposition.

2. Visa Information System (VIS).

   a. Updates and expands upon the second generation Schengen Information Systems (SIS II).

   b. Calls for a common identification system for visa data.

      Aims to develop security measures, including biometric capabilities.

   c. Also allows exchange of visitor visa data between Member States.

C. Agreements Between E.U. & U.S. on Extradition and Mutual Legal Assistance in Criminal Matters

1. Mutual Legal Assistance requests from U.S.

   a. October 16, 2001 letter from White House to President of E.U. Council listing nearly 40 proposals for E.U.-U.S. cooperation

   b. Explore especially ambiguous and dangerous proposals:

      i. "Explore alternatives to extradition including expulsion and deportation, *where legally available and more efficient*."

      ii. "Whenever possible, *permit urgent MLAT requests to be made orally*, with follow-up by formal written requests."

2. Agreement between the E.U. and the U.S. on extradition.

   a. Eases process to extradite wanted people from E.U. to the United States.

   b. Broadens the range of extraditable offenses.

3. Asserts advantages for "both sides of the Atlantic"

D. Condemns Financing of Terrorism

1. Signing the UN Convention for the Suppression of the Financing of Terrorism of December 1999 at Extraordinary Council Meeting on Sept 20–21, 2001.

> The Convention updates outdated resolutions and acknowledges the complexity of terrorist financing, mentioning that "assets of every kind, whether tangible or intangible, movable or immovable, however acquired, and legal documents or instruments in any form, including electronic or digital" would be subject to the Convention's rules. *See* Article 1, International Convention for the Suppression of the Financing of Terrorism, Adopted by the General Assembly of the United Nations in resolution 54/109 of 9 December 1999, *available at www.un.org/law/cod/finterr.htm*. The Convention became effective as of April 10, 2002.

2. Utilization of Resolution 1373 (2001)—which establishes a committee to track progress of policies against terrorist financing at 90-day intervals.

E. Report by Counter-Terrorism Committee

Highlights difficulties in implementing Resolution 1373 including: roadblocks placed by banking institutions and financial professions, the ratification of the Resolution without measures in place to enforce it in certain States, and the complexities of distinguishing between terrorism and organized crime. *See* Note by the President of the Security Council, 26 January 2004, available at *http://ods-dds-ny.un.org/doc/UNDOC/GEN/N04/219/97/PDF/N0421997.pdf?OpenElement*. Counter-Terrorism Committee reiterated its commitment to implementing the Resolution, citing the "urgency of the task." *See Id.*

F. European Security Strategy (ESS)

1. Adopted by the European Council on December 12, 2003. *See* "A Secure Europe in a Better World - a European Security Strategy," available at *http://ue.eu.int/uedocs/cmsUpload/78367.pdf*.

2. ESS Goals.

　a. Recognize the importance of security on a global level

　　"Security is a precondition of development."

　b. Improve ability to respond to threats against the E.U.

　c. Effectively utilize multilateralism to exert pressure on aggressors.

　　"Trade and development policies can be powerful tools for promoting reform."

2. Response to the ESS.

　a. Praise: provides a coherent European viewpoint.

　b. Criticism: inability of Member states to agree on direction or implementation; tension between sovereignty and process of inter-nation transparency of information and enforcement.

XI. EUROPEAN RESPONSE TO THE MARCH 11 MADRID BOMBINGS

A. Clearer articulation of need to "flex" E.U. power.

"In light of the events in Madrid, the European Council believes that full implementation of [the European Security Strategy's] measures to combat terrorism is a matter of urgency." *See* "Declaration on Combating Terrorism," Mar. 25, 2004, at *http://ue.eu.int/ueDocs/cms_Data/docs/press/Data/en/ec/79637.pdf*.

B. Appointment of Europe's first anti-terrorism chief, Gijs De Vries.

1. "There will be neither weakness nor compromise of any kind when dealing with terrorists." *Gijs De Vries*, 13 May 2004 speech.

2. "we are in this together…I am determined to push the European Union's fight against terror even further, and to do so in close co-operation with the U.S." *See* European strategy in the fight against terrorism and the co-operation with the United States, May 12, 2004, at *http://ue.eu.int/uedocs/cmsUpload/Washington,%2013%20May%202004.pdf*.

XII. ANTI-TERRORISM MEASURES OF EUROPEAN COUNTRIES

A. United Kingdom

1. "Anti-Terrorism, Crime and Security Act 2001" at *www.hmso.gov.uk/acts/acts2001/20010024.htm*.

　a. This act defines a terrorist as a person who "(a) is or has been concerned in the commission, preparation or instigation of acts of international terrorism, (b) is a member of or belongs to an international terrorist group, or (c) has links with an international terrorist group." Ch. 24, Part 4, §21(1)(2). It also contains the following provisions:

　　i. Cuts off terrorists' access to funds;

　　ii. Improves information sharing between agencies;

　　iii. Prevents terrorists' abuse of immigration and asylum laws;

　　iv. Allows for detention without trial for renewable six-month periods for suspected international terrorists who threaten national security and for whom there is no immediate prospect of removal; and

　　v. Strengthens current legislation relating to chemical, nuclear, and biological weapons and ensures the protection and security of aviation and civil nuclear sites.

　b. Sixteen foreign nationals have been identified as detained pursuant to Part 4 of the Anti-terrorism Crime and Security Act 2001, of which two left the country voluntarily. *See BBC News*, "Terror Suspects Lose Appeal," Oct. 29, 2003, at *http://news.co.uk/go/pr/fr/-/1/hi/uk/3223595.stm*.

　　i. This Act raises a number of questions about due process afforded to detainees because:

1. it permits the detention of foreign nationals without charge or trial on the basis of secret evidence.

2. So long as the government proves that the detainees have not been charged or tried, it claims there can be no judicial review to challenge the information on which their detention is based. See Audrey Gillan, "No Right to Trial for 10 Terror Suspects," *The Guardian*, Oct. 30, 2003.

3. The government "only ha[s] to prove it ha[s] 'reasonable grounds to suspect' that the men were linked with terrorism and has admitted that the evidence would not stand up in a proper court of law." *Id.*

c. In July 2002, the U.K. Special Immigration Appeals Commission ruled that the government's detention of eleven suspected foreign terrorists, imprisoned in high security jails without charges, was unlawful and discriminatory. See Audrey Gillan, "Detention of 11 Foreign Terror Suspects Unlawful, Judges Rule," *The Guardian*, July 31, 2002.

i. The government immediately appealed this decision. In October 2002, the Court of Appeal reversed the Commission's July ruling, finding that the power to detain a suspect without trial under the Anti-terrorism, Crime and Security Act was acceptable. See BBC News, "Judges Back Anti-Terror Law," Oct. 25, 2002, at *http://news.bbc.co.uk/1/hi/uk/2360319.stm*.

ii. It found that their continued detention was justified because these detainees "may" pose a threat to national security and cannot be returned to their home countries because they may be placed in harm's way.

As in U.S. cases, the Court was very deferential to the executive branch in determining who may pose a threat to national security. *Id.* The lawyers for the detainees are considering an appeal of the decision to the House of Lords. *Id.*

d. On August 11, 2004, the Court of Appeal ruled against the challenge of the suspected terrorists, detained indefinitely under the Anti-terrorism Crime and Security Act of 2001 based on evidence mostly kept secret in the interest of national security. Lawyers for the foreign nationals argued that the evidence may have been obtained through torture of detainees in military camps and should be excluded.

i. In a 2–1 decision, the court found "there was no evidence in any of the appeals that any material relied on by the secretary of state had in fact been obtained by torture." Leader, "Tortured Logic," *The Guardian* (Aug. 12, 2004) at *www.guardian.co.uk/terrorism/story/0,12780,1281297,00.html*. Nevertheless, the evidence would have been admissible as long as Britain had not "procured or connived" at the torture. *Id.* See also, Audrey Gillan, "Judges in Row Over Torture Ruling: Courts can hear evidence if abusers are not British," *The Guardian*, Aug 12, 2004, available at *www.guardian.co.uk/terrorism/story/0,12780,1281397,00.html*.

ii. Detainees plan to appeal to the House of Lords.

B. Germany

1. Only 9/11 Conviction Overturned.

a. On March 4, 2004, the federal criminal court in Germany overturned the conviction and ordered a retrial of Mounir el Motassadeq, the only person convicted in connection with the 9/11 attacks. See Luke Harding, "First and Only 9/11 Conviction Overturned By German Court," *The Guardian*, (Mar. 5, 2004).

b. Motassadeq is serving a maximum 15 year prison sentence in Hamburg, having been found guilty on over 3,000 counts of accessory to murder and giving logistical support to a Hamburg-based al-Qaida cell that included 3 of the 9/11 hijackers. *Id.*

c. Motassadeq's attorney said that he was denied a fair trial because the United States Justice Department refused him access to the transcripts of the testimony of Ramzi Binalshibh, thought to be the al-Qaida mastermind. Binalshibh allegedly told U.S. interrogators that Motassadeq did not assist the 9/11 hijackers. Binalshibh was arrested in Pakistan in 2002 and is in secret U.S. custody. The Justice Department said that Binalshibh was "not available." *Id.*

d. The same Hamburg court acquitted Abdelghani Mzoudi who was accused of identical charges for lack of evidence when a part of Binalshibh's testimony was presented to the German court under mysterious circumstances. *Id.*

e. Germany's federal prosecutor, Kay Nehm, criticized the United States for not making information available from captured suspects that could help secure their convictions; Nehm said the conduct of the United States was "incomprehensible." See Associated Press and Reuters, "German Court Overturns Only 9/11 Conviction," *MSNBC News Services*, Mar, 4, 2004.

C. U.S. Bilateral Arrangements with Pakistan

1. Since October 2, 2003, Pakistan and the United States have committed to "their bilateral cooperation in the war against terror." See *www.state.gov/r/pa/prs/ps/2003/24894.htm*.

This cooperation has led to several high-profile arrests, including that of Ramzi Binalshibh, a planner of the September 11 attacks in America.

2. Crack-down on Al-Qaeda has had intelligence slips.

a. Mohammad Naeem Noor Khan.

i. Khan was "cooperating with Pakistani authorities as part of a sting operation against Osama bin Laden's al-Qaeda network." See "Senator Asks White House to Explain Khan Link" available at *www.reuters.com/newsArticle.jhtml?type=politicsNews&storyID=5914872&src=rss/ElectionCoverage&section=news*.

ii. The release of Khan's name to the international press may have jeopardized the operation.

"The Pakistani officials said that after Khan's arrest, other al-Qaeda suspects abruptly changed their hide-outs and moved to unknown places." *See* "Leak allowed al-Qaeda suspects to escape" at *www.usatoday.com/news/world/2004-08-10-pakistan-intel_x.htm*.

D. International Criminal Court

1. Jurisdictional mandate to prosecute cases occurring within and by countries that have ratified the Rome treaty that created the ICC.

2. May try individuals, including sovereigns and members of the military for genocide, crimes against humanity, and crimes arising from armed conflicts.

3. At least 89 countries around the world have agreed to participate, including many in Europe, and the United Kingdom. *See* James Podgers, "An Unused Weapon: International Criminal Court Could Play Role in War Against Terrorism, Says New Chief Prosecutor," *ABA Journal eReport*, Sept. 19, 2003, at *www.globalpolicy.org/intljustice/icc/2003/0922iccterror.htm*.

4. U.S. opposition to the ICC is based on a fear that members of the U.S. military may face prosecution in the ICC. *Id.*

5. The United States' refusal to cooperate with the ICC may undermine the support the ICC could provide the U.S. in its efforts to combat terrorism. *Id.*

6. Sixty-six countries have urged ICC's prosecutor, Luis Moreno Ocampo, to investigate the conduct of the United States in the war against Iraq, charging that the war was an act of aggression. However, Mr. Ocampo has not initiated any preliminary investigations of the United States because the charge is not plainly within the Court's subject-matter jurisdiction. The nations that ratified the ICC treaty, Assembly of States Parties, disagreed over the definition of aggression. *Id.*

XIII. CIVIL LIBERTIES & HUMAN RIGHTS ISSUES

A. Personal Data & Privacy

"Measures used in the fight against terrorism that interfere with privacy...must be provided for by law. It must be possible to challenge the lawfulness of these measures before a court." *See* "Guidelines on Human Rights and the Fight Against Terrorism," Committee of Ministers of The *Council of Europe*, July 11, 2002, at *www.coe.int/T/E/Human_rights/h-inf%282002%298eng.pdf*.

B. Attorney-Client Privilege

1. "The Court recognises that an effective fight against terrorism requires that some of the guarantees of a fair trial may be interpreted with some flexibility." Guidelines on Human Rights and the Fight Against Terrorism at 28.

2. "The Court recognized that the interception of a letter between a prisoner—terrorist—and his lawyer is possible in certain circumstances[.]" *Id.*

Erdem v. German, No. 38321/97 (May 7, 2001) (European Court of Human Rights) Held that a Kurdish refugee of Turkey, arrested in 1988 at the German border on suspicion of being a terrorist and held for six years prior to and during trial, at which he was sentenced to an addition six years for various offenses, had been held in violation of the European Convention on Human Rights, art. V, sec. 3 (right to be brought promptly before a judge), because Germany had not cited compelling enough justifications to warrant the loss of liberty prior to trial).

Twelve Steps Toward Fulfillment in the Practice of Law

by Carl Horn, III[*]

This article focuses on life and career decisions the individual lawyer can make to enhance professional fulfillment.

The author offers only partly with tongue in cheek, the world's first 12-Step Program for Lawyers.[1] Although there is nothing magic about the delineation or order of the recommended "steps," there has been an intentional blending of the professional and the personal. The twelve steps toward greater fulfillment in the practice of law—and, of course, in life generally—are:

- Step 1. Face the facts
- Step 2. Establish clear priorities
- Step 3. Develop and practice good time management
- Step 4. Implement healthy lifestyle practices
- Step 5. Live *under* your means
- Step 6. Don't let technology control your life
- Step 7. Care about character—and conduct yourself accordingly
- Step 8. "Just say no" to some clients
- Step 9. Stay emotionally healthy
- Step 10. Embrace law as a "high calling"
- Step 11. Be generous with your time and money
- Step 12. Pace yourself for a marathon

Whether the reader is a law student making initial career decisions, an associate or partner in mid-career, or a senior practitioner, these twelve steps will help you avoid—and, if need be, reverse—a number of troubling trends.

Several assumptions underlie the recommended steps. First, there has been an attempt, to harmonize the strictly *professional* with more *personal* goals and values. The professional and personal dimensions of our lives are in unavoidable tension. Facing this tension head on, the intent has been to develop "steps" that will enhance our fulfillment not only professionally but also on a deeper personal level.

The second assumption has been the preferability of the simple and straightforward to the more complex, where that is possible. On one level, of course, the problems facing the legal profession are mind-bendingly complex, as indeed are the problems facing contemporary society generally. On the other hand, as theologian Richard John Neuhaus has reminded us, we on occasion find "simplicity on the other side of complexity."

The third assumption or organizing principle has been the need to balance objective data and recommendations on the one hand, with more subjective "steps," on the other. The observation that honestly billing more than 1,800 or 1,900 hours per year will seriously impinge on one's ability to be a sufficiently present parent or an available friend or a volunteer in the community or even a happy person— whether you agree with it or not—is more-or-less an objective one. The same is true of specific time management and minimal exercise recommendations, as well as cautions about intrusive technology, which never allows the relief from work everyone needs. On the other hand, exhortations to make significant relationships a priority, to care about character, to embrace law as a "high calling," and to pay

---

[*] This article is adapted from Chapter 4 of *LawyerLife—Finding a Life and a Higher Calling in the Practice of Law*, by Judge Carl Horn, III (© 2003 American Bar Association). Reprinted with permission. The book may be ordered online at *www.ababooks.org*; by phone, 1-800-285-2221; by fax, (312) 988-5568; or by mail, Publication Orders, P.O. Box 10892, Chicago, Illinois, 60610-0892.

Carl Horn, III has served as a U.S. Magistrate Judge for the Western District of North Carolina. A former Chief Assistant U.S. Attorney. Judge Horn spent the first 11 years after law school graduation in private practice and as a counsel to two national nonprofit organizations. He is the author of numerous books and articles, including the *Fourth Circuit Criminal Handbook*, now in its 10th edition, and is a frequent speaker at CLE and other bar-related functions. Judge Horn and his wife of 32 years have six children ages 13–27. Judge Horn can be reached at U.S. Courthouse, 401 West Trade Street, Suite 238, Charlotte, North Carolina 28202, (704) 350-7470, e-mail: *chorn@ncwd.net*.

[1] The author proposed abbreviated versions of a "12-step program" for lawyers, which included several systemic "steps" for firms, law schools, and the courts, in articles published in the 1990s by the *North Carolina Bar Journal*, the *South Carolina Lawyer*, and the ABA's *Law Practice Management* magazine. However, this is the first published "12-step program" based solely on choices faced by the individual lawyer.

attention to emotional health all tend toward the attitudinal and subjective. Although some hyper-rational lawyers may have difficulty with the latter recommendations, dismissing them as too "touchy feely," this does not make the subjective any less important. This is true, as University of Chicago Professor [of English] Richard M. Weaver urged in his book of the same title, because "ideas have consequences."[2]

The concept of law as a public service "calling" led prior generations of lawyers to volunteer countless hours to their communities, to worthy organizations and causes, and to clients unable to pay their fees. Not surprisingly, public respect for lawyers and professional "fulfillment" followed what began essentially as an idea, or a series of ideas, about what it meant to be a lawyer. Conversely, as cynicism about the higher purposes of law—and the idea in some quarters that making money is sufficient raison d'etre for the profession—have taken hold, public approval and lawyer happiness appear to have fallen.

Step 1. Face the facts

Every 12-step program begins with an exhortation to those in the targeted group to acknowledge their need. "My name is John, and I am an alcoholic." Or, I am addicted to sex or food or some other habit or compulsion. Or in current context, perhaps, I am a lawyer who went to law school (or began practice) with high ideals, intentions to live a balanced life, etc., but now ....

Survey data, anecdotal evidence, and expert opinion which collectively suggest troubling trends in the legal profession. Some commentators, particularly those writing from the academy, see the profession as dying, as "on the edge of chaos,"[3] or otherwise as being *in extremis*. Others, particularly older practitioners, lament that the profession they have proudly served has become an increasingly unprincipled, dollar-driven business,[4] express concern over decreases in collegiality, civility and "professionalism," worry about the precipitous decline in public respect, and/or simply note that they are working more but enjoying it less.

In Step 1, we are being asked to make a more personal assessment. How am I doing in light of my own values, standards, and priorities? Have they changed? Am I pleased with the balance in my professional and personal life? Are my priorities, as evidenced by how I spend my time week in and week out, consistent with any principles, dreams or ideals I once brought to the table? Am I a professional who treats colleagues—and opponents—with civility and respect? Or we might ask, if I were on trial for being a nice person, or a successful parent, or a good citizen, or [you fill in what quality or virtue *you* hope to reflect], would there be enough evidence to convict me?

A sizeable minority of the bar describes itself as dissatisfied to the point that they do not plan to practice law until retirement. In several surveys a majority would recommend against one of their own children following in their professional footsteps. And a not insignificant minority is so "miserable" they are currently being treated for clinical depression or have even been contemplating suicide.

Be honest. If you were to give yourself a "happiness check," on a one-to-ten scale, where are you? How does that compare to three years ago or five years ago? Or, for that matter, to when you were in college or law school or got married or had your first child? Are you emotionally healthy? Are you satisfied with the key relationships in your life? When you look back on these years, will you be pleased with your priorities—as evidenced by how you *actually* spent your time—or will you regret not having spent more time with your family and close friends? In short, do you feel good about where you are professionally and personally and where your life appears to be going? Again, be honest.

These are the facts we each must face, and not just once but on a regular basis, if our lives are to remain balanced and on course. Lawyers who do not ask these kinds of questions, who fail to engage in periodic introspection, are more likely to experience what Dr. Benjamin Sells has described as "the lingering feeling of emptiness despite material success."[5] Others will realize at some point that the stress in their life has grown intolerable, that in Judge Laurance H. Silberman's words they "hate

---

[2] Richard M. Weaver, *Ideas Have Consequences* (Chicago: University of Chicago Press, 1948).

[3] Mary Ann Glendon, *A Nation Under Lawyers* (Cambridge, Massachusetts: Harvard University Press, 1994), p. 3.

[4] *See, e.g.,* Sol M. Linowitz (with Martin Mayer), *The Betrayed Profession: Lawyering At The End of the Twentieth Century* (New York, NY: Charles Scribner's Sons, 1994).

[5] Benjamin Sells, *The Soul Of The Law: Understanding Lawyers And The Law* (Boston: Element Books, 1994), p. 34.

what the practice of law has become,"[6] or that their use of alcohol or even illegal drugs has moved to the danger zone.

It would be naive, of course, to suggest that all trouble can be avoided, or happiness assured, by any simple exercise. However, by honestly and openly asking the right questions, we increase our chances—that is, we take the first step—toward a balanced, fulfilling professional life.

Step 2. Establish clear priorities

Let's be realistic and honest. In the very best of times practicing law has been a challenging, time-consuming, and often difficult undertaking. The origins of the maxim about the law as a "jealous mistress" are lost in history, but it certainly predates the era of billable hour requirements, the geometric increase in large firm practice, young lawyers who require six-figure incomes to pay off five or even six-figure educational debts, and other stressors of more recent origin.

Although lawyers in prior generations worked hard, and on occasion were consumed by their work, broad dissatisfaction with the profession was simply not an issue on the table. Law has never been a nine-to-five job, but Jonathan Foreman's description of associates in his large New York firm as "wage slaves"[7] would have almost certainly fallen on deaf ears even as recently as the 1970s. And somehow the lawyers in these earlier generations still found time to serve their communities, mentor younger colleagues, be sociable with one another, and do an impressive amount of pro bono work.

What has changed? Why does it seem so excruciatingly difficult today to engage in all these laudable professional and civic activities—not to mention to find time and emotional energy for family and friends, for exercise and other "healthy lifestyle practices," or every now and then, just to "chill out"?

One major reason for the change, seldom mentioned in the laments on lost balance, is the larger-than-law demographic shift, beginning in earnest in the 1960s, from one to two wage-earner families. We must not forget that the jealous *mistress* metaphor fit, in part, because most of the lawyers were men. And, more pertinent to the point at hand, most with families to "balance": (a) had a more limited concept of their parental role as primarily "to put food on the table," and (b) enjoyed the free services of a stay-at-home mom who took care of responsibilities most contemporary couples now share. Indeed, this fundamental demographic shift is so significant and pervasive that we are almost "comparing apples to oranges" when we look to earlier generations of lawyers for inspiration or guidance.

Whether single or married, and, if married with children, whether one or two of the parents work outside the home, there is a widespread sense today that there is never enough time. And that is precisely why it is crucial to establish clear priorities. As someone once quipped, "If you don't know where you're going, any road will take you there." We must know at least where we *want* to go with our professional and personal lives—and prioritize our time accordingly.

Bruce Warnock, an Arizona lawyer and real estate developer, learned this lesson "the hard way." Giving a personal testimonial, Warnock began his contribution to the ABA's 1993 publication, "*Breaking Traditions: Work Alternatives For Lawyers,*" with an evocative question. "What do you do when you wake up one day," he asks, "and realize that your priorities have been distorted for more than twenty years?"[8]

Raised by "Depression-era parents" who instilled in him the kind of work ethic that often leads to material success, but can also lead to unhealthy workaholism, Warnock's wake-up call came in the form of "three cataclysmic events" in a single year: his partner in the development company had a nervous breakdown, his wife of sixteen years and the mother of his two children was diagnosed with cancer, and the real estate market in which he was heavily invested began what was to become "its tremendous plummet."[9]

Warnock elected to learn and grow from these life-shaking events. Beginning with "a concerted program to get [his] priorities in order," he quickly realized that while he was working twelve-plus hours a day, six or seven days a week, his daughters

---

[6] Laurence H. Silberman, "Will Lawyering Strangle Democratic Capitalism?: A Retrospective," 21 Harv. J. L. & Pub. Pol'y 607, 615 (1998).

[7] Jonathan Foreman, "My Life as an Associate," *City Journal* (Winter 1997), p. 89.

[8] Bruce Warnock, "A Professional Metamorphosis: From Workaholic to Part-Time Lawyer," in *Breaking Traditions: Work Alternatives For Lawyers* (Chicago: Amer. Bar Ass'n, 1993), p. 49.

[9] *Ibid.*

and wife had been growing and developing largely without him. "I felt a little like Rip Van Winkle," Warnock reports. "Where had the years gone since I rocked them to sleep?"[10]

Brian Warnock is one of the lucky ones. He "woke up" after only twenty years, before it was too late to rekindle relationships with the family he always considered, at least in the abstract, to be the primary reason he was working so long and so hard. Others are less lucky because, as San Francisco lawyer Michael Traynor reflected toward the end of his career, the child-raising years slip away in a blur if we are not careful. Writing in the *Vanderbilt Law Review* in 1999 (when he was in his late 60s), Traynor gave some retrospective advice every parent should heed:

> I will emphasize that the years with your children fly by in an instant, that they and time with them are precious, and that I wish I had spent more. Whenever you can, tell the god of money and the god of ambition, who is no less voracious, that you and your kids are going to fly a kite or build a snowman.[11]

The bottom line: to avoid later life regrets, realize now that the time you spend with your children will be remembered as "precious"—and as far more valuable than more money or any temporary career achievement you may have to forego. Make spending time with your children a top priority, and be sure your daily and weekly schedules reflect it.

This does not mean that lawyers, with or without children, should not be prepared to work very hard. It simply means that, if we aim to live balanced lives, lines must be drawn beyond which we are not willing to go, at least not on a regular basis. In other words, living a balanced life—in which quality time is regularly saved for our families and other close relationships—should itself become one of our top priorities. And when people or pressures repeatedly push us in a contrary direction, we must learn to say politely but firmly, "Sorry, that part of me is not for sale."

Again, let's be realistic and honest: having enough money is important. In fact, let's go a step further and agree that making enough money should be one of our "clearly established priorities." But, of course, the proper priority in a balanced life that should be given to making *enough* money must not become a license for workaholism or what one commentator called a "money-centered world view." Money is a means to an end. If balance and happiness are among our life goals, we must be vigilant not to allow it to become an end in itself.[12]

Ronald H. Kessel, then Managing Partner of Palmer & Dodge in Boston, made this point at a meeting of the Womens' Bar Association of Massachusetts: "Be prepared to make less. It's not the end of the world. You don't have to make more and more money at the price of being miserable."[13]

Alan Dershowitz recounts friends and former students who have turned down jobs they had always wanted because they "can't afford" the reduced income. Dershowitz points to "the irony ... that [those] who turned down judgeships or other dream jobs were richer when they had less money and poorer when they had more."[14]

Dershowitz asserts that "too many rich people ... end up living financially *dependent* lives,"[15] and that

---

[10] *Ibid.*, p. 50.

[11] Michael Traynor, "The Pursuit of Happiness," 52 Vand. L. Rev. 1025, 1030–31 (May 1999).

[12] In Professor Patrick J. Schiltz' provocative article discussed in Chapters 2 and 3, "On Being a Happy, Healthy, and Ethical Member of an Unhappy, Unhealthy, and Unethical Profession," 52 Vand. L. Rev. 871 (May 1999), the author suggests that it is more than the desire for money that fuels the workaholism of many lawyers. Noting that lawyers will work absurdly long hours to earn incremental income they really do not need, Schiltz hypothesizes that for some it is a competitive "game"—akin to academic "competitions," and then competitions for clerkships and the "best" jobs, at which they have excelled in the past—"[a]nd money is how the score is kept in that game." *Id.* at 905.

Professor Schiltz concludes:

> It is not because these lawyers *need the money*. Any of these lawyers could lose every penny of his savings and see his annual income reduced by two-thirds and still live much more comfortably than the vast majority of Americans. What's driving these lawyers is the desire to *win the game*. These lawyers have spent their entire lives competing against others and measuring their worth by how well they do in the competitions. And now that they are working in a law firm, money is the way they keep score. Money is what tells them if they're more successful than the lawyer in the next office—or in the next office building—or in the next town .... For many, many lawyers, it's that simple.

Id. at 906 (emphasis in original).

[13] Quoted in Dick Dahl, "The Trouble With Lawyers," *The Boston Globe Magazine*, Apr. 14, 1996, p. 33.

[14] Alan Dershowitz, *Letters to a Young Lawyer* (New York, NY: Basic Books, 2001).

[15] *Ibid.*, p. 35 (emphasis in original).

"[w]hen money enslaves rather than liberates, something is wrong."[16] Badly wrong.

Of course, you should expect to work very hard, and sometimes this will require "long hours at the office (and terrifically long hours when you have a case about to try or a deal about to close),"[17] but if we are to realize professional fulfillment, if we hope to be happy establishing clear priorities is a must.

Step 3. Develop and practice good time management

Turning our attention from somewhat subjective values and priorities, the more pragmatically inclined will be pleased to note that our next step—developing and practicing good time management—is about as practical as it gets. Here, we simply agree that *whatever* time we spend on our work should be arranged for maximum productivity.

In the "olden days," this was simply referred to as being efficient or "well organized;" somewhere along the way, experts emerged in what came to be called "time management." Like experts in organizing closets or garages, personal trainers, etc., some experts in time management can be quite helpful, even if they essentially offer common sense solutions that many of our predecessors discovered instinctively or by trial and error.

There are certain basic organizational insights and habits, formerly thought to be within lay expertise, that you can begin to apply immediately.

One book that is full of practical insights on how to use time more efficiently is Alec Mackenzie's *The Time Trap*.[18] It was the first published in 1990 by the American Management Association. Lawyers will find Mackenzie's discussion of the top twenty "time wasters" particularly pertinent and helpful. According to the author, the key impediments to our efficiency at work are:

1. Management by Crisis
2. Telephone Interruptions
3. Inadequate Planning
4. Attempting Too Much
5. Drop-in Visitors
6. Ineffective Delegation
7. Personal Disorganization
8. Lack of Self-Discipline
9. Inability to Say "No"
10. Procrastination
11. Meetings
12. Paper Work
13. Unfinished Tasks
14. Inadequate Staff
15. Socializing
16. Confused Authority
17. Poor Communication
18. Inadequate Controls
19. Incomplete Information
20. Travel[19]

Of course, certain points in any general discussion of time management will be more applicable to law practice than others, but Mackenzie's recommendations are a must read for any lawyer—from the "organizational challenged" to those, like your author, for whom efficiency and organization come more naturally.

There are at least five areas in which many lawyers could begin to make significant progress simply by paying closer attention. They are: (1) better planning; (2) minimizing interruptions, by phone or in person; (3) more careful scheduling/planning of meetings; (4) mastering the paper flow; and (5) more thoughtful and efficient delegation. Although not intended as a substitute for more in-depth analysis by the experts, it is hoped that even cursory discussion of these "time wasters" will convince the reader of the efficacy and potential of what we are here calling "Step 3."

In her contribution to the ABA's 1997 publication *Living With The Law: Strategies To Avoid Burnout And Create Balance*, time management expert Margaret S. Spencer emphasizes the central importance of better planning.

"Preparing and following a daily, written, prioritized 'to-do' list is the single most powerful time management technique," Spencer has concluded.[20] Otherwise, "you end up working on whatever pro-

---

[16] *Ibid.*

[17] *Ibid.*

[18] Alec Mackenzie, *The Time Trap* (New York, NY: American Management Association, 1990).

[19] *Ibid.*

[20] Margaret S. Spencer, "Time Management," in *Living With the Law: Strategies to Avoid Burnout and Create Balance* (Chicago: Amer. Bar Ass'n, 1997), p. 27.

ject pops into your mind first, or whatever project is most noticeable on your desk, rather than a project you have consciously decided is the most important."[21] Taking a step back from what has been called "the tyranny of the urgent" to plan how our limited time *should* be spent is also "the best way to minimize the possibility a task will be overlooked. In other words, a good to-do list helps you see the forest *and* the trees."[22]

Spencer suggests six steps toward creation and maintenance of an effective to-do list. Although there is nothing sacrosanct about the individual steps, and some may find them too detailed or cumbersome, there is also much substance in her detailed recommendations, and those with busy practices may want to appropriate most or all of them.

"First," Spencer counsels every busy lawyer, "make a written list of all the projects and tasks that you 'must' do, in the order that they come to mind, leaving a wide margin on the left-hand side of the paper .... List each project in discrete sections that can be completed in an hour or less. For example, instead of listing 'prepare memorandum of points and authorities,' write something like 'legal research for memo—bias issue' ..., 'draft first section of memo,' and so on. Cutting each project into bite-size chunks gives a clearer picture of the work to be done, helps you schedule your work realistically ... [and] makes it a less likely target for procrastination."[23]

"Second, go through this general list, assigning each project a priority level of A, B, C, or D, and writing the letter *in pencil* in the left-hand margin.[24] Spencer explains:

> A-level tasks are those that are both urgent and important (*i.e.*, tasks that must be completed within the next few days to avoid serious negative consequences), such as drafting direct examination questions for a trial set for next week. B-level tasks are important but not urgent (*i.e.*, tasks that must be completed at some point beyond the next few days to avoid serious negative consequences), such as planning a general litigation strategy for a new case. C-level tasks are those minor matters that are urgent but not particularly important (*i.e.*, tasks that, if not completed at some point in the very near future, would yield minor negative consequences), such as responding to an invitation to a function in which you are not particularly interested. D-level tasks are neither urgent nor important (*i.e.*, tasks that can be left undone indefinitely with only minor negative consequences), such as going through your address files to delete the names of people with whom you are no longer in contact.[25]

Author's note: Whether one utilizes these precise categories (or even, for that matter, these six steps) is less important than that written, prioritized planning become an essential part of the daily work routine.

"Third," Spencer continues, "within each priority category, number each task (again, in the left margin and in pencil) according to its relative importance and the order in which logic requires the task to be done."[26] Spencer notes that this will help you focus, for example, on the need to delegate a portion of a project which may be a lower priority for you, but which needs prompt attention by someone in order for the overall project to be completed on time. In any event, at the conclusion of this step,

> "each item on your list will have a unique letter and number combination, such as A1, B1, and so forth."[27]

"Fourth, from this general list, prepare a separate, shorter written list, which will constitute your daily to-do list. Include only those tasks that you realistically think you can complete that day, keeping in mind other commitments such as appointments and meetings."[28]

"The fifth step is to start with project A1, and—as far as possible given the nature of your practice—*stay with it until it is finished*. Continue with A2, A3, and so on, checking off each task as you complete it, until you finish all the A-level tasks."[29]

Next, we proceed with "the B-level tasks, again *sticking with each task until it is done*. C-level projects, which are usually such tasks as dictating a letter, returning a phone call, or paying a bill, can be done during the transition time between the important projects, or during those times (such as just after

---

[21] *Ibid.*, p. 28.
[22] *Ibid.*
[23] *Ibid.* (emphasis in original).
[24] *Ibid.*
[25] *Ibid.*, pp. 28–29 (emphasis in original).
[26] *Ibid.*, p. 29.
[27] *Ibid.*
[28] *Ibid.*
[29] *Ibid.* (emphasis in original).

lunch) when you know you are at your least productive."[30]

Spencer is a realist, recognizing that to-do lists will frequently have to be amended as "new tasks" or even "emergencies" come up. Rather than becoming unfocused and sidetracked by the unexpected, however, she counsels lawyers to plug the unplanned for work in *according to the priority it objectively deserves*. That which is really an emergency, for example, would likely be given an A1 priority. On the other hand, unexpected work which would have been given a lower priority had you known about it in advance should not be elevated to a higher priority simply because it caught you by surprise.

Finally, "[a]s the sixth and last step, at the end of the day (or whenever you make your next to-do list), go back to your general list, cross off all the tasks you completed that day, add whatever new tasks arose that day, reprioritize tasks as necessary, and make a new daily to-do list according to the steps previously described."[31]

Your author has been using a streamlined version of Margaret Spencer's prioritized to-do list for many years, and highly recommends it. As has been noted, it is not the precise way it is created or used that makes having a "daily plan" such a valuable time management tool. Rather, it is the fact that we are able, daily, to step back from the deluge of demands and pressures and decide which work deserves our limited time and energy.

My own daily and weekly planning includes elements and nuances some readers may find useful. First, I have daily plans (on 8-1/2" x 11" lined paper) for two to three weeks ahead at any given time. Of course, they are skeletal two to three weeks out and must be amended as new appointments or work arise. Every Thursday or Friday, usually at the end of the day once it quiets down, I go through the week-at-a-glance calendar West Publishing provides, and create another week (the third week out) of daily plans. One of the benefits of looking several weeks ahead is that it frequently points to preparatory work (or errands or calls) that need to be noted for action a week or two earlier.

Centered at the top of each daily plan I write and underline the day and date. On the left side I record, in red ink, any appointment, engagement, or event—basically anytime I am expected to be somewhere, including in chambers, at a particular time. Below that I record, in blue ink, the files, projects, "action items," etc., on which I plan to work that day. About half-way down the sheet I write and underline "Calls," and then record them in pencil (with numbers, an added efficiency you will learn to appreciate). Finally, on the right side of the sheet I record any errands I hope to run or things I need to remember to do when I get home. (I also keep a 3" x 5" card in my shirt pocket for errands and at-home entries. As long as I write it down on my daily plan or the 3" x 5" card, I can relax and usually avoid unwelcome "surprises.")

One feature of my approach on which Ms. Spencer is silent, but which I strongly recommend, is the inclusion of personal and work-related to-do items on a single daily plan. For example, if one of my children has an athletic or other event, it goes in red. If I have agreed to write a letter of recommendation for a family friend, it goes in blue. Likewise, personal phone calls and errands are entered on a single daily plan. There is just one of each of us, with limited hours and energy to give, and I find that this kind of integration of professional life and equally important personal obligations is essential to a sense of being "successful" at either.

Several other brief suggestions regarding planning, in no particular order: (1) Keep a master annual calendar of key birthdays of family and friends, and enter them in your new calendar each year—both on the day of and sufficiently ahead to send a gift or card. (2) Always carry a 3" x 5" card and a pen, even on weekends, so you can make a note of things that come to mind (and then forget them), note errands and be more efficient in running them, etc. (3) Keep a separate list of the work you have assigned to others (their abbreviated "to-do list"), and mark items off as they are completed. (This has the double benefit of taking those items off *your* list and making you a more efficient supervisor.) At the end of each day, transfer any remaining items to tomorrow's daily plan. (5) And then go home, feel satisfied about a good day's work, and resist any nagging thought that you should have done more. If you have planned well and worked efficiently for the appointed time, there is little constructive about these worrisome thoughts. You have worked enough.

Making progress on the second and third time wasters— interruptions and meetings—also requires

---

[30] *Ibid.* (emphasis in original).
[31] *Ibid.*

a clear, prioritized plan for our work. Only then can a reasoned decision be made about whether to take the phone call, agree to meet, delegate to a secretary or associate, etc. In other words, without a daily plan we have no way of evaluating whether the unexpected claim on our time advances the "big picture" ball, or is a digression to be postponed or avoided altogether. Although this is a simple concept with which it is hard to disagree, it is frequently neglected in actual practice.

As every time management expert will confirm, how we handle telephone calls is of tremendous importance. This includes whether and when to accept calls, how best to screen calls, by whom and when calls are returned, and how much time we spend on a particular call. And while answers to these questions are to some degree a matter of personal style and preference, there are inherent efficiencies to keep clearly in mind as we determine what works best for us.

The principal efficiency enhancer in regard to telephone calls is simple: to the extent possible, avoid interruptions while working on priority projects during the most productive period of your day. This will require a good call screening system, preferably by a person rather than a machine, and a healthy measure of diplomacy. Some calls have to be taken, of course, but you may be surprised how few that turns out to be. And for those clients or others who are unreasonably offended by your eminently reasonable efforts to use time more wisely, perhaps you should skip directly to Step 8 ("Just say no" to some clients)!

The importance of having a good secretary, someone who projects warmth and competence *and* can efficiently handle what would otherwise become interruptions, cannot be overemphasized. If you have this kind of working relationship already, be thankful. And be sure to show it financially and by regular, thoughtful expressions of personal gratitude. If not, you should make finding and training a good secretary one of your "A1" priorities.

Once it is determined which interruptions should be blocked, whether they present by phone or in person, as many as possible should be handled by your secretary or an associate. ("Ms. Lawyer is not available right now. Could I help you?") Others, like the talkative coworker or friend, can be dealt with during what you decide is properly "down time." Some calls will have to be returned personally, but if you know the subject of the inquiry in advance—something a well-trained secretary will find out and can give you, frequently with a proposed response—you can also significantly reduce the time you spend on the *necessary* calls. And you can save all this time and prevent many concentration-breaking interruptions without offending or appearing to be less "available," at least to those callers or erstwhile visitors who are themselves reasonable.

Like all "best laid plans," even the most efficient approach to telephone calls will not prevent a certain amount of time and energy loss playing "phone tag." However, as Margaret Spencer observes, several small steps will go a long way toward reducing this residual annoyance. First, return calls as promptly as you can, consistent with the previously recommended approach—not days later, for example. Second, if you know what the call was about and can leave a message with the likely answer, there may be no need for a follow-up call. Third, if you jot down or otherwise have a written response in hand, you will probably convey it more efficiently, whether you are speaking to a person or a machine. And fourth, if you must leave a message requesting a return call, "include the specific time or times you are most likely to be available [to receive it]."[32]

As with interruptions generally, we can only determine whether it is advisable to set up or attend a meeting if we first have a clear, prioritized plan for our daily work. The plan is the big picture; meetings are details that only make good sense from a time management perspective if they fit into it.

Many meetings are scheduled unnecessarily, that is, the perceived need for the meeting could be satisfied, for example, by letter or a 20-minute conference call. Some meetings are planned prematurely, before the issues at hand are sufficiently ripe to allow for their efficient resolution. And even those meetings which are properly scheduled often lack a clearly defined agenda, which almost always results in more time being spent on nonessential tangents than is justified or reasonable.

A word to the wise: before you set up or agree to attend a meeting, decide that its purpose is consistent with your own work plan. Assuming you answer this question in the affirmative, ask yourself whether a meeting is really necessary, who should attend, and whether the timing is right. And finally, if preliminary analysis yields a green light, either prepare a clearly defined agenda for the meeting, or

---

[32] Spencer, *supra* note 20, at 32.

insist that someone else prepares one—and then stick to it.

A fourth area in which many lawyers could save considerable time is in the handling and processing of "the plethora of paper that continually crosses [our] desks."[33] The key principles here are: (1) touch the paper the minimum number of times (where possible, just once); read and deal with "the plethora of paper" in a time and manner consistent with your written daily plan, not allowing paper itself to become an inefficient interruption; and (3) whatever you do, don't get buried in it.

The first step toward time efficiency in handling paper is deciding how to sort it, and a close second step is determining when to review and deal with it.

Margaret Spencer suggests sorting papers initially into three categories: "(1) to file, (2) to read, and (3) administrative."[34] There may be different or additional categories that work better for you, of course. But whatever categories you choose for initial sorting, efficiency lies in selecting the right time or times to attack the paper monster and then spending the least possible time on each item.

Spencer encourages lawyers to "[r]esist the temptation to spend more than a few seconds with any item until you have gone through the entire pile."[35] Like many rules there are exceptions to this one, but it is generally good advice. In any event, the idea is to go through "the daily deluge"[36] quickly, throwing away (or preferably, putting in a recycling bin) what we do not need to keep, and sorting the rest according to time sensitivity and our own pre-existing priorities.

We have all seen lawyers' desks covered with clutter, there will be readers of this article, some of whom are very fine lawyers, who fall in that category, but I will offer this advice to all: you will save time and *feel* more caught up and organized, if you avoid even *the appearance* of being buried in paper work.

A fifth time waster afflicting many lawyers is insufficient attention given to how and when to delegate. The value of a good secretary, who becomes in highest form almost an alter ego, has been extolled. This point cannot be emphasized enough. Similar praise and commendation can be given, from a time management perspective alone, to well-trained paralegals and administrative assistants.

For those with the luxury of associates (or partners) to whom work can be delegated, the same principles apply. Conversely, if "you live by the rule that the way to get things done right is to do them yourself," as Dr. Amiram Elwork put it in "*Stress Management For Lawyers: How To Increase Personal & Professional Satisfaction In The Law*,"[37] get over it. The time and energy you alone have to give can and will soon run out. What you can accomplish by the thoughtful and efficient delegation to others is significantly less limited.

Dr. Elwork is absolutely correct that an inability to delegate efficiently "can be a most debilitating and time wasting habit."[38] He is also correct that if we "hire the right people, [are] clear in [our] instructions, and create a supportive psychological environment" we are far better off "liv[ing] by a different rule: anything that can be done by others should be done by them."[39]

The bottom line: those who learn to delegate effectively will free up many of their own hours and see their productivity significantly rise. Who, exercising reasonable judgment, would decline that kind of bargain?

Whether the individual lawyer relies on expert advice or goes it alone, arranging our limited time for maximum productivity is an important step toward fulfillment in the contemporary practice.

Step 4. Implement healthy lifestyle practices

I believe it was the North Carolina Bar Association's Report of a 1989 study that first used the phrase "healthy lifestyle practices." Reporting in 1991 on a statewide survey distributed by its Quality of Life Task Force two years earlier, the authors noted a positive correlation between lawyers who self-reported a sense of "subjective well-being" and those who engaged in certain habits or practices the reporters deemed "healthy."

The reader will probably not be surprised that "regular exercise" was the first healthy practice

---

[33] *Ibid.*, p. 30.
[34] *Ibid.*
[35] *Ibid.*
[36] *Ibid.*

[37] Amiram Elwork (with contributions by Douglas R. Marlowe), *Stress Management for Lawyers: How to Increase Personal & Professional Satisfaction in the Law* (Gwynedd, PA: The Vorkell Group, 1997) (Second Edition), p. 139.
[38] *Ibid.*
[39] *Ibid.*, pp. 139–40.

noted (based on the highest correlation with those reporting "subjective well-being"), but may find the somewhat eclectic list that followed more noteworthy. According to the North Carolina Bar Association Report, the other regular practices which were predictors of contentment or "well-being" (in their order) were: attending religious services, personal prayer, having hobbies, engaging in outdoor recreation, pleasure reading, and taking *weeks* of vacation. In a word, the lawyers with other serious interests—those who successfully resisted the "all work and no play" syndrome—also considered themselves the happiest.

Of course, exercise is a "no brainer." We all know we need it, and every medical report on exercise extols its positive effects on health and longevity. And yet, what scant data there is suggests that about "[h]alf of lawyers do *not* exercise regularly."[40]

Margaret S. Spencer, the lawyer-turned-time management expert cited in the previous "step," regards exercise as "a necessary time commitment" on a par with the many office-bound tasks we have to juggle.[41] Indeed, as Spencer observed, the more demands and pressure we face, the greater need we have for the stress-relieving effects of a good workout:

> Being in good physical shape can make it much easier to handle these periods of extreme stress and can also make you feel better and more energetic during periods of normal stress. You can *always* make time to exercise once you realize that a moderate amount ... of vigorous, aerobic exercise gives you so much energy that it more than compensates for the time you spend exercising.[42]

Lawyers who already exercise will affirm its paradoxical time-expanding qualities, partly due to the calming effect of the endorphins it dispatches to our tired and overworked brains. But even if this were not the case, there is simply no excuse for anyone who cares about their health not *to make time* for regular exercise.

As to the beneficial effects of religious or spiritual practices, the reader will find further support for this observation in the fine work of Steven Keeva, Assistant Managing Editor of the *ABA Journal*. Beginning with a series of articles, a number of which are available on his Web site (*www.transformingpractices.com*), Keeva explores this idea more systematically in his 1999 book, *Transforming Practices: Finding Joy And Satisfaction In The Legal Life*.[43] Defining "spiritual practices" very broadly, Keeva believes they will "bring out the best in you and help you to know parts of yourself that have been overlooked or pushed aside in response to the demands of a frantic professional life. It will move you toward wholeness, toward accepting yourself for all that you are, so that you can bring your heart and soul to work, find the joy in it, and have more to give to others."[44]

If that sounds appealing, you may want to consider implementing some or all of Keeva's recommended steps "toward balance in your life":

- Spend some time thinking about what parts of yourself you're neglecting. Your body? Your spiritual side? Your need for friendship, love, or intimacy? Your need for connection with your past and your life story?

- Take ten minutes each morning to think about the big picture. Readings from books on spirituality can be helpful.

- Take some time to become aware of your concept of the divine and its place in your life.

- Map out a balanced day, with time allotted for your financial, physical, emotional, and spiritual needs.

- Allow yourself to do nothing for five minutes at least once a day.

- Ask yourself a simple question: How could I spend my days in a way that would make me feel excited about waking up in the morning? The answer may help lead you toward more balance in your life.

- Try this balancing exercise: For the next seven days, keep a diary of your personal and professional time. Notice how much time you devote to each aspect of your life. Then ask yourself if you'd find any adjustments to your time allocation advisable. Are you investing your time in

---

[40] Schiltz, *supra* note 12, at 880 n. 60, citing the *North Carolina Bar Association's Report of the Quality of Life Task Force and Recommendations* (1991), p. 4; and Young Lawyers Div., American Bar Ass'n, *The State of the Legal Profession 1990* (1991), p. 51 (emphasis added).

[41] Spencer, *supra* note 20, at 34.

[42] *Ibid.*

[43] Steven Keeva, *Transforming Practices: Finding Joy and Satisfaction in the Legal Life* (Chicago: Contemporary Books, 1999).

[44] *Ibid*, p. 28.

those people, places, and things that you treasure most deeply?

- Don't wait for a huge chunk of free time to materialize before you try these suggestions; find the time where you are now, in the present.[45]

Or, better still, buy Keeva's book and absorb dozens of similarly pithy insights.

Like the exhortation to exercise regularly, the value of the other "healthy lifestyle practices" are not the stuff of which controversy is made. They are common sense. Don't work yourself to death. Get a life. Develop hobbies or other serious, non-work-related interests. Lose yourself in a good book. Keep in touch with your family and friends. Take enough vacation to recharge your batteries. Simple ideas all, but essential if we are to achieve the kind of balanced fulfillment for which many lawyers are properly striving.

Step 5. Live under your means

The next step is like these previously made points—it implicates priorities and calls on the individual lawyer to make choices—but it may also be more difficult to put into practice. This is particularly true for those who graduate from law school with large educational debts (an irreversible fact). It is also true for those who have made the dubious (but potentially reversible) decision to buy into lifestyles they cannot afford without becoming what Jonathan Foreman calls "wage slaves."[46]

It is doubtful that many who borrow substantial sums to attend college or law school realize how graduating with a large debt can limit choices, but that is precisely what it does. Unlike the decision whether to buy a more prestigious address or a more expensive car, borrowing for educational purposes is often seen as a "necessity." And for some it truly may be.

The fact that borrowing may be (or has been) necessary does not prevent the cycle identified by the ABA's 2000 Pulse Study—the debt-driven need for a high salary leading to unreasonable work demands leading to discontent or worse—from occurring. As the Pulse Study described it, "[y]oung attorneys are often attracted to these positions because the high salaries allow them to more quickly pay off debt owed for law school.... Yet these same attorneys, many of whom were the best and the brightest in their respective law school classes, find practicing law [in firms paying the highest salaries] anything but stimulating."[47] In fact, many become positively miserable.

Those who make the unwise, although thoroughly understandable decision to move too quickly from the genteel poverty of the student life into a lifestyle they cannot yet afford are buying a lot more than they realize. They are buying into another cycle, as Stanford Law Professor Deborah L. Rhode put it, in which "desires, once satisfied, beget more desires" and yet "often do not yield enduring satisfactions."[48] And, more pertinent to the matter at hand, they are also—usually without realizing it—dramatically limiting their own options.

In Step 5 we seek to head this cycle off before it begins, and if it has begun, to do whatever we can to reverse it. If you or one of your children are considering how much to borrow for college or law school, do not make the decision lightly. Ask whether attending the much more expensive private school is really worth being saddled with the extra debt *for years* following graduation (and it may, in fact, be worth it—the point here is not to make the decision without carefully considering the real-life consequences). The graduating law student or young associate who thinks whatever starting salary will make their heart's desires immediately affordable should run for cover!

The core insight here is that living *under* your means is the path to financial freedom, the path of maximum options—including the option of telling "Caligula" to go to hell, if necessary—and paradoxically perhaps, even the way to maximize our material pleasures. By controlling our expenses and saving a substantial part of what we make, when we *are* able to afford the nicer car or go on a great vacation (which we will have paid for in advance)—or, for that matter, when we make a generous contribution to a worthy cause—the pleasure will not be compromised by the stress inherent in being overextended financially.

Realistically, just as work expands to fill the time, so our financial "needs" have a tendency to

---

[45] Ibid. p. 28.

[46] Foreman, *supra* note 7, at 91.

[47] American Bar Ass'n, *The Pulse of the Profession* (November 22, 2000), p. 26.

[48] Deborah L. Rhode, *In the Interests of Justice: Reforming the Legal Profession* (New York, NY: Oxford University Press, 2000), p. 32.

expand and consume all we make—and sometimes a good portion of what we hope to make in the future. Cars now cost more than houses did when the author graduated from law school, (in 1976). The upshot is that, unless we actively struggle against it, we will find ourselves engaging in consumer spending that severely limits our ability to choose a healthier, more balanced life. How, after all, can we say "No" to more fee-generating work when we have all those bills to pay?

But if we are to live a balanced life we must learn to say "No" not only to more work, but also to the consumer spending that seems to make imbalance a necessity. By controlling our spending, we can significantly reduce the financial pressures that stress us out and push an increasing number over the edge. We can take "Step 5" toward fulfillment in the contemporary practice of law. We can live under our means.

Step 6. Don't let technology control your life

Some years ago a speaker held forth on how three technological innovations, also known as "modern conveniences," had actually robbed us of a great deal of our free time. The three culprits were the telephone, air conditioning, and what was then called "the Xerox machine."

It was one of those talks that made you smile and think, "I never thought of it that way." Although it is a good bet that few, if any, in the audience used these conveniences less following the presentation, it certainly made you think. Unlike more predictable personal visits, the telephone had rendered us "on call" at almost any time (although I do remember being taught as a child never to call anyone at home after 9:00 p.m., and as a young lawyer not to call anyone at the office before 9:00 a.m.). Air conditioning, especially in the South, extended our nine-to-ten-month work year—court shut down, and many lawyers went to the beach, lake, or mountains during the hottest part of the summer—to twelve. And the transition from carbon paper to copier greatly expanded our concept of who "needs to know" about various documents, with all that entails. One does not have to be a Luddite[49] to get the point: technology is, as the ABA Pulse Study described it in 2000, a "double-edged sword."[50]

And, of course, the technological innovations have continued unabated. As will be the case with many readers, our children were more adept with the computer before they got out of grade school than we parents will probably ever be. But even for us relative Neanderthals, the computer is an omnipresent part of our daily lives. Virtually all lawyers (and judges and law professors) now do legal research online or on a CD, not with books or in a library. E-mail is the preferred way to communicate with many clients and lawyers, and indeed, some clients require it. And the Internet is a must-use resource from the various research sites to information on expert witnesses to the ability to retrieve or file documents. And even as this is being written, as Bob Dylan sang to us boomers, "These times they are [still] a changin."

So what is wrong with all that? Nothing really wrong; and even if there were some preferable features of the earlier approach—having days instead of minutes to respond to communications, for example—we will never put the technological Genie back in the bottle. Time and technology will continue to move rapidly along, with or without us, as it did after Ned Ludd and those named for him took to destroying "laborsaving" machinery in 18th and 19th Century England.[51]

We can, however, note the additional pressure proximately caused by technology, and seek to humanize it a bit. And we can take Step 6, that is, we can refuse to let technology invade and control every inch of our lives.

Here is how the ABA Pulse Study described pressures caused by the "growing dependence on technology":

- Lawyers feel compelled to stay up on technology, yet they don't know where to turn.
- Attorneys are also finding it increasingly difficult to mentally disengage or escape from work when at home or on vacation.

---

[49] The original Luddites were 19th Century English workers who destroyed "laborsaving" machinery as a protest. They were perjoritively called Luddites in memory of Ned Ludd, an Englishman who had destroyed machinery for similar reasons in the 18th Century. Today the term "Luddite" is
continued

used, *inter alia*, to refer to those who oppose technological change generally.

[50] American Bar Ass'n, *supra* note 47, at 32.

[51] *See* note 49.

- Less personalized communication both diminishes attorneys' ability to develop relationships with clients and can lead to miscommunication.
- Work itself has become more rushed and less considered.
- Instantaneous access to information pushes performance standards higher:
  - Clients expect fast turnaround on research and the remittance of documents.
  - Courts and clients expect legal work to reflect the most up-to-date decisions posted on the Internet.[52]

The Pulse Study also noted the negative impact technology-related pressures were having on professional satisfaction:

- Practicing law is less personal and more mechanized.
- Younger attorneys often spend the bulk of their time in front of a computer screen, which is less stimulating and intrinsically satisfying.
- Attorneys find it increasingly difficult to put their stamp of professionalism on their work.[53]

Or, as one lawyer in a focus group—described as a "Firm Decision-maker" in Sacramento, California—put it, the problem is *too much* information. This lawyer reports, for example, receiving about 150 e-mails a day, on which he must spend up to "an hour every day just going through them. That type of information is an information glut ... I don't seem to ever get away from it."[54]

Think about it. If this lawyer left his computer at the office and took a two-week vacation, as he or she certainly should from time to time, upon returning to the office there would be over 3,000 e-mails, which would take about a day-and-a-half simply to go through and read. Is it technologically backwards to say this is "just nuts?"

The Pulse Study also elaborated on the effect the many hours spent glued to the computer is having on professional satisfaction, and not surprisingly, the news is not good:

> Except for attorneys who are involved in trial work, most attorneys spend the bulk of their first years sitting, day after day, in front of a computer terminal conducting somewhat tedious tasks—creating/filling out forms, researching issues, reviewing documents, etc. There is little opportunity to interact with—and thus learn from—other attorneys. Because these mundane tasks are the very source of billable hours, young attorneys also feel guilty about spending any time away from their desks. And, in law firms where new attorneys are paid high salaries, how much time one spends away from the computer "not working" is carefully scrutinized.[55]

This lack of collegiality, not to mention human contact with actual clients, catches many newly admitted lawyers by surprise. "One thing ... I was not prepared for," one "New Bar Admittee" in Chicago told an ABA focus group, was "sitting in your office by yourself, alone, all day long, with a max of five minutes of human contact. I didn't think it would be like that. I wasn't prepared mentally and emotionally for that."[56]

Nor is the daily dose of technology necessarily over when it is finally time to go home. There is always the home computer, or a laptop or notebook computer to be taken home to "finish up." Many lawyers are expected to go nowhere without a cell phone, beeper, or both, in case someone needs to reach them. And others are expected to check voice mail and e-mail regularly, even if further work has to wait until "first thing in the morning." (Dare you be so lax?)

Again, the Pulse Study—rightly calling technology "both a blessing and a curse"—draws an accurate picture of the dilemma faced by the contemporary lawyer who hopes to excel professionally, but also wants to have "a life":

> On the one hand, laptops, beepers, cell phones and other technological gadgetry allow these responsibility-laden attorneys to take work home with them so they won't miss their daughter's soccer game or their son's Boy Scout meeting. Technology also allows them to operate more efficiently which, at least in theory, frees up time they can spend with their families or on personal pursuits. The downside, of course, is that these very advancements have blurred the lines between office and home. Now it is impossible to escape the demands of the office. Many attorneys

---

[52] American Bar Ass'n, *supra* note 47, at 32.
[53] *Ibid.*
[54] *Ibid.*

[55] *Ibid.*, p. 40.
[56] *Ibid.*

feel enslaved to check voice mail and e-mail regularly. Even those who have established boundaries realize these tenets may or may not be respected by clients or colleagues.[57]

Technology *is* both a blessing and a curse. Some clients and partners expect to be given home phone numbers, cell phone numbers, and beepers—and proceed to use them liberally. Expectations that associates and even partners will be in regular touch with the office electronically, wherever they are and whatever they are doing, are clearly communicated. Can any professional advancement, any interim material acquisition, really be worth this kind of omnipresent invasion of our privacy and personal space?

The answer, class, is "Of course not!" Or, if you wish, stronger language to that effect.

So how do we counter the technology-driven pressure to be, in effect, on duty or on call "24/7"? Although it is no easy project, and to the extent we are attempting to roll back our current over-availability it may be even more difficult, it starts with drawing a line. As in the decision about how many hours to spend at the office generally, we must each decide how much of us is "for sale." And then if our clients, employers, or partners do not like it, tough luck.

Once we get up the courage to draw the line—and it will take courage—two basic things can happen. Those who have been applying this kind of pervasive pressure might realize we can perform adequately without being at their beck and call one hundred percent of the time. In that event we will have successfully adjusted their unreasonable expectations and gotten back that part of our personal lives we never should have given up. The other thing that can happen, of course, is that we might lose clients or even lose our jobs. Although this would no doubt be a temporary hardship, things will eventually fall into place—and be far better, overall, when they do. Remember, we are not advocating being lazy or shirking duty here. We are talking about working long and hard, but at some point realizing that we share every human being's need for private space.

How we do that precisely is something each individual must work out. Some get up early and work, either at home or in their offices, so they can have dinner with their families most evenings. Others decline to carry cell phones or beepers, or check e-mail or voice mail, much of the time they are away from the office. The author knows a family that takes the phone off the hook for a brief time in the evenings to allow the family some uninterrupted time together. But whatever our particular strategy, the core objective is the same: to establish boundaries which prevent technology from controlling our lives, Step 6 toward fulfillment in the contemporary practice of law.

Step 7. Care about character—and conduct yourself accordingly

"Let me tell you how you will start acting unethically," Professor Patrick J. Schiltz addresses law students. "It will begin with your time sheets."[58] Schiltz' prediction of what might follow is eerily prescient:

> One day, not too long after you start practicing law, you will sit down at the end of a long, tiring day, and you just won't have much to show for your efforts in terms of billable hours. It will be near the end of the month. You will know that all of the partners will be looking at your monthly time report in a few days, so what you'll do is pad your time sheet just a bit. Maybe you will bill a client for ninety minutes for a task that really took you only sixty minutes to perform. However, you will promise yourself that you will repay the client at the first opportunity by doing thirty minutes of work for the client for "free." In this way, you will be "borrowing," not "stealing."
>
> And then what will happen is that it will become easier and easier to take these little loans against future work. And then, after a while, you will stop paying back these little loans. You will convince yourself that, although you billed for ninety minutes and spent only sixty minutes on the project, you did such good work that your client should pay a bit more for it. After all, your billing rate is awfully low, and your client is awfully rich.
>
> And then you will pad more and more—every two minute telephone conversation will go down on the sheet as ten minutes, every three hour research project will go down with an extra quarter hour or so. You will continue to rationalize your dishonesty to yourself in various ways until one day you stop doing even that. And, before long— it won't take you much more than three or four

---

[57] *Ibid.*, p. 63.

[58] Schiltz, *supra* note 12, at 917.

years—you will be stealing from your clients almost every day, and you won't even notice it.[59]

Or, to put it in philosophical jargon, once we start down the slippery slope of ethical compromise—lying, cheating, or stealing just a little, perhaps—it is awfully difficult to prevent a full slide into shameless dishonesty.

If our aim is fulfillment in the practice of law, or in life generally, we must not let that happen. If we steal from our clients, a little or a lot, it will become increasingly difficult to feel good about who we are and what we do for a living, to "look ourselves in the mirror," or to "sleep well at night." We will become more cynical about the whole idea of right and wrong, condemning at least in our minds "moral absolutists" who might take issue with our real-world pragmatism. And an overall sense of fulfillment, difficult to achieve at best, will become more elusive still.

Professor Schiltz also warns the law student looking ahead at his or her career about "becom[ing] a liar."[60] Here is his similar take on the contours of that slippery slope:

> A deadline will come up one day, and, for reasons that are not entirely your fault, you will not be able to meet it. So you will call your senior partner or your client and make up a white lie for why you missed the deadline. And then you will get busy and a partner will ask whether you proofread a lengthy prospectus and you will say yes, even though you didn't. And then you will be drafting a brief and you will quote language from a Supreme Court opinion even though you will know that, when read in context, the language does not remotely suggest what you are implying it suggests. And then, in preparing a client for a deposition, you will help the client to formulate an answer to a difficult question that will likely be asked—an answer that will be "legally accurate" but that will mislead your opponent. And then you will be reading through a big box of your client's documents—a box that has not been opened in twenty years—and you will find a document that would hurt your client's case, but that no one except you knows exists, and you will simply "forget" to produce it in response to your opponent's discovery requests.[61]

"Do you see what will happen?" the Professor rhetorically intones. "After a couple of years of this, you won't even notice that you are lying and cheating and stealing every day that you practice law."[62] A little padding of the time sheet here, a half truth or "little white lie to cover a missed deadline there" will have fundamentally changed "your entire frame of [moral] reference."[63]

Sadly, lawyers who slide all the way into this amoral abyss will have adopted "a set of values that embodies not what is right or wrong, but what is profitable, what [they] can get away with."[64]

Do not let it happen to you, and if compromised ethics have already infected "the hundreds of mundane things that [we lawyers] do almost unthinkingly every day,"[65] vow and strive to return to a more solid ethical and moral foundation. However much pressure is being applied, "[d]o not pad your time sheets—even once. And do not tell lies to partners or clients or opposing counsel. And do not misrepresent legal authority to judges. And do not break your promises. And do not do anything else that is contrary to the values you now hold."[66] Or, if you have already gone a way down the slippery slope and reform is necessary, return and "hold on for dear life" to the values you were taught and never should have compromised.

Of course, there is more to having good character than not lying, cheating, or stealing. Presumably a lawyer with good character, whether or not a religious person, will apply what has come to be known as the Golden Rule ("Do unto others as you would have them do unto you"—not, as a cynic once quipped, *before* they do unto you.")

If more lawyers would accept and apply this simple precept—treating others as they would wish to be treated—many of the ills inherent in contemporary practice would be addressed *ipso facto*. Certainly, the return to collegiality and civility, a core concern of the "professionalism movement," would be. Ditto for the prompt return of phone calls and

---

[59] *Ibid.*
[60] *Ibid.*

[61] *Ibid.*, p. 917–18.
[62] *Ibid.*, p. 918.
[63] *Ibid.*
[64] *Ibid.*
[65] *Ibid.*, p. 949.
[66] *Ibid.*, p. 950.

response to correspondence, full cooperation during discovery, and the general need to reduce aggression and stress, which is "over the top" for altogether too many practitioners.

The ABA Pulse Study noted as what it called "an erosion of professional courtesy and sense of community" in the contemporary practice.[67] Professor Roger E. Schechter called it "the civility crises" in his 1997 article, "Changing Law Schools To Make Less Nasty Lawyers."[68] Professor Schechter describes the perceived problem as lawyers who are "increasingly prone to behave as combatants, refusing to extend common courtesies to one another."

It is behavior that is sufficiently pervasive that in one survey "half the lawyers responding characterized their professional colleagues as 'obnoxious.'"[69]

The ABA's Pulse Study notes the "erosion of ... common courtesy," which has led to a "less pleasant and more stressed work environment" for many lawyers, the 2000 report explains:

- In the past, attorneys from various professional backgrounds would get together in more relaxed settings—bar meetings, the lawyer's room at the courthouse, etc.—where they could get to know one another on a more personal basis. It was in this setting that codes of behavior were established and conveyed to younger attorneys.
- While a sense of community still exists, it now occurs at a specialty level.
- Lawyers today think of themselves as "trial lawyers," "patent specialists," or "defense attorneys," beholden only to the rules of their specific community.
- Younger attorneys, who have never been taught by mentors or the community at large about the professional codes of behavior, may confuse advocacy with aggression.[70]

The result of this "erosion in professional courtesy" is more than just the absence of the camaraderie enjoyed in years past. Can contemporary lawyers do better on the character/professional relations front? Of course we can, much better, in fact. We can vow to do what most of us already know is right: we can strive to conduct ourselves honorably, which means refusing to lie, cheat or steal—however much pressure we are under, or how "profitable" the wrong choice may appear to be at that moment.

And we can adopt the simple but profound teaching of the Golden Rule: that we should treat others, including opposing counsel, as we ourselves would like to be treated. If we do that—refusing to start down the slippery slope of compromised ethics, and treating others with civility and respect—we will like what we see when we look in the mirror. If we care about our character and conduct ourselves accordingly, we will be able to sleep well at night. And we will have taken one more important step toward finding satisfaction and fulfillment in the practice of law.

Step 8. "Just say no" to some clients

There is no doubt attorney-client relations have changed significantly. And like those in lawyering generally, the changes in clients and client relations have not generally been for the better.

The parallel changes in lawyering and clients make it difficult to discuss one without continual reference to the other, almost like hearing "both sides" following an argument between two children. "Ok, you did this, and you did that. I don't care if A or B. From now on X, Y, and Z." In other words, before stones are thrown at the unreasonable or unethical demands of some clients, lawyers must be sure their own glass house is in order.

Traditional exhortations to lawyers, like those of Ambassador Sol M. Linowitz "not [to] undertake the representation of someone he does not trust and whose story he does not believe,"[71] almost strike the contemporary ear as naive and quaint. But Ambassador Linowitz is onto something that is still relevant to the topic at hand. There remains a kernel of truth in the conclusion of Roy Grutman, a senior partner in a New York megafirm, that "accepting a client is ultimately a moral decision."[72]

---

[67] American Bar Ass'n, *supra* note 47, at 34.

[68] Roger E. Schechter, "Changing Law Schools to Make Less Nasty Lawyers," 10 Geo. J. Legal Ethics 367, 378 (Winter 1997). Schechter is a Professor of Law at George Washington University.

[69] *Ibid.*, p. 394 n. 47.

[70] American Bar Ass'n, *supra* note 47, at 34.

[71] Sol M. Linowitz (with Martin Mayer), *The Betrayed Profession: Lawyering at the End of the Twentieth Century* (New York, NY: Charles Scribner's Sons, 1994), p. 31.

[72] *Ibid.*, quoting Roy Grutman and Bill Thomas, *Lawyers And Thieves* (New York, NY: Simon & Schuster, 1990), p. 28.

One factor overlooked by this more cynical approach to client selection is the lack of satisfaction a lawyer with decent values will likely experience in advocating his various unreasonable causes and positions—unless, of course, the lawyer is as big an asshole as the "ideal client." But alas, we are getting ahead of ourselves.

Pleading for a return to value-based client selection, Ambassador Linowitz urges that "[g]ood lawyers don't have to take bad clients."[73] He relates a conversation with Edward Bennett Williams in which the famous trial lawyer was asked about his representation of certain sordid characters. "Everyone is entitled to a lawyer," Williams defended himself (with some justification). "Yes," came the more traditional response, "but they are not entitled to *you*."[74]

Fast-forwarding two or three decades, Linowitz points to the savings-and-loan scandal as being "laced with stories about the participation of reputable law firms that knew their clients were doing improper things but tried to squeeze their actions into the framework of permissive government regulations so they could be, with luck, legally defensible."[75] Exercising 20-20 hindsight, he notes that regulators subsequently decided both "that the dishonesty [of the savings-and-loan employees] was punishable" and "that the lawyers bear some responsibility for abetting it."[76] Having heard President George W. denounce trial lawyers in a State of the Union message, for which he received a bipartisan standing ovation, one has to wonder how long aggressive prosecutors will give lawyers the traditional benefit of the doubt in deciding who to charge as a "co-conspirator" in more politically-driven initiatives.

Again, Ambassador Linowitz expresses the traditional view, which will not comfort lawyers tempted to walk close to the frequently fuzzy line between zealous advocacy and abetting a fraud:

[I]n the end professionals have to stand responsible for their own actions, and the cry "My client made me do it" must fall on deaf ears.

This is not to suggest that lawyers should shy away from politically unpopular causes or clients, or even be less zealous in their advocacy, but fundamental self-interest requires some very clear ethical thinking as we step closer to this line. The limited point here is that lawyers who fail to maintain high ethical standards and appropriate professional distance from what a politically motivated prosecutor might regard as "deception" could find *themselves* in need of counsel. Right or wrong, that is particularly true in today's anti-lawyer political environment.

While most lawyers will not get close enough to this line to have a reasonable fear of criminal prosecution, many more describe the attorney-client relationship as increasingly stressful and problematic. Walt Bachman summarily calls it "the most stressful aspect of lawyering."[77]

The ABA Pulse Study describes how increased client influence over "how legal projects are priced and executed" has become a major "pressure point":

- Clients tend to be project, not relationship-focused.

- Projects are often bid out to multiple firms rather than turning to one trusted counselor.

- There is an increasing desire for project fees which can be budgeted versus billable hours, with law firms assuming the risk if projects require more effort than anticipated.

- Clients also demand fast turnaround and 24/7 access to attorneys, at least via e-mail.

- Many want to be directly involved in the process.

- Billing is carefully scrutinized.

- Larger clients may require firms to follow formal billing procedures specific to their organization's requirements.

- Lack of uniformity in billing procedures means firms often have to utilize multiple billing approaches.[78]

Whether "increasingly demanding clients" were caused in whole or in part by increasingly greedy, dishonest lawyers is beside the point here. The impact on professional satisfaction, like the proverbial rain in the *Bible*, has fallen "on the just and the unjust."[79] According to the Pulse Study, this means:

- More time/resources spent on administrative tasks and relationship management

---

[73] Linowitz, *supra* note 85, at 30.

[74] *Ibid.*, p. 31.

[75] *Ibid.* (emphasis in original).

[76] *Ibid.*, pp. 34–35.

[77] Walt Bachman, *Law v. Life: What Lawyers are Afraid to Say about the Legal Profession* (Rhinebeck, NY: Four Directions Press, 1995), p. 135.

[78] American Bar Ass'n, *supra* note 47, at 30.

[79] *See* Matthew 5:45.

- Less control over the pace of work
- Less ability to escape the pressures of the job
- Ambiguity as to what and how to bill
- Lower profits/job, requiring attorneys to take on more work
- Feeling more like a "hired gun" versus a respected counselor.[80]

Or, as a California lawyer told one of the ABA focus groups, "it strikes me that the clients are shopping on eBay for their next lawyer."[81]

Steven Keeva introduces us to Sheldon Tashman a New York litigator who ultimately decided it was in his best interest, as they tell school kids in regard to sex and drugs, to "just say no" to some clients. Tashman, once took any case that walked through the door, has since become a personal injuries lawyer who "will not take a case he doesn't believe in."[82]

"The law has many temptations that lack integrity," Tashman concluded. "There's a temptation to make a case out of nothing, to make a living out of situations that aren't real, to not be ethical."[83] Admitting "certain things [which] weren't really right" in his past, he cites "trouble sleeping" and the spectre of his son seeing an unfavorable newspaper story as the dual motivation for changes in his professional course.[84] Tashman quickly discovered that the peace of mind attending higher ethics and more careful client selection were well worth what they cost him in lost fees.

Keeva suggests a broader and deeper look at the client's motivation, expectations, and best interest (broadly defined). Among other questions, Keeva suggests that lawyers consider at the outset:

- Why has the client come?
- What role does he want me to take?
- Are my words consistent with my values?
- Have I made clear what I see both his and my own role(s) to be in this relationship?
- Have I made clear where my loyalties lie?

- Have I been clear about the range of options, both legal and nonlegal, that may be available?[85]

As the representation continues, Keeva encourages lawyers who hope for improved relationships with their clients to ask, *among other things*:

- Have I been clear so far about what I see as the merits and deficiencies in the case the client thinks he has?
- Does the client seem open to striving for a win/win solution?
- Is he willing to take any responsibility for the problem? —Can he admit that there were things he could have done that might have prevented the current problem?
- Is the client deluding himself about any aspect of the case?
- What ways of looking at this case might locate deeper implications? For example, are there family implications that may at first not be apparent?

To summarize "Step 8," there is more stress than there once was in attorney-client relations. Part of this is the fault of lawyers, particularly greedy, dishonest lawyers. But wherever relative fault lies, we can increase the inherent satisfaction in the attorney-client relationship by keeping in mind a few key principles.

First, we must be scrupulously honest with our clients, including but not limited to the work we choose to do and how it is billed. Second, we need to be exceedingly careful not to cross ethical lines and to keep a measure of professional distance, particularly where an objective third party might see our client's conduct as "deceptive." Third, we should strive to provide wise counsel, which often requires more of a "big picture" approach to problem solving and conflict resolution. And finally, we will simply have to "just say no" to some clients.

Step 9. Stay emotionally healthy

How we spend the hours of our lives is not the only balance we must strike. Finding balance between the rational/cognitive/left brain elements of human experience—where many lawyers are at their best—and the "softer" right brain counterbalances: including feelings, emotion, "heart," and imagination, is just as important. In a word, it is crucial that we stay emotionally healthy.

---

[80] American Bar Ass'n, *supra* note 47, at 30.
[81] *Ibid.*
[82] Quoted in Keeva, *supra* note 43, at 198.
[83] *Ibid.*, pp. 198–99.
[84] *Ibid.*, p. 199.

[85] Keeva, *supra* note 43, at 200–01.

Lawyers who achieve professional success, but who are *not* emotionally balanced and healthy, will frequently realize that "something is missing." Some seek professional help, particularly if the result is clinical depression, a failed marriage, or some other personal crisis. Others may muddle along in what Benjamin Sells calls a "state of mild torpor"[86] for years.

As Dr. Sells analyzes the problem, by prolonged over-emphasis on the rational and the argumentative, many "lawyers have become abstracted from the world of actual experience.... Whether in terms of feeling like a fungible component in a big law firm machine, or a sideline spectator of one's own family life, or like an amoral technician servicing the bottom line ... lawyers feel dissociated from daily life—*including themselves*."[87] At its worst, this can leave even highly successful lawyers feeling "lonely ... exiled, rejected by their fellow citizens."[88]

But whether or not it devolves to that point, many lawyers need "[t]o re-establish contact with the ground of actual experience, [to] break through the abstractions that separate them from air below the clouds. They must come back to earth, where the air is thicker and more life-sustaining."[89] According to Sells, "this means that lawyers need to educate their passions and invigorate their imaginations with the same dedication they apply to sharpening their analytic skills."[90]

As Professor Walter Bennett sees it, the goal is no less than "wholeness as a human being," which may require "a reorientation of the soul ..., a reopening of the intellectual and emotional gates that so many people begin to shut in law school."[91] George W. Kaufman, who conducts workshops for unhappy or stressed-out lawyers,[92] would agree. Noting the importance of "intimacy" to happiness, and the need to be in touch with feelings and emotions to achieve it, Kaufman traces the imbalance he has observed in many lawyers back to his years at Yale Law School—from 1959 to 1962! "Only once in my three years at law school," he writes, "did I witness a professor blush because he had revealed a deeply personal side of himself, and I never observed any teachers or students express feelings with the same fervor they expounded facts."[93]

As it turns out, a hyper-rationalist approach to education and life distorts more than the individual personality. It also limits our ability to grasp the real meaning of many human experiences. "Feelings and emotions are part of our human makeup [which] give us information in a way that is different from the way we gather information through our intellect," Kaufman notes."[94] Imbalance occurs in the lives and personalities of many lawyers, beginning in law school, because "[o]ur training honors our cognitive skills and dismisses information gathered through other channels. As such, we tend to exploit our rational capacities and ignore other parts of ourselves that offer different ways of learning."[95]

In an article titled "A Symphony Of Silence,"[96] Steven Keeva likens lawyers with undeveloped or atrophied inner lives to music that is off-key and lacking rhythm. "Nearly all that is audible," he concludes, (comparing the profession at large to a symphony orchestra) "is shrill, frenetic and in the upper registers. The bass line seems to be missing.... There's something wrong with the rhythm too. There are too few rests. Music without silence grows tedious and exhausting; it gives the imagination no room to breathe."[97]

Keeva's prescription for lawyers who have focused excessively "on striving and achieving," who find themselves mired in "tedious and exhausting" pursuit of "airtight, left brain solutions at the expense of feeling and intuition," is what he broadly calls "inner work."[98] Acknowledging that ours is "a culture that rewards workoholism and downplays the value of stillness and reflection," Keeva urges law-

---

[86] Sells, *supra* note 5, at 177.

[87] Ibid., pp. 176–77 (emphasis in original).

[88] Ibid., p. 176.

[89] Ibid., p. 178.

[90] Ibid., pp. 178–79.

[91] Walter Bennett, *The Lawyer's Myth: Reviving Ideals in the Legal Profession* (Chicago: The University of Chicago Press, 2001), pp. ix, 2.

[92] *See* text in Chapter 2 at note 113.

[93] George W. Kaufman, *The Lawyer's Guide to Balancing Life and Work: Taking the Stress Out of Success* (Chicago: American Bar Association, 1999), p. 13.

[94] *Ibid.*

[95] *Ibid.*

[96] Steven Keeva, "A Symphony of Silence," *California Law Week*, Aug. 9, 1999, p. 31.

[97] *Ibid.*

[98] *Ibid.*

yers who hope for happiness to reconnect with these kinder, gentler elements of the human experience.[99]

In *The Lawyer's Guide To Balancing Life And Work: Taking The Stress Out Of Success*, George Kaufman recognizes that some lawyers feel "happy" when levels of professional success, such as making partner, are reached. For these, "there has been a joining of success and happiness. For others, the gulf between success and happiness is deep."[100] Kaufman's response, like Steven Keeva's exhortation to engage in "inner work," is not rocket science. "When I began my career," Kaufman writes, "I assumed that success would yield happiness. It doesn't. If happiness is to be a career goal, it must be separately addressed."[101]

In his thirty-five years in practice, Kaufman certainly knew lawyers who "owned" their values and had well-integrated personalities, that is, lawyers who were emotionally healthy. But he also encountered those who were professionally successful, yet "enjoy[ed] no sense of well-being," who felt "trapped by the work they [did]," and many others whose "work life ha[d] invaded their privacy."[102] He writes, for example, about a lawyer acquaintance "who, when admitted to partnership in a prestigious law firm, was overwhelmed with sadness and dread. Eight years of toil had produced membership in an exclusive club. But the work he endured to achieve that membership was work he would need to endure forever to keep that membership in good standing."[103]

Kaufman promotes emotional health through a series of simple exercises. In one, he invites participants to consider the opportunity costs (which he calls "losses") of a demanding professional life. "Those losses started with compromises we made as we attempted to juggle work, play, family, and self. If the term 'loss' seems too stark to describe your process, consider what you may have compromised or surrendered to succeed at work."[104]

Kaufman makes an interesting observation about a preliminary hurdle in getting lawyers to describe their feelings. "Losses are connected to our feelings," he explains. "But when I ask lawyers to describe those feelings, most deny their existence. In fact, whenever I ask lawyers to tell me their feelings, they respond by telling me their thoughts."[105] But although they may be deeply buried, getting back in touch with feelings about these "losses" or opportunity costs—from harm to an intimate relationship, to an inability to pursue a hobby or do volunteer work, to missing a child's birthday—is a necessary ingredient of emotional health.

In another exercise, Kaufman encourages lawyers to reflect on their ten most important values. To set the reflection in motion—and, hopefully, to engage the right-brain imagination—Kaufman offers a non-exclusive list of values we may want to consider:[106]

Love	Freedom	Security	Play
Power	Comfort	Competence	Exercise
Growth	Joy	Creativity	Vegging Out
Acceptance	Support	Warmth	Pride
Gratefulness	Honesty	Balance	Romance
Justice	Serenity	Humility	Frivolity
Trust	Fulfillment	Success	Spontaneity
Intimacy	Adventure	Passion	Perfection
Health	Service	Achievement	Appreciation
Humor	Harmony	Winning	Conscientiousness
Focus	Kindness	Appreciation	Wealth
Integrity	Desire	Presence	Aggressiveness
Honor	Family	Change	Tenacity
Beauty	Truthfulness	Understanding	Practicality
Expediency	Inquiry	Compassion	Loyalty

Of course, while some values are certainly more commendable than others, the purpose of this exercise is not to tell us what our values should be. Rather, the purpose here is to cause us to reflect on what our foundational values *are*—and then to be honest with ourselves about whether and how well we are putting them into practice.

However clear our "values" or pure our priorities, the high stress level at which many lawyers operate week after week will make emotional health and balance difficult to achieve. Fortunately, there is help available here, too, but as in the related issues we have already addressed—like establishing clear priorities, developing and practicing good time management, implementing healthy lifestyle practices, living under our means, not letting technology control our lives, and just saying "no" to some clients—the stress problem will not resolve on its own. Like

---

[99] *Ibid.*

[100] Kaufman, *supra* note 93, at 52.

[101] *Ibid.*

[102] *Ibid.*

[103] *Ibid.*, p. 57.

[104] *Ibid.*, p. 78.

[105] *Ibid.*, p. 81.

[106] *Ibid.*, p. 154.

the other issues, reducing excessive stress is an ongoing struggle we must actively engage.

Peter N. Kutulakis, Professor of Law and Vice Dean at the Dickenson School of Law in Carlisle, Pennsylvania, is one of a growing number of experts in "stress management" specifically for lawyers. In his contribution to the ABA's 1997 book, "*Living With The Law: Strategies To Avoid Burnout And Create Balance,*" Professor Kutulakis (who holds law and counseling degrees) suggests four key areas in which lawyers need to practice effective stress management: (1) Managing Your Body; (2) Managing Your Personal and Emotional Life: (3) Managing Relations with Your Clients; and (4) Managing Relations with Your Coworkers.[107] As in Dr. Amiram Elwork's helpful book, "*Stress Management For Lawyers: How To Increase Personal & Professional Satisfaction In The Law,*"[108] Kutulakis' recommendations range from reorienting fundamental priorities and values to simple but effective relaxation techniques.

To reduce stress, Professor Kutulakis recommends several strategies which by now should be familiar: balancing work and personal life, regular exercise, saying "no" to the demands of some clients, and effective time management.[109] But both he and Dr. Elwork bring their treatment/therapy training to the conversation, also recommending conscious relaxation, deep breathing, visualization, biofeedback, and what Kutulakis calls "thought stopping."[110] Lawyers suffering from high stress should consider these recommendations, as well as the very similar "Stress-Reducing Suggestions" in George Kaufman's materials.[111]

If we are to find fulfillment in law or life, we must take Step 9. We must seek a healthy balance between our rational, cognitive sides, on the one hand, and our feelings, emotions, hearts, and imaginations on the other. We must pursue balance not only in how we spend the limited hours of our lives but also between our outer and inner selves. In a word, we must strive to stay emotionally healthy.

Step 10. Embrace law as a "high calling"

Yale Law School's Dean Anthony Kronman observed: the [spiritual] "crisis has been brought about, by the demise of an older set of values that until quite recently played a vital role in defining the aspirations of American lawyers."[112] And at the heart of this "older set of values" was an *assumption* that the best lawyer was "not simply an accomplished technician but a person of prudence or practical wisdom as well ... a wisdom about human beings and their tangled affairs that anyone who wishes to provide real deliberative counsel must possess."[113]

It is not our purpose here to re-discuss this historical or philosophical point, but to suggest its connection with professional satisfaction and fulfillment—a connection Dean Kronman also clearly sees. "To those who shared this view it seemed obvious that a lawyer's life could be deeply fulfilling. For the character-virtue of practical wisdom is a central human excellence that has an intrinsic value of its own. So long as the cultivation of this virtue remained an important professional ideal, lawyers could therefore be confident that their work had intrinsic value, too."[114]

Lovely old words: wisdom, virtue, character. Hardly ones that come immediately to mind when the contemporary lawyer is considered, but words or ideals from which much else good in the practice of law once flowed. Among them: the ideal of the seasoned lawyer as a wise counselor, or even per Abraham Lincoln's good counsel, a "peacemaker"; lawyers, in Professor Deborah Rhodes' words, who have been "architects of a governmental structure that is a model for much of the world" and "leaders in virtually all major movements for social justice in the nation's history";[115] and countless lawyers in cities and towns across America, like those chronicled by Professor Walter Bennett and his students in their "oral histories," who "were living lives dedicated to a higher purpose, who loved what they were doing, and who found intellectual richness and creativity in lawyers' work."[116]

---

[107] Peter Kutulakis, "Stress Management Checklists," in *Living With the Law: Strategies to Avoid Burnout and Create Balance* (Chicago: Amer. Bar Ass'n, 1997), pp. 81–83.

[108] Elwork, *supra* note 37.

[109] Kutulakis, *supra* note 107.

[110] *Ibid; accord* Elwork, *supra* note 37, at 44.

[111] Kaufman, *supra* note 93, at 127–31.

[112] Anthony T. Kronman, *The Lost Lawyer: Failing Ideals of the Legal Profession* (Cambridge, Massachusetts: The Belknap Press of Harvard University Press, 1993), pp. 1–2.

[113] *Ibid*, p. 2.

[114] *Ibid.*, pp. 2–3.

[115] Rhode, *supra* note 48, at 3.

[116] Bennett, *supra* note 91, at 6.

Having absorbed so much bad news about unhappy lawyers, so many lawyer jokes, so much "bitching and moaning," Professor Bennett reports "experienc[ing] something close to euphoria" when he discovered, *inter alia*, that there were still "lawyers and judges who were proud of being members of the profession, who felt that being a lawyer involved a deep moral commitment, that it was a position not only of prestige, but of honor."[117] In other words, Professor Bennett and his students discovered lawyers and judges who, consciously or unconsciously, had embraced law as a high calling.

Of course, if we take this higher road—if we embrace law as a calling "that involve[s] a deep moral commitment"[118]—there are a number of things we will instinctively understand we must *not* do. We will not, for example, lie or even make misleading representations to courts. We will not treat opposing counsel in a manner which we would not want ourselves to be treated. We will not cheat or steal from our clients by doing unnecessary work or padding our billing records. And we will not take on work that we find morally offensive just because "everyone deserves a lawyer"—or, for that matter, because we could use the extra money.

Sadly, this has not been the direction of what we euphemistically (if not cynically) still call "legal ethics" in more recent decades. As Professor Mary Ann Glendon points out, we have come philosophical light years from the 1950s when corporate lawyers at least "sometimes ... [served as] 'conscience' to big business."[119] Putting the profession-wide fear of making value-judgments, God forbid, in historical perspective, Glendon observes:

> The first ABA Canons (adopted in 1908) held up a robust model of a lawyer who was no mere tool of the client: a lawyer "advances the honor of his profession and the best interests of his client when he renders service or gives advice tending to impress upon the client and his undertaking exact compliance with the strictest principles of moral law." In the 1960s, old-fashioned terms like "honor" and "principles of moral law" vanished, but the role of adviser and co-deliberator was still promoted: "A lawyer should exert his best efforts to insure that decisions of his client are made only after the client has been informed of relevant considerations. A lawyer ought to initiate this process if the client does not do so. Advice of a lawyer need not be confined to purely legal considerations.... In assisting his clients to reach a proper decision, it is often desirable for a lawyer to point out those factors which may lead to a decision that is morally just as well as legally permissible." In 1983, however, that mild encouragement to moral deliberation with clients was scrapped in favor of a provision that merely permits lawyers to refer to "relevant" factors: "In rendering advice, a lawyer may refer not only to law but to other considerations such as moral, economic, social and political factors, that may be relevant to the client's situation." Like Betty Crocker, the wise counselor has gotten slimmer over the years.[120]

In fact, as Professor Glendon later also notes, "[t]he most hotly debated issue in connection with the 1983 Rules ... was whether a lawyer should be required, rather than merely permitted, to disclose information he has reason to believe is necessary to prevent a client from causing *death* or *serious bodily harm* to another person."[121] Those advocating a morally-based "do the right thing" requirement soundly lost to what Professor Glendon describes as "the advocates of iron clad client confidentiality."[122]

With all due respect to the good men and women involved in the 1983 debate, that this was even a close call—death or serious bodily harm versus client confidentiality—is itself astounding. Can there be any question, when lawyer thinking strays that far from the "common good," why public opinion of lawyers has continued to plummet? Where are the ideals, or even what Dean Kronman calls "practical wisdom," in this bloodless, value-free calculus?

Dean Anthony T. Kronman is correct in connecting the collapse of historical ideals to the loss of "the professional self-confidence [they] once sustained."[123] It follows, if we are to have realistic hopes for regaining "professional self-confidence," that we must reaffirm ideals that transcend self-interest—including our individual and profession-wide commitment to the "common good." We must not allow the legal profession to become an amoral, dollar-driven business; indeed, we should not be

---

[117] *Ibid.*

[118] *Ibid.*

[119] Glendon, *supra* note 3, at 75.

[120] *Ibid.*, pp. 79–80 (internal notes omitted).

[121] *Ibid.*, p. 81.

[122] *Ibid.*

[123] Kronman, *supra* note 112, at 3.

afraid to make value-based decisions or give advice grounded in moral conviction. In short, if we are to find fulfillment in the practice of law, we must take Step 10: we must embrace law as a high calling.

Step 11. Be generous with your time and money

G. K. Chesterton, the prolific British writer and polemicist, had a keen eye for the paradox. And no paradox lurking in life's lessons caught his eye more frequently than the inverse relationship between selfish materialism and happiness.

Most of us realize, at least in our better moments, that money and material acquisitions will not give us lasting satisfaction—but lots, present company included, give it a good faith effort! The lucky ones, like Bruce Warnock,[124] ultimately realize that happiness lies elsewhere and, in fact, that devoting too much of our time and energy to acquiring will yield the opposite result.

We know, too, that the simple pronouncement of St. Paul that "it is more blessed to give than to receive,"[125] is profoundly true, and that there is no "blessedness" (translated elsewhere as "happiness") in being a miser. Indeed, it is no coincidence that "miser" and "miserable" come from the same Latin root word.

Legal writing that attempts to make this point—that lawyers should be more generous with their time and money—tends to remain more narrowly focused on *pro bono* work. This is good counsel, as far as it goes, and more of us should strive to meet or exceed the ABA's suggested goal (at least fifty hours of *pro bono* work per year). As Professor Deborah L. Rhode notes, "[f]ew lawyers come close," and "[o]nly about a third of the nation's five hundred largest firms have agreed to participate in the ABA Pro Bono Challenge, which requires a minimum annual contribution of three percent of the firm's total billable hours."[126] In his article, "A Lawyer's Duty to Serve the Public Good," U.S. Circuit Judge Harry T. Edwards properly laments not only the reduction in *pro bono* practice, but also the declining number of law school graduates choosing public service careers.[127]

But the declining commitment to *pro bono* work and public service is more derivative than central to the point we are trying to make here. In some ways—Chesterton would have loved this—our primary point here is more selfish, namely, that being generous with our time and money will make us feel better about our profession and our lives generally. In a word, giving generously will make us happier.

More central to our intended point is Steven Keeva's encouragement to develop a "helping heart."[128] He explains:

> In every tradition that emphasizes the importance of the inner life, compassion and service are held up as preeminent virtues. Those who, through the ages, have been revered for their wisdom and empathy—the Gandhis and the Martin Luther Kings of this world, to name but two recent examples—have often been people who believed that the very purpose of life is to be of service to others.
>
> Today's lawyers, being overwhelmingly inclined to minimize the importance of their inner experience, are more apt to see personal enrichment as their purpose, at least in their professional lives.[129]

To avoid suffering the misery of the miser, Keeva recommends a very simple exercise he calls "At Your Service":

> Freely giving your time and energy to others will repay you tenfold. You might consider looking for opportunities each week (or even every day) to perform random, anonymous acts of kindness. It's the holding of doors for others, picking up what someone else dropped, helping an elderly person across the street, or simply offering an encouraging smile that eventually help us to dissolve the boundaries that keep us feeling separate from one another. It will make you feel better and may come to have an impact on the way your practice law.[130]

Of course, the specific charity or "acts of kindness" in which we engage is less important than developing an unselfish attitude. The essential point is, if fulfillment is one of our goals, after we provide for ourselves and our families, we will get more sat-

---

[124] *See* text at notes 8 through 10.
[125] Acts 20:35.
[126] Rhode, *supra* note 48, at 37.
[127] Harry T. Edwards, "A Lawyer's Duty to Serve the Public Good," 65 N.Y.U. L. Rev. 1148, 1152–54 (1990).

---

[128] Keeva, *supra* note 43, at 133.
[129] *Ibid.*
[130] *Ibid.*, p. 134.

isfaction out of generously giving than we will from hoarding.

Keeva points to Mahatma Gandhi and Martin Luther King. The one who comes to my mind is Mother Theresa, the diminutive Yugoslavian peasant who moved to Calcutta to serve the poorest of the poor. Although most of us are not saints, we can all learn from those who are. And who could look at Mother Theresa—who died owning little more than her familiar blue and white sari and her Rosary beads—and doubt that she had discovered a joy in life that eludes most contemporary Americans?

What Mother Theresa and others devoted to a charitable way of life discover is that it is indeed more blessed—happier—to give than to receive. Lawyers who are fortunate enough to make more money than they need should apply this important life lesson by taking Step 11, that is, by looking for opportunities to share their time, talents, and resources with others.

Step 12. Pace yourself for a marathon

If you have taken Steps 1 through 11, you are already well on your way to Step 12: pacing yourself "for a marathon." Clear priorities that balance work and personal lives, effective time management, healthy lifestyle habits and practices, resisting the most intrusive technology, dealing with excessive stress, and being more selective about clients and cases are each important steps toward our last goal: a sustainable pace.

Conversely, if you are working so many hours that you consistently come home exhausted (or so distracted you cannot enjoy family or friends outside of work), if you have not established clear priorities, if you are a poor time manager, if you seldom get a good aerobic workout, if your consumer spending is out-of-control, if you can never get away from the beeper, cell phone and computer for "down time," if stress is eating you up, , you should probably deal with these issues first. Any one of these, left unattended for too long, is inconsistent with our ultimate goal, which is a healthy, well-balanced life.

As we consider Step 12—pacing yourself for a marathon—some of the previously made points warrant re-mention. Professor Schiltz's advice not to let yourself "be purchased at auction like a prize hog" or to "choose one law firm over another because of a $3,000 difference in starting salary"[131] is sound.

Rather, make it clear from the outset—in your own mind first, and then with any prospective employer or partner—that only so much of you is "for sale." Make it clear that quality of life matters to you, that you intend to work hard and "pursue excellence" professionally, but not to sacrifice important relationships and other essential elements of a healthy, balanced life.

Professor Dershowitz in *Letters To A Young Lawyer*,[132] observes that "[e]very book, painting, symphony or speech could be improved. The search for perfection is illusory and has no end."[133]

He is absolutely correct, as is Dr. Elwork in concluding that "[s]ince perfection does not exist, perfectionists are doomed to be perpetually frustrated."[134]

In a word, pursuing excellence is consistent with a sustainable pace while the futile attempt to achieve perfection is not. "Given these distinctions, choosing to strive for excellence rather than perfection has important implications for how much job satisfaction you derive and how successful you become."[135] Strive for professional excellence, but be wary of any tendency you may have toward perfectionism.

Emotional health and balance is another important element of a sustainable pace. And because many of us depend upon warm relationships with children, and later grandchildren, for emotional strength, we should keep in mind San Francisco lawyer Michael Traynor's late-life observation "that the years with your children fly by in an instant."[136] Many will also want to take to heart Traynor's wise counsel, "[w]henever you can, [to] tell the god of money and the god of ambition, who is no less voracious, that you and your kids are going to fly a kite or build a snowman."[137]

The simple but important point here is that we are more likely to be emotionally balanced and healthy if we enjoy warm, loving relationships with those closest to us. This may not be spouses, children, or grandchildren in a particular case, of course, although for many it will be. But whoever they are, if those closest to us are having to remind us to "stop

---

[131] *See* text at note 12.

[132] Dershowitz, *supra* note 14, at 77–78.

[133] Dershowitz, *supra* note 14, at 77–78.

[134] Elwork, *supra* note 37, at 153.

[135] *Ibid.*

[136] Traynor, *supra* note 11, at 1030–31.

[137] *Ibid.*

talking like a damn lawyer" too often, this may well be an area of our lives that needs attention.

Professor Dershowitz's observation that the wealthiest people tend to take the shortest vacations[138] brings us to another important point, if a sustainable pace is the goal. The point here is about as straightforward as it gets: take it. All of it. You need it. The office and the practice will survive. And you will return refreshed, batteries recharged, with more enthusiasm and energy for your work. In fact, taking regular vacations will not only give you a sustainable pace, they will make you a better lawyer.

Finally, since we are using an athletic metaphor for what we are calling "Step 12," we will end with another exhortation to exercise regularly. It was no fluke that the North Carolina Bar Association's Quality of Life Task Force discovered, out of all the "lifestyle practices" examined, the highest correlation between lawyers who got "regular exercise" and those who self-reported a sense of "subjective well-being."[139]

David B. Myers reviewed a number of psychological studies related to what made people "happy" in preparing to write his 1992 book, *The Pursuit of Happiness: Who Is Happy And Why*."[140] As summarized by Dr. Elwork, the number one factor noted as contributing to "happiness" was "physical health and fitness."[141] The bottom line: lawyers who exercise regularly enjoy its stress-relieving effects, and are generally able to keep work pressures and demands in better perspective. If you have not done so already, make a commitment now to join them.

As we close this article, it is necessary to state what will be obvious to many readers, namely, that this first-ever "12-Step Program For Lawyers" is a career-long project. Except for the extraordinarily well-disciplined, and perhaps the most saintly, these are challenges and issues with which we can expect to struggle for the rest of our lives. But, thankfully, they are not impossible struggles, and if we diligently take these "steps," we can realistically expect to move closer to our goal: finding balanced success—and fulfillment—in the practice of law.

---

[138] Dershowitz, *supra* note 14, at 35.

[139] *See* text in Step 4, *supra*.

[140] David G. Myers, *The Pursuit of Happiness: Who Is Happy And Why* (Morrow, 1992; Avon, 1993).

[141] Elwork, *supra* note 37, at 157.

A TESTIMONIAL
THE PATH OF AN IMMIGRATION ATTORNEY

by Elizabeth Gervais-Gruen[*]

When I was 8 years old, I knew that I wanted to be an attorney. Thereafter, when I was on my way to college, I tried to prepare myself with the kind of courses that would be of most advantage for entrance to college and law school.

For some years prior to practicing immigration law, my practice was in municipal law. I now limit my practice to immigration and nationality law, but have no limitation beyond that. However, I impose a limitation as to my clientele. I choose to represent only those people who, in my opinion, have the capacity to become good citizens and whose stories are credible. In this way, after providing complete and accurate documentation, I have every reason to expect an affirmative decision. As to choice of clients, I have erred occasionally, but not enough times to change my pattern of selection. Before I accept a case, I make certain it is a case I want. I make sure it is a just case and one that should be decided in my client's favor. I believe that if I combine my efforts, my accumulated experience, and the law with clear documentation, the case should be decided in favor of my client.

I do not think of myself as a woman attorney. I am a woman, and I am an attorney. I enjoy being a woman. I enjoy being an attorney. There were only two women in my law school class of 200. When I graduated from law school, I found I was in a world of men. I did not find any discrimination in the courtroom, although I have seen plenty of it since that time. In relation to the Immigration and Nationality Service, there was no discrimination at all because I was a woman.

I continue to play an active role in structuring immigration policy as an active member of the American Immigration Lawyers Association and cofounder of its Carolinas Chapter. AILA is in touch with our representatives on Capitol Hill. I am constantly in touch with my representatives, both in Washington, D.C., and in the state, seeking their aid as needed. I am equally active in this respect in my own community.

When I was chair of the Immigration and Nationality Committee of the North Carolina Bar Association, one aspect of immigration law that troubled me was the effect of a guilty plea in a criminal case on an alien's subsequent application for naturalization. Some aliens who were charged with crimes were advised by their attorneys to plead guilty and did so in the belief that, after they paid the fines and court costs, the criminal charge would be settled and the file closed. Later, the aliens would discover that their criminal convictions had to be divulged with adverse consequences when they applied for naturalization, and needed to show good moral character. I felt strongly that an alien should be advised of the implications of the guilty plea on a subsequent naturalization application. As a result, I asked that the North Carolina law be amended so that an alien would receive such a warning.

The North Carolina Bar Association voted to include my proposed amendment with other amendments presented to the legislature for consideration. The General Assembly passed my amendment and it is now a part of the North Carolina General Statutes. Today, the voices of those who wish to restrict immigration have become louder. Since September 11, 2001, under the standard of "Beware the Terrorist," we have seen more and more restrictions and more and more removal of rights; even listening to confidential attorney-client conversations is permitted.

We must stand against restrictions to the end that justice, immigrant rights, and our rights are not

---

[*] **Elizabeth Gervais Gruen** practices immigration and naturalization law in Chapel Hill, North Carolina; she is a former member of AILA's Board of Governors and is a founding member and former Chapter Chair of the Carolinas Chapter. Gervais-Gruen has practiced law for 70 years; the last 48 of which have been limited to immigration. She is nationally recognized for mentoring generations of immigration attorneys.

(**Editor's note**: Gervais-Gruen has expressed the sentiment that when she mentors attorneys, she is rewarded far beyond her efforts. Judge Carl Horn, III's provocative article suggests that many personal and professional aspects contribute to a successful lawyer's life; among these elements are mentoring and pro bono service. To this list, the editors would add client advocacy.)

trampled upon. We must all stand for national security, but with it must come justice for all. If we are to be a land of immigrants, and we are the hosts, we should be welcoming hosts—not restrictive hosts. We should be hosts with open arms and offer even-handed justice to all, so that we may live together in a secure country. If we remove/deport an immigrant because he or she did not report a change of address within 10 days as required by the law, we harm ourselves in our own eyes and the eyes of the world. To combat a backlash against immigrants, I consider it my responsibility to make clear what immigrants offer to this country, the many fields in which they are important to this country, and the areas of endeavor in which jobs would not be filled without immigrants—such as contractors and landscapers, to mention but a few.

I like the field of immigration law. I like the work everyday. It is this that gives me the energy to continue. When I am asked why I have not retired, I can honestly reply that knowledge of immigration law is a high skill, a skill I possess, which causes me to be good for my clients, and, in turn, they are good for me. I hope that I have the opportunity to continue in this path, the path that gives me pleasure each day I work.

A Testimonial
My Name Is Lynn, and I am a Volunteer

by C. Lynn Calder*

In affirmation of the preceding article of Carl Horn, III, "Twelve Steps Toward Fulfillment in the Practice of Law," I am writing to encourage every reader to practice Step 11, "Be Generous with your time (and money)." Volunteer your time to "immigration law" and feel good about it. This article will provide you with solid reasons and testimonial to convince you to contribute your time, talents, skills, and energy (and maybe money) more often to pro bono clients and the greater immigrant community.

Recognizing the need for members of the bar to volunteer, the ABA has issued a "Pro Bono Challenge," which calls on leaders of the nation's top 500 law firms to adopt goals for pro bono hours equivalent to 3 to 5 percent of the firm's total billable hours.

Congratulations to AILA members who exceed that amount already; other members are encouraged to accept and fulfill this ABA challenge.

VOLUNTEER WITHIN YOUR PROFESSION

Most, if not all of us, volunteer in some way—whether it is joining the Parent Teachers Association (PTA), teaching at a children's religious school, hosting a social event to raise money for the local symphony, or hammering nails to build a Habitat for Humanity home. We have passions and we want to express them. Giving of time, talent, and money to benefit immigration law and immigrants is another way to practice volunteerism. We can volunteer within our own profession in numerous ways: agree to represent a VAWA client pro bono; offer free consultation time at a local Hispanic-sponsored "Ask the Lawyer Day"; speak at a church about immigration law; write an amicus curiae brief; mentor a nonimmigration attorney who has accepted a pro bono asylum case; or raise money for a pro-immigration political candidate.

In the March/April 2003 issue of AILA's *Immigration Law Today*, Miami AILA member Mary Kramer explained why she volunteers[1]:

> The benefit of pro bono work is the same as the benefit of doing community service. Life is not just about going to work and collecting a wage. It's also not just about loving and helping one's own family. I like to embrace life and all it has to offer. That means respecting others who are not as fortunate as you, helping others move forward in life, lending a hand. I cannot change the world, but I can do my own little part. Working on worthwhile pro bono cases is a way of doing my part.

A reason, then, to contribute within your own profession is to satisfy your desire to give of yourself and do good work in the community. And so many opportunities come right across your desk.

VOLUNTEER TO ADVANCE YOUR CAREER

Another reason to contribute time, talent, and energy is to advance your own career. Many years ago, as I was beginning to practice in immigration court, I was asked to screen "incarcerated alien" cases at our state prison where deportation hearings were held. Relief was sometimes available in these pre-IIRAIRA cases; and even if no relief was available, inmates were in dire need of file review and immigration advice.

---

* For over 15 years, **C. Lynn Calder** has practiced in all areas of immigration law with Allen and Pinnix, P.A., located in Raleigh, North Carolina. She is a Trustee Emeritus of the American Immigration Law Foundation and a past chair of the AILA Carolinas Chapter and the North Carolina Bar Association Immigration and Nationality Law Committee. Calder regularly participates as faculty for AILA, N.C. Bar Association, N.C. Academy of Trial Lawyers, and law school continuing legal education programs; and she has taught immigration law at N.C. Central University Law School. She is a North Carolina Board-Certified Specialist in immigration law and serves on the North Carolina State Bar Immigration Specialization Committee. Calder is included in *Best Lawyers* for immigration law.

---

[1] "Up Close and Personal with Mary Kramer and Alsy Lomangino of the South Florida AILA Legal Assistance Project," 22 *Immigration Law Today* (March/April 2003) p. 30.

As a bimonthly volunteer, I had the opportunity to interact in a positive way with the then-INS trial attorney (in our case, often the district counsel), the immigration judge, and prison officers. I learned a great deal quickly about the criminal immigration practice and developed long-term professional friendships. Occasionally, the cases produced a paying client—many times, there are family members able to pay an attorney, and the case was worth defending. Sometimes I would choose to accept representation of an inmate on a pro bono basis because he or she had relief but no money. In every way but financial, the pro bono cases were as profitable as the paid ones.

Volunteering within the immigration law field can expand your expertise, introduce you to colleagues and potential clients, and help make your presence (and availability) known to the community.

VOLUNTEER TO FEEL GOOD ABOUT YOURSELF

Carl Horn mentions pro bono work as something that we all know we need to do. But think about it as more than just something we need to do. Eating broccoli is something we need to do, yet it encourages few of us to want to go to work in the morning.

Pro bono representation typically falls into one of three categories:

1. One type includes those matters we wholeheartedly find to be compelling and worthy of our help. We know up-front that the potential client cannot afford our services (or rent or food for their family); and we agree to represent them on a no fee basis. We might or might not bill for expenses. We feel good when we accept the case. We can help the client, and our work might have broader implications with regard to protecting the state of immigration law.

2. A second category includes those cases we agree to accept on a reduced fee basis. These are similar to the first type. These cases involve worthy clients and issues, but we feel some fee can be paid. Perhaps the church is passing the hat, a benefactor is involved, or the client has limited income. We can still feel good that we are doing the right thing, and maybe feel a little less guilty about the hours being taken away from full "billables." Furthermore, the client will be invested in the effort; often a client who pays something for legal service will take that service more seriously.

3. Finally, there are the "pro bono" cases we hadn't planned on. These are the cases that began as "full fee" but the client can no longer afford the attorney's fee. We have to decide whether to withdraw or continue to represent the client on a no fee or reduced fee basis.

Carl Horn indicates that "being generous with our time and money will make us feel better about our profession and our lives generally. In a word, giving generously will make us happier." Stated another way, pro bono representation of clients can make us feel happier. Rather than begrudgingly accepting the client who cannot pay anything or must pay a lower fee, or reluctantly continuing with a client who can no longer pay, we can choose to embrace these opportunities. We can accept the decision we have made and feel good about our giving back to the profession. The low fee or "post-retainer" no or low fee client is as much a pro bono case as any other. We can feel proud about all of our pro bono representation, enjoy the commitment we have made to those clients, and feel good about giving something back.

GIVE SOMETHING BACK

When I was eight months pregnant and having early contractions, I received a notice from the Board of Immigration Appeals (BIA) that a pro bono case I had taken many years earlier had been chosen for oral argument. Certain issues in the case needed to be further addressed; and losing on one issue in the case could have affected general availability of §212(h) relief. I was referred to Tom Hutchins, an AILA member in Virginia, who might be willing to assist me.[2]

Tom immediately came to my client's rescue. He researched cases from across the country and across administrative agencies and prepared a masterful supplemental argument. He spent countless hours on the phone and e-mail with me for background information and with experts within immigration "litigation" circles, who suggested ways to present arguments. With Tom doing most of the work, a supplemental brief was timely submitted.

---

[2] Thomas Hutchins was the recipient of the 2000 *AILA Pro Bono Award*.

When the oral argument notice came and I had just delivered my daughter, I again sought help. Based on the expert legal work that Tom had accomplished, AILA member Mary Kramer agreed to present the oral argument, which was to be held in her home city of Miami. Every observation, including that of the BIA Chairman Paul Schmidt, was that Mary delivered a magnificent oral argument. Because of the willingness of Tom Hutchins and Mary Kramer, the Board ruled in our favor, foreclosing a nightmare decision against §212(h) relief had the appeal been dismissed.

Tom Hutchins and Mary Kramer are my personal heroes, as they are heroes of countless immigrants. Tom and Mary are AILA practitioners and volunteers.

Few of us practice immigration law just for the money—it is far too complex and frustrating a practice to do that. Most of us practice immigration law because, at some fundamental level, we love it and are compelled to do so. Express your passion about immigration law and immigrants through volunteerism as well as through paid legal practice. Volunteer—feel good about yourself. In the words of Mary Kramer, "[t]hose of us who have been fortunate in our lives—and I've been extremely fortunate—should give something back. In the end, we only win again."

A TESTIMONIAL
IMMIGRATION ADVOCACY IS A MATTER OF PROFESSIONAL RESPONSIBILITY

*by John L. Pinnix**

It is safe to assume that many AILA attorneys embarked on their legal careers without the slightest premonition of what the practice of law would be like, much less that they would become immigration attorneys.

At the end of his career, Clarence Darrow wrote that he disliked the practice of law yet he was fascinated by the idea of the law; by the time he understood what the practice was about, "I was in too deep to get out."

Yet Darrow, the "Attorney for the Damned," inspired generations of students in the first half of the 20th century to enter the law profession. Idyllic portrayal of fictional and real life attorneys in the media age undoubtedly influenced more recent generations to go to law school. In the 1950s, the television version of Erle Stanley Gardner's "Perry Mason" launched an ancillary speaking career for Raymond Burr—before "real" bar associations. During the Civil Rights era, it was Atticus Finch. In more recent years, the characters in "L.A. Law," "Law and Order," and "The Practice" influenced, for better or worse, the public's perception of attorneys.

---

* **John L. Pinnix** is a past president of the American Immigration Lawyers Association (2002–2003) and a founding member of AILA's Carolinas Chapter. He attained B.A. and M.A. degrees in History at the University of North Carolina at Greensboro and his J.D. at the Wake Forest University School of Law. He has served as an adjunct professor at North Carolina Central University School of Law and as a Senior Lecturing Fellow at Duke University School of Law. Pinnix is a principal in the Raleigh law firm, Allen and Pinnix, P.A., and is a North Carolina Board-Certified Immigration Specialist.

This article updates and continues a "call to action" by the author in "Immigration Advocacy is a Matter of Professional Responsibility" (*AILA Dispatch*, July/August 2000); "Advocacy: When the Going Gets Tough, The Tough Must Get Going" (*AILA Dispatch*, October 2000); "Shifting Sands, Cloudy Tea Leaves—Immigration Advocacy for 2001 and Beyond" (*AILA Dispatch*, January/February 2001); and "Members Tool Up Advocacy Efforts as Crucial Issues Reach Congress" (*AILA Dispatch*, September 2001).

The summer I took the bar exam, future attorneys throughout America were glued to the Watergate hearings and fixated on a "country lawyer," Sam J. Ervin, Jr.—"the last founding father."

Although economics will always attract the talented and ambitious to legal careers, the highest aspirations of our profession are not monetary. This is certainly true in the immigration field.

While many areas of immigration practice have flourished in the last decade, I still believe that few of us are in immigration just for the money. Most immigration attorneys could more profitably put their energies and legal talents to work elsewhere.

I believe that an immigration practice lets us indulge the fundamental reasons we were attracted to the law: helping others, securing justice, and making the system work. For many years, the North Carolina Academy of Trial Lawyers' motto was, "Lawyers Helping People"; helping people is the essence of what immigration law is about.

As attorneys, certainly as immigration attorneys, we are advocates. Advocacy is the essence of our professional existence. We analyze our case, prepare it, and, consistent with the law and the applicable rules of ethics and practice, try to pursue it in the way most advantageous to our clients. Not only is this why we are retained, it goes to the very core of our professional responsibility.

But sometimes there are roadblocks: there is no remedy, there is nothing you can file, and litigation is impractical. After you have consulted with your client, you determine that in your best professional estimation—due to the passage of legislation such as IIRAIRA or the USA PATRIOT Act, or a recent adverse court decision—the client is Simply Out of Luck.

Tragic and mischievous scenarios seem infinite: a school cannot offer a key course because of the H-1B cap; a derivative E-2 who inadvertently overstayed but is now eligible for a green card has to consular process and wait abroad a year or more to see if a waiver of the 10-year bar will be granted; a

30-year-old misdemeanor conviction renders the mother of three U.S. citizen children inadmissible.

You tell your client "sorry," or "sit tight, AILA is working on it," or "maybe later." Then you move on to a matter where there is a remedy. Right?

Wrong! At the point you move on, just hoping that AILA—or the immigration fairy—will bring a better tomorrow, you are very arguably abdicating your professional responsibility to your client.

The American Immigration Lawyers Association has a talented and highly effective advocacy staff. But the chance that the message of our still comparatively small, affinity bar will be heard and acted on by Congress does not depend on AILA's staff and finite resources, but on the commitment of AILA's members. More precisely, the chance our message will change the law depends on our members energizing themselves and their clients to drive home our compelling and righteous message.

The late Justice Sam J. Ervin, III, Senator Ervin's son, once asked me why certain attorneys wanted to become judges when they seem reluctant to make decisions. I have a similar question about immigration attorneys who are reluctant to advocate.

In "Imagination Advocacy is a Matter of Professional Responsibility" (*AILA Dispatch,* July/August 2000), I noted that attorneys are natural advocates; in fact, it is our second nature. We, and our clients, can and must educate the public and our elected officials as to the evils of restrictive legislation; if we do not make this our cause and accept this challenge, no one will, and the harm will be irreparable.

I never have mastered the art of screening my calls, so virtually every day of my professional life I meet or speak with the employer, spouse, pastor, neighbor, or friend of a long time—albeit undocumented—resident.

The person who contacts me wants to help "get papers" for a key employee, wife, parent, or friend. They are astounded to learn that under current U.S. law, there is nothing that can be done to help the foreign national, even if the person is married to a U.S. citizen and is the parent of U.S. citizen children. September 11 in no way abated the tide that craves amelioration of harsh laws and demands a system that will provide fundamental fairness to this generation of immigrants.

Just because there is no solution today doesn't mean there is no hope. You, your clients, and their friends can help, right now. The tool for victory is already in our own hands: advocacy.

Among the most cited political quotes of the 20th Century is the late Speaker of the House Tip O'Neal's gem: "All politics is local." This is not a cliché but an eternal truth of American politics.

Our most effective tool for persuasion is to present the real-life concerns of our clients who are not only business, civic, and religious groups, and American families—they are also constituents. There is simply no stronger weapon than going to our elected officials with our clients' compelling stories.

Incredibly, some immigration attorneys seem to think they have no political access. Nothing could be further from the truth. Immigration attorneys are important in their own right. Our opinions do matter. We are practicing in a cutting-edge niche of the legal profession. Not only that, each of us represents *premium clients*: opinion makers, civic and religious leaders, educators, investors, and family, refugee and human rights advocates. We represent core, key, influential constituents that every political leader must take into account.

The tools immigration attorneys need for lobbying are readily available from AILA, AILF and AILF's Immigration Policy Center. These tools can be accessed instantly via AILA's InfoNet: position papers, draft letters to members of Congress and the media, and score cards to instantly determine the voting record of every member of Congress. Many of the advocacy documents are translated into Spanish.

Give your clients, and everyone interested in the welfare of your clients, a list of the names and addresses of your state's congressional delegation and provide them with draft advocacy letters that are instantly available through InfoNet. Give them the Capitol Hill switchboard number, (202) 224-3121; and the White House: (202) 456-1414. Have them log on to *www.aila.org* (the public site) and click on "Write to Congress" to access the ability to immediately "Take Action" and send letters via e-mail to their members of Congress.